The Oneness Motif in the Fourth Gospel

Motif Analysis
and
Exegetical Probe into the Theology of John

by

Mark L. Appold

WIPF & STOCK · Eugene, Oregon

Appold, Mark L.
The oneness motif in the fourth gospel: motif analysis and
exegetical probe into the theology of John. – 1. Aufl. –
Tübingen: Mohr, 1976.
  (Wissenschaftliche Untersuchungen zum Neuen Testament: Reihe 2; 1)

Wipf and Stock Publishers
199 W 8th Ave, Suite 3
Eugene, OR 97401

The Oneness Motif of the Fourth Gospel
Motif Analysis and Exegetical Probe into the Fourth Gospel
By Appold, Mark L.
Copyright©1976 Mohr Siebeck
ISBN 13: 978-1-61097-543-8
Publication date 6/13/2011
Previously published by J. C. B. Mohr, 1976

VORWORT DER HERAUSGEBER

Die Reihe der "Wissenschaftlichen Untersuchungen zum Neuen Testament" besteht nun seit über 25 Jahren. Als erster Band erschien 1950 die Untersuchung von K.G. Kuhn, Achtzehngebet und Vaterunser und der Reim, seither sind 17 weitere Bände nachgefolgt. Um im Blick auf die in den letzten Jahren stark gestiegenen Druckkosten die Preise auch bei kleineren Auflagen einigermaßen im Rahmen des Erträglichen zu halten, wurden seit 1970 einzelne Bände nach einer Schreibmaschinenvorlage im Offsetverfahren gedruckt. Da es wünschenswert ist, die auf diese Weise hergestellten Bände von jenen deutlicher zu unterscheiden, die in der traditionellen Ausführung erscheinen, wurde die Gründung einer einfacher ausgestatteten Zusatzreihe beschlossen, die die Bezeichnung "WUNT 2. Reihe" tragen soll. Wir freuen uns, mit der Untersuchung von Herrn Dr. Appold diese 2. Reihe der WUNT eröffnen zu können.

Die Herausgeber

ACKNOWLEDGEMENTS

This book is a slightly reworked and corrected copy of my inaugural dissertation accepted by the Faculty of Evangelical Theology at the Eberhard-Karls University of Tübingen, Germany in December, 1973. I am grateful to Prof. Dr. Martin Hengel for his supportive interest in the thesis, including also Prof. Dr. O. Michel and Prof. Dr. J. Jeremias for their acceptance of this study into the series Wissenschaftliche Untersuchungen zum Neuen Testament.

I am particularly indebted to my teacher, Prof. Dr. Ernst Käsemann, who not only gave me initial incentive for this investigation but whose own work and intense theological concern together with personal encouragement provided me with continual impetus for my extended study. My deep appreciation is further expressed to Prof. Dr. Friedrich Lang for his ready kindness and scholarly advice as well as for the personal concern he demonstrated throughout and especially as Ephorus during my first year abroad in the Evangelisches Stift Tübingen. I am also obliged to Prof. Dr. Edgar Krentz of Concordia Seminary in Exile for response and critique given in preparation of this manuscript.

Finally, I would like gratefully to acknowledge the Lutheran World Federation Exchange Program and in particular also Dr. and Mrs. Harold Hirt whose support and generous financial assistance made this study possible.

Kirksville, Missouri   Mark L. Appold
July, 1975

TABLE OF CONTENTS

INTRODUCTION TO THE PROBLEM.......................... 1
   A. THE SITUATION................................ 2
   B. AIM AND SCOPE................................ 8

PART I
THE MORPHOLOGY OF THE ONENESS MOTIF IN THE FOURTH GOSPEL

CHAPTER

  I. PRELIMINARY SURVEY OF THE PASSAGES............ 11
      A. SIGHTING THE TEXTS........................ 11
      B. OVERVIEW OF INTERPRETIVE APPROACHES....... 13

  II. ONENESS AND THE RECIPROCITY STATEMENTS........ 18
      A. RELATIONALITY BETWEEN JESUS AND GOD....... 18
      B. RELATIONALITY BETWEEN JESUS AND HIS OWN... 34

  III. ONENESS AND THE CHRISTOLOGICAL TITLES......... 48
      A. THE SON OF MAN............................ 48
      B. THE SON OF GOD............................ 55
      C. THE SON................................... 58
      D. THE CHRIST................................ 64
      E. THE PROPHET............................... 69
      F. THE KING.................................. 74
      G. OTHER DESIGNATIONS........................ 78
      H. EGO EIMI.................................. 81

  IV. ONENESS AND THE SEMEIA........................ 86
      A. THE PROBLEM............................... 86
      B. DISTINCTIVE CHARACTERISTICS OF THE SIGNS.. 88
      C. CRITICAL QUALIFICATIONS................... 94

V.	Oneness and the Passion Account...............	103
	A. PRELIMINARY REMARKS.......................	103
	B. INTEGRATION OF THE PASSION MATERIAL........	105
	C. SIGN SIGNIFICANCE OF THE TEMPLE PERICOPE..	114
	D. ARGUMENT AND STRUCTURE OF THE EXORDIAL PASSION MATERIAL...........................	121
	E. THE PASSION NARRATIVE.....................	125

PART II
THE ONENESS PASSAGES

A. Literary and Source Analysis

VI.	Aspects of the Compositional Problem and its History..	139
	A. THE PROBLEM...............................	139
	B. HISTORICAL DEVELOPMENT....................	140
	C. BULTMANN'S SYNTHESIS......................	145
	D. REACTIONS AND SHIFTS......................	148
VII.	Oneness Passages in the Departing Prayer of Jesus..	157
	A. TEXT STRUCTURE AND SOURCE ANALYSIS........	157
	1. Structural Considerations.............	157
	2. Stylistic Factors.....................	160
	3. Excursus: Religio-historical Profile of the Oneness Motif..................	163
	B. THE LITERARY CHARACTER OF CHAPTER 17......	194
	C. PROBLEMS OF INTERNAL STRUCTURE AND THEOLOGICAL VARIANCE......................	212
VIII.	The Oneness Passage in a Prophetic Statement..	237
	A. STRUCTURAL CONSIDERATIONS.................	237
	B. STYLISTIC FACTORS AND INTERNAL PROBLEMS...	239
	C. RELIGIO-HISTORICAL COMPARISONS............	243

IX. ONENESS PASSAGES IN A DISCOURSE 246
   A. CONTEXTUAL PROBLEMS 246
   B. STYLISTIC FACTORS 252
   C. THEOLOGICAL ARGUMENT 254
   D. RELIGIO-HISTORICAL CHARACTER 259

B. THEOLOGY OF THE ONENESS PASSAGES

X. THEOLOGICAL EXPLICATION 261
   A. CHRISTOLOGY AND ECCLESIOLOGY OF THE ONE-
      NESS MOTIF 262
   B. SOTERIOLOGY AND ECCLESIOLOGY OF THE ONE-
      NESS MOTIF 272
   C. ONENESS: A THEOLOGICAL ABBREVIATION 280
   D. UNIQUENESS OF THE JOHANNINE ONENESS MOTIF. 289

BIBLIOGRAPHY 295

Introduction to the Problem

The number of problems which surface and begin to multiply with any serious study of the Fourth Gospel is reminiscent of Jahweh's promise to Abraham regarding his progeny: "They would be as the stars in the heavens and as the dust particles of the earth; if anyone is able to count them, so shall their number be." D. F. Strauß's well-known dictum of the "seamless cloak of Christ" may indeed well apply to the character of the Fourth Gospel, but then to only one side. Like the tapestry, whose frontal appearance shows consistent lines and a unified picture but whose reverse side appears as a jumbled array of tangled knots and raveled threads, so the Gospel of John is distinguished by its clear and ruthlessly consistent witness as well as marked by deep aporias and questions that have been the thorn of interpretive studies for centuries. Nor are the questions and problems simply the result of academic constructions as though here were a special playground for exegetical gymnastics and mental exercises. It is rather the peculiarity of the text itself with its characteristic simplicity and complexity and its striking uniqueness in the NT canon that has continued to evoke countless and sharply contradictory heuristic attempts at clarification. Luther could express the singularity of this Gospel by designating it "das einige zarte rechte Hauptevangelium." From a kerygmatic standpoint that may be clear. And yet couched beneath the centrality of its witness remain all manner of historical and interpretational problems that continue intensively to be debated and extensively discussed.

To dwell on this fact of the abundance of problems may for some smack of a stereotyped jeremiad.[1] No apology, however, is made for joining the chorus acknowledging the weight and

---

[1] Cp. J. Becker's complaint ("Wunder und Christologie," *NTS*, 16, 1970, p. 130): "Es ist zur Zeit eine liebgewordene Gewohnheit, auf die drückende Last des noch ungelösten johanneischen Rätsels hinzuweisen."

scope of the Johannine problem. In fact, that acknowledgment marks a necessary beginning for this study and comes as the result of exegetical and existential struggle with a text for which interpretive answers are not easy to come by. To labor in the field of Johannine studies and to work through the plethora of accompanying literature is certainly in the least a humbling and an exacting experience. But for the interpreter, be he just a beginner, and particularly for one who must regularly stand in the pulpit, the task of continuing interpretation is an indispensable endeavor, even when this entails long detours and involved historical-critical constructions. Where the price is high the corresponding product may or may not be of equal value. In any case it is purchased with substantially greater care.

A. THE SITUATION

If we were to indicate some of the current contributions and trends in Johannine studies which have set the stage for this investigation,[1] then mention, first of all, would have to be made of major works during the forties and fifties under whose shadow most recent Johannine interpretation has evolved. In the Anglo-Saxon world this would include above all the expositions by C. H. Dodd,[2] E. Hoskyns,[3] and C. K. Barrett.[4] Their common concern for historicity and their extreme reserve in questions of source and redaction criticism are characteristic features. While Hoskyn's richly theological exposition demonstrates pointed disinterest in questions of tradition transmission and Johannine milieu, Dodd's platonizing interpretation, consistent with the traditional English approach, reflects substantial concern for documenting relations to the Hellenistic world. On the continent and with an influence extending far beyond, R. Bultmann's impressive commentary,[5]

---

[1] The following overview is selective and restricted only to representative commentaries and monographs. Further cp. H. Metzger, "Neuere Johannes-Forschung", *VuF*, 12, 2/1967, pp. 12-29.
[2] *The Interpretation of the Fourth Gospel*, Cambridge, 1963 and *Historical Tradition in the Fourth Gospel*, Cambridge, 1963.
[3] *The Fourth Gospel*, London, 1947.
[4] *The Gospel According to St. John*, London, 1962.
[5] *Das Evangelium des Johannes (KKNT)*, Göttingen, 1962.

as well as his discussion of the Gospel of John in his N.T. theology,[1] have maintained a pre-eminent position for more than three decades. His commentary, bolstered by numerous prior and subsequent essay studies and analyses, is truly a landmark along the way. Its strength as well as its fascination and appeal derive from a rare combination of precise methodology and exhaustive coverage that involves a bold and unified theological approach, detailed literary and source analysis, and a comprehensive utilization of comparative religious materials available at that time.

Bultmann's work synthesized lines of approach for subsequent Johannine research. As none other his commentary underscored the necessity of clarifying the nature and scope of the given traditions with which the evangelist worked and of recognizing the subtle complexity of the relationship between the prior traditive elements and the later Gospel composition. Here it was seen that while given strands of tradition set directional limits to the whole Gospel, they themselves do not simply determine its basic intention.[2] In the interaction between the two, the decisive question is how the evangelist used the material and what he wants to say with it. Bultmann's integrated approach further demonstrated that what finally counts for an exegesis of the Fourth Gospel is a delineation of the total underlying and motivating conception. Thus it will not do to answer with isolated passages or partial aspects of the Fourth Gospel unless they are related to the whole and to the center.

Indeed, Bultmann believed he had discovered that center which he defined in existential Kierkegaardian terms of paradox. The theological orientation was decidedly anthropological. The new self-understanding of faith was regarded as

---

[1] *Theology of the New Testament*, II, Chas. Scribner's Sons, c. 1955, pp. 3-99.
[2] Bultmann, *Ev Joh*, p. 6: "Und die Exegese hat die erste Aufgabe, die für den Verf. mit der Tradition, in der er steht, gegebenen Möglichkeiten des Redens aufzudecken. Was der Verf. hier und jetzt sagen will, ist freilich aus diesen Möglichkeiten nicht einfach abzuleiten; aber dem, was er sagen will, ist durch sie eine bestimmte Richtung gegeben und sind bestimmte Grenzen gesetzt..."

the decision to overcome the offense of the revelation of
God's reality encountered in the pure humanity of the earthly
Jesus. As might have been expected, Bultmann's interpreta-
tion stirred intensive reaction on all fronts. In the area
of literary and source criticism initial response appeared
above all in the larger critical works by E. Ruckstuhl[1] and B.
Noack,[2] then in the extensive assessment by D. M. Smith[3] and
most recently in monographs by R. Fortna,[4] W. Nicol,[5] and A.
Dauer.[6] In the area of comparative religious backgrounds
Bultmann's insistence on the Gnostic character of the
Johannine material was subsequently advanced in the posthu-
mously published monograph by H. Becker,[7] in the reprint of an
earlier study by E. Schweizer,[8] then in a modified sense in
the monograph studies by S. Schulz,[9] and recently in the work
by L. Schottroff.[10] Despite the demise of Reitzenstein's "redeemed redeemer" model, renewed work on the Mandaean sources
and the rising importance of the Nag Hammadi texts continued
to point to the viability of the Gnostic question for the
Fourth Gospel. In general, however, the trend during the
sixties in Johannine comparative religious investigations
e.g. by O. Böcher,[11] F. M. Braun,[12] O. Betz,[13] and H. Noetzel[14] was
the attempt to establish relationships with traditional

---

[1] *Die literarische Einheit des Johannesevangeliums*, Studia Friburgensia, n.s. 3, Freiburg/Schweiz, 1951.
[2] *Zur johanneischen Tradition*, København, 1954.
[3] *The Composition and Order of the Fourth Gospel*, N. H./ London, 1965.
[4] *The Gospel of Signs*, SNTS Monograph Ser. 11, Cambridge, 1970.
[5] *The Semeia in the Fourth Gospel*, Suppl. Nov. Test. 32, Leiden, 1972.
[6] *Die Passionsgeschichte im Johannesevangelium*, Studien z. A.u.N.T., Bd. xxx, München, 1972.
[7] *Die Reden des Johannesevangeliums und der Stil der gnostischen Offen-barungsreden*, FRLANT N.F. 50, Göttingen, 1956.
[8] *Ego Eimi*, FRLANT N.F. 38, Göttingen, 2. Aufl., 1965.
[9] *Untersuchungen zur Menschensohn-Christologie im Johannes-Evangelium*, Göttingen, 1957. *Komposition und Herkunft der johanneischen Reden*, Stuttgart, 1960. Cp. also *Das Evangelium nach Johannes*, NTD 4, Göttingen, 1972.
[10] *Der Glaubende und die feindliche Welt*, Neukirchen-Vluyn, 1970.
[11] *Der johanneische Dualismus im Zusammenhang des nachbiblischen Judentums*, Gütersloh, 1965.
[12] *Jean le Théologien II. Les grandes traditions d'Israel et l'accord des écritures selon le quatrième Evangile*, Paris, 1964.
[13] *Der Paraklet. Fürsprecher im häretischen Judentum im Johannes-evangelium und in neugefundenen griechischen Schriften*, AGSU 2, Leiden, 1963.
[14] *Christos und Dionysos*, Arbeiten zur Theologie, Stuttgart, 1960.

Jewish sources, and in studies like those of P. Borgen[1] and W. Meeks[2] to evaluate in addition the rabbinic traditions and haggadic interpretations of the O.T. as well as the Samaritan sources (so also K. Haacker[3]) or as in the study by L. J. Martyn[4] to explore the relation to the Diaspora synagogue.

It was Bultmann's theological interpretation, however, which initiated the greatest storm of response. Representative monographs by H. Holwerda,[5] L. van Hartingsveld,[6] and R. Ricca[7] attempted counter interpretations on the level of Johannine eschatology, whereas Th. Müller,[8] W. Wilkens,[9] and K. Haacker[10] sought to document a salvation-history perspective. J. Heise's study,[11] on the other hand, reflected virtual acceptance of the whole of Bultmann's interpretation. A noteworthy development in the entire discussion has been the literal blossoming of extensive studies by a growing number of Roman Catholic exegetes. In addition to two magna opera, a major uncompleted commentary by R. Schnackenburg[12] and an American counterpart by R. Brown,[13] there has appeared a steady stream of excellent and detailed monographs including those

---

[1] *Bread From Heaven*, Suppl. Nov. Test, 10, Leiden, 1965.
[2] *The Prophet-King, Moses Traditions and the Johannine Christology*, Suppl. Nov. Test., 14, Leiden, 1967.
[3] *Die Stiftung des Heils*, (Dissertation-Mainz) 1970. Haacker's study is now available in a reworked and somewhat shortened form in the series: *Arbeiten zur Theologie*, Heft 47, Stuttgart, 1972. References in this study are made to the original dissertation.
[4] *History and Theology in the Fourth Gospel*, New York, 1968.
[5] *The Holy Spirit and Eschatology in the Gospel of John*, A Critique of R. Bultmann's Eschatology, Kampen, 1959.
[6] *Die Eschatologie des Johannesevangeliums*, Eine Auseinandersetzung mit R. Bultmann, Assen, 1962.
[7] *Die Eschatologie des Vierten Evangeliums*, Frankfurt/Zürich, 1966.
[8] *Das Heilsgeschehen im Johannesevangelium*, Frankfurt/Zürich, 1961.
[9] *Die Entstehungsgeschichte des 4. Evangeliums*, Zollikon, 1958; *Zeichen und Werke*, ATANT Bd. 55, Zürich, 1969.
[10] op. cit.
[11] *Bleiben*, HUT Bd. 8, Tübingen, 1967.
[12] *Das Johannesevangelium*, I Teil, Einleitung und Kommentar zu Kap. 1-4, Herders Theol. Komm. z. NT, Bd. IV, Freiburg, 1965. II Teil, Kap 5-12, 1971.
[13] *The Gospel According to John I - XII*, The Anchor Bible, Vol. 29, New York, 1966. XIII - XXI, Vol. 29a, 1970.

of W. Thüsing,[1] J. Blank,[2] R. Borig,[3] G. Richter,[4] H. Leroy,[5] and A. Dauer.[6]

Despite its unpretentious size and appearance and what has been referred to as a "biblicistic-pietistic title,"[7] E. Käsemann's recent study,[8] now in its third printing, introduced decidedly new impulses into the Johannine discussion. This collection of former lectures crystallized with such provocative sharpness major accents of Johannine theology that not only was a basis laid for a new round in Johannine exegetical studies but a literal hornet's nest was broken into by posing the lingering questions of a previous generation in aggressively new and yet carefully modified form. In striking contiguity and yet in sharpest antithesis to Bultmann's interpretation, Käsemann called attention to the uniqueness of the Johannine witness, a uniqueness which finds concentrated expression not in the incarnation but in the testimony to the glory of Christ as the pre-existent Son of God who is one with the Father. Accordingly, the theme of the Fourth Gospel is not "and the Word became flesh" but "and we beheld his glory." With repristinated phraseology and insights of the old liberal school the Jesus of John is described as "God who strides over the earth" (so Baldensperger, Bousset, Wrede, Wetter). The life of Jesus and his appearance in the flesh are not the marks of humiliation but rather the channels of exposure which provide the possibility for communication with the alien world. History for John is not reportáge and narrative rehearsal but rather the epiphany of the Word. Thus only within the context of God's revelation is history at all possible. Here dogmatic reflection clearly dominates the

---

[1] *Die Erhöhung und Verherrlichung Jesu im Johannesevangelium*, NTA 21, 1. Münster, 1960. A second edition (1970) includes an expanded supplement dealing with the current discussion.
[2] *Krisis*, Freiburg im Breisgau, 1964.
[3] *Der Wahre Weinstock*, SANT Bd. 16, München, 1967.
[4] *Die Fußwaschung im Johannesevangelium*, Regensburg, 1967.
[5] *Rätsel und Missverständnis*, Ein Beitrag zur Formgeschichte des Johannesevangeliums, Dissertation-Tübingen, 1968.
[6] *op. cit.*
[7] So G. Bornkamm, "Zur Interpretation des Johannes-Evangeliums", *Gesammelte Aufsätze*, Bd. III, München, 1968, p. 104.
[8] *Jesu Letzter Wille Nach Johannes 17*, Tübingen, 3. Aufl, 1971. The third edition has been considerably expanded with additional footnotes.

witness, a witness whose only theme is the presence of Christ.
Nor is this presence simply postulated as bare occurrence as
though the fact alone that the Revealer came were the extent
of the proclamation. On the contrary, it is filled with content descriptive of the glory of Christ and his oneness with
the Father. Epiphany christology is the pivotal point of
Johannine theology. Conversely, John's stark dualism cannot
be understood anthropologically as a dualism of decision
since faith and unbelief appear as confirmation of decisions
that actualize a predestined and irrefrangible position. As
such, Johannine dualism is anchored in the omnipotence of the
Word manifested in the presence of the glorious Christ. To
identify the historical location of these reflections is, in
Käsemann's assessment, to point to a conventicle type of
Christianity characterized by gnosticizing tendencies and a
naive docetism. With such consistent and controversial lines
it was clear that the gauntlet had once again been thrown
down for renewed work on the Fourth Gospel. And it is not at
all surprising that in response a new dimension of an old
discussion was touched off with a growing number of contributions and reactions. While it may not be the last time that
a new beginning must be made in Johannine interpretation,[1] it
is the first time that the discussion has taken on such broad
and intensive dimensions and summoned such varied participants. Above all, it is the first time that the discussion
must encounter such a wealth of previously developed material
and decide between so many nuances and finely positioned accents.

It is against this background that this present investigation has taken its form and shape. It goes without saying
that any interpretation stands or falls by the very text it
seeks to explain. Its validity is measured directly by the
text itself. That this entails a certain amount of circularity is, of course, not to be denied. Circularity is an

---

[1] Cp. G. Bornkamm, "Zur Interpretation des Johannes-Evangelium", *op. cit.*
p. 121: "Es wird nicht das letzte Mal sein, daß wir auf dem Felde der
Johannesauslegung von vorn anfangen müssen."

inherent factor in all historical investigation.[1] What is
called for, then, is a careful examination of the particulars, a detailed textual analysis which best accounts for the
multiplicity of aspects and accords with the overall intention of the final composition. It is the center which qualifies the respective parts. Or to put it the other way around,
you cannot deal with any one of the parts in the Fourth Gospel without having to deal in some respect with the whole.
Thus, while analysis of the text's individual elements is indispensable in determining their discrete connotations, this
must not be done in isolation since their relation to the
structure and conception of the whole is decisive. For example, the Fourth Evangelist uses a variety of christological
designations such as Messiah, Christ, the Prophet, the Son of
Man, Son, and Son of God, each of which has its own distinct
provenance, original meaning, and history of tradition. To
project any one of these apart from the rest as the carrier
of Johannine christology would, however, not be valid since
it is the interrelationship of all these titles in their
present context and, above all, in their predication by the
total Johannine scheme which determines the accents and sets
the directional lines for an interpretation of the gospel's
christology. These same considerations hold true for any
analysis that proposes to explore and explicate the role and
content of a given motif. Motif analysis is an integral part
of the total interpretational task and as such helps to provide the necessary exegetical evidence for locating the interpretation most consistent with the material and the evangelist's intention.

B. AIM AND SCOPE

The following investigation undertakes to clarify the motif
of oneness in the Fourth Gospel. In view of its centrality
in John's Gospel, it is surprising that this motif has not
yet been the subject of any single extensive investigation.

---

[1] K. Haacker (*op. cit.* p. 4) engages in a gross oversimplification when
he charges that Bultmann's failing consists in giving an a priori answer
to the nature of the given traditions before exegesis of the text.

That is all the more surprising since the oneness passages have regularly attracted considerable attention in current as well as in past interpretation. This was particularly the case in the days when the terms of mysticism reflected a key approach in Johannine exegesis. No less is that the case when in current studies the question of John's relation to a docetizing christology looms up with paramount importance. Because of their uniqueness the Johannine oneness passages raise basic questions. To what extent are these passages representative for the evangelist's theological concerns? And should they be decisive, then what is the specific role and function of the motif which they express? Of course, this touches on a whole constellation of related problems. What textual evidence is there to explain the uniqueness of those elements of the oneness motif that are peculiar to John? Is the oneness motif an integrated theme in the theological plan of the Fourth Gospel or does it represent earlier or later, isolable or perhaps even disruptive tradition? What is its relation to the christology as well as to the ecclesiology and soteriology of the Gospel? Central in the response to these questions is not only a determination of the larger interpretational lines but a determination of the specific significance of the passages themselves in which the explicit term of oneness is employed in a theological sense. Here it is a question of establishing the tradition-historical place of these passages, the provenance of the motif, and its theological significance in relation to the larger context of the Gospel. These are the questions that will provide the framework and the scope of our investigation.

The study is divided into two major parts. Part one is aimed at tracing the morphology of the oneness motif in terms of the Gospel's major theological orientation. The introductory chapter provides a preliminary survey of those passages which explicitly use the term of oneness. Coupled with this is a brief historical overview of representative interpretational approaches. Then in the succeeding four chapters the following areas --the reciprocity statements, the christological titles, the semeia, and the passion account-- are respectively examined in order to gain an overall picture of the shape and function of the oneness motif as it relates to these basic areas. Here the decisive question asked consists in the extent to which the motif is embedded in the theology and structure of the Gospel and whether or not it plays a determinative role in reflecting the direction of the evangelist's witness. Of major concern in the investigation is the type of christology that is represented. The fact that christology forms the core of the Gospel's substance has been often and variously acknowledged. Whether or not it can be maintained that this christology is developed from the standpoint of the oneness motif is the crucial issue considered in this section.

Part two of the investigation is devoted to a study of the oneness passages themselves. After an introductory chapter dealing with an overview of the Johannine compositional problem, the oneness texts are analyzed from a literary and structural standpoint in the attempt to establish the nature of the composition or tradition in which the motif is located. The analysis proceeds along form-critical, stylistic, and religio-historical lines coupled with an investigation of the context in which the texts are located. The concluding chapter presents the theological explication of the oneness motif in the respective passages with particular emphasis on the relation to and the consequences for the evangelist's christology, soteriology, and ecclesiology. Of final concern is a summary comparison of the significance of the oneness motif in John with the occurrence of oneness themes in the rest of the NT and Ignatius.

PART I

THE MORPHOLOGY OF THE ONENESS MOTIF IN THE FOURTH GOSPEL

Chapter 1: Preliminary Survey of the Passages

A. SIGHTING THE TEXTS

Εἷs is used throughout the Fourth Gospel, as elsewhere in the NT, in the everyday sense as an equivalent for the indefinite article or in a specifically numerical sense as one in contrast to more than one. In the following seven verses, however, its usage in the numerical sense has strong theological connotations. In 10:16 the feminine and masculine adjectival form appear in the formula: "One flock, one Shepherd." The theological import of the usage here has both ecclesiological and christological significance. It is ecclesiological in that the character of the gathering of the believers is described. The future goal is pointed to where the chosen who hear the voice of the Shepherd will be one, free from the threats of the hostile world. The usage is, furthermore, christological in that the exclusiveness of Jesus as the Shepherd is expressed. The polemical claim is that there are not many shepherds but only one. Correspondingly, the nature of the gathering of those who hear the voice of the one Shepherd is also oneness. In the remaining passages the neuter singular of εἷς is always used. Never does the noun form ἑνότης appear. It is not metaphysical entities or static states of being that are described but always relations and events. Thus in 10:30 the relation between Christ and the Father is described in terms of oneness. Here the oneness motif appears as an explicit christological denominator. Dogma and kerygma interchange as the answer is given to the question, "Who is Jesus?" A soteriological function is also implicit. For whoever wants to see and to receive the works of the Father must see and receive them through the Son.

In 11:52 the purpose why the one man Jesus should die (par. 18:14) is paralleled with the explanation that the children of God should be gathered into one. Here in a passage somewhat analogous to 10:16 the oneness motif carries ecclesiological as well as soteriological significance and is oriented to a future goal descriptive of the heavenly reality that characterizes the unity of the gathered and chosen believers. Similarly in 17:11, where Jesus prays for the predestined that they may be one even as He and the Father are one, the oneness motif is used ecclesiologically and soteriologically to express the integration of the chosen believers into the projection of the pre-existent glory and unity of Jesus who is one with the Father. Thus the unity of the Father and the Son is understood and proclaimed as the sole basis for the unity of the church. In the most extensive and in many respects the crowning passage in the three verses in 17:21-23 the various accents of the oneness theme are alternately repeated and summarily reinforced. Again a future aspect is noted as Jesus prays for those who are yet to believe and asks that all be one, yes completely one after the pattern of his own oneness with the Father. The reasons for Jesus' unity with the Father are not reflected on. They are already presupposed in the pre-existent and eternal relations now made manifest in the revelation. In a sense the whole Gospel plan is summed up in the petition: "that they may be one as we are one." Here the εἷς motif serves as an abbreviation for Johannine christology by proclaiming who Jesus is, viz. the Revealer who is one with the Father. Likewise, the motif serves to express the meaning of the salvation event and the purpose of Jesus' mission, viz. the integration of the believers into the projected oneness of Father and Son so that they, the chosen ones, remain the recipients of divine love and glory. The resulting ecclesiological solidarity rests on a continuing encounter with the word and expresses itself in witness to the world. In summary, then, we may provisionally conclude that at least the following dimensions substantially constitute the oneness motif's basic orientation: 1) its christological use as a revelatory indicator expressing the unique relation of Jesus to the Father; 2) its soteriological significance in indicating that the possibility of faith exists only in response to and in oneness with the heavenly reality manifested in the works of Father and Son; 3) its ecclesiological significance in describing the solidary character of the chosen ones.[1] Of course, the extent to which these interpretations hold true must be tested in the following study.

B. OVERVIEW OF INTERPRETIVE APPROACHES

As noted previously, there has as yet been no single extensive study devoted specifically to the theme of oneness as a basic Johannine motif.[2] Nevertheless, the significance of John's use of the oneness theme has in varying degrees always been recognized and has led to often widely divergent interpretations. Two generations ago the predominant approach in Johannine studies was to see in the oneness passages the characteristic expression for the mystical form and substance of the Gospel. In fact, the Fourth Evangelist was often regarded as "the greatest of Christian mystics" and his Gospel as naturalizing the mystic form of religion within Christianity.[3] Thus it was customary to view Jesus as the mystagogue who mediates incorporation into the Divine through the visio Dei. The prayer that the initiates become one reflects the

---

[1] The only other passage in John where εἷς has theological implications is 8:41 where the Jews respond: "We have one Father, even God." Its usage here is formally parallel to 10:16 but is otherwise extraneous to the Johannine oneness complex since the evangelist shows no interest in using the oneness term to express the monotheistic aspect of faith.
[2] E. Stauffer's article on εἷς (ThWB II, pp. 432-440) deals primarily with the Pauline passages and touches on the Joh. verses only in passing without disclosing their specific meaning or the larger function of oneness in John. J. L. D'Aragon's essay ("La Notion johannique de l'unité", Sciences Ecclesiastique, 11, 1, 1959, pp. 111-119) avoids the problem of Joh. oneness. D'Aragon's study is essentially nothing more than a compendium of passages demonstrating the relation of oneness to the expressions of reciprocal knowledge, love, and immanence. J. F. Randall's unpublished dissertation (The Theme of Unity in John XVII: 20-23. Its Background and Meaning, Université Catholique de Louvain, 1962) deals only with the verses in ch. 17 and further attempts to document the character of the literary genus of farewell discourses and their religio-historical relation to the theme of unity.
[3] Cp. W. Howard, The Fourth Gospel in Recent Criticism and Interpretation, London, 1955. p. 150; 241. W. Bousset, Kyrios Christos, Göttingen, 5. Aufl., 1965. pp. 168f.

culminating apotheosis.¹ Jesus mediates to others the relation in which he stands with the Father. Union with God and mutual immanence are the decisive marks of this approach. A prevailing aspect of the mystically oriented and idealistic interpretation is the pronounced emphasis on the ethical character of the oneness motif.² Thus C. H. Dodd, for example, contends that the indwelling of man in God and God in man is coupled with the insistence on the deed. The idea in which both these strains meet is that of divine ἀγάπη.³ Accordingly, the accent is on a personal union of love whereby the realization of oneness is understood as the copy of a divine archetype, the reflection of a timeless reality. How strongly Dodd is determined by a platonizing and idealistic interpretation could hardly be clearer. W. Thüsing insists that the Johannine oneness of Father and Son is essentially a oneness of love and will which finds its deepest expression in Jesus' obedience unto death and the sacrifice on the cross.⁴ C. K. Barrett proposes an organic connection with the OT to the extent that "the unity of God now means the unity of Father and Son, and the command to love the neighbour becomes the requirement of mutual love within the Church."⁵ Here there are many variations on the same theme. E. Percy finds the declaration of Jesus' oneness with the Father a self-evident and thoroughly natural expression for "Jesus' consciousness of his calling."⁶ W. Bauer understands the oneness relationship between Jesus and the believers essentially in moral terms

---

[1] H. Holtzmann, *Lehrbuch der n.t. Theologie II*, Tübingen, 2. Aufl., 1911. p. 424, believed to be able to recognize the marks of the progressive mystic steps from purification to the final consummate act of ἐποπτεία.
[2] Cp. W. Heitmüller, *Das Johannesevangelium*, Die Schriften des NT IV, Göttingen, 3. Aufl., 1918. pp. 21, 30: "Tiefste Tiefe und höchste Höhe innerlichster, persönlichster Mystik...Höhepunkt der ethischen Religion schlechthin."
[3] C. H. Dodd, *Interpretation*, p. 199.
[4] W. Thüsing, *Herrlichkeit und Einheit*, Eine Auslegung des hohenpriesterlichen Gebetes Jesu, Düsseldorf, 1962. Cp. also F. Büchsel, *Das Evangelium nach Johannes*, NTD IV, Göttingen, 1946. p. 492: "...Vielmehr ist das ewige Verhältnis zwischen Vater und Sohne Liebe, d.h. etwas Persönliches und Sittliches." So also F. Mußner, ΖΩΗ *Die Anschauung vom "Leben" im Vierten Evangelium*, München, 1952. p. 154: "Die mittelbare 'unio mystica' mit Gott darf freilich nicht in einem psychologisch-ekstatischen Sinn, sondern in einem personal-ethischen verstanden werden."
[5] C. K. Barrett, *St. John*, p. 25; cp. also Hoskyns, *op. cit.* p. 390.
[6] E. Percy, *Untersuchungen über den Ursprung der johanneischen Theologie*, Lund, 1939. p. 204.

since "relations to God and Christ are established through the keeping of the commandments."[1] Moving basically within the same thought constellation is S. Hanson's interpretation which places the oneness relationships into the category of "the identity of representation."[2] Thus the Father sends the Son and in His love He is loyal to Him. Similarly the Church represents Christ through obedience and fidelity.

Often coupled with the ethical aspect is what many interpreters refer to as the metaphysical or ontological intent of the oneness statements. Thus it is maintained that the ethical oneness is based on Jesus' metaphysical unity with the Father.[3] "Then John's thought about Jesus is not so much functional as it is essential."[4] His intention would be to describe Jesus' ontological relation to the Father whereby the basis would be laid for the later theology of the Trinity.[5] From here it is only a short step to correspondent talk of the ontological structure of the one Mater Ecclesia in which the believer has an ontological part.[6] Ecumenical implications have also been noted. Thus it is said that the Johannine oneness idea implies the true unity of all Christians without any confessional barriers.[7] Or it is said that the "Trinity's mutual interpenetration", implicit in the Johannine passages, "must be reflected in the One Church, in whose common life all the distinct churches should share by intercommunion, mutual recognition, and interchange of ministries."[8] Others are careful to note that oneness for John is

---

[1] W. Bauer, *Das Johannesevangelium*, Handb.NT 6, Tübingen, 3. Aufl., 1933. p. 249.
[2] *The Unity of the Church in the New Testament*, Acta Seminarii Neotestamentici Upsaliensis 14, Uppsala, 1946. p. 146f.
[3] F. Mußner, op. cit, p. 79; W. Bauer, *Joh. Ev*, p. 84; O. Betz, op. cit, p. 166.
[4] C. Barrett, *St. John*, p. 45; Cp. also J. Blank, *Krisis*, p. 112.
[5] Cp. T. E. Pollard, "The Exegesis of John X:30 in the Early Trinitarian Controversies," *NTS* (3), 1956/57. pp. 334-349. *Johannine Christology and the Early Church*, Cambridge, 1970. J. Giblet, "La Sainte Trinité selon l'Evangile de saint Jean," *Lumiere et Vie* (29), 1956. pp. 98ff.
[6] So G. Behler, *Die Abschiedsworte des Herrn*, Johannesevangelium Kapitel 13-17, Salzburg, 1962. p. 283f.
[7] B. Schwank, "Damit alle eins seien," Joh. 17:20-26, *Sein und Sendung*, (28), 1963. p. 531.
[8] T. E. Pollard, "That They All May Be One" Jn. xvii.21 and the Unity of the Church. *Expository Times* (70,5) 1959. pp. 149f.

not uniformity nor can it be established through organizations, institutions, or dogmas. Not a perceptible phenomenon of the world, it is instead an eschatological event which is realized only in the word of proclamation in which the Revealer is present.[1] Lest that be understood only as an inner unity in the tradition of word and faith, objection is raised that the unity of the church can never be detached from the unity of Father and Son which establishes the oneness of believers.[2] Here oneness is understood in antithesis to terrestial phenomena as a heavenly reality whose presence among men can be had only as a projection from the heavenly realm. Participation in that oneness follows as a result of remaining in the Word and is made possible only to the extent that one is determined by that Word. This accent, however, is shifted when, for example, it is maintained that "the human world has in itself something latent which makes it possible for the human beings to receive the Divine gift."[3] In that case the oneness theme receives a decidedly anthropological center.

Other dimensions claimed for the Johannine oneness motif include sacramental aspects. Eucharistic overtones are detected by some as constitutive elements in the motif's intention.[4] A salvation-history perspective is apparent when it is maintained that the basic interest of the motif is to underscore the historical uniqueness and singularity of the cross event as well as the intercessory position of Jesus which is established by virtue of his historical work.[5] Here oneness among the believers is understood in an organic sense and as part of a rectilinear development of the "new humanity" and "body" themes which appear in the Pauline traditions.[6] A final aspect to be mentioned in this overview stems from the attempt to explain why the oneness theme appears in John with such emphasis. E. Schweizer maintains that the reason is to be found in the fact that the unity of the church had become

---

[1] So R. Bultmann, *Ev. Joh*, p. 393f.
[2] E. Käsemann, *Letzter Wille*, p. 142.
[3] H. Odeberg, *The Fourth Gospel*, Amsterdam, 2. Aufl., 1968. p. 146.
[4] Cp. J. L. D'Aragon, *op. cit.*, p. 117; R. Brown, *John* I, p. 443; G. Behler, *op. cit.*, p. 302: "Einheit ist die Wirkung der heiligen Eucharistie."
[5] E. Stauffer, *art. cit.*, *ThWB* II, p. 438.
[6] E. Stauffer, *loc. cit.*

such a burning problem.¹ Thus the roots for the use and development of the oneness theme in John would lie primarily in anti-heretical polemic and in the insistence that a united front be presented in witness to the world.²

In the foregoing we have in summary fashion touched upon a variety of representative accents and approaches developed in the interpretation of the Johannine oneness motif. They help accentuate the nature and the scope of the problem before us by demonstrating the variance and the contradictory positions that have been set forth. Whether any one of these interpretations or any other is valid or untenable must be tested by the text and by an analysis of the related particulars. However, before going into a more thorough investigation of the specific passages containing the term εἷς, we will first explore the role and shape of the motif in its broader perspective as it is implicitly suggested in other areas of the Gospel.

---

[1] "Der Kirchenbegriff bei Johannes," *Neotestamentica*, Zürich/Stuttgart, 1963. p. 263.
[2] Cp. G. Wetter, *Der Sohn Gottes*, FRLANT N.F. 9, Göttingen, 1916. p. 167.

Chapter II: Oneness and the Reciprocity Statements

A. RELATIONALITY BETWEEN JESUS AND GOD

One of the most striking features of the Johannine discourse material is the repeated appearance of statements in reciprocal form describing the relation between Jesus and the Father and between Jesus and the believers. In no other place in the NT do reciprocity statements appear in such massive concentration and frequency as they do in John. Here their function is distinctly unique. That is evident, first of all, in those statements which pertain to Jesus' relation to the Father. Though descriptive in nature, these statements are clearly not meant to convey a body of knowledge or teachings with progressing and developing lines of thought since all the statements revolve essentially around one and the same theme. In fact, not only their formal structure but their meaning as well move in a circle. All these statements appear as words of Jesus occurring in contexts that range from polemical situations of conflict to detached dialogue with the disciples. And yet in every instance they are words which emanate from and point back to the speaker himself. The thrust is to indicate that he is the center. He is the pivotal point of authentic relations between man and God because he stands in perfect unity with the Father. Thus Jesus can say that if anyone has known him, he has known the Father (14:7). To see Jesus, not with empirical vision but with faith perception, is the same thing as seeing the Father (14:9). Reciprocal statements like these are reflected on theologically with a variety of changing terms and pictures. The reason why it is Jesus and not another who is the way to the Father is because it is only Jesus of whom it can be said that the Father is in him and he in the Father (10:38; 14:10, 11). Never is that kind of reciprocity in the Gospel extended to anyone else. Only Jesus stands in perfect solidarity with the Father. This same relation is described again, this time from the standpoint of "knowing", when Jesus declares that the Father knows him and he knows the Father (10:15). The circular and self-authenticating explanation given for this mutuality of knowledge is found in Jesus' statement: "I know him for I come from him..." (7:29). Correspondingly it is the Father who knows the Son because it is the Father who has sent him. For this reason Jesus can say to the hostile unbelieving world: "If you knew me you would know Him who sent me" (8:19). Where else could such formulations derive except from the conviction that Jesus and God are one?

The sending motif, touched on in the last verse, also plays an important role in the reciprocity statements. The Father sends the Son to do the works which the Father has given him to complete (5:36). As the Sent One the Son can only do what has been given to him (17:4). He can only do what the Father does (5:19), only speak what he has seen with the Father (8:38) and declare what he has heard from Him (8:26). In turn, Jesus' works bear witness that he is sent from the Father (5:36). Conversely, the Father who sent him bears witness to Jesus (5:37). In the sending mission the mutual exchange of work and witness underscores the underlying theme of Jesus' oneness with the Father. This is the relation which further motivates the declaration in 7:16f., where Jesus states that his teaching is not his own but his who sent him. Anyone who speaks on his own seeks his own renown. But he who seeks the renown of him who sent him is true. In other words, Jesus is true, viz. he speaks the truth he was sent to speak and is therefore faithful and reliable simply by virtue of his claim that his teaching is not his own. Likewise the Father who sent him is true (7:28; 8:26). In other words, He is true because His witness through the Son He sent is faithful and reliable. The truth of Jesus and the Father rests in the common origin and purpose of the Father's sending and the Son's being sent. The same theme is underscored when Jesus declares that he does not seek his own will but the will of him who sent him (5:30). Jesus' will is the Father's will and the Father's will is Jesus' will. For this reason it is not Jesus alone who judges, but rather Jesus and he who sent him (8:16). Or to put it in another way, just as the Father raises the dead and gives them life so also the Son gives life to whom he will (5:21). He is able to do that because he has life in himself just as the Father has life in himself (5:26). In all of these reciprocity statements the underlying theme repeatedly and variously expressed is clearly the oneness of Father and Son.

This very oneness, however, appears problematic when measured against accents inherent in the structure and background of the sending motif. It has long been recognized that the frequent use of the formula-like participial construction, ὁ πέμψας με, and corresponding phrases utilizing the verbs πέμπειν and ἀποστέλλειν play a constitutive role in the Fourth Gospel.[1] Yet to make the motif of "sending" and the "sent one" the one central theme and basis of the Gospel, as Bultmann suggests,[2] is neither warranted nor tenable. Despite its importance and peculiarity as a Johannine formula, it is by no means inclusive enough in meaning and orientation to serve as the integrating center of the Gospel and as a key for grasping the specificity of its christology. Furthermore, the motif is also used to describe the work of John the Baptist (1:6,33: 3:28) and is not singularly christological in use.[3] If a reason were to be given why the sending motif plays such a prominent role in the reciprocity statements, as elsewhere in the Gospel, the most compelling cause would be found in

---

[1] Already E. Norden (*Agnostos Theos*, Darmstadt, 3. Aufl., 1956. p. 382) called attention to the frequency and stereotyped nature of the phrase. Similarly Bultmann (*Ev Joh*, p. 186 n. 3) who lists 17 occurrences for ὁ πέμψας με, ca. 6 occurrences (depending on manuscript variations) for ὁ πέμψας με πατήρ, and another 15 occurrences for related phrases expressing the sending action of the Father. See also Ricca, *op. cit.*, p. 108. E. Haenchen, "Der Vater, der mich gesandt hat", *Gott und Mensch*, Tübingen, 1965. pp. 68-77.

[2] "Die Bedeutung der neuerschlossenen mandäischen und manichäischen Quellen für das Verständnis des Johannesevangeliums", *Exegetica*, Tübingen, 1967. p. 57: "Was ist seine zentrale Anschauung, seine Grundkonzeption? Zweifellos muß sie in dem immer wiederholten Satz stecken, daß Jesus der Gesandte Gottes sei..."

[3] K. Haacker's reference (*op. cit.*, p. 140) to Mk. 11:27-33 where in the question of authority Jesus aligns himself with John the Baptist does not really apply here since the account and its parallels all occur outside of the context of the sending motif. To speak of "Kontinuität in der Umformung" has no real basis.

the revelational character of the motif.¹ And yet the basic
structure of the sending - sent concept poses a problem. Its
orientation, as its history in Hellenistic and Jewish traditions illustrates, indicates that the agent or emissary who
has been authorized and empowered to carry out the mandate
for which he had been sent is not the principal or sovereign
figure but instead occupies a more or less secondary position?
As such, the emissary receives his authority from another and
has subordinate, deputy-like significance. But precisely
that aspect is foreign to the Johannine conception which reflects, as the reciprocity statements already indicate, a
pronounced emphasis on the oneness of Father and Son.³ When,
therefore, the ὁ πέμψας με πατήρ phrase is isolated as the
characteristic expression of Johannine christology and interpreted predominantly in terms of an obedient emissary relationship expressed in service and an act of love,⁴ then an

---

¹ The juristic aspects which answer to the question of authority (cp.
Rengstorf, ThWB I, p. 414f.) and also the suggestion of origin (cp.
Bultmann, Ev Joh, p. 30 n. 2) are component parts of the revelational
character of the motif.
² In cynic-Stoic literature the authority of the emissary or messenger
may derive from his own subjective initiative or self-consciousness (cp.
Rengstorf, ThWB I, p. 398). In general, however, the emissary is simply
a representative of the monarch or the one who sent him and therefore has
a secondary, derivative position. Also in Gnosis, where the term is a
favorite expression, the divine emissary is sent by "the highest God" thus
implicitly suggesting a subordinal position for the messenger although
here the idea of consubstantiality may considerably alter the circumstance
(cp. W. Bauer, Joh Ev, p. 58). In rabbinic traditions the emissary may be
viewed as equal to the one who sent him. Here equality is conceived of in
terms of an identity of representation. (cp. Billerbeck, Kommentar zum
NT aus Talmud und Midrash, München, 1961. Bd. I, p. 590; Bd. II, pp. 167,
466. In OT and Jewish traditions generally the emissary has a subordinate position in relation to the sender. P. Borgen, "God's Agent in the
Fourth Gospel: Religions in Antiquity," Essays in Memory of E. R.
Goodenough, Leiden, 1968. pp. 143f. summarizes thus: "there are striking similarities between the halakhic principles of agency and ideas in
the Fourth Gospel as (a) the unity between the agent and his sender; (b)
although the agent is subordinate; (c) the obedience of the agent to the
will of the sender; (d) the task of the agent in lawsuit; (e) his return
and reporting back to the sender; (f) his appointing of other agents as
an extension of his own mission in time and space."
³ Cogent is Rengstorf's observation (ThWB I, p. 405): "Von ihr aus (sc.
der wesenhaften Einheit Jesu mit Gott) haben in bestimmten Zusammenhängen
ἀποστέλλειν und πέμπειν ihre eigenartige Prägung im 4. Ev. empfangen,
nicht aber haben sie umgekehrt die joh. Christologie mitgeformt." Further,
Käsemann, Letzter Wille, p. 25. Contra Dodd, Interpretation, p. 254.
⁴ So E. Haenchen, "Der Vater, der mich gesandt hat," op. cit. Again in
"Vom Wandel des Jesusbildes in der frühen Gemeinde," Verborum Veritas,
Festschrift für G. Stählin, Wuppertal, 1970. p. 12.

accent shift is introduced which is not wholly compatible with the Johannine conception. John's christology leaves no room for even incipient subordinationism. Jesus is not just the Father's authorized representative or agent. For John he is not simply the man specially qualified by God. While it is true that he can do nothing of his own (8:28), still he is understood as the one who gives life <u>to whom he will</u> (5:21). In fact, he has the power to lay down his own life and to take it up again (10:18; cp. also 2:19). In the case of the religio-historical analogies, the essence of the emissary is to point back to the one who sent him. But in John's Gospel this relation receives a vital added qualification. Not only can it be said of Jesus that he points back to the Father and makes him known (1:18) or that no one comes to the Father except through the Son (14:6), but also conversely that no one hears and learns from the Father without coming to Jesus (6:45). In other words, the Father points only to the Son. It is the possibility of this reverse statement which underscores the full dialectic of a relation which is not one-sidedly balanced but mutually and reciprocally conditioned. Thus the same honor which accords the Father is also to be given to the Son and, vice versa, whoever does not honor the Son does not honor the Father who sent him (5:23). This constant interchange and reciprocity reinforce the fact that the sending motif must be understood in the light of Jesus' oneness with the Father.[1] From this standpoint it receives its specifically Johannine character and in referring to his origin and commissioning by the Father documents Jesus' complete solidarity with God.

The dialectic of oneness is further qualified and reflected

---

[1] Typical of the blurring which so often occurs at this point is Hoskyn's insistence (*op. cit.*, p. 267f.) that Jesus' mission properly rests in his knowledge of the Father and in the Father's love for the Son whereby the knowledge of the Son is finally dependent on the love of the Father for the Son. Similarly Barrett, *St. John* p. 201 who describes the mission of Jesus as "the fruit of submission." Haenchen too ("Vom Wandel," *op. cit.*, p. 12) makes common cause with this interpretation but errs when he regards the oneness theme as restricted to 10:30 and 17:11, 21f.

on in terms of the theme of ἔργα.¹ Its reciprocal aspect is expressed when Jesus declares, "My Father is working still, and I am working" (5:17). The intention of the statement is pointedly displayed when the Jews respond with the charge that Jesus is making himself equal with God (5:18). The works which Jesus does disclose who he is. Just as the works of the world disclose its essential and constitutive opposition to the Revealer (7:7) so the works of God (9:3) disclose the revelational activity of the Father in the Son and express their essential solidarity.² Jesus can therefore say: 'Even though you do not believe me, believe the works that you may know and understand that the Father is in me and I am in the Father" (10:38). In other words, though formally distinct, the works of Jesus express his essential identity since they have been given him by the Father and disclose his oneness relation with the Father. In this sense the works of Jesus are parallel to his words.³ For if anyone does not keep Jesus' words, it is not Jesus who judges him (12:47; cp. also 8:16); rather the word which Jesus has spoken --a word which he has received-- will be that person's judge on the last day (12:48). The initial thrust of these statements is to underscore that what Jesus is he is by virtue of what he has received. The words he speaks he has heard from the Father (12:49) and the works he does have been given him (5:36). He does them "in the name of the Father" (10:25) and they have their origin ἐκ τοῦ πατρός. The words and works of Jesus are, therefore, inseparably bound to the Father. But since the Father has given them only to the Son, those same words and works are inseparably bound to the Son. They are a connecting link between Father and Son. If, as we said before, what Jesus is is determined by what he has received, then it must

---

[1] Since the ἔργα have an origin distinct from the σημεῖα (cp. R. Fortna, "Source and Redaction in the Fourth Gospel's Portrayal of Jesus' Signs", JBL (89), 1970. pp. 151ff.) and have a broader scope of meaning (not clearly recognized by G. Bertram, ThWB II, p. 639), the two terms will be considered separately.
[2] This orientation of Jesus' ἔργα is well recognized by W. Wilkens, Zeichen und Werke, p. 85. Wilkens fails, however, to draw sharply the consequences for his overall interpretation.
[3] Cp. Bultmann, Theol. of the NT, II, p. 60.

also be seen that what he has received is determined by his oneness with the Father.[1] The resulting reciprocity of ἔργα can not be understood platonically in terms of archetype and copy but rather must be seen in terms of mutuality. If it is the work of the Son, then it is also equally the work of the Father. In short, the identity and reciprocity of ἔργα[2] testify to the perfect solidarity between Father and Son.

Frequently coupled with the theme of Jesus' works is the motif of μαρτυρία.[3] This opens still another aspect to the Johannine constellation of reciprocity statements. The dialectic maintained evidences an advanced stage of theological reflection. On the one hand, Jesus states that if he bears witness to himself, then his witness is not true (5:31). True, rather, is the witness of the Father which is given concerning the Son (5:32). Jesus repeatedly points beyond himself. With almost monotonous persistency it is emphasized that he can do nothing of his own accord (5:19) and that he does not act or speak on his own authority (8:28; 14:10). The immediate impact of these declarations is to point beyond the simple earthly sphere. Historical phenomena are in themselves empty and always open to misunderstanding to the degree that they are not qualified by God's clarity and doxa from beyond. Similarly, the witness of the fathers (7:19f.) and the prophets (8:52f.) or the witness of John the Baptist (1:32f.) are never final instances in themselves but receive validity only when they point beyond themselves and open the way to the

---

[1] Contra Dodd, *Interpretation*, p. 327, who maintains that the identity of work is conditioned, on the Son's part, by unqualified obedience and, on the Father's part, by his perfect love for the Son. Dodd fails to recognize that the repeated references to Jesus' selfless action --he can do nothing on his own authority (5:30; 8:28; 12:49); he does not seek his own will (5:30)-- are not descriptive of unqualified obedience or of the relinquishment of Jesus' power and will but are descriptive of his perfect relation with the Father. W. Thüsing (*Erhöhung und Verherrlichung*, p. 71) likewise obscures the Johannine intention when he maintains: Wenn der Sohn den Willen des Vaters tut, so is damit immer der Verzicht auf den eigenen Willen gemeint. Dieser Verzicht wird dadurch ausgedrückt, daß der Sohn nicht von sich aus handelt." The categories of obedience and relinquishment are foreign to John's description of Jesus.
[2] τὰ ἔργα can also be summed up simply as τὸ ἔργον (4:34; 17:4) since the works of Jesus given to him by the Father are really only one: the saving manifestation of God's presence.
[3] Cp. Schnackenburg, *Joh Ev*, I. p. 347f.

reality of God's presence.[1] Thus when Jesus insists that his witness to himself is not true (5:31), what is being said is that the earthly sphere, when separated from God's revelation, is empty and not true, viz. it is illusory and does not have the character of reality. This thought is now further developed. For even though Jesus can maintain that when he bears witness to himself, his testimony is not true, we find further statements which assert precisely the opposite. Before the Pharisees Jesus declares: "Even if I do bear witness to myself, my testimony is true" (8:14). Similarly he can maintain that it is the works which he has done and which no one else did which exposed the sin of the world (14:24). How is this formal contradiction to be explained? The relation becomes clear when the reasons are considered why Jesus' self-testimony is said to be true. It is true because Jesus knows where he has come from and where he is going (8:14). He knows that he has always been with the Father. That's why his claims are absolutely exclusive. Jesus is a stranger to the world because his real origin and home are other-worldly. His witness is true precisely because the works which he does are done in the Father's name (10:25). In short, it is the Father who is working in him; therefore Jesus' witness is true inasmuch as it is the Father's witness.[2] In all of this circularity of thought the one integrating center which motivates the statements is consistently the same: Jesus' inseparable oneness with the Father. In this way the character of the revelation is also described. In the final analysis it can only be said that God bears witness to himself. His word demonstrates its validity in the self-evident quality and sufficiency of the revelation.[3]

---

[1] Käsemann (*Letzter Wille*, p: 94) rightly notes in this connection that even as the fathers can be quoted against Christ (8:33ff.) or the proclamation of the Church can threaten to supplant Christ, so the claim of the earthly Jesus can appear incredible to the one or mislead the other through illusions of salvation. Even the incarnation remains vague and contradictory as long as it is not penetrated by a faith which realizes the glory of Jesus and all glory only in Jesus.
[2] Cp. Blank, *Krisis*, p. 204: "Jesus bezeugt sich selbst nur so, daß er ineins damit Gott den Vater bezeugt und sich selbst als Sohn."
[3] When E. Schweizer ("Jesus der Zeuge Gottes," *Studies in John*, Suppl. Nov. Test., 24, Leiden, 1970. pp. 161-168) in a surprising about-face from his *Ego Eimi* study, now contends that Jesus for John was not the

ONENESS AND THE RECIPROCITY STATEMENTS

Integral to the reciprocity statements is also the centrally important motif of δόξα. As with the other reciprocally described terms already referred to, δόξα too is employed against the background of the oneness between Father and Son. The clearest formulation of this appears in the hymn-like passage in 13:31f. where Jesus declares that the Son of Man is now glorified, and in him God is glorified. If God is glorified in him, God will also glorify him in himself, and glorify him at once. Here Jesus' glorification as the Son of Man is identified with the glorification of God. The glorification of both constitutes a unity. The glory which Jesus receives does not qualify his relation to the Father. Rather his relation of oneness to the Father qualifies the glory that is given him (17:24) and makes it identical to the glory of the Father. Since in the Fourth Gospel Jesus' oneness relation with the Father is never described as being broken or even diminished, his glory correspondingly is always consistent and is never relinquished.[1] Precisely this point is reinforced with the

---

Revealer but rather "the Witness of God," he has chosen a very problematic designation which introduces accents not basically congruent with the Johannine presentation of revelation. This revelation is self-authenticating precisely because it is rooted in the oneness of Father and Son. Never in the Fourth Gospel is Jesus explicitly described as a witness for God. In fact, the term μάρτυς is never used in John. Instead of Jesus witnessing to God, it is said that the Father bears witness to the Son (5:32,37; 8:18), that the Paraclete bears witness to him (15:26), that John the Baptist bears witness to him (1:7) and likewise the crowd (12:17); the Scriptures bear witness to him (5:39) and finally that Jesus himself and his works bear witness to himself (5:36; 8:14; 10:25). The christological direction of all these statements is obvious. And yet Jesus' self-witness consists only in what he has heard and seen (3:32) and in the works which the Father has given him to do (5:36). In this sense it may indeed be said that Jesus bears witness to God, but it is a self-witness possible only because of his oneness with the Father. The nature of this oneness relation is obscured when Schweizer reduces its meaning merely to "a unity of will, complete trust in the Father, and faithful obedience" (167). Not only does he ignore the forensic and juristic background of the concept of witness, but interpreting primarily from the standpoint of Jesus' via dolorosa, he introduces an accent shift not compatible with the Johannine conception. While it is true that the Johannine congregation may be characterized by faith struggle and persecution (15:9f.; 16:1,32), it is not the characteristic understanding of the Johannine Christ that he is the searching Shepherd who consoles the doubters and empathizes with their faith problems because he himself has gone the way of passion and pain.
[1] W. Thüsing (Erhöhung und Verherrlichung, p. 206f.) fails to recognize this when in the interpretation of 17:5 he maintains that through Jesus' request for glorification Jesus is to receive a status which he did not have on earth. Thüsing goes on to say that the earthly Jesus is referred

juxtaposition of the aorist and the future tenses in the 13:31f. passage. The interchangeable glory manifested in the past is not separate or qualitatively different from the interchangeable glory to be manifested in the future. They are rather aspects of the one event.[1]

This same relation is emphasized in the answer to the prayer in 12:38 where Jesus asks that the Father's name be glorified. To glorify the Father's name is tantamount to glorifying Jesus himself. When the heavenly voice replies: καὶ ἐδόξασα καὶ πάλιν δοξάσω, the juxtaposed aorist and future again point to the unity of the glorification which is not developmental or changed by temporal demarcations. The essence of the thought sequence implied in these verses is this: the Father glorifies himself in that he glorifies the Son. Since this glorification occurs in the Son, it has revelational significance. Because God sent Jesus as Revealer[2] he glorified his own name. And when it is said that God will glorify

---

to as the pre-existent one but never as παρὰ σοί (the Father). But what sense can it possibly have to press the meaning of the locality aspect of "being with the Father" by restricting this to the pre- and post-earthly existence of Jesus when likewise for and during his earthly ministry Jesus declares: "I and the Father are one" (10:30) or when he asks, "Do you not believe that I am in the Father and the Father in me?" (14:10,11; cp. also 10:38). The incontrovertible import of these passages is to indicate that Jesus' oneness with the Father is never interrupted even in his earthly ministry. The principal difference between παρὰ τῷ πατρί in history and beyond history does not consist in a status change for Jesus but in the changed circumstances surrounding his one status in solidarity with the Father. In history Jesus' glory is constantly contested and called into question by a hostile world whereas beyond history in his pre- and post-earthly existence his glory remains unchallenged. For this reason it is not clear, and at best inconsistent, when W. Wilkens (Zeichen und Werke, p. 111) maintains that Thüsing's observations at this point are correct even though Wilkens rightly insists that Jesus' glory cannot be understood kenotically in John.
[1] Cp. Bultmann, Ev Joh, p. 402: "Es ist jenes νῦν, in dem Vergangenheit und Zukunft aneinandergebunden sind..."
[2] In a programmatic attempt to locate the key for understanding John's concentrated christology, K. Haacker (Die Stiftung des Heils, cp. p. 246) polemicizes against the term "revealer" and suggests instead the category of "the founder" (der Stifter). If any one concept were ever singularly inadequate to convey the complexities and the uniqueness of Johannine christology, then certainly Haacker's choice meets the requirements. Not only is the phenomenology and structure of the concept of "founding" theologically foreign to the Johannine conception but also the terminology is nowhere even suggested despite Haacker's proposed Moses-Christ analogy. The reciprocity statements alone argue against the use of the concept, and it is significant that Haacker's analysis ignores this aspect.

it again, this means nothing other than that Jesus continues as Revealer even through his death. It is the Johannine understanding of Jesus' death which gives the δόξα theme its strikingly unique significance. From the outset Jesus' crucifixion is regarded as his exaltation. ὑψωθῆναι (3:14; 8:28; 12:32) is the characteristic expression for Jesus' death on the cross. Apart from ch. 19, the account of the crucifixion scene, σταυρός and σταυρωθῆναι are never used even though the cross as such is repeatedly referred to throughout the Gospel.[1] But these references are consistently made in terms of Jesus' elevation, his being lifted up, or in terms of the related description of his glorification. Accordingly Jesus' death is not understood as a descent into disgrace or as separation from God but as ascent and elevation to victory and glory, a confirmation of his oneness with the Father. While δοξασθῆναι is a much broader term and is not entirely synonymous with ὑψωθῆναι, it too describes the exaltation significance of the cross but does so in sharpest and most characteristic fashion. The hour of Jesus' death is defined simply as the hour of glorification (7:39; 12:16, 23; 13:31f.; 17:1,5). Jesus' crucifixion manifests the glory which the Father has given him. Two essential points emerge here as constitutive and bear further consideration. First of all, it is again made clear that the cross is not understood as a tragic catastrophe. The elements of humiliation and God-forsakenness have been stripped away and in their place are seen glory and exaltation. The traditional sequential approach as represented e.g. in Lk. 24:26 where the risen Lord asks, "Was it not necessary that the Christ should suffer these things and enter into his glory?" is not at all expressed in the Johannine scheme. In

---

[1] G. Klein's response to F. Hahn's study in *Evangelisch-Katholischer Kommentar zum NT*, Vorarbeiten Heft 2, 1970, p. 132, is hardly tenable when he observes that if passion motifs are scattered throughout John's Gospel, this would argue against understanding John's christology as docetizing. In reply it must be remembered that not the quantity and distribution of passion themes are decisive, but rather the manner in which they are used and understood. Even for the Gnostics the passion themes, albeit thoroughly recast for their own purposes, were nevertheless repeated topics of discussion. Cp. K. Beyschlag, "Zur Simon-Magus-Frage," *ZThK* 68/4, 1971, p. 417f. and A. Böhlig, "Christentum und Gnosis im Ägypterevangelium," *Christentum und Gnosis*, Beih. 37 z. ZNW, 1969, p. 11.

John the cross is not seen as the first step or condition for Jesus' entrance into a state of glory. Already the cross itself is enveloped in glory and marks an epiphany of victory and power.[1]

The second point that needs to be considered here is the place of the cross in relation to the ministry of Jesus. The fact that Jesus' glorification, as noted above, is emphatically localized at the point of the cross raises the question whether or not there is a progressive-linear dimension inherent in the reciprocal manifestation of God's glory in Christ. The problem is accentuated by passages such as 7:39 where, in obvious reference to the cross event, it is stated that Jesus was not yet glorified (cp. also 12:16). In his detailed analysis of the Johannine δόξα motif Thüsing consistently maintains the presence of a developmental process in the manifestation of God's glory whereby two major stages or periods set the lines of demarcation. The first stage, embracing Jesus' earthly work, is to have reached its culmination in the obedient death on the cross. The second and greater stage, analogous to the growth of the seed, is to be equated with the post-Easter, Spirit-filled works of the Church which keep on increasing until completion in the final consummation.[2] But

---

[1] Blank (*Krisis*, p. 269, n. 12) legitimately criticizes Bultmann for misplacing the accent in explaining the meaning of the cross thus: "the hour of δοξασθῆναι is the hour of the Passion" (*Ev Joh*, p. 324). Instead, Blank formulates the other way around: "the hour of the Passion is already the hour of δοξασθῆναι." Conzelmann's objection (*An Outline of the Theology of the New Testament*, New York and Evanston, 1969, p. 343) that the two formulations are not really alternatives is made from the standpoint of a harmonizing interest. Furthermore, his intimation that Blank's judgment is made in the light of catholic dogma is, at least at this point, unfounded.

[2] Although he fails to draw the consequences, even Thüsing (*Verherrlichung und Erhöhung*, p. 201) concedes that a sharp differentiation between the two stages cannot be made: "daß zwischen diesen beiden Stadien eine Analogiebeziehung besteht und daß das Heilswerk der beiden Stadien in joh. Sicht eine Einheit bildet." Blank's critique of Thüsing is thoroughly justified in insisting that according to John the work of revelation is only a single work (cp. *Krisis*, p. 269). But Blank, on the other hand, is not consistent when he maintains that Jesus' glorification is bound to a particular moment in history where his glory begins (p. 270): "Damit ist zugleich die geschichtliche Konkretheit des Menschensohnes gegeben; denn die ganze Rede hat nur dann einen Sinn, wenn derjenige, von dem die Rede ist, etwas bekommen soll, was er solange, bis die Stunde kam, in dieser (definitiven) Form nicht gehabt hatte." It is not surprising, then, when Blank without warrant introduces the Suffering Servant theology of Is. 52-53:12 as background for the glorification motif of John (p. 271). The same orientation is maintained by Dodd, *Interpretation*, p. 374.

the imposition of this kind of divisional scheme is basically incongruent with the Johannine conception. This is apparent on at least three counts. 1) Already the incarnation is understood not as a preliminary and veiled event but in the continuity of God's presence as the projection of His eternal glory (1:14b).[1] 2) Similarly, the words and works of the earthly Jesus are seen as manifestations of the same glory (2:11; 8:54; 17:4). Precisely this is underscored when in anticipation of the raising of Lazarus Jesus declares: "This illness is not unto death; it is for the glory of God, so that the Son of God may be glorified by means of it" (11:4). In other words, Jesus' glorification is not identified only with the cross but is evidenced in his prior work as a continuing reality.[2] Even before Good Friday and Easter, he is the Resurrection and the Life. 3) Furthermore, as was noted with the juxtaposition of aorist and future in 12:28 and 13:31f., past and future are bound together as respective aspects of a single event. Thus when Jesus refers to his accomplished work which manifested the Father's glory (17:4), he points to his whole past work of revelation. That this revelation also has a future is indicated by references to the "greater works" (14:13; 15:8) and to the testimony of the Spirit (16:4) all of which glorify the Son and the Father in the Son. Significant, however, is that these chronological aspects are not theologically distinguished as qualitatively different so far as they pertain to the revelatory work of Jesus.[3]

While there are formal differences in time and place in the

---

[1] The incarnate Jesus is the pre-existent Christ. Therefore there is no need in John for mention of the virgin birth or for a proclamation act at Jesus' baptism. Cp. E. Fascher, "Christologie und Gnosis im vierten Evangelium," *ThLZ* (93), No. 10, 1968, p. 726.
[2] Cogent treatment of the Johannine time scheme is given by L. Schottroff, "Heil als innerweltliche Entweltlichung," *Novum Testamentum*, XI, Leiden, 1969, p. 295.
[3] The responses of the believer and the growth of the church may legitimately be viewed from the standpoint of sequential development. But for John it is not valid to project a developmental pattern back onto the nature and revelatory activity of Christ. Cp. Bultmann, "Zur Interpretation des Johannesevangeliums," *ThLZ* (87) 1962, p. 4. In short, we may formulate thus: the Revealer is the constant; response to him is the variable.

manifestation of God's doxa, there is no principal difference in the character of its christological disclosure. Jesus comes and he goes; he is sent and he returns; but his glory, though extending into different spheres, remains the same. The words and works of the earthly Jesus do not have preliminary character in John. They are not simply an anticipation of the glorification of the cross. Just as the cross is surrounded with the glory which Jesus had before the world was made (17:5), so also his ministry, as that of the incarnated Logos, appears as the continuation of pre-existent glory. What is meant by saying that the glory of the incarnation and crucifixion is conditioned by changes in time and place is illustrated, first of all, by the incarnation of the Word. Incarnation does not signal a divestiture of glory but rather the Word's singular entrance into the world which is thereby exposed to the manifestation of God's presence in Christ.[1] Correspondingly the passion and crucifixion are characterized not by renunciation and suffering[2] but rather by passage from the alien world and return to the home that is free from the hostility of the cosmos.[3] For this reason the cross receives

---

[1] The incarnation means a change in locale for the Logos. Because the Logos enters the world, the character of the world is brought to light and confirmed as sinful. Sin is the result of the world's encounter with and rejection of the Logos. And yet by the same token the world was already sinful before the appearance of Jesus; otherwise the incarnation would be meaningless. (cp. Conzelmann, *Outline*, p. 353). This same dialectic pervades the entire Gospel and results in a unique integration of time dimensions so that formal temporal demarcations lose their significance. Pre- and post-resurrection experiences are telescoped into one. It is not the evangelist's intention to elevate the period from the incarnation to cross as the middle point of history. In fact, it is the characteristic feature of his Gospel that it is not developed and unfolded from a history of salvation perspective. The conceptuality for this is notably absent. W. Wilkens (*Zeichen und Werke*, p. 136) does not do justice to the specific accents of John when he insists on introducing the terms of historical development and e.g. maintains: "Wie die Präexistenz Jesu durch den Logos-Titel bezeichnet wurde, so ist für seine Postexistenz der Titel des Parakleten bezeichnend. Durch beide Titel hebt der Evangelist Präexistenz und Postexistenz scharf von der Zeit der Inkarnation ab. Wilkens then identifies the time of incarnation as "Mitte der Zeit" (p.166).
[2] Against Dodd (*Interpretation*, p. 208) who speaks of Jesus' "self-devotion to death in love for mankind" and Barrett (*St. John*, p. 354) who in reference to the passion speaks of "human anxiety" and "God's strength made perfect in weakness."
[3] W. Bauer, *Joh. Ev.*, p. 176: "Der Tod Jesu ist kein σκάνδαλον sondern Eingangspforte zur δόξα für ihn." Cp. also Käsemann, *Letzter Wille*, pp. 49f.

its culminant significance. It is the point of Jesus' departure which signals final κρίσις for the world (7:33f.; 8:21) as well as also κρίσις for the disciples (13:33). In this sense the cross receives its character as the definitive glorification of Jesus because he departs not as one who remains in death but as the continuing Giver of life. Or to put it in another way, the culminating importance of the cross lies not in the fact that Jesus receives glory which he never had before but in the fact that he departs with the same glory he always had. Because Jesus' glorification is so emphatically identified with his departure[1] the conditions of faith in him are clearly spelled out. There is no way to the exalted Christ except through the cross, that is to say, except in terms of his going away, on the one hand, and his continuing glory on the other. This is why there is κρίσις even for the disciples, a problem which is particularly central to the farewell discourses.

To ask for the motivating cause for this kind of high christology and the unique usage of the δόξα theme as a reciprocal description for Father and Son and as a basic motif in which Jesus' cross and death find expression is to point to the central theme of oneness between Father and Son.[2] This is the same oneness which also appears at the heart of the reciprocal use of the ἀγάπη motif. Reference is made, first of all, to a reverse statement indicating the interchangeability resulting from oneness. Jesus declares that hating him is equal to hating his Father (15:23). In hating Jesus, the Jews, as representatives of the world, hated the very Father in whom they claimed to believe. Thus sin is exposed in one's relation to Jesus since Jesus is one with the Father. Conversely, it can be said that if anyone loves Jesus, that person will be loved by the Father (16:27) and Jesus will love him and disclose himself to him (14:21,23). This reciprocity

---

[1] H. Leroy, *Rätsel und Missverständnis*, p. 59: "Das Kreuz ist ja für den joh. Offenbarer zum unumgänglichen Mittel der Rückkehr in die δόξα geworden."

[2] Wilkens (*Zeichen und Werke*, p. 110) is to be concurred with here: "Das Einssein von Vater und Sohn wird so scharf herausgearbeitet wie in keinem anderen Evangelium."

of love does not create the relation but is possible only because of Jesus' prior oneness with the Father. The sequence in these verses helps to make this clear. Of the one who loves Jesus it is not said, first of all, that Jesus loves him but rather first that the Father will love him. Emphasized here is the fact that the Father's revelation takes place in Jesus. In fact, Jesus is in the Father (14:20); Jesus proceeds from him and is sent from him (8:42). Therefore the relation of love to Jesus demands the reaction of the Father since the reciprocity of love is qualified precisely by Jesus' oneness with the Father. It is only because of this oneness that it can be said that the Father loves the Son (3:35; 10:17;[1] 15:9; 17:23,24,26) and that the Son loves the Father (14:31) or that whoever loves the Son is loved by the Father (14:21) and for whomever God is indeed Father that person will necessarily love the Son (8:42).

In our consideration thus far the Johannine reciprocity statements and the corresponding motifs around which they are built have dealt with explicating the relation between the Father and Jesus. Our review has shown that they are decidedly christological in orientation to the extent that they lay basic lines and detail accents and nuances descriptive of God's revelation in Christ. We have further seen that their integrating center is the oneness between Father and Son. Thus it may be said that the factors of mutual knowledge, glory, love, witness, and work, together with the theme of sending are not the qualifiers of Jesus' oneness with God but that precisely the opposite is true. It is rather the unity between Father and Son which determines the meaning and scope of the reciprocity statements and their related motifs and which qualifies the intention and character of their declarations. It is because of this oneness that the christology of the Fourth Gospel appears so high and exalted. Its heartbeat

---

[1] Here the thought cannot be that Jesus must win the love of the Father by laying down his life. The Father loved him already before the foundations of the world (17:24). Hence the reverse of the first statement could be maintained, viz. that because the Father loved Jesus he laid down his life. As such, the Father's love would be an expression of his oneness with Jesus.

lies in the theme of perfect solidarity between the Father and the Son.

B. RELATIONALITY BETWEEN JESUS AND HIS OWN

The second major complex of reciprocity statements centers around the relation between Jesus and the believers as well as also the inner relation among the believers. The oneness which characterizes the relation of the Father and His Revealer is here extended to cover the relation of the Revealer and those who have been given to him, viz. the believers. Whereas the relation between the Father and the Son was described in terms of a oneness that is given, complete, and continuing and which accordingly qualifies the mutually interchangeable attributes and works, the relation between the Son and the believers is described in terms of a oneness which, although given and predestined, nevertheless must be kept and repeatedly confirmed. It is characterized by a future aspect which necessitates the imperative to keep on remaining in the Word. The reciprocity statements which were considered in the preceding section were christological in character. The statements which now follow are soteriological and ecclesiological in nature.

It is significant to note that just as the oneness relation between God and the Word was already signaled in the Prologue (1:1-5)[1] and then followed with various explications in the Gospel, as e.g. expressed in the christological reciprocity statements, so also the theme of oneness between the Revealer and the believers is implicitly contained in the Prologue. World and man, which exist through the Logos (1:3), are in darkness when they are not in Him and He in them.[2] The light

---

[1] v. 5 as a parallel to v. 14 implies the historical appearance of Jesus and indicates that already the initial statements of the Prologue cannot be restricted to a trans-historical dimension. Past and present are bound together "sub specie aeternitatis." Consequently, the oneness of the pre-existent Logos with God cannot be separated from the oneness of the Incarnated Logos with the Father. Cp. Käsemann, "Aufbau und Anliegen des johanneischen Prologs," *Exegetische Versuche und Besinnungen*, Bd. II, Göttingen, 1964, pp. 160f.

[2] The implicit reciprocity of these verses is recognized by Chr. Demke, "Der sogenannte Logos-Hymnus im Johannes-Prolog," *ZNW* (58), 1967, p. 57.

shines ἐν τῇ σκοτίᾳ (1:5a) which neither grasps nor extinguishes the life which was ἐν αὐτῷ (1:4a). For that which was created, real life exists only in the Logos[1] which is the light that shines in the darkness. When man receives the light (1:12), then he receives a new point of origin (ἐκ θεοῦ ἐγεννήθησαν, 1:13). In receiving power (ἐξουσία) to become a child of God (1:12), he cannot remain in the sphere of darkness. Rejection of the Revealer constitutes darkness and darkness in turn means to live under the sway of death. In the Logos, on the other hand, there is life.[2] Light and life are the manifestations of God in Christ and disclose the nature of darkness. Where the revelation, however, is accepted, man's origin is disclosed as being from God and his relation to the Revealer is bridged. Thus already in the opening verses of the Gospel decisive aspects of man's relationship to God, to the world, and to himself are defined and are made the basis for the soteriology that is expressed in the corresponding reciprocity statements which describe the oneness relation between Revealer and the believers.

There are different aspects which contribute to the description of this relation, but its basic character and orientation are most succinctly expressed when Jesus declares, "Because I live you will live also" (14:19).[3] The life of the believer is established through the resurrection life of Christ. Christ's life has causative and formative function. Because Jesus lives his disciples can live, and only he is a disciple who knows that Jesus lives, who in other words, knows and believes that Jesus is the glorified one. This same interchange is expressed in the terms of reciprocal knowledge when

---

[1] K. Aland's exhaustive study ("Eine Untersuchung zu Joh. 1:3,4. Über die Bedeutung eines Punktes," ZNW (59), 1968, pp. 174-209) virtually secures the originality of the controversial reading which places the period after ἕν and identifies ὃ γέγονεν with the following verse (1:4) so that the exclusiveness of the ἐν αὐτῷ in relation to that which is created is thereby emphasized. Cp. similarly Bultmann, Ev Joh, p. 21.
[2] Apart from the Logos there is no life. Dodd's (Interpretation, p. 280) idealizing interpretation is untenable: "The idea of an incarnation of the λόγος as creative reason...is prepared for in the thought of the Logos immanent in man."
[3] Here is another clear example of how in John the time dimensions are telescoped into one. Even before the resurrection Jesus speaks as the Resurrected One.

Jesus says, "I know my own and my own know me" (10:14). The nature of the relation described here is not an *unio mystica* with merging identities but rather a oneness in which both sides are mutually qualified in the following way. Jesus is qualified by his own and knows them not because of their knowledge of him but because he is sent to them and gives himself completely for them. Correspondingly, his own know him and are qualified by him because of his knowledge of them. As a result of this kind of mutuality the reaction from the world to Jesus applies also to the believers. Thus Jesus declares: "If they persecuted me, they will persecute you; if they kept my word, they will keep yours also" (15:20). Conversely, it can be said, "If the world hates you, know that it has hated me before it hated you" (15:18). Again, significant in the relationship here is the priority accorded Jesus. The world's reaction to the disciples is triggered first of all by its reaction to Jesus. This is John's way of emphasizing that christology is at the center.

Other passages need to be noted in this complex as well. They underscore the expanded scope of the reciprocal relationship between Jesus and his own as being simultaneously a relation with the Father. Thus when Jesus says, "...he who receives anyone whom I send, receives me; and he who receives me, receives him who sent me" (13:20),[1] it is made clear that because Jesus and the Father are one, the believers's relation is not to the Revealer alone but equally to the Father. The same relation is expressed when Jesus prays for his own and recognizes that all who belong to him belong at the same time to the Father, and those who belong to the Father belong likewise to him (17:10). On the other hand, when the Father's love which characterizes his relation to the Son is also in the believers, then it is Jesus who is in them (17:26). Or when anyone loves Jesus, it is the Father who loves him in return (16:27). The import of these statements is, first of all, again to emphasize the absence of any disparity in the

---

[1] The parallel but independent variant of the synoptic tradition in Mt.10:40 and Lk.10:16 (cp. Bultmann, *Die Geschichte der synoptischen Tradition*, FRLANT N.F. 12, Göttingen, 1961, p. 152f.) implies that the emissary is identical in meaning and purpose to the one who sent him.

oneness between the Father and the Son. And yet in John that
is understood dialectically. Whereas Jesus consistently is
identified as one with God, he is, nevertheless, at the same
time differentiated (ὅτι ὁ πατὴρ μείζων μού ἐστιν! 14:28). Jesus
is the Sent One; he is the Revealer. That is to say, God is
not accessible apart from Jesus. Direct relationship with
the Father is impossible except through him who is directly
related to the Father, namely the Son.[1] Just as God is available not directly but only through Jesus, so it can be said
for the believer of John's church and the subsequent church
that there is no direct relation to Jesus except in terms of
faith. The believer's oneness relation to Jesus, unlike the
perfect solidarity that exists between Father and Son, is
measured by the faith response to the Word and is therefore
open-ended and future oriented. It is significant that this
basis of the believer's oneness relation with Jesus is described in terms of promise when e.g. Jesus declares: "In
that day you will know that I am in my Father, and you in me,
and I in you" (14:20). Of course, the relation is present
reality but only from the perspective of "that day" which is
to say, from the perspective of faith in the Exalted One.
Finally, it may be said that the faith relation, which begins
with the recognition of who Jesus is, is conditioned by its
ultimate goal where Jesus prepares a promised place for his
own that where he is they may also be (14:3).[2] In the meantime solidarity with the Revealer must be renewed and continually realized in repeated confrontation with his revelation.

It is against this background that the remaining reciprocity statements depicting oneness with the Revealer and among

---

[1] Cp. Conzelmann (Outline, p. 335): "...in the revealer God really appears...God does not appear directly but only in the revealer."
[2] Untenable is L. Schottroff's conclusion ("Heil als innerweltliche Entweltlichung," op. cit., p. 297): "Jedoch deutet Johannes dieses individuelle futurische Heilsgeschehen ganz im Sinne seines präsentischen, innerweltlichen Erlösungsverständnisses." 14:4ff. polemicize against the assumption that the present is only an anticipation of salvation but do not argue for the exclusiveness of an inner-worldly salvation. If 14:2f. were to be understood as Schottroff proposes, and the exclusiveness of the present were an issue, then the explication in 14:4ff. would have to read differently. For an overview of the conflicting interpretations at this point see H. Leroy, Rätsel und Missverständnis, p. 53 n. 3.

the believers are to be understood. The central motifs in these statements are those of abiding and loving. Characteristic for their structure is the paranetic and imperative form. Thus Jesus can say: "A new commandment I give to you that you love one another; even as I have loved you that you also love one another (13:34; cp. also 15:12). Love is exclusive and does not apply to the world but only to those who are in the bond of love patterned after the oneness relation in which the Father loves the Son. Therefore Jesus can further say: "As the Father has loved me, so I have loved you; abide in my love" (15:9). The appeal to remain in love and to reflect the love of Jesus by loving the brother does not appear in isolation, as though here were an independent factor on which the reception of God's revelation could be based. On the contrary, the appeal to be engaged continually in mutual love is the necessary consequence of life in faith and has its causal priority in the activity of the Revealer.[1] In

---

[1] J. Becker ("Die Abschiedsreden Jesu im Johannesevangelium," *ZNW* (61), 1970, pp. 215-246) makes a strong case for isolating ch. 15 with its pronounced statements on agape relations as a later redactional addition which not only derives from a theological situation similar to that of I John and different from the intention of the Fourth Evangelist but also which gives such prominence to paranetic demands that indicative and imperative are confused and the *solus Christus* emphasis of chs. 13 and 14 is *nolens volens* modified so that ethical behavior becomes an additional condition for salvation, replacing the priority of the work of the Revealer. While it is beyond the scope of our present investigation to enter into a thorough literary analysis of ch. 15, the following theological points, which argue against Becker's interpretation, need to be considered. His observations, on the one hand, are certainly correct that by itself ch. 15 reflects a "situationless" character, that it is not marked by a smooth progression of thought, or that even its terminology at times is unjohannine (so also Heise, *Bleiben*, p. 87 n. 191). But to conclude with Becker that ch. 15 is therefore extraneous to the farewell discourses is unwarranted. The topic of the continuing work and presence of the Revealer in terms of the life and relationships of those who are his own is an essential theme of the farewell discourses. The "greater works" of 14:12 are essentially equivalent to the "bearing fruit" of 15:2ff. which together with the emphasis on "abiding" and "continuing" underscore the farewell orientation of ch. 15. Whereas the predominance of the imperative in ch. 15 is admittedly striking, it must be noted that ἀγαπᾶν and μένειν are not isolated and required as bare deeds but are qualified by the strong indicatives in 15:3,16a, and in the declaration that without Christ the disciples can do nothing (15:4). Furthermore, the certainty of prayer being answered (14:12c,13) can hardly be said to be the result of Jesus' statement "I go to the Father" and thus constitutively different in ch. 14 from the certainty described in 15:7,16c where contingency is attached to abiding and bearing fruit, since in both cases the causal factor lies in the activity of the Revealer who is already glorified.

fact, for the Fourth Evangelist faith and love coincide since both are conditioned and motivated in response to the Word. Continuing in love is defined as "keeping the commandment" (15:10; 14:15). Similarly Jesus can say: "If a man loves me, he will keep my word" (14:23). Consequently, keeping his commandments and keeping his word are understood as a unity.[1] But since faith itself, as the fundamental relation to Jesus, is also understood as keeping his word (8:31), it is clear that faith and love in their determination by the word form an inseparable unity. Admittedly, the term faith is not so much as even mentioned in ch. 15 where the imperative to love is most fully developed. But that can be no justification to isolate ἀγάπη as simply an ethical category since the possibility of reciprocal love among the believers is given only as a continuation of the love between Father and Son (14:31; 15:9) made known in the revelation of Jesus for his own. Here it must be remembered that Jesus is speaking to those who are already his own and who have received the gift of his work. Thus the appeal to love one another is not an appeal for tolerance and patience in respecting the rights of another by imitating a noble moral example but rather a summons to stay with the Word which creates the relation in the first place and out of which arises the necessity to serve one another (14:12). The appeal is not an exhortation to begin loving or to do one's own meritorious part[2] but to continue in the reciprocity of loving which has its beginning in the oneness of Father and Son.[3] Those who are loved love and are bound

---

[1] Inconsistent with Johannine usage is Riesenfeld's contention (ThWB VIII, p. 144) that τηρεῖν means the conserving of catechetical tradition. Such an early catholicizing accent is notably absent in John (against K. Haacker, Die Stiftung des Heils, p. 115). "Keeping the word and the commandments" is not the Johannine equivalent for transmitting and preserving a body of normative tradition but rather gives expression to continuing in the word event through which one is integrated into the relationship given by Father and Son who make their home with the believer (14:23f.).
[2] Contra Wikenhauser, Das Evangelium nach Johannes, (RNT 4), Regensburg, 1961, p. 285: "Wenn Jesus nun von den Jüngern verlangt, in der von ihm empfangenen Liebe zu verharren, so fordert er damit von ihnen, daß sie sich der Fortdauer dieses Geliebtwerdens wert machen."
[3] The oneness of love is not mystical in nature as Mußner (op. cit., p. 158): "ἀγάπη und unio mystica gehören bei Johannes zusammen." Nor can it be said that ἀγάπη leads to life and fellowship with God. It is rather the received Word which creates ἀγάπη and life.

together by the same love with which they were loved. In short, ἀγάπη for John designates the oneness established by the Word as a projection of the oneness of love between Father and Son. Only as a projection of that oneness is real love at all possible.

The same orientation is also maintained in terms of the reciprocity of μένειν, which likewise receives a prominent place in ch. 15. Thus Jesus can entreat the believers: "Abide in me <u>and</u> I in you (15:4). Here καί has a causal comparative accent as is indicated not only by the grammatical sense (Jesus is not entreating himself) but also by the following interpretation which reinforces the priority of the work of Christ: "Unless you abide in me," Jesus says, you cannot bear fruit (v. 4) for "apart from me you can do nothing" (v. 5). The fact that this takes place within the context of a reciprocal relation already established is indicated when Jesus says, "You are already made clean by the word which I have spoken to you" (15:3) and "you did not choose me, but I chose you (15:6).[1] Significant also is the conditional declaration: "If you abide in me," (v.7) which is not followed by "and I in you" but rather by "and my words abide in you." Abiding consequently is understood not as an ethical response characterized by loyalty and faithfulness[2] but as a situation and an event in which the words of Christ remain in the believers. Abiding is not the condition for receiving the words of Christ. Rather receiving the words of Christ is the condition for abiding. Similar to the use of ἀγαπᾶν, abiding and believing in their determination by the Word form an inseparable unity. Essentially the same is maintained when Jesus declares that whoever loves him, keeps his words (14:23) and when he asserts, "If you abide in me and my words abide

---

[1] Cp. Heise, *Bleiben*, p. 173: "Entscheidend für das Verständnis von μένειν ist, daß es die Jünger sind, zu denen Jesus sagt, "bleibet in mir," und daß er gerade indem er dies sagt, ihnen ein enues Sein zuspricht, sie auf dieses neue Sein hin anspricht."
[2] Bultmann (*Ev Joh*, pp. 332; 411) speaks of the character of μένειν in terms of a demand for "loyalty." But even as he himself concedes that μένειν here is not a matter of "eines Sich-einsetzens für die Sache" or a "Treueverhältnis zwischen Personen" it would seem better to avoid the term of loyalty altogether. Cp. further Käsemann, *Letzter Wille*, p. 112.

in you..." (15:7).[1] It is the centrality and omnipotence of
the heavenly Word which creates real relationships and makes
ἀγαπᾶν and μένειν possible in the earthly sphere. The imperatives for μένειν and ἀγαπᾶν, then, are not so much appeals
and exhortations as they are the demarcations which provide
the lines within which the disciples may realize the promise
of their Lord. Because Jesus abides in his own they may a-
bide in him.[2] Because Jesus as the projection of heavenly
oneness loves his own, they may be one with Him and with one
another in love. Since this relationship of faith is always
threatened by the encroachments of an alien world, it is a
relationship which must be constantly renewed and which can
be renewed only by continuing in Jesus. Thus the function of
the reciprocity form is clear. By giving expression to the
fact that the work of the Revealer is always directed toward
man, it simultaneously emphasizes that this work is appropri-
ated only by continuing with the Revealer.

The only other occurrence of μένειν in reciprocal form appears in the disputed sacramental passage in 6:51-58,[3] where

---

[1] K. Haacker (Die Stiftung, p. 118) blurs the individual accents and
disregards the significance of contexts when he simply equates 15:7 and
8:31 with 2 John 9. Nowhere does the Evangelist indicate that "keeping
Jesus' words" is equivalent to preserving a particular tradition and
above all not in 15:7 where the reciprocal statements underscore the directness and dynamic of the relation to Jesus (cp. E. Schweizer, "Der
Kirchenbegriff bei Johannes," op. cit., p. 267) which derives from the
presence of his words in the believers. The ῥήματα are not simply specific sayings and precepts of Jesus (against Barrett, St. John, p. 396),
but rather they are "the words of eternal life" (6:63) which is the one
Word --Christ. Appropriately, Heise (Bleiben, p. 73): "Es handelt sich
um ein Wort, das ein Geschehen ansagt." Heise's repeated identification
of the Word as the "Word of love," however, represents an accent shift
that obscures the lines maintained in the Gospel.
[2] Jesus' abiding becomes reality wherever he is heard and received. Cp.
Käsemann, Letzter Wille, p. 96. Haacker's critique at this point is weak
(Die Stiftung, pp. 120-123) because it fails fully to recognize that for
John the earthly Jesus is already the exalted Christ precisely because
Jesus and the Father are one. Thus the word of Jesus, which is the point
of reference for the μένειν ἐν αὐτῷ, cannot be equated on a one dimen-
sional level with the historical ipsissima verba. To be sure, the Spirit
brings to remembrance all that Jesus said (14:26), but what was said was
for John said by the exalted and pre-existent Son who in his oneness with
the Father spans all time dimensions.
[3] v. 51 has been variously divided depending on whether already b or
first c is to be understood sacramentally. Since b, however, may best be
understood as a summary of the preceding, it generally is not joined with
the eucharistic unit.

Jesus declares: "He who eats my flesh and drinks my blood abides in me and I in him (v. 56). The independent nature of this passage has often been cause to isolate the verses, together with the mutual immanence formula in v. 56, as a later addition basically inconsistent with the evangelist's original intention. In the ensuing debate over the authenticity and meaning of vs. 51-58 almost every imaginable detail and aspect has been explored and scrutinized.[1] Despite repeated attempts to defend the original literary unity of the chapter,[2] there is growing concensus that vs. 51-58 contain an originally independent and separate tradition. Coupled with this is the recognition that these verses constitute an undeniably clear reference to the Eucharist and can hardly be understood merely metaphorically as a continuation of the bread of life theme developed in the preceding verses.[3] Even when the presence of eucharistic overtones in the rest of the chapter is granted,[4] the eucharistic character of vs. 51-58 is

---

[1] For a concise overview of the various interpretations see S. Schulz, *Untersuchungen zur Menschensohn-Christologie*, p. 116 and H. Leroy, *Rätsel u. Mißverständnis*, p. 110f.

[2] In a series of carefully worked out studies P. Borgen (*Bread from Heaven*; also "The Unity of the Discourse in John 6," *ZNW*, 50, 1959, pp. 277-78; "Observations on the Midrashic Character of John 6," *ZNW*, 54, 1963, pp. 232-240) contends that Jn. 6:31-58 is a closed literary unity structured on the basis of a common homiletic pattern found in Philo and in Palestinian midrashim. Following this scheme, vs. 31-33 are said to form the opening statement and v. 58 the closing statement of a planned, unified homiletic composition originating with one writer. The conclusiveness of Borgen's argument is severly shaken, however, when one realizes that his literary criteria can be applied to 6:31-51b as well without including the disputed passage in vs. 51-58. Cp. critique by R. Brown, *John*, p. 294 and G. Richter, "Zur Formgeschichte und literarischen Einheit von Joh. 6:31-58," *ZNW*, 60, 1969, pp. 21-55.

[3] The opposite is maintained by H. Odeberg (*The Fourth Gospel*, p. 239) who defends the thematic unity of the chapter and sees vs. 51-58 as lending a realistic emphasis to the actuality of the spiritual world (eating and drinking are metaphors for real believing) and thus concludes that "no part of the discourse...can primarily refer to the sacrament of the Eucharist." Similarly, P. Borgen (*Bread from Heaven*) with slightly shifted accents insists that the entire discourse is a demonstration of the reality of the incarnation of Jesus.

[4] Note esp. 6:11,23. Cp. here W. Bauer, *Joh. Ev.*, p. 99. Bornkamm ("Die eucharistische Rede im Johannes-Evangelium," *Geschichte und Glaube*, Bd. III, pp. 60-67) rightly notes, however, that traces of eucharistic speech here do not exceed those of the syn. accounts of the miraculous feedings. R. Brown (*John,I*, p. 286), on the other hand, clearly overextends the case when he presses for eucharistic undertones "in the multiplication, the transitional verses (22-24), the introduction to the discourse, and the body of the discourse (35-50)."

so pronounced and the disjuncture between 51c and the preceding, as well as between 6:63 and the preceding, so sharp that the passage, despite common features with the rest of the chapter, gives the impression of a separate unit and suggests independent provenance. This is reinforced through the introduction of the following new elements which do not occur in the rest of the chapter: σάρξ, αἷμα, ὁ υἱὸς τοῦ ἀνθρώπου, φαγεῖν (τρώγειν) τὴν σάρκα, πίνειν τὸ αἷμα, and ἄρτον διδόναι. Considering that otherwise the sacraments exercise no explicit role in the Fourth Gospel and are most notably absent precisely in those places where one would most expect to find them, it would seem compelling to regard the presence of 6:51c - 58 as the corrective measure of a later redactor intent on providing a missing note to harmonize with current church practice or perhaps to consolidate the front against a docetically understood Christ.[1] Such an assumption, however, is not necessary and may in the end amount to more of a convenient evasion than to a critical accounting. If 6:51c - 58 contain liturgically preformed tradition, as is suggested above all by the structured formulations in vs. 54-56,[2] we may see reflected here elements of a particular understanding of the Eucharist.[3]

The decisive question, however, is why such pronounced eucharistic tradition should be incorporated at this point? We must, first of all, note the significance of the indentification between the chapter's dominant theme of spiritual or heavenly bread and the eucharistic termini of flesh (v. 51c) and flesh and blood (v. 58).[4] The bread motif of the discourse

---

[1] So Bultmann, Ev Joh, p. 162; Bornkamm, "Die eucharistische Rede," op. cit., p. 67; H. Koester, "Geschichte und Kultus im Johannesevangelium und bei Ignatius von Antiochien," ZThK, 54, 1957, pp. 56-69.
[2] Whereas these verses more strongly reflect set eucharistic formulations based in the liturgy rather than in homiletic construction (against J. Jeremias, "Joh. 6:51c - 58 --redaktionell?" ZNW, 44, 1952/53, p. 256f.), there is no basis to characterize them as hymnic tradition with parallel-structured strophes (so Leroy, Rätsel, p. 117). Parallelism is present but only in a loosely knit construction.
[3] Cp. E. Schweizer, "Das joh. Zeugnis vom Herrenmahl," Neotestamentica, p. 395: "Es scheint mir durchaus möglich, daß hinter diesen Worten schon eine Tradition steckt, die das Herrenmahl sehr massiv als göttliche Speise im hellenistischen Sinn verstanden hat."
[4] The antecedent of οὗτος is clearly the ἐμέ of v. 57 which is further explicated in terms of the σάρξ and αἷμα of v. 56.

is understood throughout as the ἄρτος of the heavenly world. Jesus himself is that bread which came down from heaven (6:38, 41, 50, 51). As the Bread of Life he does not belong to the world, but comes from the Father with whom he is one. Into this context now are inserted elements of fixed eucharistic tradition (vs. 54-56) which are integrated through the statements in vs. 51ff. and vs. 57f.[1] The intention is a polemical one designed to show that the Eucharist must be interpreted in the light of the bread of life theology developed in the preceding discourse together with the critique in vs. 60ff. Consequently, what we have in vs. 51-58 need not be a later redaction meant to compensate for the absence of the account of the institution in ch. 13, nor is it the Johannine counterpart to the Synoptic and Pauline account of the Eucharist,[2] but rather an independent interpretation of the sacrament as celebrated in the Johannine community and as seen against the background of its inner-church struggles.[3] The interpretation fostered here is intended specifically as a corrective measure[4]

---

[1] As a transitional statement, v. 51c, which makes the first mention of σάρξ, is hardly a culmination to the preceding discourse (against H. Schürmann, "Joh. 6:51c —ein Schlüssel zur grossen joh. Brotrede," BZ, N.F. 2, 1958, pp. 244-262; D. M. Smith, Composition and Order, p. 147) but rather an introduction to the eucharistic segment. With this transition the gift (ἄρτος τοῦ θεοῦ) is identified with the Giver (ἄρτος ὃν ἐγὼ δώσω) and is further identified with eucharistic σάρξ. As the question of the Jews indicates (v.52), the σάρξ of v. 51c cannot be a reference to the cross but must be understood eucharistically as τὴν σάρκα φαγεῖν. The abruptness of the change from spiritual bread to sacramental flesh underscores the force of the dialectic. The integration of thought, however, is clearly evidenced by the progression and interchange of verbs: from φαγεῖν τὸν ἄρτον, v. 50 (the bread which comes down from heaven —then equated with σάρξ, v. 51c) to φαγεῖν τὴν σάρκα, v. 52 (sacramental flesh) to τρώγειν τὴν σάρκα, v. 54 (pronounced sacramental eating) to τρώγειν τὸν ἄρτον, v. 58 (sacramental eating identified with the interpretive and qualifying term ἄρτος. Cp. L. Goppelt, τρώγειν, ThWB, VIII, 236.
[2] Against R. Brown, John, I, p. 285: "It is possible that we have preserved in v. 51 the Johannine form of the words of institution."
[3] Cp. Käsemann, Letzter Wille, p. 73.
[4] Bornkamm's objection ("Die eucharistische Rede," op. cit., p. 65) that vs. 51c-56 are not formulated as a corrective overlooks the fact that these verses (esp. vs. 54-56) consist primarily of preformed set liturgical formulation. The corrective is given in vs. 53 and 57f. and above all in the preceding and subsequent statements on the bread that comes from heaven and the flesh which is of no avail. To say with Bornkamm that vs. 60ff. evidence absolutely no reference to vs. 51-58 is unwarranted. Granted that the immediate connection is with the thought developed in vs. 32-51a, this does not negate the interpreting function for the intervening eucharistic segment, particularly in view of the connecting links of the terms "Son of Man" and "flesh."

against a crass sacramentalism which would reduce the Eucharist as a φάρμακον ἀθανασίας to a manipulable possession which in itself would secure the salvation of the believer. This kind of sacramentalism is countered by the revelational theology developed in terms of the Bread of Life motif and applied to the understanding of the Eucharist. Thus the intention of vs. 51-58 is not anti-docetic! The σκληρὸς λόγος of v. 60 is not the offense of Jesus in the flesh mediated through sacramental eating and drinking but the Jesus of glory who is one with the Father and who cannot be controlled and sacramentally made available at will.[2] Just as the character of the λόγος σὰρξ ἐγένετο is its manifestation of glory so the character of the sacramental σάρξ and αἷμα is determined by the heavenly bread (vs. 51c.58) which has divine origin (v.58) and by the Son of Man (v. 53) whose home is in the world above.[3]

Qualified by this polemicizing critique, the sacrament is made to point beyond itself to the Revealer who is at the

---

[1] Against E. Schweizer, Das joh. Zeugnis vom Herrenmahl," *op. cit.*, p. 394. P. Borgen, *Bread from Heaven*, pp. 179-187. Also Richter, "Zur Formgeschichte u. lit. Einheit," *op. cit.*, p. 46.

[2] The corrective force of the revelational bread theology as applied to an uncontrolled sacramentalism is the essence of the hard saying. The schism of v. 61 is not due to a reference to the death of Jesus since this is nowhere a point of issue in the context (against E. Schweizer, σάρξ *ThWB*, VII, p. 104 n. 309). W. Wilkens, *Zeichen und Werke*, p. 159, n. 8 rightly recognizes that the place of 6:51c - 58 is not in the pursuit of a particular sacramental interest but rather in the "Erhärtung des Ärgernischarakters der joh. Christologie..." Wilkens misinterprets the character of this christology, however, when he speaks of the claim of Jesus as the son of Joseph, the Word of God become *flesh*. Just the opposite is the point of ch. 6 which identifies the offense of Jesus not in his earthly fleshly character (vs. 42f.) but in his heavenly divine origin. Appropriate is C.F.D. Moule's observation ("The Individualism of the Fourth Gospel," *Nov. Test.*, 5, 1962, p. 185): "perhaps the Fourth Evangelist is consciously and deliberately interpreting the sacraments themselves in terms of other categories rather than interpreting other categories by means of the sacraments."

[3] G. Richter's contention ("Zur Formgeschichte u. lit. Einheit," *op. cit.*, p. 37) that the Son of Man designation in v. 53 does not pertain to Jesus as a divine being is unwarranted. Furthermore, Richter proceeds on a methodological false basis when he elevates 20:31 to the position of an exclusive criterion, compliance to which determines whether or not a passage is original or redactional. 20:31 is itself tradition-historically conditioned (cp. Fortna, *The Gospel of Signs*, p. 197f.) and its applicability as a standard for determining what was original or secondary to the evangelist's intention cannot be maintained.

same time the Revelation, to the Giver who is likewise the Gift. The cultic-ritual formulations of eating flesh and drinking blood are retained but receive here an emphatically conditioned orientation inasmuch as they are determined by the bread and spirit statements of the context.¹ The strict dichotomy between flesh and spirit (6:63; also 3:6) as applied to the eucharistic verses is not meant to document the mode of Jesus' sacramental presence, but instead to express the conditions of his availability. His availability is not produced from below but given from above. To receive Jesus from above and thus to meet him also in the Eucharist demands a faith relationship without which he cannot be had. It is in this light that the mutual immanence formula of v. 56 must also be understood. In its pre-Johannine context it may well have had the meaning of mutual incorporation of substance. Here its orientation, however, is distinctly different as the verse serves to explicate the relationship of faith.² Real sacramental eating and drinking presuppose a faith relation to the Revealer. To the participant in the Eucharist as to each believer the promise is given that he abides in Christ and Christ in him.³ It is not the eating and drinking which serve as the condition for this mutual abiding since only he receives the eucharistic Christ who receives him as τὸν ἄρτον ἐκ τοῦ οὐρανοῦ τὸν ἀληθινόν, viz. as a gift from above. Thus within a polemical setting the christological and faith priorities are maintained here for the reciprocity of μένειν as they were in ch. 15.

SUMMARY: In this section we have reviewed the various ways in which the reciprocity statements, so uniquely characteristic

---

[1] Excellently formulated by H. Leroy, *Rätsel*, p. 122: "...dann kann die 'Härte' der Rede nicht im Sprechen vom τρώγειν (φαγεῖν) τὴν σάρκα liegen, denn diese Formulierung und die damit verbundene Sakramentstheologie --handfester Sakramentalismus gnostischer Prägung! --ist ja längst Gemeindebesitz! Vielmehr ist die Härte in der korrigierenden Einführung der ἄρτος -Theologie in das Sakramentsverständnis zu sehen."
[2] Against J. Heise (*Bleiben*, p. 93) who uncritically adopts Bultmann's literary proposals and therefore relegates the reciprocity formula here to a redactional addition inconsistent with the evangelist's intention.
[3] In his zeal to establish connections everywhere with the OT R. Brown (*John*, I, p. 293) suggests a reflection here of the OT covenant theme in Jer. 24:7 and 31:33. Unwarranted!

for John, are used in relation to the oneness motif. We have seen how as christological formulations they serve to give expression to the oneness between Father and Son which, because it is revelational, is always oriented to man. As a result, the reciprocity statements appear also in soteriological and ecclesiological contexts describing the relation among believers and their relation to the Revealer. These statements cannot be isolated from the first since they are the necessary consequences of the reciprocity between Father and Son precisely because this oneness is revelational. For this reason the paranetic and sacramental aspects of the Johannine reciprocity relations are not extraneous but essential to the oneness motif. They have their roots in the priority of Jesus' oneness with the Father.

Chapter III: Oneness and the Christological Titles

A. THE SON OF MAN

The Johannine Son of Man sayings form our first point of reference. Distinctly different from their synoptic counterparts[1] and stripped of their otherwise characteristically apocalyptic features, the Johannine Son of Man designations occur thirteen times (incl. the stronger variant reading in 9:35) scattered throughout the first thirteen chapters. Whereas their respective literary contexts may give the first impression of a fragmentary character,[2] closer examination reveals an integrating unity which binds the various passages together. Our purpose here will be to specify the nature of that integrating factor.

In the continuing debate over the place and original scope of the Son of Man passage in 5:27-29 in its relation to the larger christological discourse in ch. 5,[3] there is increasing agreement that while the passage syntactically is loosely connected with its context and most probably constituted or at least contained separate elements of prior tradition, perhaps as independent segments or as an already unified logion,[4] its present theological correspondence to the motif complex of the chapter is not essentially broken or inconsistent. Isolated, the Son of Man figure in v. 27 with its emphasis on

---

[1] W. Bauer, *Joh. Ev.*, p. 42: "Die im 4. Evangelium 12 mal (gegen 69 mal bei den Synoptikern) auftretende Selbstbezeichnung Jesu als ὁ υἱὸς τοῦ ἀνθρώπου kann betrachtet werden ohne Rücksicht auf den älteren, bei den Synoptikern vorliegenden Sprachgebrauch." Contrariwise, cp. Schnackenburg, *Joh. Ev.*, I, pp. 417-420. S. Smalley, "The Johannine Son of Man Sayings," *NTS*, 15, 1969, p. 298.
[2] So Schulz, *Untersuchungen zur Menschensohn-Christologie*, p. 123.
[3] Following a long list of predecessors, Bultmann (*Ev Joh*, p. 195) designates v. 27 as "unnötig und nachklappend." Similarly, although with different consequences, R. Schnackenburg (*Joh. Ev.*, II, p. 147) identifies vs. 27b-29 as redaction. Contrary positions are maintained by R. Brown, *John*, I, p. 197 and J. Blank, *Krisis*, p. 159. W. Bauer, *Joh. Ev.*, p. 87: "Für Jo ergab sich wohl kein Widerspruch." For an overview of the discussion cp. S. Schulz, *Untersuchungen*, p. 111.
[4] Cp. G. Iber, *Überlieferungsgeschichtliche Untersuchungen zum Begriff des Menschensohnes im Neuen Testament*, Heidelberg/Dissertation, 1953, p.118.

the judging function is strongly reminiscent of the Daniel 7:
13f. conception. Similarly, v. 28f. with its emphasis on the
resurrection to life and the resurrection to judgment and its
proximity to Daniel 12:2 reflects clear apocalyptic tradition.
Although the initial contrast seems stark, the introduction
of these features can hardly be understood as a reaction or
harmonizing attempt meant to provide a counterbalance with
aspects of traditional apocalypticism since those elements
are not at all developed or dwelt upon.[1] If the passage was
incorporated by the evangelist, then it was evidently intended as a reinforcement for the judgment, life and hearing
themes of the preceding verses as well as also simultaneously
as a critique against an unqualified futuristic eschatology.[2]
Beyond that, however, the sterotyped formulations of vs. 27 -
29 have no function and when isolated appear at best as rem-
nants of a pre-Johannine view.[3]

It is significant that the theme of judging was already
struck in v. 22. Since, as stated there, it is not the Father
who judges but rather the Son, judgment is not separated from
the revelation but occurs as the reverse function of the life-
giving work of the Son. The reason for judgment is explained
in v. 24 in terms of man's response to the Jesus' word. He
who hears Jesus' word and believes him who sent him has already eternal life and does not pass into judgment. The resurrection is present reality! And yet the gift of resurrection life is not part of an automatic process. If hearing
the word and believing means life now, then refusal to hear
and to believe mean judgment now. Judgment follows with necessary consequence as the reverse side of the prior life-
giving function of the Son. It should be noted that while a
future orientation is implicit in v. 25 (the hour is coming),[4]

---

[1] Cp. C. Colpe, ὁ υἱὸς τοῦ ἀνθρώπου, ThWB VIII, p. 469.
[2] S. Schulz (Das Ev. nach Joh, p. 91) speaks of a "stillschweigende Umdeutung."
[3] Käsemann, "Zur Johannes-Interpretation in England," Exegetische Versuche, II, p. 147f, can legitimately speak of these formulations as not being "organisch wie etwa bei Paulus oder im ganzen übrigen NT mit denen der präsentischen Eschatologie verbunden sind, sondern so etwas wie ein Appendix."
[4] Even Bultmann (Ev Joh, p. 194 n.2) concedes: "...die Eliminierung des künftigen Gerichts bedeutet nicht die Eliminierung der Zukunft überhaupt im mystischen Jetzt."

it is not developed but rather qualified with unprecedented insistence that the hour is now. This emphasis on the present reality is a predominant concern of the evangelist. Into this thought pattern now is inserted the Son of Man segment (vs. 27-29) so that just as vs. 24-26 correspond to v. 21, so vs. 27-29 correspond to vs. 22ff.[1] The impact of this sequence of verses and their thematic integration is to indicate that the Son of Man figure in v. 27 is to be understood in the light of the dominant "Son" motif and of the present realization of life which the Son gives. If Jesus is given authority to judge <u>because</u> he is the Son of Man (v. 27),[2] he is the Son of Man <u>because</u> as recipient of judgment from the Father he is first of all the Giver of life just as the Father raises the dead and gives life (v. 21). To identify the motivating impulse which facilitated this kind of reinterpretation, in which originally apocalyptically colored traditions were given a decidedly new orientation, is to point to the singularly most pervasive reflection in the Fourth Gospel, the reflection on Jesus' oneness with the Father. Significantly, this theme of oneness was signaled at the beginning of the discourse (v. 17). As the substructure of the subsequent development of thought, it gives new direction to the stereotyped formulations by orienting them to a oneness christology.

In his conversation with the man healed of congenital blindness, Jesus asks him if he believes in the Son of Man (9:35). The healed man had already confessed Jesus as a "prophet" (v. 17) and as "one from God" (v. 33). In the affirmation to the Son of Man question (v. 38), a confessional climax is reached

---

[1] The inner coherence of these verses is detailed in the analysis by G. Iber, *op. cit.*, p. 128ff.
[2] Since the Son of Man designation of v. 27 is characterized by heavenly qualities, the designation is not tantamount in meaning to "man" (cp. Schnackenburg, *Joh. Ev.*, I, p. 415; also Colpe, *ThWB*, VIII, p. 422) nor can it be understood as a reference to the humanity of Jesus (contra Blank, *Krisis*, p. 159. Barrett, *St. John*, p. 60: "In John...Son of Man (means) one who shares the nature of man."). The significance of the anarthrous υἱὸς ἀνθρώπου lies less in the parallel to Dn. 7:13 than in the indication of Jesus' uniqueness. So A. Schlatter, *Der Evangelist Johannes*, Stuttgart, 1930. p. 152: "υἱὸς ἀνθρώπου ...ist gesagt, weil in diesem Zusammenhang seine Einzigkeit völlig deutlich ist. Die entsteht aus der Einzigkeit seiner Gottessohnschaft."

whereby the Son of Man designation not only incorporates the
thrust of the two earlier confessions but qualifies and goes
beyond them in emphasizing the absolute character of him
whose presence and word are the cause of healing. The judging
theme implicit in the traditional Son of Man concept is picked
up and developed in vs. 39ff., where, however, it is not made
to refer to a future event, let alone an apocalyptic drama,
but rather to present judgment in terms of the continuing
guilt of the Pharisees (v. 41).[2] Here again is evidence showing how the Son of Man term is recast and utilized in the
specific interest of Johannine christology where it becomes a
carrier for the descriptive meaning of the heavenly and healing presence of Jesus within the contemporary dimension.

The judgment motif appears in connection with the Son of
Man term once again in 12:34.[3] The exaltation of the Son of
Man signals the judgment of this world. Consistent with the
previous emphasis, this judgment is not lodged in the future
but realized now (v. 31). The new accent associated here
with the Son of Man term is the exaltation theme. This accent had already been introduced in Jesus' conversation with
Nicodemus, where the Son of Man is identified as the one who
must be lifted up (3:14). The same motif appears in 8:28
where Jesus declares: "When you have lifted up the Son of

---

[1] The textual variant for 9:35 which reads "Son of God" instead of the
more strongly attested "Son of Man" captures well, nevertheless, the intended thrust of the question.
[2] Whereas J. L. Martyn (*History and Theology in the Fourth Gospel*, New
York, 1968, p. 133) rightly recognizes the contemporary level of the
judgment brought by the Son of Man, and with justification speaks of the
church-synagogue tension of the evangelist's day as being decisive in determining the formulation of the account, still it is forced and contrived to view the bulk of the dramatic construction of ch. 9 as deriving
from a contemporary healing and dispute event (p.10ff.) in the evangelist's church.
[3] Here the Son of Man term is used in contrast to the figure of a national Davidic Messiah (against Colpe, *ThWB*, VIII, p. 471)to show that
the work of Jesus was inconsistent with Jewish messianic presuppositions
(cp. Barrett, *St. John*, p. 357). At best it could be said that an apocalyptic element is retained, not in the question of the Jews, but in the
judgment theme of v. 31 and may have facilitated the introduction of the
Son of Man term in v. 34 which appears to be a synthesis of set tradition
and free composition (see Schulz, *Untersuchungen*, p. 120). And yet the
apocalyptic theme of judgment, while formally retained, is radically reinterpreted. Cp. W. Bousset, *Kyrios Christos*, p. 156.

Man, then you will know that I am he."¹ Of importance is the fact that all three passages do not speak of Jesus being elevated to the status of Son of Man but rather that as the Son of Man he is elevated or lifted up. In other words, the Son of Man is already an exalted figure. Since nowhere in extra-biblical literature or even in the Synoptics do we find a clear parallel to the formulation describing the exaltation of the Son of Man,² it seems reasonable to assume that we find in the Johannine passages a specific interpretive concern of the evangelist and the community which he represents. Here the "lifting up"³ theme serves in the first instance to explicate the Revealer's return from the world to his heavenly home. As such, its primary meaning is to indicate a change in place. But another dimension is added here, viz. its application to the cross.⁴ Contrary to its use in the rest of the NT Gospel tradition, where ὑψοῦν refers to the ascension and the exaltation of Christ into power and glory as a termination of his state of humiliation, in John the "lifting up" theme is made to refer already to the cross. For John, as we have already seen, there is notably no reflection on the cross as a point of degradation.⁵ Instead it is understood as the point of

---

[1] Significant in this verse is the equivalence drawn between the Son of Man term and the revelatory formula ἐγώ εἰμι.
[2] Blank, *Krisis*, p. 81: "Gegenüber einer verbreiteten Auffassung ist vor allem darauf hinzuweisen, daß die Erhöhungsterminologie ihren ursprunglichen Sitz nicht im Anschauungskreis des 'Menschensohnes' hat." Also Schulz, *Untersuchungen*, p. 105. Disputed is the passage in Eth. Enoch 70f. (Cp. Colpe, *ThWB*, VIII, pp. 428; 471 n. 451). In Gnostic texts the Primal Man figure may be described as descending and ascending but never as "being lifted up." (Cp. Bultmann, "Die Bdtg. d. mand. und manich. Quellen," *op. cit.*, p. 83).
[3] Schulz, *Untersuchungen*, p. 122f. contends that since 3:14 was an independent pre-Johannine logion which combined the ὑψοῦν motif with the Son of Man title, 8:28 and 12:34, which are more fragmentary in character, do not represent closed pre-formed logia but rather the composition of the evangelist who borrowed the ὑψοῦν - υἱὸς τοῦ ἀνθρώπου relation from 3:14.
[4] Cp. G. Bertram, ὑψόω, *ThWB*, VIII, p. 608: "Im Joh. Ev. ist ὑψόω wohl an allen Stellen, an denen es vorkommt (3:14; 8:28; 12:32,34) bewußt doppelsinnig gebraucht." Also Schnackenburg, *Joh. Ev.*, II, Exkurs 13. Untenable is Odeberg's contention (*The Fourth Gospel*, p. 99) that the "lifting up" motif refers to a spiritual experience with the believer in which the Son of Man is united with him and...is elevated in the believer's experience.
[5] Contra Barrett (*St.John*, p. 61) who maintains that the ascent of the Son of Man is understood paradoxically in John both as an ascent into glory but also as a "plunge into the depths of humanity." Blank (*Krisis*, p. 82) who, despite his recognition that John's theology of the cross is a

departure for the exalted Son of Man, and as such is incorporated into an epiphany christology which presents the saving work in terms of the manifestation of God's presence. This shift in meaning raises the question how it was possible for the expression of exaltation, which in the christologies of the nascent church otherwise always referred to Jesus' appointment to the sovereignty of the heavenly kyrios, here with unprecedented change to be applied to the cross? The motivation may be seen in implications of the oneness motif. When it is said that the Son of Man must be lifted up, this signals the departure of him who has always been one with the Father. Since for John this oneness is never diminished, the cross must also be viewed accordingly not as an intervening break but as the point of return for the exalted Son of Man. For the same reason Jesus speaks as the one who is already ascended, when to Nicodemus he declares: "No one has ascended into heaven but he who descended from heaven, the Son of Man" (3:13).[1] Similarly in the much disputed passage in 1:51, where a variety of tradition-historical motifs converge,[2] the essential thrust is to confirm the continuing unity between God and the Son of Man. Syntactically, 1:51 evidences the character of an independent logion, and its incorporation into the Nathanael pericope reflects the consistent concerns of

---

theology of glory, (p. 271) nevertheless maintains that the concept of exaltation is understandable only from the standpoint of a prior humiliation and that therefore the Johannine Son of Man must go the way of passion to cross as the "Servant of God." (p. 85). Dodd (*Interpretation*, p. 247) also insists on introducing the Isaianic servant theology (esp. Is. 52:13) as background. The result is "eisegesis" instead of exegesis.

[1] J. L. Martyn (*History and Theology*, p. 133): "...he (Jesus) speaks... as though he were already exalted to heaven." Blank (*Krisis*, p. 77) presses the meaning of the sequence ascent-descent and therefore identifies "das Christusgeschehen als das absolute und einzige Heilsgeschehen." That certainly is a constitutive moment although its appropriate derivation lies in the oneness of the Son of Man with God. This passage can hardly be said to be parallel in intent to Eph. 4:9f. (contra Haacker, *Die Stiftung*, p. 142) where the *katabasis* is not revelatory in character but descriptive of the total victory of the Exalted One. Odeberg suggests (*The Fourth Gospel*, pp. 72-98) that inherent in 3:13 is a polemic against the traditions of ascensions into heaven by great saints, patriarchs, and prophets of old. Similarly Meeks, *The Prophet-King*, pp. 299ff. If so, the polemic derives from the absolute uniqueness of the Johannine Son of Man.

[2] Cp. F. Hahn, *Christologische Hoheitstitel*, FRLANT 86, Göttingen, 1963, p. 39 n.6. Also Schulz, *Untersuchungen*, p. 97f. Colpe, *ThWB*, VIII, p. 472.

the Johannine Son of Man christology[1] which is to give expression to the uninterrupted heavenly nature and contemporary dimension of the work and person of the Revealer.

Even when additional motifs are added to the Son of Man figure, the basic orientation remains the same. Thus the two passages (12:23; 13:31f.), which speak of the glorification of the Son of Man, add nothing essentially new, but only reinforce the witness that the passion and death of Jesus are also moments of glory. Here exaltation and glorification may be seen as the concurrent, mutually conditioned aspects of the same event. Consequently, in the strict sense of the word, it cannot be said that Jesus' exaltation on the cross leads to glory[2] since the hour of the passion is already the hour of glory. The attachment of the δοξασθῆναι theme to the Son of Man figure is furthermore important from the standpoint of the time dimensions involved. Whereas apocalyptic tradition identifies the glorification of the Son of Man with his future enthronement (Eth. Enoch 51,3; 55,4; 61,8), the glorification of the Son of Man in John, as particularly the hymnic segment in 13:31f. indicates, spans past, present, and future and further demonstrates that the glory which applies to the Son of Man applies simultaneously to the Father. This interpretive development is possible because the Son of Man

---

[1] Drawing on the Primal Man speculations from a variety of Hellenistic documents, Dodd suggests (*Interpretation*, p. 244) "that for John the Son of Man is the ἀληθινὸς ἄνθρωπος, the real or archetypal Man, or the Platonic Idea of Man" and that as such he is "the inclusive representative of ideal or redeemed humanity." Similarly, Odeberg (*The Fourth Gospel*, p. 40) speaks of the inclusive nature of the Son of Man term whereby the believers are incorporated into the unity of "the Man." Granted that Gnostic elements flowed into an admixture background for the Johannine Son of Man sayings (cp. Bultmann, "Die Bdtg. d. mand. u. manich. Quellen," *op. cit.*, p. 96; *Ev Joh*, p. 74. Colpe, *ThWB*, VIII, p. 422; and against Schulz, *Untersuchungen*, *passim*, who maintains a rectilinear development from apocalyptic to Gnostic interpretation), still there is no indication whatever in the text that the Son of Man is to be understood as a corporate being. The Son of Man term in John has a singular, christological function. The title is applied only to Jesus (cp. Bultmann, *Ev Joh*, p. 74 n.4). As such, the Son of Man is not a man among others, or even the representative or spiritually all-inclusive Man, but rather God manifest in the human sphere. (Cp. Käsemann, *Letzter Wille*, p. 35).

[2] Contra W. Kümmel, *Die Theologie des Neuen Testaments*, NTD Ergänzungsreihe 3, Göttingen, 1969, p. 246: "seine Herrlichkeit ...wird erst durch den Tod des Menschen Jesus vollendet."

is consistently understood as a heavenly being who is one with the Father. For this reason also it can be said that when the Son of Man ascends, he returns to where he was before (6:62). Because his origin is heavenly the food which he gives is also heavenly (6:27) and consequently qualifies also the eucharistic food as flesh and blood not of a manipulatable, controllable possession but of the heavenly Son of Man (6:53). In conclusion it may be said that, whether adopted as previously set tradition or recast into new form, the distinctive features of the Johannine Son of Man figure can be best accounted for as deriving from the community's reflection on and conviction of Jesus' oneness with God.

B. THE SON OF GOD

Already the sheer frequency of the ὁ υἱός as a christological designation indicates the importance of the role it plays in the Fourth Gospel. Whereas the absolute form of ὁ υἱός occurs in the Synoptics in only three separate instances (Mt.11:27 par. Mk.13:32 par. and Mt.28:19), in Paul once (I Cor.15:28), and five times in the Epistle to the Hebrews (1:2,8; 3:6; 5:8; 7:28 --all anarthrous except 1:8), it is employed eighteen times in John's Gospel. Even that statistic is not completely revealing since the profuse use of the πατήρ designation[1] also implies the son relationship without explicitly using the term son. In fact, it can be said that the Father - Son relationship appears as one of the most constitutive and significant features of Johannine theology.[2] Why is precisely this terminology of Father and Son so integral to the Johannine conception?[3] The question is all the

---

[1] Cp. G. Schrenk, πατήρ, ThWB, V, p. 996. πατήρ formulations occur 50+.
[2] Schnackenburg, Joh. Ev., II, p. 151: "Das 'Vater-Sohn Verhältnis' ist der Schlüssel zum Verständnis des joh. Jesus..." C. H. Dodd, Interpretation, p. 253: "Certainly there is no other writing known to me in which the idea of divine sonship is treated with anything like such fullness and precision."
[3] Clarification of this question is fundamental to our study. Here F. Hahn's observation ("Methodenprobleme einer Christologie des NT," VuF, 2/1970, p. 10 n.16): "daß die älteste christologische Überlieferung vornehmlich in Vorstellungskomplexen ihren Ausdruck fand, die durch Hoheitstitel geprägt waren." needs to be balanced with Balz's demand (Methodische Probleme der neutestamentlichen Christologie, WMANT 25, Neukirchen, 1967,

more acute when we take into consideration the varying tradition-historical backgrounds of the son designation in its absolute sense and in the form of "Son of God." Although both forms are intimately related and virtually interchangeable in the Fourth Gospel, each form, colored by separate prior developments which must not be indiscriminately mixed, needs to be considered independently.[1]

The old debate about the background of the Son of God designation --whether of Palestinian or Hellenistic derivation--[2] need not concern us in depth here. Important rather is the contrast with the different aspects peculiar to the respective stages of tradition-historical development within the primitive Christian communities. If the Son of God title developed in early Palestinian Christianity primarily within the context of an adoptianistic christology, and if in Hellenistic Jewish Christianity a different profile emerged with the incursion of θεῖος ἀνήρ motifs, whereby emphasis was laid on the Spirit-powered endowment of Jesus to perform authenticating mighty works, and if in Hellentistic Gentile Christianity greater concern was manifested for the aspects of substance and essence,[3] then it is significant that none of these factors appear in conjunction with the Johannine use of the Son of God designation. In John the title has been given a unique function and can be used as a self-evident designation

---

p. 21: "Die Untersuchung der Würdetitel muß ergänzt werden durch die Untersuchung der christologischen Motive und der Vorstellungen --zunächst ohne Bindung an einen bestimmten Titel. Es wird dabei die Frage zu klären sein, ob nicht in der n.t.lichen Christusverkündigung bestimmte Titel auswechselbar sind und von einer Vorstellung in eine andere hinüberwandern können."

[1] This distinction is ignored in Schulz's otherwise careful analysis of what he calls the "son theme-tradition." (*Untersuchungen*, pp. 124ff.

[2] Cp. Bultmann, *Theology of the NT*, I, pp. 130f.

[3] This development is traced in detail by F. Hahn, *Hoheitstitel*, pp. 280-319. In critical reaction P. Vielhauer ("Ein Weg zur neutestamentlichen Christologie?" *Ev. Theol.*, 1/2 1965, pp. 65-69) rightly challenges Hahn's working principle which presupposes a chronological rectilinear sequence from the Palestinian community to Hellenistic Jewish Christianity to a final stage represented by Gentile Christianity. This kind of schematic succession minimizes the problem of simultaneous developments. Thus the delay of the parusia need not necessarily be the presupposition for the development of a theology of exaltation nor functional statements the prior stage for essential or ontological ones. See also D. Georgi, "Der vorpaulinische Hymnus Phil. 2:6-11," in *Zeit und Geschichte*, Tübingen, 1964, p.292.

for Jesus without any further reflection on the predominant aspects which distinguished its development elsewhere. Here the use of the title reflects an established confessional position and gives clear expression to the faith conviction that Jesus is one with God.[1] There is no real reflection on how, when, or under what circumstances this is the case -- whether because of virgin birth, a proclamatory act at baptism, miracles,[2] resurrection confirmation or whatever. Because he is always one with God, Jesus can always be described as the Son of God. Therefore his glory as the Son of God is interchangeable with the glory ascribed to God (11:4) and just as the Father gives life to the dead (5:21) so the dead which hear the voice of the Son of God will live (5:25). Significant for the remaining passages is the fact that the title appears predominantly in confessional contexts, often as the object of the verb of believing or as the criterion by which the absolute uniqueness of Jesus is determined.[3] Thus not <u>believing</u> in the name of the only Son of God (3:18) means condemnation. Conversely, Martha confesses, in response to Jesus' declaration "I am the Resurrection and the Life," that she <u>believes</u> Jesus is the Son of God (11:27). And so the evangelist closes his Gospel with the words "that you may <u>believe</u> that Jesus is the Christ, the Son of God"(20:31).

In pointing to the uniqueness of Jesus, the ὁ υἱὸς τοῦ θεοῦ title further evidences its character as a confessional standard which not only delineates the response to the identity of Jesus but serves also as the measure by which unbelief is exposed and judged. Thus John the Baptist points beyond himself and gives witness that Jesus is the Son of God (1:34). Prompted by Jesus' display of preternatural foreknowledge, Nathanael confesses that Jesus is the Son of God (1:49). Because Jesus himself declares and demonstrates that he is the

---

[1] Therefore Jesus can be described as the one from above (8:23) who is not of this world (17:16) and who after his earthly mission returns to the Father (13:1; 16:28). Cp. Bousset, *Kyrios Christos*, p. 156.
[2] The miraculous semeia in John never evoke the response of "Son of God." And yet 1:49 and 20:31 suggest that the title was associated with this skein of tradition.
[3] Cp. E. Schweizer, υἱός, *ThWB*, VIII, p. 389: "Der Sohn Gottes als Inhalt des Bekenntnisses." Further, L. Schottroff, *Der Glaubende*, p. 290.

Son of God (10:36; 19:7), the hostile reaction of the Jews is stirred and leads to Jesus' arrest and crucifixion, which paradoxically signals judgment for the unbelieving world. In all of these instances there is nothing in the text to suggest that Jesus in any sense <u>became</u> the Son of God or that the title is meant to describe a metaphysical union with God. Instead, the evangelist's usage of the title reflects a decidedly functional orientation in explicating the revelational character of Jesus and his heavenly divine nature. As such, the title appears as an integral expression of a theology which has at its root the proclamation that Jesus and God are one.[1]

C. THE SON

Additional accents are added to this motif complex through the absolute use of the term ὁ υἱός. A kind of transition from the "Son of God" to the "Son" usages is provided by the passage which declares that God gave his only Son and sent His Son into the world (3:16f.). Whereas in all of the other Son passages the term "Son" is used in counter-relation to the "Father," here alone it appears in relation to God.[2] That is significant insofar as it points to a traditional thought pattern represented also in Gal.4:4f. and Rom.8:3f. as well as in I Jn.4:9 where God, and not the Father as subject, sends the Son.[3] A prima facie case could be made for identifying these passages with Jn. 3:16f. and referring them to a common root of prior tradition in which the sending of God's Son was described in terms analogous to the sending of pre-

---

[1] In detailing the nature of that oneness, it is not warranted to play out functional against essential aspects. Cp. F. Hahn ("Methodenprobleme," *op. cit.*, p. 38): "Es wäre falsch, wollte man eine dieser Aussagereihen verselbstständigen und etwa die funktionalen Aussagen wegen ihrer a.t. lichen Vorgeschichte als normativ ansehen... Was die funktionalen und die Wesensaussagen miteinander verbindet ist gerade der personale Aspekt, denn keinesfalls sind funktionale Aussagen im Gegensatz zu personalen Aussagen zu verstehen."
[2] The "Son" in 3:36 appears in a context with both Father and God and would offer the only variation.
[3] The fact that related expansions of the same thought occur in clauses like "He whom God has sent" (3:34; cp. also 8:42; 6:29) does not detract from the uniqueness of the "God sending His Son" formula in 3:16.

existent Wisdom (Wisd.9:9). Although pre-existence is not an issue in both the Pauline and Johannine references, still it is a factor in the overall christologies of both Paul and John. As in I Jn.4:9 together with Gal.4:4 and Rom.8:3, where the sending formulation is implicitly tied in with the meaning of the cross (cp. also Mk.12:1-9), so John 3:16f. too evidences an implicit reference to the cross.[1] And yet the accents are fundamentally different. In the Pauline passages subjection to the Law is the qualifying theme and in I Jn.4: 10 it is the expiatory offering for sin. These accents are notably absent in Jn.3:16f. where the sending theme (διδόναι and ἀποστέλλειν), insofar as it relates to the cross, is predicated neither by OT Law / sacrifice themes[2] nor by temporal eschatological categories but by spatial ones (καταβαίνειν, ὑψωθῆναι, etc.) which combine with the soteriological themes of God's love and the response of faith that leads to eternal life or to the disclosure of the world's hostility that ends in condemnation. Although the theme of God sending his Son, as developed in 3:16f., reflects typically Johannine literary and thematic features, the formulation of the passage retains nonetheless a discrete and separate character when compared with the remaining usages of the absolute ὁ υἱός, since the other usages always appear in contexts relating to the Father and furthermore do not occur in conjunction with the ἀποστέλλειν motif.[3]

The highest concentration of occurrences of "the Son" designation is found in 5:19-26 (8x) and in 3:35f. (3x). Both of these complexes are distinguished by the theme of the Father's transfer or delegation of power and authority to the

---

[1] Reference to the cross is not implicit in the ἔδωκεν of 3:16 (against Kramer, op. cit., p. 113) which, as the parallel in v.17 demonstrates, is to be understood simply in the sense of sending (cp. W. Bauer, Joh. Ev., p. 57) just as the Father gives the Paraclete (14:16) by sending him (14: 26; 15:26). The inference to the cross in 3:16 is gained from the context, specifically from 3:14f.
[2] S. Schulz (Untersuchungen, p. 141 and Komposition und Herkunft, p. 135) can give no convincing documentation for his contention that 3:16 must have its roots "in der Opfer-und Sühnetradition des AT."
[3] C. H. Dodd (Interpretation, p. 225) blurs the lines of tradition-historical development when he isolates the sending motif and concludes with the imprecise generalization that "John has deliberately moulded the idea of the Son of God in the first instance upon the (OT) prophetic model."

Son. Despite the attempt to see in this feature a justification for postulating an original apocalyptic background for both complexes,¹ it should be remembered that neither the fatherhood of God nor the designation of the savior as the "Son" has roots in apocalyptic thought. The structural and formal affinity, on the other hand, to Gnostic thought patterns is so evident,² that the supposition of apocalyptic Son of Man provenance for these υἱός statements hardly seems likely. Consequently, what we have represented in these passages are not the direct products of an apocalyptic Son of Man christology modified by later additions accruing in the process of interpretation³ so that a rectilinear development results from a Palestinian to a Hellenistic stage. Rather, just the reverse seems to be the case in that a christology of exaltation grew with Gnostic formulations and expanded with traces of traditional apocalyptic terminology. Furthermore, although the tradition-historical process underlying the line of development for the "Son" designation no doubt was given significant impulses from the tradition of Jesus' characteristic use of אבא, it can hardly be maintained that the Johannine use of the ὁ υἱός designation, therefore, derives directly from a "son-consciousness" of Jesus.⁴ The so-called Johannine logion in Mt. 11:27 and Lk. 10:22 provides another factor

---

¹ So Schulz, *Untersuchungen*, pp. 124-139, who identifies these passages as originally independent logia deriving in their earliest stage of formation from apocalyptic thought. Similarly E. Schweizer, *ThWB*, VIII, p. 375 postulates an apocalyptic origin. On the other hand, the "delegation" motif can also be termed a characteristically Gnostic theme. Cp. Bultmann, *Ev Joh*, p. 188 n. 3.
² In addition to the parallels listed by Bultmann, *Ev Joh*, p. 119 n.3 and W. Bauer, *Joh. Ev.*, p. 38, see the compilation of pertinent Coptic-Gnostic texts by Schnackenburg, *Joh. Ev.*, II, pp. 163f.
³ Against Schulz's programmatic conclusion (*Untersuchungen*, p. 138: "Nicht die Menschensohn-Christologie und die damit verbundene endzeitliche Eschatoloige stellen einen 'Zusatz' dar, sondern vom Interpretationsprozeß aus gesehen eher die gegenwärtige Eschatologie."
⁴ Against Blank, *Krisis*, p. 162, who argues that "der Gebrauch des Sohnes-Namens für Jesus auf Jesus selbst zurückgeht." Similarly B.M.F. van Iersel, *'Der Sohn' in den synoptischen Jesusworten*, Suppl. Nov. Test, III, Leiden, 1961, who maintains that the Son of God title was a derivation of the authentic "Son" designation. Also W. Grundmann, "Mt.11:27 und die joh. 'Der Vater-der Sohn' Stellen," *NTS*, 12, 1965/66, p. 46. The evidence does not point to a straight line derivational development but rather to a simultaneous formation of independent levels of tradition which were subsequently fused. Cp. Hahn, *Hoheitstitel*, p. 329 and Ph. Vielhauer, *op. cit.*, p. 70.

which needs to be considered here. Representing an independent strain of tradition,[1] this synoptic passage relates the Father's delegation of power and authority in a fashion similar to Jn. 3:35f. and 5:19ff. to the reciprocity between Father and Son. All things have been given to Jesus by the Father (Mt. 11:27a and Jn. 3:35). The orientation to the Father is more strongly accentuated in the synoptic logion, however, than is the case in the Johannine usage which reflects elements of further development. Thus, whereas in the Q passage it can be said that no one knows the Son except the Father, in John this knowledge is extended to include the believers (cp. 10:14f.).[2] Eternal life is tied to faith in the Son (3:36), for whoever believes in the Son has eternal life. The revelational uniqueness of the Son derives from his absolute solidarity with the Father. In the Q logion the orientation is more in the direction of the πάντα μοι παρεδόθη,[3] where the Son appears as God's representative in the world. In John, on the other hand, these same thoughts are further qualified with statements underscoring the reciprocity of the judging and life-giving work of the Father and the Son. The Son is, to be sure, the revelational agent of the Father, but more than that, the Son has life in himself (5:26), has all judgment (5:22), and gives life to whom he will (5:21).

Compared with the absolute use of ὁ υἱός elsewhere in the NT the uniqueness of the Johannine usage clearly stands out. Elsewhere either the relation to the traditional Son of Man christology is determinative (I Thess. 1:10) and apocalyptic and subordinational motifs set the tone (I Cor. 15:28; Mk. 13:32) or the designation is used for a title of exaltation as in Hebrews but yet not within a context of relationality to the Father.[4] What originally may have been a subordinational

---

[1] U. Wilckens, σοφία, ThWB, VII, p. 517, identifies Mt. 11:27 as part of an originally unified segment consisting of three logia in vs. 25-30. Wisdom motifs are characteristic for the passage. Cp. also E. Norden, *Agnostos Theos*, pp. 277ff.
[2] F. Hahn, *Hoheitstitel*, p. 330.
[3] Cp. Schnackenburg, *Joh. Ev.*, II, p. 159.
[4] Cp. E. Käsemann, *Das Wandernde Gottesvolk*, FRLANT 55, Göttingen, 1961, pp. 71f. and E. Grässer, "Der Hebräerbrief 1938-1963," *Theol. Rund.*, 30, 1964, p. 221. In Hebrews the Son's rank is a high priestly rank. Furthermore, it can be said, "although he was a Son, he learned obedience through what he suffered" (5:8).

note may still be echoed in Jn. 5:19, but significantly that aspect is not at all developed. Instead, the emphasis is consistently such that in the Son it is always and really the Father who confronts man. The delegation of power and authority to the Son is not descriptive of a one-time event but rather illustrative of a continuing relation in which the Father loves the Son (3:35; 5:20) and in which the Son always does what the Father does (5:19). Therefore whoever disobeys the Son receives the wrath of God (3:36). Conversely, whoever honors the Father must honor the Son (5:23). It is not as though the Father receives final honor, as in Phil. 2:11b,[1] since in John equivalent honor must be given both the Father and the Son. For this reason the glorification of the Son who returns to the Father means simultaneously the glorification of the Father (17:1) not only in respect to the meaning of the death of Jesus but also in regard to the μείζονα ἔργα of the church (14:12f.). Since Jesus is the Only Begotten (1:14,18)[2] who is εἰς τὸν κόλπον τοῦ πατρός (1:18) and therefore continually in closest communion with the Father, he is consequently like the son who continues forever (8:35). Furthermore, the offer of eternal life is always given when one confronts the Son (6:40),[3] for it is only the Son who really sets men free (8:36).[4]

Taken together these passages demonstrate the unique tradition-historical position of the Johannine "Son" designations. In John the term is more than a title of exaltation

---

[1] Cp. O. Michel, ὁμολογέω, ThWB, V. p. 214; E. Schweizer, ThWB, VIII, p.385.
[2] Against the background of an Isaac-Christ typology, Th. C. De Kruijf, "The Glory of the Only Son," Studies in John, Suppl. Nov. Test, XXIV, Leiden, 1970, pp. 111-123, attempts to make a case for understanding μονογενής more as a soteriological term than as a christological one. His contention, however, lacks convincing support since in all four occurrences (Jn. 1:14, 18; 3:16, 18) the theme of death and sacrifice is either absent (1:14, 16) or not the primary orientation (3:16, 18). Further, see Schnackenburg, Joh. Ev., II, p. 155.
[3] As the Revealer who brings life, the Son continues to reflect the will of the Father. Again it is significant that instead of a one-time event, it is the continuing will of the Father in the Son's revelation that is spoken of.
[4] Implicit in the Son usage in this passage are the accents of sovereignty and freedom. Cp. Rengstorf, δοῦλος, ThWB, II, p. 279. Also A. Böhlig, "Vom 'Knecht' zum 'Sohn'," Wissenschaftliche Zeitschrift d. M. Luther-Universität, Reihe 6, 1957, p. 590.

since it is consistently used within contexts designating a relation between the Father and the Son. Accordingly, the Son is not an independent figure but one with the Father. The Son has meaning only in relation to the Father. Therefore the Son is described as having his legitimation from the Father. Conversely, the Father does not appear as an isolated figure but in a oneness relationship to the Son. God's meaning as Father cannot be separated from his relation to the Son. Therefore the fatherhood of God is described as contingent on the revelation that is realized in his Son. This oneness is not acquired or ephemeral in nature so that it could be achieved or terminated. And even though the revelation is realized in time, the oneness relation between Father and Son, which it presupposes, is rooted in eternity; it is pre-existent and continuing. Nor, finally, can it be said that the usage of the Son title serves to delineate the humanity of Jesus[1] as the everyday usage in the traditional elements in 1:45 and in 6:42 suggests. On the contrary, the absolute use of ὁ υἱός regularly points to Jesus as a heavenly being who brings judgment and life because he is one with the Father. The striking contrast with traditional messianic and Son of Man conceptions underscores the independency of the Johannine usage as well as its uniqueness. In John the titles of "Son" and "Son of God," despite originally varying orientations, coalesce in meaning. The possibility for this

---

[1] W. G. Kümmel, *Die Theologie des N T*, p. 241, insists that inherent in the Johannine conception of the divine Son who possesses supernatural knowledge about man (1:47f. 4:24f. 13:18f.) and who knows in advance the outcome of events yet to come (13:11), who walks on water (6:19) and through closed doors (20:19), and who performs powerful, demonstrative miracles is also a deliberate emphasis on the humanness of Jesus. Thus Jesus is thirsty (4:7) and hungry (4:31). He is tired (4:6), weeps (11:35), and shows anger (11:33). He even changes his plans (7:8,10). Kümmel, et al., would like to understand these aspects as an intentional counterbalance to the picture of the divine Son (cp. esp. C. H. Dodd, *Historical Tradition*, p. 236 n.1). This position, however, overlooks the fact that these descriptive references of Jesus the man all occur in the narrative portions of previous tradition. As such, they complement the narration but are not further reflected on or interpreted as is the case with Jesus' divinity. For this reason it is not legitimate to lift them out as dominant or characteristic features meant to harmonize the Johannine presentation of Christ. Further significant is that even when Jesus is described as tired, thirsty, and hungry, he appears as one who has a different drink and food to give than the material forms talked about.

synthesis, which also includes the Johannine Son of Man title,[1] lies within the presuppositions of John's oneness christology. These presuppositions form the motivating factors for the adoption of traditional forms and their adaptation to comply with the evangelist's witness.

D. THE CHRIST

The remaining christological titles of the Fourth Gospel fall essentially within the same pattern: the consolidation of traditions of differing provenance assimilated and synthesized in the interests of a distinct, christological point of view. This, of course, does not mean that they entirely lose their originally discrete connotations. On the contrary, these distinctions are to an extent noticeably maintained. Already in the very first chapter, which displays such a disproportionately heavy concentration of varying titles (λόγος, ἀμνός τοῦ θεοῦ, Μεσσίας - Χριστός, κύριος, ὁ προφήτης, βασιλεύς) in addition to the Son of God, Son, and Son of Man titles already considered,[2] differentiations between contrasting eschatological figures are not disregarded. Similarly in 7:40f. e.g. a clear difference is asserted between "the prophet" and "the Christ." Significantly all of these remaining titles occur in statements made by others, and in contrast to the "Son of Man," "Son of God," and "Son" complex, never are used in the words of Jesus. This would seem initially to indicate that for the evangelist they are not as central to the christology of the Gospel as the υἱός forms. Also to be noted is the fact that these titles occur by and large with a polemical orientation and in contexts which implicitly reflect a variety of current eschatological views and beliefs with which the evangelist takes issue. They are, as it were, designations which from his perspective need further comment and qualification not because they are wrong or to be denied but because they are not entirely adequate and are open to too much misunderstanding. Behind them stand varying messianic

---

[1] Cp. E. Freed, "The Son of Man in the Fourth Gospel," *JBL*, 86, 1967, p. 403.
[2] Cp. Schnackenburg, *Ev. Joh.*, I, pp. 321-328 (Exkurs 3). Also C. H. Dodd, *Interpretation*, p. 346.

expectations which may be illustrative of aspects of the Jewish-Christian debate of the time. Here, however, they are adopted and through reorientation and reinterpretation given a new direction to correspond more completely to the real authority and status of the Revealer to whom they point. The extent and manner in which this takes place reveals further the nature of the process we have already seen at work in which traditional forms, without further reflection on their original implications, are made to conform to the fundamental shape of the Fourth Gospel's christology.

We turn our attention, first of all, to what in OT and Jewish thought was the most basic designation for God's eschatological agent, viz. the term ὁ χριστός, the Anointed One, the Messiah. Just as much as a variety of different motifs and accents went into the making and formative development of this designation in its usage for a national royal or a universal apocalyptic figure who would act on God's behalf,[1] so little can we say that John's usage of the term presupposes a uniform Jewish doctrine of the Messiah. The distinct Jewishness of the term is underscored by the fact that the evangelist on both occasions of its occurrence translates the transliteration of Μεσσίας from the Hebrew into its Greek counterpart ὁ χριστός (1:41; 4:25). Also of note is the fact that the term occupies such a prominent place in the arguments used by the Jews for whom the technical issue of the Messiah's authentication was of paramount importance.[2] The first occurrence of the designation comes in the Jew's confrontation with John the Baptist where the question of identity is raised and he is asked whether he is the Christ (1:20,25). The addition of the names "Elijah" and "the prophet" as part of the same question reflects the variety in Jewish messianic expectation. None of these terms, however, is further developed in the discussion. The Baptist simply refuses to ascribe to himself any messianic dignity and instead points beyond

---

[1] Cp. F. Hahn, *Hoheitstitel*, pp. 135-225.
[2] Cp. R. Schnackenburg, "Die Messiasfrage im Johannesevangelium," *Neutestamentliche Aufsätze*, (Festschrift J. Schmid), Regensburg, 1963, pp. 240-264.

himself to the One who would come after him (1:27; also 3:28).[1] But the matter does not rest there. He gives further witness. But in his testimony he does not use the same terminology that had been applied to him. In other words, the Baptist does not point to Jesus and say, "He is the Christ!" Instead, his witness is, "I have seen and borne witness that this is the Son of God" (1:34). It is on this level that the messianic designation of "the Christ" reaches its fullest dimension.[2] It is placed on a new trajectory and receives its significance within the context of a oneness christology.

This line of development may be clearly observed in 7:25ff. Again the question of the Messiah forms the center of the Jewish discussion. A mixture of messianic speculations is considered. When the Christ appears, no one will know where he comes from (7:27b).[3] But since it is common knowledge where Jesus comes from, how can he be the Christ (7:27a)! The second problem raised is that of miracles. "When the Christ appears, will he do more signs than this man has done?" (7:31).[4] Finally, the discussion is led by some of the people

---

[1] Since Jesus is identified with the Prophet by the people in the crowd (6:14; 7:40ff.), it is clear why the Baptist is presented as refusing this title for himself. But since Jesus is never identified in terms of an eschatological Elijah, the question is raised why the Baptist refuses this designation also, particularly since the Elijah typology was otherwise so readily applied to the Baptist in the early Christian communities (cp. Hahn, *Hoheitstitel*, pp. 371-380). In Justin's *Dialogus cum Tryphone* the tradition is discussed of the Messiah who has no power until Elijah anoints him. With some justification M. deJonge ("Jewish Expectations about the 'Messiah' according to the Fourth Gospel," *NTS*, 19,3, 1973, pp. 246-270) points to this tradition as helping to explain the Johannine text. Indeed, if calling John Elijah did imply a dependency of Jesus on Elijah, then it is clear why the Baptist could not be identified with this figure.

[2] M. deJonge ("Jewish Expectations," *op. cit.*, p. 250) rightly points out that the entire section of 1:19-50 stands between 1:18 and 1:51 both of which deal with the heavenly status of the One to whom all of the designations in the intervening section point.

[3] The tradition in 7:27 of the hidden origin of the Messiah (IV Ezra 7:28; Syr. Baruch 29:3) seems to conflict with the position represented in 7:42 that the Messiah would stem from the house of David (II Sam. 7:12; Is. 11:1) and be born in Bethlehem (Micah 5:1). Apart from the possibility of having here two separate and independent traditions is also the possibility that behind 7:27 stands the tradition of the Messiah who tarries unrecognized on earth until the time of his public disclosure (cp. Billerbeck, *op. cit.*, II, pp. 488f.

[4] It has often been pointed out that the Davidic Messiah was not expected to be a miracle worker even though miracles were thought of in

into another aspect of the question of origin. The Jews know
the Messiah's genealogy. He must stem from David's line and
be born in the village of Bethlehem (7:42). At the same time
the Jews realize that neither of these stipulations applies
to Jesus, for he is the son of Joseph (6:42) and comes from
Nazareth. Furthermore, what good can come out of Nazareth
(1:46)? In fact, no prophet is to rise from Galilee (7:52).
How then can Jesus be the Messiah? Significantly, Jesus enters the Messiah discussion of the Jews at the point of the
question of origin (7:27f.).[1] Instead of referring to standard messianic qualifications, he speaks of his mission and
the oneness relation with the Father which this presupposes.
At stake is not the correctness of exegesis --the Jews were
quite right in their interpretation of the physical lineage
of the Christ-- but at stake is the recognition of Jesus'
real nature. Therefore the discussion of genealogy (7:42) is
superfluous since a knowledge of Jesus' physical descent does
not guarantee recognition of his spiritual descent.[2] Thus the
polemic in this passage is not simply against a Davidic and
Judean ideology of the Messiah since as the reinterpretation
makes clear neither the southern nor the northern origin of

Jewish belief as a characteristic feature of the messianic times as e.g.
in Is. 35:5f. where God is the author of mighty works, not, however, a
messiah. (Cp. Bultmann, *Geschichte d. syn. Tradition*, p. 275; Billerbeck,
op. cit., I, p. 593; C. Burger, *Jesus als Davidsohn*, FRLANT, Göttingen,
1970). On the other hand, miracles and signs were frequently associated
with the expectation of a Mosaic eschatological prophet (Hahn, *Hoheitstitel*, p. 219; Meeks, *The Prophet-King*, p. 164). Consequently, what we
have represented in Jn. 7:31 is either an amalgamation of the roles which
the Mosaic-like Prophet and the Messiah were expected to exercise in an
eschatological future (so Martyn, *History and Theology*, p. 88) or, as
seems more likely, we have an instance of reflections that derive not
from Jewish but from a Christian Messiah dogma (so Schnackenburg, *Ev. Joh.*,
II, p. 206 and M. deJonge, "Jewish Expectations," *op. cit.*, p. 258.

[1] This is typical for the pattern followed in John where the question of
origin is always a deciding issue. Thus e.g. Nicodemus addresses Jesus
not simply as "teacher" equal in status to his own position but as "teacher come from God." (Cp. Bornkamm, "Der Paraklet im Joh. Ev." *Gesammelte
Aufsätze*, III, p. 81). Correspondingly, it is said of the believer: "He
who is of God, hears God's words."

[2] This technique of misunderstanding is basic to the composition of the
evangelist. It derives from the conviction that there is no understanding of the Scriptures apart from faith in the divine Christ. (Cp. Conzelmann, *Outline*, p. 338. Also Leroy, *Rätsel*, p. 189.) Therefore John's
tenet can be that the OT promises not only the Messiah but in doing so
promises Jesus (5:39).

the Christ is of real importance in comparison with Jesus' heavenly origin. In all of this the realignment of terminological meaning is clear. Jesus himself does not use the term ὁ χριστός nor, on the other hand, does he deny its applicability. Instead, the new dimensions are staked out in which the term must be understood. This pattern is continued in 10:24 where the Jews ask Jesus point blank whether or not he is the Christ. Instead of giving a direct answer, the terms are changed and Jesus, in pointing to his works, begins a discourse which culminates in the declaration: "I and the Father are one" (10:30). Here is where the ὁ χριστός designation receives its proper orientation. Similarly in 12:34, where in the question of "the Christ who remains forever" the Messiah figure is interchanged unexpectedly with the Son of Man figure, no direct answer is provided for the question that had been raised. The implication is that the content with which the questioners filled their messianic terms needs to be altered. Where that is not the case, their statements betray a fundamental misunderstanding.[1]

So far we have considered the ὁ χριστός designation as used by representatives of the Jews. It is important to see that the title can be used not only as a criterion of identity but also from a confessional standpoint as a statement of faith, although, once again, always in contexts which indicate that further qualification is necessary.[2] Thus Andrew confesses, "We have found the Messiah" (1:41). The title here appears

---

[1] Integral to this passage is the typical Johannine irony with which the scene is constructed. The believer already knows that "the Christ remains forever." In the mouth of the Jews, however, these same words, supported by the Scriptures (the closest parallel is Ps. 89:37; cp. W. C. Unnik, "The Quotation from the OT in John 12:34," *Nov. Test.*, 3, 1959, pp. 174-179. Other parallels given by Schlatter, *Der Evangelist*, p. 213.) constitute a misunderstanding of who the Messiah is because they fail to recognize his self-authenticating claim of oneness with the Father.
[2] 9:22 e.g. reflects aspects of the contemporary Jewish-Christian debate of John's day, where the confession that Jesus is the Christ was viewed as a normative faith statement both from the standpoint of the synagogue as well as from the Christian community. John's reluctance, however, to adopt the title without further qualification is demonstrated in his deliberate attempt to reorientate or substitute as e.g. in Peter's confession (6:68), where instead of the confession, "You are the Christ" (Mk. 8:28) we read: "You are the Holy One of God" viz. Jesus is the completely Transcendent One. Further, see W. Kümmel, *Theol. d. NT.*, p. 238.

on a similar level as the subsequent confession made in
Philip's response: "We have found him of whom Moses in the
law and also in the prophets wrote" (1:45) and then in Nathanael's declaration: "You are the Son of God! You are the
King of Israel!" (1:45). The direction given these variant
terms, already narrowed by Nathanael's confession of the Son
of God, is further set by the concluding statement on the Son
of Man who is in constant communion with the heavenly world
(1:51). This is not to say that the Son of Man title as such
supersedes all the rest. It is rather the directional line
which is important, a directional line which points to the
divine status of Jesus who is one with the Father. Similarly,
when Martha confesses her faith (11:27), she declares she believes that Jesus is the Christ, the Son of God, he who is
coming into the world. The same co-ordination between Christ
and Son of God appears finally in 20:30 where the purpose of
Jesus' signs is described as causing faith "that Jesus is the
Christ, the Son of God." Even where the designation "Christ"
is formalized and used as a proper name (1:17; 17:3), its contextual setting points beyond traditional messianic expectations by adding qualifying statements which speak of the Son's
continual communion with the Father (1:18) and which relate
co-ordinately "the only true God" with "Jesus Christ whom
thou has sent." (17:3).

E. THE PROPHET

With the confession of the Samaritan whoman who declares,
"I know that the Messiah is coming ...when he comes, he will
show us all things." (4:25; similarly the question in 4:29)
an additional consideration is brought into play which again
reflects the amalgamation process at work in the evangelist's
use of eschatological titles. This is the only instance in
John where Jesus accepts the Messiah title as a self-designation
(4:26). But significantly he does so with the inclusion of
the final clause ἀναγγελεῖ ἡμῖν ἅπαντα. These words are reminiscent of prophetic activity, where the prophet is viewed as
possessing the capacity to penetrate through human thought as

well as to know the outcome of events in advance.[1] Indeed, this corresponds to the description of Jesus, who knows everything that will befall him (18:4), and who tells his disciples of events before they happen so that when they do take place, the disciples may believe (14:29; 13:19; 16:4). All of this raises the question of the significance of the prophet designation for the Fourth Gospel and the relation of this term to the constellation of Messiah statements discussed above. Twice Jesus is directly acclaimed as "a prophet," once by the Samaritan woman, who, because Jesus told her all that she ever did (4:39), declares: "Sir, I perceive that you are a prophet" (4:19), and secondly by the blind man, who, when asked about his reaction to the One who healed him, confesses, "He is a prophet" (9:17). Of significance is the fact that the statement by the Samaritan woman is further on qualified by her reference to the Messiah (4:25) and by her question: "Can this be the Christ?" (4:29). That indeed is surprising, since the term מָשִׁיחַ is not a Samaritan designation and before the 16th century does not even occur in Samaritan sources, which are quite clear in demonstrating that the Samaritan understanding or concept of the one who is to come is unlike the concept represented in Judaism or Christianity.[2] Here we have a clear instance of how terminologies of varying eschatological import overlap and coalesce because of the evangelist's specific christological point of view by which variant forms are levelled whenever they appear inadequate to express the real status of Jesus. Similarly, when the man healed of blindness confesses that Jesus is a prophet, this designation, even though a real and true prophet is meant,[3]

---

[1] Cp. Lk. 7:39ff. Further, cp. Billerbeck, *op. cit.*, II, p. 133. G. Friedrich, προφήτης, *ThWB*, VI, p. 845. Odeberg (*The Fourth Gospel*, p. 187) conjectures for this passage that "the real intention is perhaps the identification of the Samaritan Messiah (Taheb) with the historical χριστός of the Christians."
[2] Cp. J. Macdonald, *The Theology of the Samaritans*, London, 1964, p. 361. Also H. G. Kippenberg, *Religionsgeschichtliche Versuche und Vorarbeiten*, 30, Berlin-New York, 1971, pp. 276-305.
[3] Martyn (*History and Theology*, p. 102) takes this instance to be a reference to "the prophet" tradition. The absence of the definite article (9:17) plus the fact that although the figure of Moses in some traditions had certain characteristics of the θεῖος ἀνήρ, these are never described as healing qualities, makes Martyn's assumption unlikely.

is, as it were, not left to stand but rather paves the way for the fuller subsequent recognition that Jesus comes from God (9:33) and that he is the Son of Man (9:35f.), a term, which as we have seen, points to the heavenly nature of Jesus who is one with the Father.

Of particular interest are the two instances where Jesus is referred to as "the prophet," that is, the eschatological prophet par excellence. In response to Jesus' miraculous feeding of the 5000, the crowd declares, "This indeed is 'the prophet' who is to come into the world" (6:14). After hearing Jesus' enigmatic reference concerning rivers of living water flowing out of the heart of the believer (7:38), some of the people identify Jesus as "the Prophet" (7:40) in contradistinction to "the Christ." Here ὁ προφήτης appears as a separate and distinct eschatological figure as also the questions addressed to John the Baptist (1:21,25) indicate. Although extensive investigations have been devoted to the clarification of this figure, an exact delineation still remains problematic.

Frequent attempts have been made to establish parallels with the Hellenistic θεῖος ανήρ figures who were often called prophets and who were characterized by extraordinary powers to heal and to foreknow events.[1] While "the prophet" in John is not explicitly predicated as a wonder worker or as one who possesses supernatural knowledge and clairvoyant powers, still it should be noted that the term occurs in contexts where such an identification seems intended. Thus in response to the feeding miracle, the crowd declares, "This indeed is the prophet" (6:14). As a result of his being healed, the former blind man confesses, "He is a prophet" (9:17). Or again, because Jesus discloses with precision the background of the Samaritan woman, she is moved to conclude: "I perceive that you are a prophet" (4:19). Here the analogies between John's use of the prophet designation and functions ascribed to divine prophets in Hellenistic piety seem evident. It is the

---

[1] Cp. L. Bieler, ΘΕΙΟΣ ΑΝΗΡ, Darmstadt, 1967, pp. 73-122. G. Wetter, Der Sohn Gottes, pp. 64-73. W. Bauer, Joh. Ev., Exkurs zu 'Der Prophet' pp. 32f. D. Tiede, The Charismatic Figure as Miracle Worker, SBL Diss. Series I, Montana, 1973.

absolute use of ὁ προφήτης (1:21,25; 6:14; 7:40) which argues against further affinity to the Hellenistic figures and which, in fact, appears as decidedly anti-Hellenistic.[1]

This in turn has given added incentive to investigate the varying expectations in Jewish thought of an eschatological prophet figure, who in analogy to the Dt. 18:15 passage is variously described as another Moses or who in reference to the Mal. 3 figure is thought of as an Elijah redivivus.[2] While both of these figures experienced at points a mutually dependent development in the pertinent literature, their usage in John appears separate. "The prophet" is spoken of as an eschatological prophet like Moses nowhere explicitly appears in the OT,[3] scattered strands of a Mosaic-Prophet tradition can be traced from the intertestamental period, where the hope for a prophet to come is reflected in the Maccabean struggle (I Macc. 4:46; 14:41; cp. also 9:27),[4] through the Qumran community where a prophet like Moses is spoken of, similar to John, as distinct from the Messiah (I QS 9:10f. 4Q test.)[5] Of special significance is the central role which the expectation of the Prophet like Moses occupied in Samaritanism. The sources which mention the Samaritan Taheb generally agree in making him the eschatological Mosaic Prophet although it should be noted that the interrelationship is varied and not always clear, apart from the fact that other traditions are ascribed to the Taheb as well.[6]

Returning to the Fourth Gospel, it is evident that one of

---

[1] So E. Fascher, ΠΡΟΦΗΤΗΣ, Giessen, 1927, pp. 288ff.
[2] F. Hahn, *Hoheitstitel*, pp. 351-380. J. Jeremias, Μωυσῆς, *ThWB*, IV, p. 862f. Cp. the quote of Gförer in footnote 125: "Es gibt keine andere Stelle in den Büchern des alten Bundes, welche um Christi Zeit so entschieden, und von so Vielen auf den Messias bezogen worden wäre, als Deut. 18:15."
[3] Dt. 18:15,18 is not eschatologically formulated but deals rather with the continuing charismatic leadership of Israel Cp. G. v. Rad, *Old Testament Theology*, I, Edinburgh/London, 1963, p. 99). Disputed is the relation of the Suffering Servant figure of Deutero-Isaiah to the prophet figure. (Cp. Hahn, *loc. cit.*)
[4] Cp. R. Meyer, προφήτης, *ThWB* VI, pp. 816ff.
[5] Consider also the two messianic revolutionaries, Theudas and the Egyptian, who Josephus says (*Ant.* 20. 97, 169) were called prophets. See Billerbeck, *op. cit.*, II, pp. 479f.
[6] Texts discussed in Meeks, *The Prophet-King*, pp. 216-257.

the constitutive elements in the evangelist's use of the prophet designation is a basic Moses typology.[1] This is corroborated by the role elsewhere ascribed to Moses in John's Gospel[2] as seen on the following counts. In the arguments of the Jews Moses always appears as the normative figure because God had spoken to him (9:29), and had given him the Law (7: 19) which cannot be broken (5:10; 7:23). Since they consider themselves capable of keeping this Law, the Jews place their hope on Moses (5:45) and hold themselves to be his disciples (9:28). Not all of these statements are antithetical to the position of the Johannine community. The evangelist too accepts the premise that the Law was given through Moses (1: 17). But company is parted, from the standpoint of the synagogue, in the conviction that Moses wrote of Jesus (1:45; 5:39) and that if one really believed Moses, he would have to believe Jesus (5:46). A similar doubleness is also maintained in the Moses typology, which in John is both thetical and antithetical in character. Both the synagogue and the Christians of John's church evidently accept the validity of some relation between Moses and the eschatological messiah but evaluate the relationship in fundamentally different ways. This has the following consequence for John. On the one hand, the evangelist can react positively to Jewish Moses typology by accepting the validity of a relationship between an act of Moses and of Jesus. For "just as Moses lifted up the serpent in the wilderness, so also must the Son of Man be lifted up" (3:14). But the lines are reversed in the case of Jesus' bread miracle where the typology is understood antithetically.[3] For "it was not Moses who gave you the bread from heaven; my Father gives you the true bread from heaven" (6:32).

It is against the background of these developmental lines that the use of the prophet designation can be more clearly understood. If Jesus' feeding of the 5000 is suggestive of

---
[1] Cp. H. Teeple, *The Mosaic Eschatological Prophet*, JBL Monograph Series X.
[2] Absurd is K. Haacker's contention (*Die Stiftung*, p. 57f.) that Moses' role is best encompassed by the term "Stiftung" and that for John the analogy between Moses and Jesus consists in this "daß beide...Stifter sind."
[3] G. Friedrich, *ThWB*, VI, p. 848.

the manna miracle associated with Moses, then the confessional response that Jesus indeed is ὁ προφήτης has by analogy the implication that he is the prophet like Moses (6:14). Furthermore, should Jesus' Scriptural quote about the rivers of living water flowing out of the heart of the believer (7:38) be an implicit reference to the water miracle of Moses,[1] then the reaction of some of the people that this is really the prophet (7:40) may likewise be understood typologically against the background of the Mosaic Prophet tradition. What is important for our investigation is to see that in none of these cases is the typology in John, despite its confessional character, left to stand as an adequate response descriptive of the real status of Jesus. The people's confession that Jesus is the prophet leads them to seek him as the one who gives bread, not heavenly bread, but the bread that perishes. In doing so they miss the real point of the sign, which is not the Mosaic-Prophet/Christ typology, but rather the heavenly status of him who can say, "I am the bread of Life" (6:35). In the pericope in 7:40f. the declaration that Jesus is the prophet implies for the Jews that what really is at stake is a matter of interpretation (7:52). Again the evangelist makes clear that the point is missed. The recognition of who Jesus is derives from his self-authenticating presence and word (8:13f.) and is not a matter of exegetical correctness.[2] It is finally significant that in all of these passages Jesus does not appear as a new Moses and that where the prophet designation is used it is always subject to further qualification. The reason for this lies within the evangelist's christological presuppositions. Those presuppositions do not derive from a prophetic christology but rather from a christology of oneness which identifies Jesus as the heavenly person who is one with God.

F. THE KING

A final factor in this complex of material needs to be
---
[1] A. Schlatter, *Der Evangelist*, p. 200.
[2] This transition pattern from the level of traditional eschatological considerations to the level of the heavenly status and presence of Jesus is excellently demonstrated in diagram form in Martyn's investigation, *History and Theology*, pp. 122-25.

considered, and that is the connection made between the
prophet and the king in 6:14,15. The question raised by this
connection, which occurs explicitly only here, is this: how
is it possible for the evangelist to use a designation so integral to the concept of Davidic messianology, namely "the
king," and identify this term with "the Prophet" when elsewhere in the Fourth Gospel the "Messiah" and the "Prophet"
are viewed as distinct figures? Is this usage indicative of
the evangelist's tendency to level and to mix eschatological
terms, as we have already observed in other instances? Or
does it represent a deliberate attempt to speak in categories
of a prophetic royal messianology, reminiscent of certain
Moses traditions in Jewish and Samaritan thought, where the
kingly and prophetic functions of Moses together with the
Sinai theophany, understood as Moses' ascent into heaven and
enthronement there, play a constitutive role?[1] If the latter
is true, the further question needs to be asked whether or
not elements of a prophetic royal messianology constitute
formative lines or a pattern for the development of the evangelist's christology. Now it is true that the designations
"king" and "King of the Jews" play an important part in John's
Passion narrative, occurring there 12 times.[2] The occurrences,
however, derive primarily from previous tradition[3] which the
evangelist adopted and reinforced to accord with his basic
theme of Jesus' passion as glorification. Beyond the original political connotation of the king designation and the
ironic equivocation with which it is used in the Passion narrative, the main thrust of the term for the evangelist lies
in the witness to the dignity of Jesus who is not of this
world but comes from above. There is no indication that underlying this usage were elements of a Moses typology, particularly also since Jesus is not tried as a false prophet,

---

[1] The latter is the thesis carefully defended by W. Meeks, *The Prophet-King*.
[2] The term "King of the Jews" (6 x) is not an eschatological designation and does not stem from Jewish messianic ideology nor for that matter from early Christian titular usage. Nevertheless, it is used interchangeably here with the title "king" (6 x).
[3] Cp. the detailed analysis by A. Dauer, *Passionsgeschichte*, pp. 122f. 127, 129f. 174f. 179, which locates the king motif in essentially prior tradition. Similarly, Bultmann, *Ev Joh*, p. 503. Haenchen, "Jesus vor Pilatus (Joh.18:28-19:15)," *Gott und Mensch*, p. 152.

or even for that matter as a messianic pretender in the traditional sense, but rather as one who makes himself the Son of God (19:7).[1] Hence it is not warranted to link up the Passion narrative use of the king designation, which has a distinctly independent character, with the prophet-king sequence in 6:14f. as though underlying all of these occurrences were a common pattern of allusions to the Mosaic prophet or to his opposite, the false prophet of Dt. 13 and 18.

In this context the occurrence of "the King of Israel" designation must also be considered.[2] The term appears twice, once in the confessional response of Nathanael at the beginning of Jesus' appearing before the world (1:49) and again at the end (12:13) in the acclamation of the pilgrims at Jesus' final entry into Jerusalem. In both cases traditional material is involved.[3] It is clear that the original connotation of the King of Israel title was determined by a distinctly Davidic messianology. Significant for the evangelist's use of the term, however, is again the implicit reorientation that takes place. As the true Israelite and hence the prototypic representative of the Christian believer, Nathanael uses initially a characteristic messianic term in confessing that Jesus is the King of Israel. But the conjunction of this designation with the Son of God title indicates, as we observed earlier, an important shift, which in turn is further qualified in the succeeding verses 50 and 51. What inspired Nathanael's initial confession was Jesus' mysterious knowledge of him. But Jesus goes on to say that Nathanael will see still greater things; he will see heaven opened and the angels of God ascending and descending on the Son of Man.

---

[1] Against Meeks (*The Prophet-King*, esp. pp. 59-87) who attempts to link up kingship and prophecy motifs as a central theme in John. Meeks insists on trying to detect royalty accents in the Good Shepherd account in ch. 10 (where, however, they are notably absent!) and conjoining these with the king motif in the Passion narrative against the background of the prophetic tradition of Dt. 18:15. Similarly, the attempt is made to establish a connection between the first trial of Jesus before the high priest and the prophet themes of ch. 7.
[2] K. L. Schmidt, βασιλεύς, *ThWB*, I, p. 578: "Wenn der eigentliche mit dem Königstitel verbundene Messiasanspruch unterstrichen sein soll, muß statt der Juden Israel genannt werden."
[3] Cp. analysis by Bultmann, *Ev Joh*, p. 319. Also Dodd, *Hist. Tradition*, pp. 152ff.

Seeing here means faith perception, a seeing of who Jesus really is, namely one who is in continual communion with the world beyond (1:51). Consequently, the King of Israel title is not given independent weight and import but is made subordinate to the evangelist's christology of oneness in which Jesus is depicted not as the royal messianic successor to David or as a Mosaic King figure but as a heavenly being who is one with the Father. Similarly in the scene of Jesus' triumphal entry into Jerusalem where the crowd, motivated in part by its witness of the miracle of Lazarus raised from the dead, now proclaims Jesus as King of Israel (12:13). In comparison with the synoptic accounts, the Johannine version gives pronounced emphasis to the kingship of Jesus.[1] The emphasis is thoroughly consistent with the evangelist's view of the exalted Christ. But again qualifications are introduced. It is not expressly stated that the crowd misunderstood Jesus in acclaiming him as king but neither is their confession pointed to as a model or normative expression. The direction is given rather in the response of the disciples. For the disciples, we are told, did not understand the statements about Jesus' kingship at first, but only when Jesus was glorified (12:16). In other words, only from the standpoint of Jesus' departure and out of the perspective of the community's post-resurrection faith, which recognized the origin and status of Jesus as of Him who is one with the Father, can the acclamation of king be appropriately understood.

From here we may return to 6:14f. The implied association of "the prophet who is to come into the world" and "the king" comes as a surprise, since from a contextual and tradition-historical point of view the motivation for "the prophet" response is implicitly prepared for with the feeding miracle (Moses - prophet - manna miracle) whereas the same cannot be said for the messianic king title (6:15). The break remains unless there is an ad hoc fusion of two separate usages without special regard for their originally discrete connotations

---

[1] This may be seen e.g. in the use of the Zech. reference. Whereas for Mt. the humility motif is retained, thus portraying Jesus as a lowly King (Mt. 21:5) in John it is deleted and Jesus is presented as the victorious king.

or unless the king designation is a deliberate addition by the evangelist and is intended as a critique of the people's acclamation of prophet which appeared in the traditional material adopted by the evangelist.[1] The only other alternative would be to see a connection between the evangelist's usage here and certain Moses traditions in which prophetic and royal functions combine. Even if all this should be the case, there is no warrant to read accents of royalty into other passages where "the prophet" occurs or, vice versa, accents of prophetic function into the other occurrences of the king title as though there were a uniform pattern deriving from a prophetic royal figure which was constitutive for the formation of Johannine christology. The cumulative evidence, if not artificially forced, argues instead for separate connotations. Furthermore, just as the king title has at best "intermediate" force and is consequently reoriented through contextual associations or through qualifying formulations,[2] so also the "prophet-king" designation, assuming that the two terms belong together, receives no primary function. In fact, it is expressly not accepted by Jesus. In answer to the attempt to make him (prophet)-king, Jesus withdraws by himself to the hills (6:15b). This is significant if for no reason than to reinforce the pattern which we have all along observed in which eschatological titles of varying provenance are made subordinate to John's basic christological intention. That intention is clearly not developed along the lines of a royal prophetic image but along lines which depict Jesus as one with the Father. Here we have not royal prophetic christology but oneness christology.

G. OTHER DESIGNATIONS

The function and centrality of the oneness theme as a christological motif is further evidenced in the evangelist's use of still other traditional designations which appear scattered throughout his Gospel. Peculiar to the Fourth Gospel

---

[1] Cp. Fortna, *The Gospel of Signs*, p. 60; Nicol, *Semeia*, p. 34.
[2] Jesus' kingship is not radically redefined in terms of the mission of the prophet, as Meeks (*The Prophet-King*, p. 67) contends but rather in terms of the exalted figure of Him who is one with the Father.

is the title "Lamb of God" which John the Baptist uses twice (1:29,36) in pointing to the identity of Jesus. Appearing in these two isolated instances and never again referred to in the Gospel, this designation clearly has its roots in given tradition. Various backgrounds have been proposed ranging from the OT expiatory sacrifices, the Paschal lamb, the lamb of the Suffering Servant tradition in Is. 53, to the victorious lamb in apocalyptic texts.[1] None of these proposals is without major difficulties and, what is more important, none of the accents suggested by them plays a functional role in the Fourth Gospel.[2] Here again, context is decisive.[3] Sacrificial or servant themes nowhere come into play. In his subsequent witness the Baptist instead gives his own explanation of how the Lamb of God designation is to be understood when he concludes: "I have seen and borne witness that this is the Son of God" (1:34).

The solitary occurrence of "the Savior of the world" title (4:42) likewise derives from John's given tradition and together with the other terms already considered indicates the breadth of the evangelist's titular resources. Thoroughly Hellenistic in character, the title here has no independent force except to indicate that of all the savior possibilities Jesus alone is ἀληθῶς ὁ σωτὴρ τοῦ κόσμου.

---

[1] For an analysis of these respective positions and their problems, cp. Dodd, *Interpretation*, pp. 230-236; Schnackenburg, *Joh. Ev.*, I, pp. 284-288; J. Jeremias, ἀμνός, *ThWB*, I, p. 342f. Bultmann, *Ev Joh*, p. 66f.

[2] Attractive though Dodd's suggestion of the conquering lamb may be, the reconstruction is too problematic and tenuous to be considered as a fixed concept underlying the evangelist's use. Cp. Barrett, "The Lamb of God," *NTS*, 1954/55, pp. 210-218. Similarly, the popular thesis that John developed the Lamb of God designation with reference to the Passover (2:13,23; 6:4; 11:55; 12:1; 13:1; 18:28,39; 19:14), thus implying a Passover Lamb typology, cannot be substantiated. Granted that certain allusions to this theme are present, it must nevertheless be recognized that they play no central role in the theological schema of the Gospel. Contra Wilkens, *Die Entstehungsgeschichte;* also *Zeichen und Werke*, pp. 74ff. Cp. Dauer's excellent critique of the Passover Lamb typology in John (*Passionsgeschichte*, pp. 132-143).

[3] Th. Müller (*Heilsgeschehen*, p. 39) fails to draw the consequences from his observation, "Der Kontext freilich ergibt kaum etwas für das Verständnis des Satzes." The absence of any further comment is in itself significant. Nor is it warranted to emphasize the phrase alone, ascribing central importance to an isolated liturgical formulation whose terminology and import hardly coincide with the overall Johannine scheme.

Conspicuous by its virtual absence is the otherwise popular title of κύριος. It occurs frequently as a standard form of address but only in scattered instances as a name designation for Jesus (4:1; 6:23; 11:2), most notably in consecutive sequence for the risen Christ (20:2,13,18,25) and then with climactic force in Thomas' confession: "My Lord and my God" (20:28).[1] Only conjecture can account for the absence of more frequent use,[2] although it may well be that the connotation of independent sovereignty associated with the term "lord" was not congenial to the evangelist's understanding of the uniqueness of Jesus whom he describes pre-eminently in relational terms with the Father. Furthermore, John's reluctant usage may also be indicative of a trend in which κύριος, as a titular designation with confessional import, began to recede in usage in favor of more specific designations.

Reference here must also be made to the Logos title. Although it appears only in the Prologue, the absolute and personified use of ὁ λόγος, as the introductory title ascribed to Jesus, has long been recognized as central in anticipating the christological concerns that follow in the Gospel. Without going into the complex problems of the inner-relationship and meaning of the component parts of the Prologue or into the problematic historical derivation of the Logos title,[3] reference is made first of all to the self-evidence and directness with which the title appears. Its meaning appears presupposed, and the figure it represents is introduced as though this were common knowledge for the Johannine community. Jesus is not mentioned, but of course it is all along understood that he is the Logos. Nor are any explanations or definitions of the nature of the Logos provided apart from statements indicating that the Logos is a pre-existent heavenly

---

[1] Kümmel (*Theol. d. NT.*, p. 245) raises the question why John avoids the designation "Lord" for the earthly Jesus but uses it repeatedly for the Risen Christ as though there were a *deliberate* distinction being made. Kümmel thereby overlooks 4:1 and 6:23 plus the fact that the occurrences of κύριος in the Easter account derive from given tradition.
[2] Bousset, *Kyrios Christos*, p. 155, surmises that the absence is due to what he calls John's "Christ-mysticism" where Jesus is made to say: "You are my friends...No longer do I call you servants" (15:14f.).
[3] Cp. Schulz, *Komposition und Herkunft*, pp. 7-56; Bultmann, *Ev Joh*, pp. 5-19. *ThWB*, IV, pp. 76ff.

being not as a derivation from God, or as the Logos of God, but rather in absolute terms as ὁ λόγος, identical with God[1] and yet differentiated from Him. The differentiation is explicated in terms of revelation, of shining in the darkness, of coming to his own home, of being rejected and received. But the revelation is never separated from the Revealer just as the Revealer is never detached from his heavenly status since he is "the Logos." This is what gives shape and form to the meaning of the incarnation. That is why the believing community can respond by saying: "We beheld his glory" (1: 14). The function of the Logos, his creating and revealing work, testify to who he is. His identity, however, is never open to question for those who have seen his glory. This is made clear in the Prologue's concluding verse. God's exegete can be only one, namely, the only Son, he who is in the bosom of the Father. Thus in exemplary fashion the evangelist's use of the Logos title provides an almost perfect paradigm for the essential concerns of the oneness motif which underlies the directional formation and reorientation of the christological titles.

H. EGO EIMI

Our final division in this section deals with the unparalleled "I am" statements. They represent one of the most outstanding crystallizations of the christological import of the oneness motif. Who else can categorically raise the exclusive claim of the absolute ἐγώ εἰμι except he who is one with the Father? Much discussion in the pertinent literature has been devoted to clarification of the tradition-historical roots and the pre-Johannine background of these statements which divide essentially into two categories: the absolute

---

[1] Contra E. Haenchen, "Probleme des joh. Prologs," *Gott und Mensch*, p. 123, who picks up an interpretation already suggested by Origin (*Commentary*, II, 2) and maintains a distinction between ὁ θεός in Jn. 1:1b and θεός in 1:1c, concluding that θεός in 1:1c, similar to Philo's use in *de Somn*. 1,299, is tantamount to θεῖος and that therefore the evangelist does not identify the Logos with God but implies rather a subordinate relation (cp. also Haenchen, "Aus der Literatur Zum Joh. Ev. 1929-1956," *Theol. Rund.*, 23/4, 1956, p. 335). However, the absolute use of "the Logos" who was in the beginning with God speaks against a relation of subordination. Further, see Chr. Demke, "Der sog. Logos-Hymnus," *op. cit.*, p.51 n. 44.

use of ἐγώ εἰμι (6:20; 8:24,28,58; 13:19; 18:5,6,8) and ἐγώ εἰμι with a descriptive predicate (6:35,48,51; 8:12; 10:7,9, 11,14; 11:25; 14:6; 15:1,5). These clarificatory attempts basically entail exploration of parallels between John's absolute use of ἐγώ εἰμι and OT theophany themes (Gen. 28:13; Ex. 3:14; Is. 45:5)[1] as well as the relation of the unique structural form of the statements to affinitive speech types in a variety of Hellenistic and Gnostic texts.[2] An additional aid in the discussion has also been the distinction made in ascertaining whether the ἐγώ εἰμι formula is a term of presentation, qualification, identification, or recognition.[3] While it is not always possible to maintain clear-cut lines of differentiation between these respective usages and mixtures at times ensue, still the overall thrust in John remains clear. Here it would be well to bear in mind the basic functional aspects that emerge with the evangelist's reflection on the meaning of the ἐγώ εἰμι statements.

In those places where Jesus simply identifies himself with the words ἐγώ εἰμι, considerably more seems intended than mere perceptual identification. Walking on the sea of Galilee, he identifies himself to his disciples with the words (6:20): ἐγώ εἰμι which amount to an epiphany event, a disclosure of divine presence. The same is the case in the response to the soldiers who came to arrest him (18:5,6,8). The reply of ἐγώ εἰμι has such transparent force in disclosing the divine presence of him who is to be taken that the soldiers draw back and fall to the ground. In other places the absolute use of ἐγώ εἰμι takes on the character of a title where it is equated with predications delineating the one who is not of this world but who comes from above (8:23,24), the exalted Son of Man (8:28). The equation is further made with predications of pre-existent status (8:58) and connected with omniscient qualities (13:19). Here functions are ascribed to the ἐγώ εἰμι

---

[1] H. Zimmermann, "Das absolute Ἐγώ εἰμι als die neutestamentliche Offenbarungsformel," *Biblische Zeitschrift*, (N.F.4), 1960, pp. 54-69 and 266-276.
[2] Cp. H. Becker, *Die Reden*. E. Schweizer, *Ego Eimi*. S. Schulz, *Komposition und Herkunft*.
[3] Bultmann, *Ev Joh*, p. 167. Bultmann identifies the majority of the I am statements as recognition formulas where the predicate is the ἐγώ and answers to the claim of exclusiveness.

statements that are wholly in keeping with John's high christology where Jesus is consistently understood in divine terms.

In those instances where Jesus' ἐγώ εἰμι statements are connected with predicate nominatives, the specific accents lie particularly on the absolute exclusiveness of his claims. Here a whole variety of different images and pictures is used in describing how the revelation takes place.[1] Thus Jesus can say, "I am the bread of life," "the light of the world," "the true vine," etc. Significantly these images are not used merely as metaphors or as parabolic points of comparison but as actual speech.[2] The different areas which they describe denote the full and absolute significance which can be equated with Jesus only. Two functions of this kind of equation are evident. First of all, it makes the revealer identical with the revelation, the giver with the gift. Jesus does not give some-thing; he gives himself (6:35,48,51). He does not merely point to the possibility of life; he is life (11:25). He does not impart information about truth for He himself is truth (14:6). The second function of the equation is to underscore the absoluteness of Jesus' claims. Bread that is physically eaten including even manna from heaven (6:49) is restricted and terrestial; only Jesus alone is living bread (6:48,51). There are many doors and many shepherds, but Jesus alone is "the door" (10:9) and "the Good Shepherd" (10:11). Apart from the true vine, which he is, no one can do anything (15:1,5).

The offense of such exclusiveness is evident. It triggers the reaction of the unbelieving world which rightly perceives that such exclusiveness is tantamount to making one's self equal with God (10:33) and therefore asks, "Is not this Jesus the son of Joseph?" (6:41). And yet the objection is not answered on that level as though the man Jesus would now have to be documented with authenticating credentials. The "paradox" does not consist in the son of Joseph placing exclusive

---
[1] Unclear is how Conzelmann (*Outline*, p. 350) can maintain that John achieves particularization by foregoing the use of imagery. On the contrary, the evangelist uses constantly changing pictures as the I am statements alone demonstrate.
[2] Cp. E. Schweizer, *Ego Eimi*, pp. 112-124.

claims[1] but rather in divine election ("All that the Father gives me will come to me" 6:37; "You do not believe because you do not belong to my sheep" 10:26) and in the self-authenticating presence of him who is one with the Father.

The starting point for an understanding of the "I am" statements lies consequently in the evangelist's christology. The functions associated with these statements --their epiphany character and their absolute claims identifying gift and giver-- appear as the logical consequence of a faith which sees Jesus uncompromisingly in heavenly and divine terms. It is not as though the community's reflections on the ἐγώ εἰμι statements have as their goal the establishment of Jesus' claim of oneness with the Father; on the contrary, they derive from the given conviction that Jesus, though differentiated from, is identical with God.[2] This is further substantiated by the fact that for John not only the resurrection, Pentecost, and parusia but also Jesus' early life all converge into one so that throughout it is the heavenly Christ who speaks. Seen from this perspective, it is clear why Jesus, consistent with the orientation given to the other designations already considered, can appear in absolute terms as the "I am." Here the interpretation of Jesus is put into his own words. And yet, even though this interpretation is

---

[1] Contra Wilkens (*Zeichen und Werke*, p. 95) who maintains that the offense of Jesus' claim of exclusiveness consists in the fact that the claim is raised by Jesus as the son of Joseph, viz. as mere man, and thus has an implicit anti-docetic intention. If that were the case, then the argument developed by the evangelist would have to proceed along fundamentally different lines. There is no attempt to demonstrate that the "man" Jesus is "paradoxically" divine. Furthermore, in view of the levelling process that takes place in John, it cannot be maintained that the "I am" statements represent a final level of christological intensification (p. 91) so that they categorically supersede the other christological designations. Whereas a kind of progression may seem to be operative for the account in ch. 6, the same cannot be held for the other occurrences of the "I am" statements. In this regard it may also be added that the different stages of the dialogue between Jesus and the Jews in ch. 6 can hardly be understood as a deliberate attempt on the part of the evangelist to document the historical character of the faith event in antithesis to a Gnostic understanding. Here Wilkens engages more in eisegesis than in exegesis.

[2] The contrary maintained by Schnackenburg (*Joh. Ev.*, II, p. 69): "Aber man würde den Gebrauch der anspruchsvollen Formel im Munde des joh. Jesus mißverstehen, wollte man sie als Identifizierung mit Gott deuten."

integral to the traditional confession and faith of the community,[1] if that faith is understood merely as self-disclosure and unveiling of one's self,[2] then it, as such, does not mark the cause of the interpretation but already a part of the response. The new self-understanding of faith is the result of confrontation with the presence of Christ and not vice versa the presence of Christ a result of faith. In short, the primacy of christology is maintained. Its specific character as oneness christology underlies the nature and function of the ἐγώ εἰμι statements and provides the inner motivation for the reorientation given to the traditional christological titles.

---

[1] Cp. Haacker (*Die Stiftung*, p. 90): "Dabei wird aus dem σὺ εἶ der Akklamation bzw. dem οὗτός ἐστιν der Proklamation das ἐγώ εἰμι der Selbstverkündigung.

[2] So Conzelmann (*Outline*, p. 350) who in this respect does not go beyond Bultmann.

Chapter IV: Oneness and the Semeia

A. THE PROBLEM

Peculiar to the Fourth Gospel is the use of the term σημεῖον for the miracles of Jesus. Never does the term occur in the Synoptics as a description of Jesus' mighty works except in a negative sense (e.g. Lk. 23:8) or as a description of the miracles by which false prophets try to legitimize themselves (Mk. 13:22). When asked to prove his credentials by performing some sign, Jesus always flatly refuses (Mk. 8:11). In John, on the other hand, the term σημεῖον is the one specific designation consistently used for Jesus' miracles[1] even though the Greek word normally does not mean miracle.[2] Of crucial importance is the dialectical manner with which the understanding of the semeia is developed in the Fourth Gospel. In the first instance they are thought of as providing legitimation for the one who performs them (2:18; 3:22; 6:30; 7:31; 9:16; 10:41; 11:47). Two of Jesus' miracles are specifically called semeia, one in a straightforward sense of semeion = miracle (4:54) and another interpretively signaling Jesus' glory (2:11). The aim of the semeia is to inspire faith (20:30). Indeed, response to the semeia of Jesus is noted as a response of faith (2:11c; 4:53b; 6:2,14), but qualifications can be added, putting a negative accent on the quality of faith involved (2:23) or even summarily designating the response as unbelief (12:37). When put into the words of Jesus (4:48; 6:26), the term semeion has a distinctly critical

---

[1] Significantly, semeia are applied only to Jesus. John the Baptist can do no sign (10:41). The first two miracles are explicitly designated as semeia (2:11; 4:54). The bread miracle (6:14), the healing of the blind man (9:16), and the raising of Lazarus from the dead (12:18) are likewise referred to as semeia. Only the healing of the man with a 38-year illness (referred to, however, as ἔργον) and the walking on the sea of Galilee do not receive specific mention as semeia. Cp. Schnackenburg, *Joh. Ev.*, I, p. 345.

[2] Cp. Rengstorf σημεῖον, *ThWB*, VII, pp. 200ff. R. Formesyn, "Le sèmeion johannique et le sèmeion hellenistique," *Ephemerides Theologicae Louvanienses*, 38, 1962, p. 882.

connotation indicating that the simple equivalence of perceivable miracle and semeion is not sufficient unless it points beyond itself to a deeper meaning. When these various usages are drawn together, it is evident that two different levels of understanding are operative. On the one level semeion is equated with mere miracle and is accepted on face value as a demonstration of divine power. On the other level, critique is introduced indicating that the semeion has basically a symbolic role and suggesting that occurrence and interpretation need to be held apart. The ensuing dialectic in the Fourth Gospel is particularly revealing for our investigation since this dialectic reflects developmental lines that help to clarify the specific christological concerns of the evangelist. Essentially the same pattern may be observed here as was noted in the evangelist's use of christological titles. This, however, is not surprising since the bulk of those titles, with the notable exception of the Son of Man and Son-Father complex, is embedded in the semeia material.

There is little dispute that the Johannine semeion accounts have their roots in prior tradition. The numbering of the initial two miracles despite the mention of intervening signs (2:23; 4:45),[1] the inappropriateness of 20:30 as a closing to the Gospel in its present form compared with the verse's suitability as a termination for an account of miracles,[2] plus the presence of an inner tension in the Gospel between the two apparently conflicting views of the meaning of miracle all have lent credibility to the widely accepted thesis that the form of John's given material was a signs source.[3] Determination of the scope, structural shape, and sequence of such a source has been notoriously difficult,[4] and it cannot be our

---

[1] O. Michel, "Der Anfang der Zeichen Jesu," *Die Leibhaftigkeit des Wortes,* (Festgabe für O. Köberle), Hamburg, 1958, pp. 15-22, assigns only the first two miracle accounts to the source. H. Conzelmann (*Outline*, p. 345) regards the term semeion as completely redactional but offers no substantiation.
[2] Cp. J. Becker, Wunder und Christologie," *op. cit.*, p. 133.
[3] Contrary positions are, of course, still maintained. Thus Blank, *Krisis,* p. 20. K. Hanhart, "The Structure of John 1:35-IV:54," *Studies in John,* Leiden, 1970. Wilkens, *Zeichen und Werke,* p. 30. W. Kümmel, *Einleitung in das NT,* begr. v. P. Feine und J. Behm, völlig neu bearbeitet von W. Kümmel, Aufl. 13, Heidelberg, 1964, pp. 146f.
[4] The most recent attempts at a more precise delineation are the carefully

goal at this point to enter into a detailed discussion of those respective problems. Our aim is rather to trace out representative lines of development in the interaction between the evangelist's composition and his use of traditional material. In this way we will be able to determine more clearly the function of the oneness motif in its relation to the semeia of Jesus.

B. DISTINCTIVE CHARACTERISTICS OF THE SIGNS

First of all, we need to note the distinctive characteristics of the semeia as described in John. One of the most outstanding features is their demonstrative character in displaying the power of Jesus.[1] Whereas in the Synoptics emphasis is on healing the blind and raising the dead out of compassion (Mt. 20:34; Lk. 7:13) and exorcizing demons as a sign of the inauguration of God's kingdom (Mt. 1:15 - 28), these accents are notably absent in John. Here Jesus does not perform miracles in order to banish sin and evil. The miracles are not pointers to the eschatological kingdom work of God,[2] but rather they call singular attention to the power of Jesus. At the wedding in Cana where Jesus changes water into wine

---

documented and researched studies by F. Fortna, *The Gospel of Signs*, and W. Nicol, *Semeia*. Cp. further the review by J. Robinson, *Entwicklungslinien durch die Welt des frühen Christentums*, Tübingen, 1971, pp. 223-241.
[1] This aspect is given due treatment particularly in Strathmann's commentary, *Das Evangelium nach Johannes*, NTD, Göttingen, 1951, ad loc. W. Wilkens (*Zeichen und Werke*, pp. 30-45) too gives major attention to this theme but takes unwarranted lit. liberties in assigning the bulk of these characteristics to the evangelist. (Cp. Fortna's review article, "W. Wilken's Further Contribution to Johannine Studies," *JBL*, 89, 1970, pp. 457-462.) Bultmann, on the other hand, maintains --and this is a decisive factor in his whole interpretation of John-- that the miracles do not occur "with demonstrative obtrusiveness" (*Theol. NT.*, II, p. 45). They are rather "pictures and symbols" with a hidden meaning and not with open manifestation (p. 44f.). Similarly R. Brown, *John*, I, p. 526, contends that the primary function of the miracles is one of symbolism. J. P. Charlier, "La notion de signe dans le IV evangile," *Revue des Sciences Philosophiques et Theologiques*, 43, 1959, p. 442, concludes that a sign is "une manifestation voilee de la doxa du Christ." So also Dodd (*Interpretation*, pp. 297ff.) who bases his whole interpretation of the signs on the platonic relation between archetypal timeless realities and their material reflections.
[2] D. Wead (*The Literary Devices in John's Gospel*, Basel, 1970, p. 26) shows little insight into the character of the Johannine signs when with synoptic terminology he concludes: "They (the semeia) pointed to the new age then breaking into history." Apart from this, Wead's Baseler dissertation is much too imprecise to be of real value.

(2:1ff.), a miracle which D. Strauß with some justification once termed "a luxury miracle," attention is centered on Jesus who in sovereign awareness of his own time disdains the initiative taken by his mother, and then under the guise of lending a helping hand, discloses his creation power[1] in what is explicitly understood as an epiphany of glory[2] inspiring the disciples to believe. What is important to note is that the additions of vs. 4 and 11b by the evangelist[3] underscore his agreement with the demonstrative character of the miracle. Compared with the synoptic variants in Mt. 8:5-13 and Lk. 7: 1-10, the Johannine account of the healing of the nobleman's son (4:46ff.) is unique in its emphasis on the miraculous. Care is taken to point out that the hour when Jesus had spoken was the exact hour when the fever had left the boy (4: 52f.). Furthermore, the additional mention by the evangelist that Jesus was in Cana, whereas the nobleman's son lay at the point of death in Capernaum, helps to underscore the greatness of the miracle[4] by drawing attention to the distance involved. The response to the demonstration of such divine power is again faith. Not only does the nobleman believe but his household does so as well (4:54). In the healing account of the man ill for 38 years (5:1-9), Jesus gives evidence of his preternatural power to know the condition of the man even before speaking with him. Then without even making a specific request or giving some expression of faith, the man is

---

[1] Cp. Noetzel, *Christos und Dionysos*, p. 48 who terms this sign an eschatological "Schöpfungswunder." E. Käsemann, "Aufbau und Anliegen," *op. cit.*, p. 176: "Alles kommt darauf an, Jesu Wunder recht zu verstehen, nämlich als Hinweise auf den Schöpfer, der seine Herrlichkeit offenbart."
[2] Significant is that the miracle, similar to 11:4,40, is not merely a demonstration of miracle-power but a demonstration of glory. Bultmann understandably disputes this (*Ev Joh*, p. 83) by insisting that the demonstrative power cannot be identified with the doxa but is only a basically inadequate picture or symbol for the same. L. Schottroff goes a step further (*Der Glaubende*, p. 261) by maintaining that the evangelist sharply distinguishes between the inner-worldly thaumaturge and the other-worldly revealer. If that were the case, how could the doxa of Jesus' life be emphatically mentioned in connection with miracle?
[3] Cp. the analyses by Fortna, *The Gospel of Signs*, pp. 29-38 and Nicol, *Semeia*, p. 30f.
[4] Bultmann, *Ev Joh*, p. 151. E. Haenchen, "Johanneische Probleme," *Gott und Mensch*, p. 87.

immediately healed as a demonstration of Jesus' divine power.[1] The demonstration is publicly witnessed, and because it occurred on a Sabbath day provokes the hostile reaction of the Jews similar to the reactions recorded in 9:1ff. and 11:1ff. The demonstrative character is further evident in the feeding miracle (6:1-15). Again a comparison with the synoptic variants reveals the idiosyncrasies of the Johannine account. Whereas in Mk. 6:35 the situation is described as critical because the place was isolated and the hour was late, or as in Mk. 8:2f. where the crowd had been with Jesus for three days and couldn't simply be sent home without anything to eat since they would collapse for hunger along the way, none of these factors enter the scene in John's account. Here the feeding miracle is evoked not in response to the people's need. Rather it appears unmotivated except to serve as a demonstration of Jesus miraculous power.[2] Accordingly, the people, moved by such an exhibition of divine might, acclaim Jesus as the prophet and want to make him their king. Again, in the account of Jesus walking on the sea (6:16-21), emphasis is laid on the demonstrative act of manifestation. Since it is not in response to the disciples' distress that Jesus appears (as in Mk. 6:48), it is not surprising that stilling the wind is not at all a factor in John's account.[3] Instead, Jesus simply appears and miraculously the boat is immediately on the shore.[4] Here the miracle of the instant landing is clearly related to the power of Jesus' divine presence. It is this demonstrative power which is further at work in Jesus' healing of the man blind from birth (9:1-41). Again Jesus takes the initiative and displays his control over defects

---

[1] Strathmann, *Johannes*, p. 99: The man is "nur Objekt, das Jesus auswählt, um an ihm am Sabbat einen dem Konflikt heraufbeschwörenden Beweis seines göttlichen Wirkens zu vollziehen." Similarly, S. Schulz, *Johannes*, p. 84.
[2] Haenchen, "Johanneische Probleme," *op. cit.*, p. 92. Strathmann, *Johannes*, pp. 111f.
[3] Wilken's suggestion (*Zeichen und Werke*, p. 52) that reference to the night hour (6:16) was a deliberate formulation "aus Perspektive der Kreuzesnacht" is too subtle to merit serious consideration.
[4] The unmotivated addition in 6:17c, the mention of distance in v. 18, and the connection with the instant landing all make Dodd's contention more than unlikely (*Hist. Trad.*, p. 198) that miracle is not the main motive of the account and that instead of Jesus walking on (ἐπί) the sea, he was merely walking by the sea. Contra cp. Bultmann, *Ev Joh*, p. 159f.

not simply incurred but congenitally determined. If 9:3 is
an addition by the evangelist,[1] we may see there a reinforcement of his understanding of the demonstrative character of
Jesus' act: "that the works of God might be manifest..." The
climax of Jesus' miracles is properly seen in his raising of
Lazarus (11:1-41). Just as the first miracle was described
as a manifestation of glory (2:11), so the last one appears
in the same light. Lazarus' death "is for the glory of God
so that the Son of God may be glorified" (11:4). Thus Lazarus
is wakened out of sleep (11:11) as a demonstration of the
resurrection power of Jesus.

Another distinct feature of the Johannine semeia is dramatic intensification. Not only are individual aspects of the
respective miracles heightened in impact and scope but the
entire complex of recorded signs lies, as it were, on an ascending line whereby the demonstration of divine power appears increasingly greater and more wonderful. This is most
apparent with the healing miracles. First it is a young boy
who is cured at a distance, then a man ill for 38 years, then
a man blind from birth, and finally Lazarus is raised from
the dead. Individual aspects are no less conspicuous for
their heightening effect. Jesus not only changes water into
wine but in doing so provides some 120 additional gallons
(2:6) for a wedding party that already had its full. Compared with the synoptic parallel, the distance is considerably increased in the healing of the nobleman's son --Jesus
is no longer in Capernaum but in Cana. In the bread miracle
the people take as much as they want and yet twelve baskets
of fragments are left (6:13) compared with only seven in
Mk. 8:8.[2] The specification of the distance the disciples had
rowed (6:19) increases the awareness of the greatness of Jesus
walking on the sea not close to shore but way out in the deep.
The blind man did not become blind later on in life but is
blind from birth. Finally, Lazarus' body, already four days
in the grave, had begun to deteriorate (11:39) before Jesus

---

[1] Cp. Fortna, *The Gospel of Signs*, p. 71.
[2] Even though the respective pericopes have different derivations, the validity of a comparison is not thereby precluded.

gives him life.

The character of Jesus as wonder-worker is also of importance. Although scattered references occur to "the man called Jesus" (9:11), who appears with his mother Mary and his brothers (2:1,12) and who weeps at the death of his friend Lazarus (11:35), statements reflecting the humanity of Jesus play no functional or constitutive role either in the source or in the evangelist's redaction.[1] The point of the traditional semeia material rather is to emphasize the status and power of Jesus. How could a man, even an extraordinary man, be capable of such demonstrative acts? Clearly here is one whose relation to God is unique (9:31). So wonderful are his works because of his uniqueness that they inspire the response of faith.[2] The character or nature of Jesus sets the stage for this basic pattern: miracle - believing acclamation. The affinity of this form-structural pattern to that which is operative in the tales of hellenistic θεῖος ἀνήρ figures is so compelling that the conclusion is often drawn that the θεῖος ἀνήρ concept is the proper background for understanding the role ascribed to Jesus in the semeia.[3] But here already the term σημεῖον poses a problem. The Hellenistic words for miracle -- θαῦμα, ἀρετή, and δύναμις -- are totally absent in John. The evangelist uses only σημεῖον and his interpretative

---

[1] Against J. Becker ("Wunder und Christologie," *op. cit.*, p. 138 and 147) who maintains that these statements not only played a constitutive part in the source but were reinforced by the evangelist with a deliberately antidocetic thrust. While it may indeed be said that the traditional material does not speak of Jesus' heavenly origin (although consider the implications of 1:49; 11:27; and 20:31!), it can hardly be maintained this material conversely displays an interest in developing statements that point to Jesus' humanity. Where references implying Jesus' humanity are retained by the evangelist, they are not reflected on and serve no particular function except when they become statements of the Jews. There they represent offense and express the terms of unbelief (6:42; 7:27). But even in these instances the question of how God can be equated with a man is not reflected on and the answer to the Jews is never given in terms of a human-divine paradox. Jesus' divinity so dominates his humanity that his presence is self-authenticating. Thus the reason for the Jew's unbelief comes across as a rejection that evades the light of Jesus' divinity.

[2] Cp. 2:11; 4:53; 10:42; 11:27; 20:31.

[3] Cp. above all G. Wetter, *Der Sohn Gottes*, esp. pp. 64-73. J. Becker ("Wunder und Christologie," *op. cit.*, p. 141): "Mit dem θεῖος ἀνήρ ist zugleich das Stichwort gefallen das die religionsgeschichtliche Voraussetzung der Semeiaquelle einzig und allein zutreffend erklären kann."

DISTINCTIVE CHARACTERISTICS OF THE SIGNS 93

addition ἔργον. Whereas in Hellentistic literature, as well as for that matter in the Synoptics, the response to miracle is typically some measure of astonishment and amazement, these reactions are notably absent in the Johannine semeia events. There the response instead is regularly expressed in terms of belief or in a statement using one of the traditional eschatological titles.[1] Furthermore, the θεῖος ἀνήρ affinity is hardly sufficient to explain the focal concentration in John on the one who does the miracle. The impression is gained in John that the initial purpose of the semeia is to direct all attention to him who worked them. The people and the situations in which they are presented, those who are healed or who witness one of the signs of Jesus have no independent function. They appear basically as stage props whose purpose is but to set the scene for an epiphany of the demonstrative power of Jesus. Correspondingly Jesus is never pictured as dependent on any one of the characters in the scene. Instead, he himself always takes the initiative and directs the course of action.[2] He alone is the sole author of the signs he performs.[3] With these observations we have touched upon the

---

[1] Another point of divergence from the analogy with a purely Hellenistic provenance may be seen in the number of distinctly Jewish features built into the narration of the semeia events (cp. Nicol, Semeia, pp. 53-60) although at the same time it should be remembered that a precise separation between these two areas is not always possible. Even a figure like Moses e.g. could take on many characteristics of the θεῖος ἀνήρ figure. Cp. D. Georgi, Die Gegner des Paulus im 2. Korintherbrief, WMANT, Bd. 11, Neukirchen-Vluyn, 1964, pp. 258ff.
[2] Jesus determines the hour of his miracle (2:14). His word is authoritative command (4:50; 5:8). He does not first speak to the crowds but simply and demonstratively multiplies the food and feeds the people (6:11f.). His appearance on the sea is an epiphany of which he is the center (6:20). Jesus heals the blind man without the blind man's speaking even a petitioning word (9:1ff.). Mary and Martha's request is not heeded (11:1ff.). Jesus alone determines the time of his work (11:6).
[3] If, as Fortna suggests (The Gospel of Signs, p. 230), Jesus' resurrection is to be understood as his greatest sign and was included as such in the traditional material, then it is indeed significant that nowhere does the formulation occur that God raised Jesus or even that he was raised. Instead, it is said, he must rise (20:9). Of his body Jesus says, "I will raise it up" (2:19). Apparently, however, this is not developed by the evangelist since the passive ἠγέρθη appears in 3:22 (and also in the redactional ch. 21 in v. 14). By the same token it is not warranted to conclude with Rengstorf, (ThWB, VII, p. 253): "Im Johannes-Ev ist nämlich Jesu Auferstehung von den Toten ebensowenig Jesu eigenes Werk wie sonst im NT sondern Gottes auferweckende Tat an ihn."

representative features of the traditional level of the semeia. They are demonstrative and intensified acts of divine power which derive from and point back to Jesus alone and so inspire the response of faith. Clearly it is a high christology represented here, and yet one not wholly congruent with the evangelist's theology of oneness. Consequently, the semeia are not adopted by the evangelist without significant alterations and qualifications.

C. CRITICAL QUALIFICATIONS

The qualifications become apparent when we examine, first of all, the soteriological function of the signs and follow the evangelist's answer to the question of their purpose. In the traditional material the relation between miracle and belief is evidently a simple one. Jesus' signs always inspire some measure of faith.[1] But for the evangelist the quality of this faith must be further explicated and defined. Hence a series of corrective additions. The additions result, as we shall see, from his christology. But, for the moment, we must trace the scope and interactions of his critique. Significant is that his critique is not leveled at the signs themselves but at the response of faith which they evoke. The problems are not in the miracles but in those who understand them. On the one hand, it is clear that the demonstrative power-character of the semeia is accepted by the evangelist. They are, after all, the works of God (5:17f.). If they were not understood as such, it is difficult to see why they were incorporated into the evangelist's account in the first place. He could just as easily have excluded them or, at second best,

---

[1] The healing at Bethesda (5:1ff.) and the epiphany on the sea of Galilee (6:16ff.) are the only two sign events where some response of faith is not explicitly mentioned. In 5:1ff. that may be due to its incorporation into the Sabbath debate, and in 6:16ff. to its otherwise independent character (cp. Schnackenburg, *Joh. Ev.*, I, p. 345). The negative appraisal in 12:37 at the close of Jesus' ministry, indicating that his signs were met with unbelief, was most likely not a part of the source (contra Bultmann) but represents rather an addition by the evangelist. It must be understood against the background of his dialectical presentation of the semeia. (Cp. Fortna, *The Gospel of Signs*, p. 199). To designate all of the preceding miracle faith as unbelief in a one-dimensional manner (so Charlier, "La notion de signe" *op. cit.*) is therefore untenable.

selected less powerful examples since evidently other possibilities were also at his disposal (consider the numbering which goes only to number 2 versus 2:23 and 20:30). But just the opposite is true. Not only are the signs which John incorporates the most impressive and intensified but their power and epiphany character is affirmatively reinforced through his own additions.[1] Furthermore, the evangelist does not deny the relationship between these signs and the faith which they evoke. For him the signs are indeed a basis for belief. They are not merely concessions given in the face of human weakness[2] or simply inner-worldly phenomena which cause misunderstanding and oppose heavenly reality[3] Rather they appear as essential works consistent with the nature of Jesus and constitutively related to the structure of faith[4] If that were not the case, it would be difficult to understand why he repeatedly takes sign faith for granted and above all why he would want to close his Gospel with a verse so typical for the traditional material --"these (signs) are written that you may believe that Jesus is the Christ, the Son of God..." -- and to do so without any qualifying additions.

Although signs may well be a basis for faith, the evangelist is concerned that they may also be misunderstood and result in something less than genuine faith. Here he goes beyond the intentional scope of his given material and demonstrates that signs may also fail to reveal the one to whom they point.[5] In the first mention of the Jerusalemites, who

---

[1] Unconvincing is Nicol's objection (*Semeia*, p. 138) that "John would hardly have magnified the miracles because for him the whole point of the miraculous is the historical reality of glory." Had historical realism been his criterion, then his Gospel would have received a fundamentally different shape. John's only criterion is the witness of the Paraclete, the continuing reality of the heavenly Christ.
[2] Against Bultmann, *Ev Joh*, p. 173.
[3] Against L. Schottroff, *Der Glaubende*, p. 261.
[4] Rengstorf, *ThWB*, VII, p. 249.
[5] Already in the traditional material miracles are understood as acts that have significance and a deeper meaning. This is indicated already by the very choice of the term σημεῖον instead of one of the more typical Hellenistic designations for the works of the thaumaturge. The difference then between John's use of σημεῖον and that of his source is not the difference of two different theologies, that is, an absolute distinction between "miracle" and "sign" (contra Haenchen, "Vom Wandel des Jesusbildes," *op. cit.*, p. 10) but rather one of degree. John is much more

saw the signs Jesus did and who consequently believed in his name (2:23), the qualifying addition is made "but Jesus did not trust himself to them" (2:24). The quality of their faith is thereby fundamentally called into question not because of the inadequacy of the signs but because of "what was in man" (3:25). When Nicodemus comes to Jesus by night, he comes as one who is motivated by the signs of Jesus. In fact, similar to the blind man (9:33), he recognizes that Jesus must therefore be from God (3:2). Still he remains on the side of unbelief (3:12), lodged in the sphere of the flesh (3:6) because he has not yet experienced "a birth from above" (3:5).

In 4:45 we are told of the Galileans who received Jesus because of all they had seen him do in Jerusalem. When one out of their midst, the official at Capernaum, then begs Jesus to heal his son, the critical reply, commonly recognized as a corrective addition by the evangelist,[1] is given: "Unless you see signs and wonders you will not believe" (4:48). The words serve as a sharp rebuke against a simple miracle faith that demands legitimation as a basis and ignores the reference character of signs that must be interpreted and spiritually perceived. This critique in turn is qualified by the dialectic maintained in the dublette that follows. With the evangelist's redaction in 50b it is asserted that the officer, who didn't ask for a legitimizing sign in the first place, <u>believed the word</u> which Jesus spoke. But correspondingly the closing statement of belief (v. 53), remaining from the traditional account, is left untouched resulting in the emphasis that the officer came to faith, viz. a fuller faith, <u>after he had seen the miraculous sign</u>. These two verses (50b and 53)

---

complex in his use of the term, adopting implications of the OT אות . In short, John introduces a developed critique. Cp. Fortna, "Source and Redaction in the Fourth Gospel's Portrayal of Jesus' signs," *JBL*, 89, 1970, p. 151-166.

[1] Cp. Bultmann, *Ev Joh*, p. 151. E. Schweizer, "Die Heilung des Königlichen," *Neotestamentica*, p. 411. Haenchen, "Johanneische Probleme," *op. cit.*, p. 88. This has been recently challenged by P. Meyer, "Seeing, Signs, and Sources," (reference in J. Robinson, *Entwicklungslinien*, p. 236). Linking 4:48 with 20:25 and interpreting them positively, Meyer charges that modern premises are introduced when it is maintained that the evangelist was intent on relativizing the miraculous significance of the signs.

may appear as alternatives, and yet for the evangelist they
are not played out against each other as mutually exclusive
terms but rather are understood complementarily.[1]

Further evidence for the evangelist's critical approach to
signs falsely understood is seen in the bread miracle of ch. 6.
A multitude follows Jesus because of the signs they saw him
doing (6:2). Their response at this level contains only rudimentary elements of faith. That faith is evidently strengthened through the witness of the multiplication of bread which
moved them to confess Jesus as the prophet (6:14). But when
they find Jesus on the other side of the sea, they are reprimanded by him. He disparages their sign faith and discredits
their seemingly good intentions: "You seek me not because
you saw signs, but because you ate your fill of the loaves"
(6:62). In other words, if they had really seen the sign,
that is, spiritually perceived it without separating the Giver from the gift, they would have searched Jesus out for a
different reason. But as it is, they missed the significance
of the sign and instead of seeing it as a pointer which would
bring them into confrontation with the Son of Man (6:27) they
receive it only as an innerworldly event, as an end point in
itself. Again it is clear that the problem is not in the
sign but in those who understand it.

A variation on this same pattern may be seen in the Lazarus
pericope. The impact and meaning of the miracle per se seems
defused through the advance declaration of Jesus: "I am the
resurrection and the life" (11:25).[2] But even with this implicit critique the miracle event itself retains meaning as
is indicated by Jesus' statement (an addition by the evangelist): "For your sake I am glad that I was not there, so
that you may believe" (11:14). In fact, many did believe
(11:45), all of which increased the hostile reaction of the
authorities who saw the relation between the powerful signs

---

[1] L. Schottroff (*Der Glaubende*, p. 267) must depolarize this relation
and therefore is compelled to maintain that the faith expressed in v. 53
is already "corrected faith." Nothing in the text, however, supports
that kind of interpretation.
[2] So Bultmann, *Ev Joh*, p. 307, followed by J. Becker, "Wunder und Christologie," *op. cit.*, p. 146.

Jesus was doing and the growing response of faith which they were causing (11:48). Consequently, they take counsel to put Jesus to death and Lazarus as well (12:10). But the impetus of miracle faith increases and leads to a popular movement which hails Jesus a king (12:13) and leads the Pharisees to conclude that the whole world has gone after him (12:19). In retrospect, however, John can use traditional words to place a negative judgment against this kind of miracle faith when he lets it be said: "Though he had done so many signs before them, yet they did not believe in him" (12:37f.). And yet virtually in the same breath he can go on to say: "Nevertheless many even of the authorities believed in him but...they did not confess it" (12:42). The doubleness is typical for the dialectic with which the evangelist understands the function of signs.

Implicit at this point is also the recognition that there are degrees of faith.[1] The authorities who believed but who were not ready to confess certainly were not yet at the point of full faith. Evidently they were only at the very beginning. With the possible exception of 2:11 and 4:53, the initial response to Jesus' demonstrative acts of miracle appears from the evangelist's standpoint as first steps to faith. This is the same pattern already noted to be operative in the evangelist's use of christological titles. Whereas a certain validity was granted many of the traditional eschatological titles as expressions of faith, still it was made clear that their meaning and the faith they expressed were not fully adequate. They were limited to the extent that they failed to reflect the real nature of him to whom they pointed. Therefore there was a constant process of reorientation and

---

[1] Surprisingly, Bultmann too can maintain that miracle faith need not be wrong: "aber er ist nur eine erste Zuwendung zu Jesus" (*Ev Joh*, p. 92). For John the quality of faith is indeed located on different levels. Cp. Fortna, "Source and Redaction," *op. cit.*, pp. 163ff. R. Brown, *John*, I, p. 530f. Understandably L. Schottroff disputes the degrees of faith since that would be inconsistent with the radical dualism which she holds to be constitutive for the 4.Gospel. (cp. *Der Glaubende*, pp. 251ff.) And yet it is not consequent dualism that is constitutive for John but rather christology. Against the background of the tradition-historical development of the text and its intensification through the evangelist's christology, the degrees of faith become understandable. Thus Bultmann's observation remains standing.

development at work in the text. A model example for this may be seen in the account of the blind man (ch. 9). The miracle of his healing led to a continually deepening awareness of who Jesus is. At first he knows only that "the man called Jesus" (9:11) had healed him. Then he confesses that Jesus is a prophet (9:17). Under cross-examination by the authorities he maintains that Jesus must be "from God" (9:33). But only in confrontation with Jesus himself and in answer to the question, "Do you believe in the Son of Man?" is full recognition reached: "'Lord, I believe;' and he worshipped him" (9:38). A similar less elaborate development may also be noted in the case of Nathanael (1:49ff.) as well as of the Samaritan woman and her co-villagers. In each case the initial response, motivated by a manifestation of Jesus' miraculous knowledge, is related to a further and fuller expression of faith. The highest level of faith is one not motivated by any sign at all, as Jesus' macarism in 20:29 indicates: "Blessed are those who have not seen and yet believe." But that does not rule out the function of signs as works which may lead to an understanding that Jesus is in the Father and the Father in him (10:38; 14:11).[1]

Retracing the steps we have taken up to this point, we may summarize with the following observations. Typical for the traditional semeia material which the evangelist adopts is the demonstrative power character of Jesus' miracles which evoke faith in him as an eschatological messianic figure. While the evangelist retains emphasis on miracle in its demonstrative sense and even reinforces this aspect through his own additions, he develops at the same time a pronounced critique of miracle faith by insisting that a sign must be understood in terms of its real significance; otherwise it results in something less than authentic faith or even in outright unbelief. In other words, the evangelist refuses to isolate the miracles. They are important both as events and

---

[1] John's use of the term ἔργον is his only alternative word for miracle. While ἔργον is considerably broader in scope and includes also the ῥήματα of Jesus (14:10) as well as the works of the exalted Christ manifest in the Church, it also embraces the miracles of the earthly Jesus. Cp. Nicol, *Semeia*, pp. 116ff.

also for the significance and meaning which they are meant to convey. For John this is a "both-and" and not an "either-or." The signs are not merely pictures and symbols. Neither are they dispensable occurrences for the witness of the Gospel nor are they merely legitimizing inner-worldly phenomena. Instead of polemicizing against his source,[1] the evangelist expands on accents already contained in the material, and in radicalizing its concerns he builds a critique against its inherent weaknesses.[2]

This whole process may be characterized by what could be called a kind of Johannine reductionism in which everything is virtually reduced to and concentrated on the point of contact between heavenly reality and the earthly sphere. Thus the validity of miracle and the quality and depth of faith which it awakens is measured by the extent to which it discloses who Jesus really is. Demonstrative signs of miraculous power should not really be necessary for faith (20:29; 4:48); the word alone is sufficient (4:50). This, however, can not cancel out the fact that signs nevertheless are given and that acts of miraculous power occur as pointers to the true miracle, namely the oneness of Jesus and the Father and the possibility of man's integration into that oneness (14:23).[3]

This brings into focus the basic question of this section: what is the criterion by which the evangelist both adopts and criticizes the traditional semeia material? The answer may be expressed in the following terms. First of all, emphasis on the epiphany and demonstrative character of the semeia is retained because this is wholly consistent with the evangelist's high christology where Jesus' glory is manifest to the

---

[1] So. J. Becker, "Wunder und Christologie," *op. cit.*, p. 147: "Der Evangelist polemisiert durchweg gegen die Christologie...der Semeiaquelle. ...In Joh xi ist das Wunder einerseits nicht mehr Symbol, sondern für den Glauben ein sinnleeres Geschehen."
[2] In failing to deal with the tradition-historical aspect of the problem, D. Tiede (*The Charismatic Figure*, p. 284) muddies the water of interpretation by claiming that with the semeia accounts the evangelist was seeking to control a triumphalist christology.
[3] E. Haenchen, "Johanneische Probleme," *op. cit.*, p. 88: "Wohl kann das Wunder, das Jesus in der irdischen Sphäre für jederman sichtbar vollbringt, zum Zeichen, zum Hinweis auf das wahre Wunder werden: daß wir in ihm den Vater sehen (14:9)..."

world and displayed in his works which declare that he is
sent from the Father (5:36) and that the Father may be seen
in him (14:9). Secondly, the faith inspired by the semeia
can be criticized by the evangelist, and again the criterion
is christology. Thus it is not sufficient for faith to be
directed to Jesus as to a Messiah or one of the eschatological figures. For John the accents must be fundamentally
changed. Faith must relate to the absolute and only manifestation of God in the Son whose origin is from above and
who is one with the Father. Because it is Jesus who is one
with God and not another, everything must point to him. Faith
which sees semeia only as legitimation must therefore be repudiated to the extent that it supplants the self-authenticating
Christ with self-proposed criteria that stipulate the how and
where of God's manifestation and try to reduce that manifesto a human manipulation.[1] The signs do not place God at the
disposal of man.[2] When the Jews as the representatives of the
world fail to believe, it is not because of the lack of power
or epiphany force in the signs and works of Jesus, but because they are blind (12:37) and do not belong to the sheep
of Jesus (10:25) nor have they been given to him out of the
world (17:6). These predestinatory statements derive from
concentration on the power of the Word and the centrality of
the divine Jesus who cannot be measured by human standards
and who repeatedly shatters the criteria applied by the
world. In the same way sign faith must be criticized when it
concentrates only on the gifts instead of the giver.[3] To
search Jesus out for what he can give instead of for what he
is may mean to lose sight of him altogether. He who sees the

---

[1] Cp. E. Schweizer, "Die Heilung des Königlichen," *op. cit.*, p. 413: "Es
kann sich umgehekrt im Wichtignehmen des sichtbaren Zeichens die Forderung
nach dem legitimierenden Zeichen verbergen, also die Tatsache, daß der
Mensch nicht Jesus selbst sucht, so wie dieser ihm begegnen will, sondern
ein Etwas, das er schon vorher sich zurechtgelegt hat und für dessen Wie
er die Kriterien zu besitzen meint."
[2] The evangelist's critique here demonstrates that Jesus' divinity is not
transparent in such a way that God could be seen directly and His presence
established through neutral observation. Cp. Käsemann, "Aufbau und Anliegen," *op. cit.*, pp. 174ff.
[3] Cp. E. Käsemann, *Letzter Wille*, p. 54: "Die johanneische Wunderkritik
beginnt und endet dort, wo Jesus selber um seiner Gaben willen gesucht
oder vergessen wird."

giver will also see the gifts, but he who longs only for the gifts may quite well forget the giver. The one who seeks the sign instead of Jesus misses both.

For John miracle must lead to a confrontation with him who says, "I am." If it is anything less than that, it is not real faith. At the center stands Jesus alone. Nothing dare obscure his position, not even his gifts. These particular accents become understandable against the background of John's christology. It is christology that serves as his basic criterion in the redaction and reorientation which we have traced in the use and interpretation of the semeia. Furthermore, it is a christology that receives its specific and determinative accents from the oneness motif. For where Jesus is seen as one with the Father, there it is understandable that his works are powerful demonstrations of divine glory and epiphanies of divine presence. There it is also understandable that everything must point to him as the center of revelation. Whatever threatens to obscure his primacy must be criticized. Thus the semeia provide us with another major area demonstrating the scope and functional importance of the oneness motif in determining the shape and direction of the Fourth Gospel. In short, the christological implications of the εἷς motif appear here as the singularly most important and determinative factor in the formative process of the evangelist's adoption and adaptation of the semeia.

Chapter V: Oneness and the Passion Account

A. PRELIMINARY REMARKS

We have already discussed aspects of the evangelist's unique understanding of the meaning of the cross expressed in terms of the glorification motif whereby Jesus' passion and death were described not in developmental terms of humiliation leading to exaltation, but rather as a continuing epiphany of divine glory. The question raised here is whether or not these accents are maintained with the same consistency for the narrative material of the passion account. The problem is, of course, clear and has been recognized as being especially acute precisely at this point. Is the concern to present Jesus as a dying man,[1] the victim of helplessness[2] who acquiescently submits to a destiny that has been imposed on him? Then the passion narrative would demonstrate contours obviously clashing or at least we at variance with the orientation thus far observed to be operative on the basis of the oneness motif, whereby Jesus appears in sovereign power and glory as the Son of God. Then further it would have to be maintained that the incorporation of the passion account was for the evangelist essentially a problem and that the place of the passion material in his Gospel owes more to the weight and importance of the evangelist's given material than it does to his specific theological intention.[3] The alternative and more popularly represented position would be to maintain that the Johannine passion account, if features of humiliation are consitutive in its structure and intent, presents, similar to the Synoptics and Paul, a tension which for the Fourth Evangelist would result in an unresolved but deliberate dialectic

---

[1] So Bornkamm, "Zur Interpretation des Johannesevangeliums," *op. cit.*, p. 113: "Wohl aber redet in den Abschiedreden der Sterbende... Unter diesen Aspekt rückt damit auch die nachfolgende Passionsgeschichte..."
[2] So Conzelmann, *Outline*, p. 347: "Passion —again before the public. Now they are offered nothing but helplessness."
[3] Thus Käsemann (*Letzter Wille*, p. 22) maintains that "die Einordnung der Passionsgeschichte zu einem Problem werden muß."

in which the cross is understood in terms of paradox. The often recognized fact that John speaks of the Passion Lord in kingly terms would then have to be understood at best as a kind of counterbalance in a tension which however distinct would still run roughly parallel to the traditional scheme found elsewhere in the NT.

Are these the only two alternatives possible? How is an answer to this difficult problem to be determined? Certainly not by simply pointing to the inherent tension between suffering and glory with an eye to harmonizing both against the background of the rest of the NT witness nor, on the other hand, by dismissing or playing down the significance of the place of the Passion in John's account. The problem is not on the level of varying statements which can be statistically pitted against each other but on the level of interpretation and how these statements are to be understood. Thus the attempt must be made to isolate the center of gravity from which the evangelist's distinctive lines of development and interpretation may be grasped.

The fact that John's passion narrative is in many respects set off from the synoptic versions by a distinctness all its own is commonly recognized. The decisive question then is this: which are the specific peculiarities, what is the extent of their significance, and against what background do these become intelligible? Such a delineation is possible not only because the synoptic passion accounts offer valuable points of comparison but above all because it is possible to distinguish with reasonable certainty between the evangelist's given material and his subsequent redaction. Of course, there is no final proof that John used a single unified written source for the passion.[1] But the assumption, bolstered by contextual, stylistic, and internal considerations is compelling especially since traditions of Jesus' passion were the first

---

[1] W. Kümmel, *Einleitung in das NT*, p. 147, urges his usual caution with the negative judgment: "...für die Leidensgeschichte reichen die Hinweise auf eine Sonderüberlieferung schwerlich aus, um eine zusammenhängende schriftliche Vorlage neben der Kenntnis des Mk und Lk zu erweisen." Barrett, *John*, p. 18 contends that the Johannine passion story is essentially an edited version of the Marcan.

larger segments of Gospel material to be gathered into continuous narrative.[1] Despite varying hypotheses regarding the scope and origin of the traditional material as well as the extent of its written or oral form, recent studies on the Johannine passion narrative reflect substantial agreement in detecting a synoptically related yet independent level of tradition that was expanded and revised by the evangelist.[2] By being able to distinguish between source and redaction in a way analogous to the semeia material, a step forward can be taken in tracing the morphology of the text's development and thus in isolating the evangelist's representative concerns. Against this background we can explore the relation of the oneness motif and its implications to John's understanding of the passion.

B. INTEGRATION OF THE PASSION MATERIAL

One of the most striking features of John's use of traditional passion material is the extraordinary freedom with which he gives these traditions new form and direction and with which he transposes whole blocks of material into different settings. As a result, material originally related directly to the passion is no longer restricted to the passion account proper but extends beyond into other contexts. This is most clearly apparent in the case of the cleansing of the temple pericope (2:13-22), which in the Synoptics (Mk. 11:15ff. par.) serves as a preliminary event to the passion but which in John, while not losing elements of association to the death and resurrection of Jesus, has been displaced to the beginning of Jesus' ministry.[3] A similar example of

---

[1] On the basis of the evangelist's additions, together with details and statements that appear superfluous to the evangelist's theology, Bultmann (*Ev Joh*, pp. 489ff.) argues for an independent written tradition underlying John's account. Dodd (*Historical Tradition*, pp. 21-150) contends that the Johannine version represents an independent strain of oral tradition differing from the strains underlying the synoptics but controlled by the same general schema.
[2] F. Hahn, *Der Prozeß Jesu nach dem Johannesevangelium*, Evange.-Kath. Kommentar 2, Zürich/Köln, 1970. R. Fortna, *The Gospel of Signs*, pp. 113-158. A. Dauer, *Passionsgeschichte*. R. Brown, *John*, pp. 787ff.
[3] In the synoptic tradition the cleansing pericope is related to the last Passover, in John to the first. Furthermore, John is unique in adding the saying of the destruction of the temple, which in the Synoptics appears in

transposition may be seen in the pericope dealing with
Caiaphas' prohecy (11:47-53). Elements of original passion
material may still be seen in v. 50 and in the tradition underlying vs. 47a, 53.[1] Although the pericope may be seen as
a part of John's overall exordium to the passion, its basic
orientation has been decidedly changed not only by the evangelist's redaction and the addition particularly of v. 52 but
also by its present location which introduces a constitutive
link to Jesus' signs and to the response prompted by his
raising of Lazarus from the dead.

Further evidence for the advanced degree of the evangelist's
redactional contribution may be seen in his free formation of
the exordial passion material in chs. 11 and 12 and 13 - 17.
It can be argued that he follows a skeletal sequence represented roughly in the Marcan version, beginning with the decree of the Sanhedrin (Jn. 11:47,53/Mk. 14:1f. par.) and continuing with the anointing at Bethany (Jn. 12:1-8/Mk. 14:3-9.
par.); the last meal with the disciples (Jn. 13:2a/Mk. 14:18a
par.); (the footwashing scene derives from an independent
tradition peculiar only to John);[2] designation of the betrayer
Jn. 13:18,21b,26-27/Mk. 14:18b. par.); the prediction of
Peter's denial and the flight of the disciples (Jn. 13:37,38;
16:32/Mk. 14:27,29-31 par); and the prayer of Jesus (Jn.12:27;
17/Mk. 14:32-42 par.). If this should indeed have been the
outline provided by the evangelist's source,[3] then all the

---

varied form as part of the passion narrative (Mt. 24:2; 26:61; 27:40.par.).
The passion character of the saying in John is retained by the equation of
the temple with Jesus' body. The problems of these interrelationships
will be discussed further on in this section.
[1] Fortna (*The Gospel of Signs*, p. 148) isolates 11:47a and 53 as traditional. P. Winter (*On the Trial of Jesus*, Studia Judaica I, Berlin, 1961,
pp. 36ff.) on the other hand, regards 11:47a, 48 as traditional and vs. 50,
53, and 57 as manifesting only traces of prior tradition. F. Hahn (*Der
Prozeß Jesu*, p. 26) speaks more confidently of unified elements of prior
tradition in vs. 47-51, 53, 57 and identifies these as an original introduction to the passion account. Somewhat similarly, Fortna (*loc. cit.*)
takes 47a and 53 as fragments of John's source's introduction to the passion. Fortna, however, adds elements of the cleansing pericope (2:14-16,
18,19) to the original reconstructed introduction.
[2] The tradition was expanded by the evangelist. Cp. G. Richter, *Die
Fußwaschung im Johannesevangelium*. Also Bultmann, *Ev Joh*, pp. 351f.
[3] So particularly Fortna, *The Gospel of Signs*, pp. 241f. and F. Hahn,
Der Prozeß Jesu, p. 25.

more striking is the extent to which John expands on the material and introduces new accents resulting in a virtually complete revision. Thus consistent with his conception, a major division is made between the events included up to chapter 12 and those following in chapter 13ff. The decision by the Sanhedrin, the anointing, and the triumphal entry are all thematically bound to the evangelist's introduction of the Lazarus pericope. The result is that both chapters form a kind of unit setting the tone and direction for what is to follow as well as marking the end to Jesus' public ministry. The extent of the evangelist's theological elaboration and revision in chs. 13-17 is, with the addition of the discourse material, even more substantial.[1] Passing over the events of the last supper, which he reports with a bare circumstantial clause, John develops the foot-washing scene and particularly the ensuing discourse into major proportions. Significant finally is the singularly unique expansion given to Jesus' pre-passion prayer which, already echoed in ch. 12, is then fully developed in ch. 17.

When these observations are pulled together, the net impact is not only to underscore the freedom with the evangelist reworked, expanded, and redirected traditions dealing with the prelude to the passion but also the broad extent to which he integrates passion-related material into his Gospel plan. This integration is evidenced by a number of factors --by the distribution of passion material in different contexts (2:13-22; 11:47ff.); the references to "the hour that has not yet come" (2:3; 7:30; 8:20) and their counterpart in 12:23ff. 13:1; 17:1; by the proportionate length occupied by the leave-taking scene and the accompanying farewell discourse together with the prayer in ch. 13-17 (almost one fifth of the entire Gospel). Furthermore the integration is evidenced in the general plan of the Gospel whereby Jesus' trial is conceived of as beginning long before the official proceedings that were initiated in the court of the high priest and then of

---

[1] Cp. Dodd's splendid comparative study of this material and his detection of only scant traces common to the scheme represented by the Synoptics.(*Historical Tradition*, pp. 50-64).

Pilate.[1] Since his word and work place man in κρίσις, Jesus' public ministry consistently appears in terms of conflict and takes on all of the characteristics of an ongoing trial. Jesus' works give witness to who he is. It is a witness that comes from the Father and yet simultaneously it is Jesus' own self-witness. As such, it causes offense and leads to indictment. Reaction is provoked. Charges are levelled. The indictment, however, appears in two different dimensions. Accusations are aimed against Jesus as an offender against the law. Consequently decisions are made to kill him and to remove him from the scene. Judgment is passed. But in its reaction against Jesus and his claims, the world reveals its true nature as opposition to God and expresses the self-judgment that is inherent in its rejection of the Revealer. Actively engaged in passing judgment against Jesus, the world at the same time becomes the passive receiver of the judgment that its action implies.[2] The Jew's indictment of Jesus reverts to self-indictment.

All of the scenes of dispute can be seen on this one line of presentation. The Jew's demand for convincing testimony (1:19ff.) as well as for a legitimizing sign (2:18) signal the initial proceeding. The explosive force of the confrontation takes on formative lines in response to the healing at Bethesda. There the Jews recognize the significance of Jesus' demonstrative act with the accompanying provocative word regarding his and his Father's work (5:1-17). Accusing Jesus of abrogating OT sabbath law and of making himself equal with God, they confirm their intention to kill him (5:18). In the bread discourse at the synagogue (6:27ff.) a dispute is again kindled, and the countercharges of the Jews (6:42) reveal their unbelief. The conflict is intensified in chs. 7 and 8. At the feast of Tabernacles Jesus teaches openly. There is a

---

[1] Bultmann (Ev Joh, p. 59) recognized this correspondence as an essential feature in the structure of John's Gospel. Thus already in regard to 1:19 he observes: "Ein Vorspiel des Streites, der das ganze Leben Jesu durchzieht, begibt sich hier also, eines Streites zwischen dem christlichen Glauben und der durch das Judentum repräsentierten Welt, der ständig unter dem Bilde eines Prozeßes erscheint..." Similarly, Blank, Krisis, p. 310.

[2] Cp. Conzelmann, Outline, p. 348.

division among the people. Is Jesus the Messiah or the Prophet? Proceedings are initiated to have him arrested (7:30,32). Charges are brought against him that he has a demon (7:20; 8:48-52). Jesus' only response is his self-authenticating witness. It is a witness, however, which relegates Moses and the Law (ch. 7) and Abraham (ch. 8) to the mediate roles of witnesses pointing to Jesus. Therefore the Jews again attempt to realize their plan to kill him as they pick up stones to throw at him (8:59). In the sabbath healing of the man born blind (9:1ff.) the dispute about Jesus' identity continues. Judgment is pronounced both by the Jews in their proceedings against the healed man and so ultimately against the Healer as well as also by Jesus who defines the purpose of his coming as judgment (9:38),[1] a theme which reaches fuller explication in the final retrospect in 12:37-43. Following the shepherd discourse there is again division among the people. Some charge once more that Jesus has a demon (10:19ff.). Then at the Feast of Dedication the Witness is pressed for direct testimony: "If you are the Christ, tell us plainly" (10:24). Jesus can only refer to what he has already told them. Thus he points to his works, to the meaning of election, and to the fact that he and the Father are one (10:25-30). The reaction of the Jews is a repetition of what had already previously taken place in similar situations. They find his response blasphemous and again pick up stones to stone him (10:31).[2] The conflict reaches another peak in the reaction that follows Jesus' raising of Lazarus from the dead. Now the Sanhedrin is convened and the decree, already long since in the making, is formalized that Jesus be put to death (11:53). The decree represents an irretractable expression of unbelief which seals the judgment against Jesus. Conversely, judgment against the unbelief of the Jews is

---

[1] Cp. Barrett, *John*, p. 303: "the primary intention of the saying is to bring out the underlying meaning of the miracle and 'trial' which is also the meaning of the ministry of Jesus as a whole."

[2] F. Hahn (*Der Prozeß Jesu*, pp. 81,85) wants to view the dispute scenes on an ascending line that reaches a climax with the charge of blasphemy in 10:33. And yet this can hardly be maintained since the charges are in a sense all qualitatively the same. Already in 5:18 the Jews sought to kill Jesus and in 8:59 they want to stone him.

sealed as the closing statement to Jesus' public ministry, a reference to Isaiah 6:10, serves to indicate: "He has blinded their eyes and hardened their heart" (12:38ff.).

Now we are prepared to draw some conclusions. Seen against the background of these repeated scenes of dispute which provide a forum for the judging and the judged, the passion narrative of Jesus' trial adds nothing that in principle is new but rather continues within the same pattern established already at the beginning (1:10f.).[1] Thus it appears as a repetition or at best as a culmination point of the preceding scenes of conflict and judgment between the Revealer and the Jews. Consequently, in the trial before the high priest the whole point at issue can summarily be put into the question about Jesus' teaching and his disciples (18:19). Jesus' defense in turn is simply a referral to what he had openly spoken to the world and to what he had taught in the synagogues and in the temple (18:20). The trial, as it were, had already taken place, the charges made, the judgment passed.[2] There is no need for further elaboration in the Jewish court. The transfer to the Gentile court follows essentially the same lines, even though the expansion of the material is considerably greater. In a carefully structured sequence of events, Jesus' trial before Pilate serves to reinforce and to reveal the depth and scope of the obduracy of unbelief which continues to the last. The world has its way in judgment against the Son of God; in bitter irony it itself succumbs thereby to final judgment. Significant for our purpose here is to note the integrating force of the trial schema which

---

[1] "He came to his own home and his own people received him not." With these ominous words of the Prologue the theme is announced that is to dominate the following scenes of dispute. H. Hegermann, "Er kam in sein Eigentum," *Der Ruf Jesu und die Antwort der Gemeinde*, Festschrift für J. Jeremias, Göttingen, 1970, pp. 112-131, traces this theme as a constitutive mark of Jesus' earthly ministry and concludes (p. 126): "Nicht in einer fremden, sich zurückziehenden Überlegenheit geht Jesus den Todesweg als Sieger, sondern indem er Gericht hält über diese Welt, sie definitiv aufdeckt und überführt, jedoch sie zu retten." Hegermann, however, oversteps his case when he goes on to conclude (129) that it was the evangelist's concern to emphasize the historical particularity of the exalted Jesus in his earthly-human capacity.

[2] Cp. H. Windisch, *Johannes und die Synoptiker*, Leipzig, 1926, p. 82: "Das Verhör hatte in mehreren Akten 5:19ff. 10:22ff. bereits stattgefunden."

pervades the structure of the entire Gospel. The conflict between the accusers and the accused together with the dialectic between the Judge and the judged, all of which appear as motivating factors in the construction of the passion account of the arrest and trial, are projected back into the framework of Jesus' public ministry with such thematic consistency that the trial schema must be seen as a fundamental binding link. In this light the passion is not merely an after-thought or appendix attached to the rest of the Gospel because of the weight of prior tradition.[1] Rather it is tightly integrated into the structural presentation and provides a central point of orientation.

Recognition of this fact, however, does not help us further until we delineate more precisely the character of its function. Of importance is the manner in which the evangelist uses and integrates the trial schema. It reveals neither a concern to present a historicizing account nor the concern deliberately to reflect continuity with OT salvation-history with reference, as has often been suggested,[2] to Jahweh's contention with Israel where faithfulness to the covenant meant salvation and disobedience resulted in judgment. In fact, the salvation-history perspective appears fundamentally foreign to the evangelist's conception. Jesus "court proceeding," his contention, is to be sure with the Jews. And yet the Jews are what they are not by virtue of OT history, but only by virtue of their response to the Revealer. Thus Jesus can say, "If you were blind, you would have no guilt, but now that you say 'We see,' your guilt remains" (9:41; cp. also 15:22). Seeing the Revealer and rejecting his offer is what gives them their constitutive character. Even appeals to

---

[1] Käsemann (*Letzter Wille*, p. 22f.) short-circuits this aspect when he concludes: "Von wenigen vorausweisenden Bemerkungen abgesehen, kommt sie erst zum Schluß in den Blick. Fast möchte man sagen, sie klappe nach..."
[2] Blank's comments in his chapter on the trial of Jesus with the Jews (*Krisis*, pp. 310-315) derive from a basic salvation history point of view. Therefore he gives prior rank to God's contention with Israel and sets this as the essential background for the evangelist's use of the theme. Had the evangelist, however, used the OT sacral-judicial action between God and Israel as his pattern, then it is difficult to understand why the characteristics of a salvation-history perspective are absent in his Gospel.

Moses, the Law, and Abraham are of no consequence, since all of these instances point not to the status of the Jews but to the status of Jesus (5:46; 7:16; 8:56). Of course, when John speaks of οἱ Ἰουδαῖοι, he has reference to empirically defined people.[1] And yet the text reveals that he is not interested in presenting a historically accurate picture of the Jews at Jesus' time. The primary function of the οἱ Ἰουδαῖοι is rather paradigmatic, meant to illustrate the form and shape of unbelief. For this reason their role can converge with the role of the cosmos. The world too receives the offer of life and light, but it passes these by. Its essence consists in its refusal to hear. Precisely that essence is laid bare and brought to light in confrontation with the Revealer who propels the world to its final and consequent action of unbelief. Latent hostility against God is openly expressed in the world's judgment against Jesus, culminating in the passion, which in turn actualizes the κρίσις τοῦ κόσμου τούτου (12:31).[2]

The role of the world and its religious representatives, the Jews, is understood by the evangelist as a model that explicates the ongoing crisis of disclosure and the resulting division between faith and unbelief which takes place whenever anyone confronts Jesus. This understanding is reinforced particularly by statements in the Farewell Discourse, where the conviction and judgment of the world (16:8-11,33) are seen from the standpoint of the work of the Paraclete and the life of the post-Easter church. Hence the conflict

---

[1] The meaning of οἱ Ἰουδαῖοι in John is not uniform. Cp. Gutbrod, Ἰσραήλ, ThWB, III, p. 378. Also E. Gräßer, "Die antijüdische Polemik im Johannesevangelium," NTS 2, 1964/65, p. 76. Bultmann's conclusion (Ev Joh, p. 59) "die Ἰουδαῖοι sind eben das jüdische Volk nicht in seinem empirischen Bestande, sondern in seinem Wesen" is applicable only with qualification. It is true that for John "the Jews" are constitued by their rigid insistence on the Torah and by a self-security in the possession of revelation which blinds their eyes to the presence of God in their midst. By the same token it must be seen that the evangelist's description is motivated by concrete empirical circumstances of his situation where the division between church and Judaism had reached an advanced stage. Cp. Blank, Krisis, pp. 246-251. Striking is the formal parallel to the anti-jewish posture typical for Gnostic movements. Cp. W. Bauer, Joh. Ev., p. 31.

[2] While it is true that "the world" and "the Jews" are not simple equivalents for the evangelist, the convergence and interaction of their functional roles should not be minimized as is the tendency with Hahn's interpretation (Der Prozeß Jesu, pp. 86ff.).

between Jesus and his opponents is understood not primarily on the level of historical narrative but from the perspective of the ongoing meaning and significance of faith. In fact, the whole trial schema must be seen in this light. Its integration into John's Gospel narrative is made to conform with his revelational concept. Here its function is primarily anthropological and soteriological. The anthropological function is to detail the issues of faith as an encounter in which hostility to God is exposed and judged. Whoever refuses to receive the Word and to continue in it is unmasked as a child of the devil (8:31-47). Even faith to the extent that it falls to the assailments of the alien world is subject to similar judgment.[1] And yet implicit in the pronouncement of judgment is a soteriological function. The final goal of the sending of the Son is not condemnation but salvation (3:18). The absolute division between flesh and spirit (3:6-8) makes clear that such salvation occurs only as a new creation.[2]

If the trial schema as a basic constituent of the passion narrative as well as of the earthly ministry of Jesus functions essentially with anthropological and soteriological motivation, then the prior question still needs to be raised concerning the cause of the motivation. At what point does the conflict, inherent in the trial schema, become real? What gives rise to the crisis reaction of the Jews and the world? What generates the dialectical development of judgment? For the evangelist there can be no doubt but that the answer lies within christology. The world is placed into crisis at the point of encounter with its Creator. The decision of faith or unbelief is realized only in the face of the

---

[1] This provides the inner motivation for the Farewell Discourses which wrestle with the problem of what it means to continue in the presence of Jesus. For the evangelist the problem is anthropological —the incompleteness of faith— and not christological. Therefore it is unwarranted to conclude with Bornkamm ("Zur Interpretation des Johannesevangeliums," *op. cit.*, p. 113): Jesus geht dahin, die Welt bleibt. Nicht ihre, sondern seine Zeit endet." For John just the opposite is true. Jesus' time never ends. His departure does not mark the basis and beginning of a new time but rather evokes deepened reflection on his continuing presence.

[2] Cp. Hegermann's careful treatment of the evangelist's development of the new creation theme ("Er kam in sein Eigentum," *op. cit.*, pp. 115ff.).

self-authenticating claim of Jesus. Because he is one with the Father, Jesus' claim is absolute. His words and works have exclusive character.[1] Therefore the security and self-understanding of the Jews is placed fundamentally into question and stands opposed to the revelational claim of Jesus. According to their law he must die. The whole trial and conflict ignites at the point of Jesus' manifestation. Κρίσις is a present reality in confrontation with Jesus.[2] Consequently it is christology that serves as the anchor point which in turn gives rise to the subsequent anthropological and soteriological dimensions of the trial schema. If christology stands out as the center point and the motivating factor, then its specific accents and nature need to be further defined and clarified. This can be done on two counts. First, it will be necessary to return to our initial finding regarding the transposition of passion material into new contexts and then to identify the reasons for the evangelist's redaction. Secondly, the passion narrative proper will be examined to clarify the motivation for the idiosyncracies peculiar to John and the reason for his redactional additions.

C. SIGN SIGNIFICANCE OF THE TEMPLE PERICOPE

Our attention is turned, first of all, to the cleansing of the temple pericope in 2:13ff. In the Synoptics, as has previously been noted, this pericope occurs in connection with Jesus' final ministry in Jerusalem shortly before his arrest and trial. In John, on the other hand, it appears together with the saying about the destruction of the temple at the beginning of Jesus' ministry. Why did the evangelist place this pericope into its present context?[3] In Mk. and to a

---

[1] E. Gräßer, "Die antijüdishe Polemik," *op. cit.*, p. 90: John's Gospel is "einer der frühesten Versuche, den Absolutheitsanspruch theologisch zu fixieren." Cp. also Chr. Maurer, "Der Exclusivanspruch des Christus nach Johannes," *Studies in John*, Leiden, 1970, pp. 143-153.
[2] L. van Hartingsveld's whole study (*Eschatologie*, p. 36 *passim*) suffers fatally at this point in its failure to recognize that for John the trial motif is not motivated by the final judgment but by the present encounter with Jesus.
[3] R. Brown's (*John*, I, p. 117f.) strained historicizing attempts result in all manner of psychologizing solutions. Schnackenburg (*Joh. Ev.*, I, p. 364) is much closer to the point when he concludes: "Deswegen darf man

lesser degree in Mt. and Lk. Jesus' provocative action in the
temple is related to the decision to have him killed.¹ In
John, on the other hand, the action leads only to a question
without any planned recrimination. The Jew's question is
followed by Jesus' reply which has the character of identity
demonstration. Its orientation is disclosure and manifestation. This is the direction already given by the context.
As such ch. 2 forms a unit. The first event, Jesus' miracle
of changing water into wine, is presented as an epiphany of
glory. Whereas this manifestation is designated as the first
of Jesus' signs (2:11), the subsequent temple pericope is
presented as a prefiguration of the end -- and significantly
also within the context of sign demonstration. It could be
argued that the relation between the two events is best seen
in terms of contrasts.² Thus the wine miracle occurs in Galilee, the temple action in Jerusalem. In Cana the setting was
a festive celebration, in Jerusalem a tense dispute. In the
first event the respondents are believing disciples. In the
second event they are the Jews who become the antagonists and
the accusers. And yet it is not so much the contrasts that
are of concern for the evangelist as it is the continuity in
the demonstration and disclosure of who Jesus is.³

This becomes evident in a closer look at the second pericope proper. Compared with the Marcan version (Mk. 11:15-19)
which served as the basis for the shortened accounts in Mt.
21:12ff. and in Lk. 19:45ff., John's description of the
purging scene is more elaborate.⁴ Instead of concluding with

---

auch nicht zuerst nach dem Sinn des Anspruches in der damaligen Situation
oder nach seinem historischen Wortlaut fragen, sondern muß es aus der Intention des joh. Jesus zu verstehen trachten."
¹ Cp. Haenchen, "Johanneische Probleme," op. cit., pp. 93-101.
² So Schnackenburg, Joh. Ev., I, p. 359.
³ Barrett (St. John, p. 164) expands this continuity in terms of fulfillment to include also chs. 3 and 4. Thus he notes that "we see Jesus first
as the fulfillment of all that the Temple represented; next as the fulfillment of apocalyptic and Pharisaic Judaism (3:1-21), and of what the
Baptist told (3:22-36); then in relation to heretical Judaism (4:1-42) and
to the Gentile world (4:43-54)." And yet it is not "fulfillment" that
provides the integrating factor (as Barrett's contrived comparisons want
to indicate) but rather disclosure Cp. Bultmann, Ev Joh, pp. 77ff.
⁴ Ennumeration of the sheep and oxen, the whip of cords, and the outpour-
ing of the coins are all additional features in John's dramatic expansion.

the well-known quote from Is. 56:7 and Jer. 7:11, Jesus' words in John are part of a direct imperative reminiscent of the verse in Zech. 14:21.[1] In any case John's development of the text is unique, as evidenced by the following points. His addition, first of all, of v. 17[2] provides an OT passage of which the disciples are said to have been reminded as they reflected on the meaning of Jesus' action in the temple. Coming from an OT text which in the early church was frequently regarded as a testimonium to the passion of Christ,[3] the evangelist's addition of the Ps. 69:10 reference is significant not only in providing a Scriptural basis for Jesus' expulsion of the traders in the temple but also in placing a preparatory and implicit reference to the passion, which in turn is more fully developed in the following verses. This veiled and initial passion reference helps to reinforce the orientation which the evangelist gives the total account. The second unique feature of the Johannine account also comes in the reaction to the temple cleansing and is expressed in terms of the question of authority. The Synoptics too introduce this question, but it is differently connected and motivated. In Mk. the cursing of the fig tree incident, which had immediately preceded the temple action, is picked up again and its meaning discussed before the question of Jesus' authority is raised. Mt. conflates the fig tree incident into one account and places it after the temple cleansing. When the subsequent question of Jesus' authority is raised, the impression is left that a new scene has been posited which is initiated by Jesus' teaching (Mt. 21:23) and which has reference to the dispute with the chief priests and scribes regarding Jesus' healing of the blind and the lame (Mt. 21:14ff.) instead of

---

[1] Dodd (*Hist. Tradition*, p. 159) suggests a deliberate "concealed allusion" to this verse as an OT testimonium. Also Fortna, *The Gospel of Signs*, p. 145. Bultmann, on the other hand, concludes (*Ev Joh*, p. 87: "Allein der Text legt nicht nahe, eine solche Anspielung vorzunehmen."
[2] Haenchen's conclusion ("Joh. Probleme," *op. cit.*, p. 105) is hardly justified: "Entweder hat der Evangelist das ganze selbst gestaltet, oder aber er hat das Ganze übernommen." Wilkens (*Zeichen und Werke*, p. 62) defends the first position of the evangelist's self-composition. Bultmann (*Ev Joh*, pp. 87,89) and Fortna (*The Gospel of Signs*, p. 145f.) legitimately point to the redactional character of vs. 17 and 20-22.
[3] Cp. Dodd, *Interpretation*, p. 301.

to his temple purge. Lk. omits the fig tree account altogether and connects the question of authority even more decidedly as a response to Jesus' "teaching." John, on the other hand, is unique in directly identifying the question of authority with the demonstrative action of Jesus in the temple.

So drastic and ostensive is Jesus' temple action that the Jews are compelled to ask for his credentials. Nor are they satisfied with just clarifying information. They demand a concrete legitimizing sign! Jesus' answer in John is similarly unique. Whereas in the Synoptics the reply is in the form of a counter-question, in the Fourth Gospel Jesus responds with the saying: "Destroy this temple and in three days I will raise it up." The temple saying of Jesus is variously transmitted in the Gospel tradition.[1] In the Synoptics it occurs in the prosecution at Jesus' trial ("We have heard him say, 'I will destroy this temple made with hands and in three days I will build another not made with hands.'" Mk. 14:58 par); in the derision beneath the cross ("You who would destroy the temple and build it in three days, save yourself..." Mk. 15:29 par); and also as a prophecy of destruction in the apocalyptic discourse ("Do you see these great buildings? There will not be left one stone upon another that will not be thrown down" Mk. 13:2 par). In all of these instances the identification is one-dimensional and expresses the physical building of the temple in Jerusalem.

An important variant of the temple saying occurs in the charge of the false witness against Stephen in Acts 6:14. Here the destruction of the temple is connected with the abrogation of Mosaic tradition. Indeed, this is a point implicitly expressed in John's temple cleansing account to which the evangelist joins his form of the temple saying, emphasizing "destruction" and "raising." The implication is that Jesus' action in the temple is to be understood not simply as a reformation of existing practices but as a transformation, an anullment or destruction of the Mosaic system and

---

[1] Cp. the analysis in H. Leroy, *Rätsel*, p. 142f. Also Dodd, *Historical Tradition*, pp. 89-91.

its replacement by Jesus.[1] And yet, important though this concern may be and also logically prepared for by the allusion in the preceding Cana miracle (2:6), still it does not express the major significance of the pericope or reflect its basic orientation.[2] This is made plain, as we have seen, by the veiled reference to the passion in v. 17, the demand for a legitimizing sign, and above all by the evangelist's additions in v. 21f. In the synoptic sayings (Mk. 14:58 etc.), as shown above, the meaning of the temple is understood by its speakers in a face value fashion as the physical structure in Jerusalem. In John, however, the temple of which Jesus speaks is explicitly interpreted as his body (2:21), even though the Jews do not understand it this way. That in turn gives rise to the typical Johannine misunderstanding since they have only the building in mind. But the evangelist's intention in the equation temple = body is clear. The equation serves notice that it is the meaning of Jesus' passion that is being talked about and that significant accents are being provided for its interpretation.

Which accents are these? We have already noted that the continuity between the temple pericope and the preceding Cana miracle consists in their disclosure character manifesting who Jesus is. To what extent this character typifies the development of the text in 2:18ff. needs to be further clarified. Provoked by Jesus' demonstrative and unparalleled action in cleansing the temple, the Jews demand a legitimizing sign. Their demand is somewhat analogous to the demand in 6:30 where, following the bread miracle, the Jews also ask for a sign. There they suggest that the sign might be some manner of repetition of the Exodus manna wonder. In response Jesus does not promise a future occurrence but rather offers an interpretation of what had already taken place. In the temple pericope, on the other hand, Jesus replies to the sign

---

[1] Thus the new orientation given to the temple purge is more radical than the original intention of the source. See Haenchen, "Joh. Problem," *op. cit.*, p. 103. Strathmann, *Johannes*, p. 62.

[2] Against Dodd, *Interpretation*, p. 303, who maintains that the primary function of the Temple Cleansing is to illustrate the fundamental truth "that Christ has come to inaugurate a new order in religion." Similarly Barrett, *John*, p. 164. Also Hoskyns, *The Fourth Gospel*, p. 194.

demand by pointing metaphorically to events yet to come: his
death and resurrection. The preceding temple purge is not
the actual sign. Although it too has sign character, its
prime function is to prepare the way and to set the terms for
the sign that is to come. Of significance is the implication
that Jesus' death and resurrection fall into the category of
a "sign."[1] This is decisive for understanding the accents
which the evangelist places on the meaning of Jesus' passion
and death. If the salient feature of the Johannine sign is
its demonstrative character emphasizing the sovereign action
of a divine Jesus, then clearly this is the accent decisive
for understanding the meaning of his passion and death.

Can this demonstrative character for the passion be consistently maintained or are there qualifying factors to be
considered? On the grounds that with the semeia Jesus always
appears as the one who acts, whereas in the passion account
he is the passive receiver of action directed against him, it
has been argued that the constitutive link between Jesus'
semeia and the passion is broken.[2] Another negative argument
is to claim that for John the semeia have only reference
character, whereas Jesus' death is said to constitute the
salvational event itself.[3] In regard to the latter, however,
it is clear that John does not present Jesus' death from a
salvation-historical point of view as the center of his Gospel. The cross has significance insofar as it marks the departure of Jesus as well as final judgment for the Jews. But
it is not Jesus' death that determines his real identity.
Furthermore, it is not the significance of the cross that
predicates the semeia but rather the significance of the
semeia that predicates the cross.[4] Thus even Jesus' death is

---

[1] This is implied further by the present location of 20:31. Contra J.
Becker, "Wunder und Christologie," op. cit., p. 133 n. 3.
[2] So Rengstorf, ThWB, VII, p. 254.
[3] So Th. Müller, Das Heilsgeschehen, p. 130. Also Wilkens, Zeichen und
Werke, p. 61.
[4] In other words, Jesus' glory determines the meaning of the cross and
not vice versa. For this reason John can set passion material into the
context of signs. Wilken's conclusion (Zeichen u. Werke, p. 62,68) "daß
das Passions-und Ostergeschehen als integraler Bestandteil der Zeichen-
wirksamkeit Jesu erscheint und die Semeia Jesu von hier aus bestimmt werden" is not tenable in the second part. For John just the reverse is true.

understood as a demonstration of victory and glory, a sign of sovereign power and epiphany. From this standpoint the first objection dealing with the active and passive roles of Jesus proves to be untenable and inconsistent with the evangelist's intention. Jesus does not appear as the passive receiver but as the sovereign Lord who is actively in control. Precisely this is the point implicit in the temple saying and its interpretation in 2:18ff. With prophetic irony the imperative is given to destroy the temple. That is the work of the Jews. But just as Jesus purged the temple with ostensive sovereign action so the intentionally ambivalent command, "Destroy this temple" signifies on its deeper level that it is he who determines his own death. Thus later on he declares that he lays down his life of his own accord (10:18). At the end he independently and soveriegnly announces, "It is finished" (19:30). This same accent is carried through for an understanding of the resurrection: "in three days I will raise it up again" (2:19b). This description of the resurrection depicting Jesus as the subject is thus similar to the semeia where he likewise consistently appears as the subject of the action. Significantly, the Jews respond only to the second half of Jesus' saying, which presents Jesus on both levels of meaning (symbolized by the verbs ἐγείρειν, 2:19b, 20b - temple as body/οἰκοδομεῖν, 2:20a - temple as building) as the one who acts. Again the evangelist's intention is underscored.

Now we may briefly summarize. The temple pericope occupies a decisive position in setting determinative accents for an understanding of the death and resurrection of Jesus. Receiving direction from the connection with the signs of Jesus, these events are characterized by his sovereign action. He is in control and determines the course of what takes place. Here a christology emerges that is thoroughly consistent with and clearly based on Jesus' oneness with the Father. The fact that this oneness is not always recognized or that even the disciples recognized the significance of Jesus' word only after the resurrection (2:22) is an anthropological problem of faith. It does not detract from the nature of Jesus, who, because he is one with God, is always in control. With demonstrative sovereignty Jesus appears as the central subject

of action as he precipitates the reaction of unbelief and
discloses himself to the eyes of faith. If this is accent
that stands out in the development and meaning of John's temple pericope, then it remains for us to trace the influence
and significance of this accent in the formation of the exordial passion narrative, beginning with chapter 11.

D. ARGUMENT AND STRUCTURE OF THE EXORDIAL PASSION MATERIAL

In the argument and structure of John's passion account,
the place of the Lazarus pericope exercises a central role.
Although, as we have already seen, the trial proceedings in a
theological sense were long underway with the resolve to kill
Jesus and the blasphemy charge already formed, it is the demonstrative and dramatic raising of Lazarus from the dead that
triggers the final reaction and initiates the prelude to the
passion. This is unique to John's Gospel. Its significance
lies in the fact that the events of the passion are fundamentally tied into the meaning of the signs of Jesus. By placing
the Lazarus episode into its present location immediately before the final death plot,[1] the evangelist is able to present
this extraordinary miracle as the underlying motivation for
the events that follow.[2] Thus the passion is seen in the
light of power and glory. Jesus enters the final days as
sovereign lord over life and death. With the Lazarus miracle
as pivotal point, the subsequent events of chs. 11 and 12 are
all related in the same vein. Jesus' manifestation of glory
(11:4) in the raising of Lazarus is cause for the Sanhedrin
to be convened and for the death plot to be finalized (11:
47ff.) at which time Caiaphas made his well known prophetic
statement. Some commentators insist on seeing in this scene
and particularly in the words of Caiaphas a culmination
point emphasizing the death of Jesus as a vicarious sacrifice.[3]

---

[1] R. Fortna, *The Gospel of Signs*, p. 145, argues that the Lazarus story appears to have occupied an earlier position in the original version of the signs. If so, the evangelist's relocation of the pericope into its present place would underscore his intention to provide new motivation for the ensuing passion account.

[2] Cp. Käsemann, *Letzter Wille*, p. 24: the Lazarus miracle "eröffnet und begründet ...die Passion."

[3] This is a key to Wilken's interpretation (*Zeichen und Werke*, pp. 72-77)

And yet hardly another passage is so important for demonstrating just the opposite. These verses will be the subject of detailed analysis in the next chapters. Suffice it to point out here that with a subtle shift given to traditional material the evangelist provides a dramatically new orientation. Propitiatory sacrifice is not the decisive motif. This is superceded by the motif of God's children being gathered into one. Just as it was a demonstration of Jesus' oneness with God which led up to and motivated the Sanhedrin scene, so the prophecy is reoriented to the consequences of that oneness, namely, to gather the scattered children of God into one (11:52).

The underlying theme of high christology continues in the subsequent events. In the anointing at Bethany (12:1-8) the double mention of Lazarus' presence, unique to John's Gospel, serves to connect the scene with the preceding Lazarus pericope. The presence of Lazarus provides a visible reminder of Jesus' majestic power over death and intensifies the offensive demonstration of who Jesus is. Just as the antagonist Caiaphas unknowingly prophesied concerning the significance of Jesus' death, so the follower of Jesus, Mary, unknowingly gave proleptic expression through her action to Jesus burial.[1] Decisive for understanding her action is its kingly significance. The anointing accords the majesty of the Sovereign, a motif which again appears in the following pericope as well as throughout the passion narrative in chs. 18 and 19. Since

---

who views this passage as occupying a central position in the Gospel and links it with the Lamb of God statements in 1:29,36 together with the passover references in 18:28, 19:14, and 19:31-37 in positing a sacrificial passover lamb theology as the evangelist's central concern. Similarly Th. Müller (*Das Heilsgeschehen*, pp. 59ff.). That the evangelist made use of segments of tradition expressing vicarious atonement can, of course, not be denied. And yet they remain distinctly on the fringe and can hardly be said to be a constitutive or central factor in John's proclamation. Cp. S. Schulz, *Ev. nach Joh.*, p. 162.

[1] The meaning of Jesus' reply in 12:7 is notoriously uncertain. Cp. the extended discussion of the possibilities in Barrett, *St. John*, p. 345f.; Hoskyns, *The Fourth Gospel*, p. 416f. The sense of the passage seems best understood in affinity to the Marcan intent (Bultmann, *Ev Joh*, p. 318) although not derivative from it (Fortna, *The Gospel of Signs*, p. 151). In comparison with its interpolation into the Marcan passion narrative (cp. Dodd, *Hist. Trad.*, p. 162) the place of the anointing pericope in John's account is thematically much more tightly integrated.

Jesus ranks supreme, his death and burial are enveloped with corresponding power and resplendence.

Jesus' miraculous demonstration at the tomb of Lazarus serves also to motivate John's account of the triumphal entry into Jerusalem (12:12-19).[1] The crowd that goes out to meet Jesus goes because it has heard of the powerful sign in Bethany (12:9).[2] John's omission of the humility theme in the Zech. quote, his reference to the use of palm fronds indicative of the victory celebration of a triumphant king,[3] the acclamation of Jesus' kingship[4] all underscore motifs of sovereignty that are consistent with and determined by the high christology which motivates the formation of John's exordial passion material.

This high christology is clearly evident in the free development given to the passion prayer tradition of Jesus, traces of which may be seen in the scene following the entry into Jerusalem (12:20ff.), where Jesus addresses the crowd together with the Greeks and then in prayer speaks to his Father (12:27ff.). The prayer theme is picked up once again at the close of the Farewell Discourses in ch. 17 and serves as the framework for a summary review of Jesus' mission and its meaning for the future church. While the place of this prayer tradition and its singularly unique development in the Fourth Gospel will be the subject of detailed analysis in the following chapter, it will suffice here simply to point out its continuity with the christological accents that have been already maintained. Jesus prays and yet he prays as one who is above human conditions and who has no need to make petition. He is one with the Father so that everything he speaks is what the Father speaks and what the Father speaks is what he speaks. There is no discrepancy between them, nothing for

---

[1] Cp. Dodd, *Hist. Trad.*, pp. 152-156. E. Freed, "The Entry into Jerusalem in the Gospel of John," *JBL*, 80, 1961, pp. 329-338.
[2] In the Synoptics the presence of the crowd (in Lk. "the multitude of the disciples") is simply presupposed. The motivation for their presence is not specifically provided.
[3] Schlatter, *Der Evangelist*, p. 265. Billerbeck, *op. cit.* II, p. 548.
[4] The addition of "even the King of Israel" (12:13) is most likely due to John's source since he accepts this traditional phrase only with critical reserve.

Jesus to be attained since it has already all been given. From this standpoint Jesus also speaks the discourses in 13-16. Just as the prayer occurred not for his sake but for the sake of the people (12:30), so the discourses are given not for his sake but for the sake of the disciples. Anthropologically the Farewell Discourses serve to explicate the struggle of faith. Christologically they allow deepened reflection on the continuing presence of the exalted Christ. Thus Jesus speaks here not as the hidden Christ burdened with the anguish of impending death. His relation to the disciples is not as to those who have continued with him in *his* trials (Lk. 22:28) but as to those who need to continue with him in *their* trials. He doesn't need their comfort; they, however, need his. Jesus speaks not as one who needs strength from heaven (Lk. 22:43) or reassurance from the Father but as one can only speak when he is one with God, namely sovereignly and with an omniscience that makes him privy to the whole counsel of God as well as to the heart of man. He speaks as the triumphant Son who prepares to return to the heavenly world of glory. Nor is Jesus' presence circumscribed by temporal or local restrictions. He departs and yet he continues and is present everywhere where he is spoken and believed. With an unparalleled reduction John identifies the Spirit with the word of Jesus. The work of the Paraclete denotes the presence of Christ who continues in sovereign victory over the world.[1] If the salient christological accents of

---

[1] In his initially in 1949 published and then in 1968 revised essay ("Der Paraklet im Johannes-Evangelium" *Gesammelte Aufsätze*, III, pp. 68-89), G. Bornkamm has carefully argued that fundamental to the Johannine Paraclete sayings is the late Jewish apocalyptic forerunner-consummator motif which serves as a kind of hermeneutical key for an understanding of John's christology. With the analogy John the Baptist: Jesus = Jesus: Paraclete, whereby Jesus implicitly assumes the forerunner role which in turn is completed by the Paraclete, the "Vorläufer-Vollender" motif is said to have been adopted by the evangelist because it enabled him to give expression to the "qualitativen Unterschied eines Einst und Dann und zugleich die unlösliche Verbindung beider" (p. 86) in explicating the basic problem of the relation between the life of the earthly Jesus and the subsequent church. (Cp. also "Zur Interpretation des Joh. Evangeliums," *op. cit.*). Bornkamm goes on to concede that the forerunner motif has received a thoroughgoing revision at the hands of the evgst. so that no room is left for Jesus to appear in a subordinal role to the Paraclete. In fact, he admits just the opposite is the case. The Spirit-Paraclete is basically none other than the exalted Christ who teaches and leads the church through the Word (p. 88).

John's prelude to the passion are marked by their correspondence to the theme of Jesus' oneness with the Father, then it remains for us to examine as the final step in this chapter the extent of this correspondence in the passion narrative proper beginning with ch. 18.

E. THE PASSION NARRATIVE

Dissimilarities with the synoptic tradition again help to isolate the accents that reveal concerns peculiar to the Fourth Gospel. The uniqueness of John's account derives in part from the tradition with which he worked; yet, his own contribution is no small factor. This is particularly evident in the initial scene of arrest in 18:1-11. Here our aim is not to engage in detailed exegesis but rather to point out representative lines of development. The character of the scene is significantly set by an enumeration of the constituents of the arresting party. Not only officers from the chief priests and Pharisees, but, in contrast to the synoptic account, also a Roman cohort is included, ranging anywhere from 200 - 600 men with lanterns, torches, and weapons. Historical reminiscence can hardly be said here to dictate the account. Theological motives, on the other hand, are everywhere present. The size and force of the arresting group serve the evangelist's theological intention well. They offset the impact of Jesus' manifestation. That this is the orientation intended by the evangelist is evidenced by his additions particularly in vs. 4-9.[1] The scene now becomes an

---

If this, however, be granted, then it is difficult to see what sense at all there is in applying the forerunner scheme to Jesus in the first place. Thus Bultmann's critique remains standing (*Ev. Joh. Ergänzungsheft*, 1957, pp. 48f.): "so wäre damit doch das Vorläufer-Motiv in einer Weise umgestaltet, daß nichts mehr von ihm übrig geblieben ist." Had it nevertheless, depite his complete revision of the motif still been the evangelist's intention, as Bornkamm claims, to emphasize that the life of the earthly Jesus be understood sub specie finis, viz. from the point of the cross backwards, then it is difficult to see how the evangelist would want such far-reaching consequences to be drawn from the vestigial remains of a schema that he has otherwise so radically broken. Why would he choose such a circuitous method to express a point otherwise not maintained in his Gospel? Illuminating and ingenious though Bornkamm's arguments may be, they clearly cannot be substantiated. Cp. also Blank, *Krisis*, p. 320.
[1] Bultmann, *Ev Joh*, p. 494, identifies vs. 4-9, with the exception of vs. 4b,5, as composition by the evangelist. So also Fortna, *The Gospel of Signs*,

epiphany of Jesus' divine supremacy. It is observed that Jesus knew all along what was to befall him (v. 4). There is no indication of flight since he voluntarily and of his own sovereign will gives himself up to death (cp. also 10:18). He is clearly identified (v. 5). There is nothing to be hidden. The motivation for the traitor's kiss (Mt. 26:48-50) is removed. When Jesus presents himself with a theophanic ἐγώ εἰμι, his captors fall to the ground (v. 6).¹ Before the Son of God the world is powerless and repulsed. Those, however, who are Jesus' own are kept through the power of his word (vs. 8f.) against which the world cannot prevail. Furthermore, the captors must obey Jesus and the disciples are released. Jesus is left by himself as the central figure who alone manifests divine glory.²

The subsequent scene of Jesus' trial before the high priest, coupled with the pericope of Peter's denial (18:12-27), derives by and large from John's given tradition.³ Despite points of convergence with the Synoptics,⁴ the distinctiveness of John's account underscores its independency. Only in the Fourth Gospel do we hear of the involvement of the military (v. 12), a trial before Annas (v. 13), and mention of "the other disciple" (v. 15). In contrast to the synoptic tradition

---

p. 114f. A Dauer, *Passionsgeschichte*, pp. 22-43, argues that the entire passage is the result of the evangelist's composition. Similarly, Barrett, *St. John*, p. 431.

¹ Dodd (*Hist. Trad.*, p. 76f.), followed by Haenchen, "Historie und Geschichte in den joh. Passionsberichten," *Zur Bedeutung des Todes Jesu*, Gütersloh, 1967, p. 59) contends that behind this verse is the Psalm 35:4 and 27:2 tradition. But the contention that "the primitive conception of Christ as the Righteous Sufferer" is implicit in John's verse is unwarranted.

² Bultmann, *Ev Joh*, p. 495 n. 5: "Es soll doch wohl auch dadurch gezeigt werden, daß in allem Geschehen Jesus der Wirkende ist, daß die Passion seine δόξα offenbart."

³ Bultmann, *Ev Joh*, pp. 496-501 regards the entire section as stemming from the source with the exception of vs. 13b, 14, 16, and 24. Fortna, *The Gospel of Signs*, p. 121 reckons even vs. 13, 16, and 24 with the source but posits major rearrangement of the original text. A. Dauer, *Passionsgeschichte*, pp. 62-80 convincingly argues for the following division between source and redaction: vs. 12, 13a, 15-17, 22a, 24, (25)-27 are traditional and the remaining redactional. Similarly F. Hahn, *Der Prozeß Jesu*, pp. 57-59, ascribes vs. 13b, 14, 19b-21, 23 to the evangelist. M. Dibelius, "Die altestamentlichen Motive in der Leidensgeschichte des Petrus und des Johannes-Evangeliums," *Botschaft und Geschichte*, I, Tübingen, 1953, p. 238, regards the whole scene as essentially the evangelist's work.

⁴ Cp. Dodd, *Hist. Trad.*, pp. 82-92.

THE PASSION NARRATIVE 127

there is no reference to the Sanhedrin, no witnesses for the prosecution, no messianic profession, and no pronouncement regarding the death penalty. Only one (plural in the Syn.) of the officers strikes Jesus (v. 22) to which Jesus, however, gives sharp and peremptory reply. The formulation of the reply shows evidence of the evangelist's own hand. Indeed, this verse (23) together with vs. 19b-21 evidence redactional concerns of the evangelist[1] and as such help to give this section its distinctive character. As was noted earlier, Jesus' trial before the Jews had already in a sense taken place. The inner motivation for the court proceedings before the Sanhedrin, as e.g. described in the Synoptics, has by and large been removed.[2] Consequently, John can narrate the high priest scene with pointed brevity and orientate the real significance of the trial to the proceedings before the Gentile court of Pilate in the following pericope, where the mise-en-scène and the dialogue are generously elaborated. Important for our purpose is to see how the evangelist's additions in vs. 19b-21, 23 give the high priest scene its peculiar character and reveal the telltale signs of his christological concerns. Thus the high priest asks Jesus about his disciples and his teaching. With a sovereign command of the situation Jesus responds only to the second half of the question and refers categorically to the public and demonstrative character of his ministry: "I have spoken openly to the world and have taught in synagogues and in the temple" (v. 20). Jesus' teaching is not a code of injunctions or a body of information but he himself. It is his self-witness. Annas can give no reply. Nor is he expected to do so. As representative of

---

[1] The phrases "teaching in synagogues" and "in the temple" (v. 20) are familiar Johannine formulations (7:14, 28; 8:20). Similarly the public nature of Jesus' teaching (v. 21) which is "open" and "not in secret" (7: 26; 10:24f.) is a characteristically Johannine emphasis rooted in the antithesis between faith and unbelief (cp. H. Schlier, παρρησία, ThWB, V, p. 877f.). Jesus' reply in v. 23 is consistent with the understanding of his divine origin (cp. 8:46). Further, see F. Hahn, Der Prozeß Jesu, pp. 61-66. Also Dauer, Passionsgeschichte, pp. 79-86.
[2] And yet it would be going too far to term the scene a "farce" (so Dauer, Passionsgeschichte, p. 247). Its formal justification is provided in the sense of Nicodemus' statement in 7:51. Theologically the scene is not so much dispensable as it is repetitious.

the hostile world, he is already judged. Jesus is the victor.[1] Even the abuse metedced out by the attending officer (v.22) is sharply and provocatively countered by Jesus' self-assured reply. The orientation of the scene is obvious. Jesus speaks as one who is in control and who is beyond the intimidations and threats of his accursers. It is not his hour of κρίσις but theirs. Such christological depiction is clearly rooted in the understanding of Jesus' oneness with the Father.

The scene of the trial before Pilate (18:28 - 19:16) reflects so thoroughly such typically Johannine features that it is generally recognized as virtually impossible to effect any clear and definitive separation between source and redaction.[2] Traces of traditional material may at best be seen in the general outline of the sequence of events including scattered details and motifs that are now integrated into the narrative. Although there are points of convergence with the Marcan-Matthean account[3] as well as with material that is peculiar to Luke,[4] there are by the same token striking dissimilarities peculiar to John. These include elements of the following: the Jew's refusal to enter the praetorium (18: 28b); the initial dialogue concerning the accused (vs. 29-31); the first hearing before Pilate (vs. 34-38a); the detached action of Jesus' scourging (19:1); presentation (before the people) of the King of the Jews (v. 5); Pilate's refusal to pass judgment and the Jew's responding demand for crucifixion

---

[1] M. Dibelius, *Die Formgeschichte des Evangeliums*, Tübingen, 1961, p. 199: "im Verhör stellt Johannes Jesu 'Herrscherwürde' heraus." Dauer, *Passionsgeschichte*, p. 247: "Auch hier geht es wieder deutlich um die Überlegenheit Jesu." Haenchen, "Historie und Geschichte," *op. cit.*, p.63: "damit läßt der Erzähler Jesus als den moralischen Sieger diesen Kampfplatz verlassen."
[2] Haenchen, "Historie und Geschichte," *op. cit.*, p. 65 n.24, argues against the use of any written source at all. Despite the admission that "the source has been so reworked...as to leave it nearly unrecoverable at points," Fortna's analysis (*The Gospel of Signs*, p. 122), similar to Bultmann's results, isolates the following material as traditional: 18:28a,33b,37b, 38c-40; 19:1-3,6 (12)-14a,15,16. Dauer's detailed analysis (*Passionsgeschichte*, esp. pp. 121-132) results in essentially the same findings although he locates traces of the source in other verses as well. The net outcome, however, is the recognition that the orientation and formation of the scene is basically the evangelist's construction.
[3] Cp. Dodd, *Hist. Trad.*, pp. 96-120. F. Hahn, *Der Prozeß Jesu*, pp. 32f.
[4] The convergence is particularly apparent in the repeated expressions of Jesus' innocence.

(v. 6b, 7); Jesus' second hearing before Pilate (vs. 8-11); the charge that Pilate would not be Caesar's friend (v. 12); Jesus is led to the Lithostroton on the day of Preparation for the Passover (vs. 13, 14a); the Jews reject their King in favor of Caesar (vs. 14b, 15). As can be seen, the bulk of John's trial scene is found in his Gospel alone. Of course this does not yet answer the question of the distinction between source and redaction. Considering the planned construction of seven scenes, the expanded dialogues, the symmetry between the two hearings and the two presentations,[1] the typically Johannine stylistic features,[2] and the dramatic technique of presenting, as it were, two stages on which the action occurs,[3] it seems evident that the evangelist's own contributions form the bulk of this section and give it its distinctive character. If this be granted, then we may find in this section particularly clear lines for establishing the specific emphases and accents which the evangelist intended for an understanding of the passion.

Three theological motifs emerge here as significant, each in connection with one of the three protagonists in the trial scene, namely the Jews, Pilate, and Jesus. First of all, we observe that even though the trial takes place before Pilate, it is actually the Jews who are conceived of as leading the proceedings against Jesus. This e.g. is underscored when Jesus asks Pilate: "Do you say this of your own accord or do others say it to you about me?" (18:34). The implication is that the Jews are the real accusers.[4] Pilate is simply their pawn and provides expression --reluctantly and unwillingly-- for the judgment that has already long before taken place. Conversely, Pilate's questions and insinuations about Jesus' kingship serve to heighten the impact of the Jew's guilt. Of course, this does not mean that Pilate, on the other hand, is

---

[1] Cp. Bultmann, *Ev Joh*, pp. 501f. Meeks, *The Prophet-King*, p. 70.
[2] Detailed analysis and listing by Dauer, *Passionsgeschichte*, pp. 105ff.
[3] See esp. Dodd, *Hist. Trad.*, p. 96 and *Interpretation*, p. 315, who identifies this dramatic technique as a Johannine form used also in the dialogue material.
[4] Cp. Haenchen, "Geschichte und Historie," *op. cit.*, p. 68: "...daß Pilatus bisher nur das Sprachrohr der Juden war."

merely a marionette figure without any independent function. He too actively symbolizes the hostile forces of the world in its expression of unbelief. But the heart of that unbelief is quintessentially expressed in the reaction of the Jews whose nomistic claim of absoluteness runs in diametric opposition to the absolute claim of Jesus as the Son of God. Thus the Jew's role in Jesus' trial before Pilate is primarily theologically determined. Because Jesus encounteres them as the Son of God, their whole existence is placed into question. Their reaction against Jesus' divinity expresses a hostility that is unmasked as the deepest and most specific form of unbelief.[1] Consequently it is pre-eminently the Jews who are presented as the responsible figures for the judgment that is passed.

The role of Pilate in the hearings against Jesus is similarly determined by theological motivation. At first, Pilate is represented as acting simply out of political interest. He raises the question of Jesus' political pretensions: "Are you the king of the Jews?" (18:33). He questions the legality of Jesus' actions: "What have you done?"(18:35). Then with the query, "What is truth?" (18:38) --not the taunted question of skepticism that it is so often made out to be, but simply the expression of unbelief-- Pilate evades the real issue before him. He sees only the political character of the charges against Jesus.[2] In the second hearing Pilate's examination takes on a decidedly deeper dimension. No longer is he moved by mere political concern. Unnerved and uneased by the Jew's charge that Jesus made himself the Son of God (19:7), he now asks Jesus the loaded question: "Where are you from?" (19:9). Jesus' response is a sovereign silence, a tacit demonstration of who has the upper hand. The believer, of course, already knows where Jesus is from; namely, that he comes from the Father (13:3) and is one with God (10:30). That recognition, however, is open only to the eyes of the faith-full and closed to the unbelief of Pilate. Pilate's function here is to make that clear. In raising the question

---

[1] Cp. F. Hahn, *Der Prozeß Jesu*, p. 88.
[2] Cp. S. Schulz, *Das Ev. nach Joh.*, p. 229.

of origin, the same question which repeatedly surfaced
throughout Jesus' ministry (3:2; 7:27, 8:14; 9:29), Pilate
unknowingly steers attention to the very heart of the matter
--Jesus' heavenly nature,[1] his oneness with the Father. Similarly Pilate's questions regarding the kingship of Jesus,
though political in intent, are pregnant with overtones that
point to the sovereign status of Jesus. Thus the role of
Pilate, similar to the Jews, is to serve as witness to who
Jesus is.

The third theological motive is expressed in terms of the
role of Jesus. It has often been pointed out that the scenes
of the trial before Pilate have the character of a symbolic
sequence depicting the proclamation and enthronement of a
king.[2] Here it is Jesus' sovereign status which is the underlying concern. Thus in the first hearing (18:33-38a) in response to Pilate's question, "What have you done?" (18:35),
Jesus' reply is tantamount to a declaration of his kingship.
He does not directly say that he is the king of the Jews,[3] but
rather goes on to describe the nature of his kingship.[4] Not
of this world, his kingship has its origin in God. That, of
course, is clear for the reader of the Gospel, since it is
known that Jesus himself comes from God and returns to Him.
But Jesus' words are not accessible to everyone. Only he who
is of the truth hears his voice (18:37; cp. 8:47). Consequently, Pilate misses the real meaning of Jesus' proclamation and the trial continues.

The theme of Jesus' kingship is then developed in the
subsequent two scenes (18:38 - 19:3) in terms of Jesus'

---

[1] Bultmann, *Ev Joh,* p. 97 n.3: "durch ihren Ursprung ist eine Person oder eine Sache entscheidend qualifiziert."
[2] So Blank, "Die Verhandlung vor Pilatus Joh 18,28 - 19,16 im Lichte johanneischer Theologie," *Biblische Zeitschrift* (N.F.3), 1959, pp. 60-81. Similarly, Meeks, *The Prophet-King,* pp. 63-80. Dauer, *Passionsgeschichte,* pp. 249-279.
[3] Even Jesus' second reply in v. 37 is best understood not as a direct affirmative answer. Cp. Dodd, *Hist. Trad.,* p. 99 n.1. Brown, *John,* II, p. 853f. Contra Bultmann, *Ev Joh,* p. 506 n.7.
[4] Jesus does not respond directly to Pilate's question. Instead he leads the dialogue on his own terms --another indication of his real status. Cp. Blank, "Die Verhandlung vor Pilatus," *op. cit.,* p. 69. Dauer, *Passionsge-schichte,* p. 253: "So spricht kein Angeklagter, sondern der Herr im Bewußtsein seines Sieges."

presentation and investiture as King. Pilate's attempt to have Jesus released failed. He had presented him before the people as the King of the Jews (18:39) and yet, analogous to their final rejection in favor of Caesar (19:5), so here they refused their real King and instead chose Barabbas.[1] The scene then shifts abruptly to the scourging, which in John's account appears somewhat disconnected and is not further commented on or developed. John's real interest lies in the subsequent action of the soldiers. They crown Jesus with an acanthus garland, array him in a purple robe, and display their mock deference saying: "Hail, King of the Jews!" (19:3). The action is typically two-dimensional. For the soldiers it is pure derision. For the evangelist it is not only symbolic of the world's rejection but also emblematic of the investiture of a real sovereign.[2] The symbolic import is not to suggest that Jesus thereby becomes the king; otherwise he could not have been presented as the king of the Jews already at the start of the trial. The intent is rather to give expression to the signs which correspond to the sovereign dignity which he in his oneness with the Father has always possessed.

In the final two public presentations (19:4-7; 12-16), interspersed by the second hearing with Pilate, Jesus, who already has described his own kingship, who subsequently was presented as the King of the Jews in the amnesty scene, and who then was accorded the ensigns of royalty with the crowning, the regal vestment, and the king's greeting, is now manifested as such before the people.[3] In both cases the presentation is connected with two statements that have been the center of sharply differing interpretations. The first

---

[1] Although a motif connection between the robber (λῃστής) Barabbas and the robber (λῃστής - κλέπτης) figure in the Shepherd discourse could be maintained, it is unlikely that a deliberate parallel was intended by the evangelist with this choice of words, especially since 18:40 owes its formation to a distinct passion tradition. Meek's insistence on drawing the parallel (*The Prophet-King*, p. 68) is artificial and done more in the interest of trying to connect the king motif of the trial with the Shepherd motif in ch. 10.
[2] Cp. Blank, "Die Verhandlung vor Pilatus," *op. cit.*, p. 73. I. de la Potterie, "Jesus, roi et juge d'apres Jn. 19,13: Ἐκάθισεν ἐπὶ βήματος," *Biblica*, 41, 1960, pp. 117-147.
[3] Dauer, *Passionsgeschichte*, pp. 250, 263 in concert with J. Blank speaks of this scene as a "Königsepiphanie" and "Königsakklamation."

statement is Pilate's proclamation: "Here is the man" (19:5). Many commentators have seen in this statement a reference to the complete humiliation of Jesus,[1] the ultimate paradox of Jesus' claim, the extreme consequence of the ὁ λόγος σάρξ ἐγένετο.[2] Others have regarded the designation as an eschatological title[3] depicting messianic rank. Both interpretations are highly unlikely. There is nothing to suggest that anything other is meant than simply the person of Jesus. (cp. Mt. 26:72). If a theological implication were intended --and this cannot be excluded in view of the planned structure of the scene and the double meaning of Johannine usages-- then its orientation would be reasonably gained from the statement's counterpart in 19:14 where Pilate proclaims: "Here is your king!"[4] There is a distinct parallelism between the two presentation statements (vs. 5 and 14) and their respective scenes. This, coupled with the overall contextual import of the king motif, provides cumulative evidence that the ecce homo statement, far from being an expression of contempt in the face of utter humiliation, refers rather to "this Jesus" who is the exalted sovereign. To see Jesus as the supreme Sovereign is to see him from the standpoint of faith. For this reason the unbelieving Jews respond to the manifestations of the king's majesty with acclamations demanding his crucifixion (19:6,15).

The fact that Jesus is really the Sovereign is reinforced with climactic emphasis in the final presentation scene (19: 12-16) where "Pilate sat down on the judgment seat" and made

---

[1] Cp. G. Sevenster, "Remarks on the Humanity of Jesus," *Studies in John*, 1970, p. 193: "the man who has profoundly absorbed himself into the life of human sin, accomplishing with obedience a work of redemption in bearing the load others should bear." Barrett, *St. John*, p. 450: "Jesus, in his complete humiliation, is set forth as the heavenly Man."

[2] Bultmann, *Ev Joh*, p. 510: "Da seht die Jammergestalt! Im Sinne des Evglisten ist damit die ganze Paradoxie des Anspruches Jesu zu einem ungeheuren Bilde gestaltet."

[3] Meeks, *The Prophet-King*, p. 70.

[4] Brown's suggestion (*John*, II, p. 890) that the ecce homo statement may derive from John's tradition is certainly warranted. Had John been creating freely, then v. 4 would have been an ideal place for Pilate to say, as he does in v. 14, "Behold your king." By the same token it is clear that the evangelist wants v. 4 to be understood in the light of v. 14, since v.14 is paradigmatically consistent with the overall orientation of the whole trial scene.

the last presentation on "the day of Preparation for the Passover" at "about the sixth hour" (19:14). Both of these significant references form the second point over which there have been sharply differing interpretations. A case can be made for understanding the καθίζειν of v. 13b in a transitive sense, whereby Pilate, instead of seating himself seats Jesus on the tribunal, where Jesus symbolically enthroned as king exercises simultaneously his role as Judge of the world.[1] Although grammatically the transitive reading could be a possibility, and the anarthrous use of ἐπὶ βήματος is reminiscent of juridic formulations suggesting the action of a judge,[2] still the context, despite the constitutive role of the κρίσις theme, does not support making the judgeship of Jesus a leitmotif coordinate with his kingship. The sovereignty aspect retains priority. The unbelieving Jews receive judgment because they reject their king. Furthermore, Jesus is not enthroned on the judgment bench of the Romans but on the cross.[3] For this reason the transitive reading of καθίζειν involves not only "an unnecessary subtlety"[4] but shifts the accents sufficiently as to be inconsistent with the Johannine intention. The intransitive reading, on the other hand, is not only grammatically easier and preferable but makes perfectly good sense as is. Even though he does not himself pass sentence directly, Pilate takes his seat on the tribunal in his official capacity as judge. In that capacity as authorized secular representative he says to the Jews, "Here is your king." Thus the world unwittingly but officially and demonstratively gives recognition to Jesus' sovereignty.

The sovereignty theme is reinforced through the added note fixing the time of the final presentation. It was the sixth hour on the day of Preparation for the Passover, that is, the

---

[1] Arguments for the transitive reading have a long history (cp. Bultmann, *Ev Joh*, p. 514) and have recently been most eloquently defended in the article by de la Potterie, "Jésus roi et juge," *op. cit*. In favor of the transitive reading cp. also Haenchen, "Jesus vor Pilatus," *Gott und Mensch*, p. 153. Also Meeks, *The Prophet-King*, pp. 73f.
[2] See de la Potterie, *loc. cit.*
[3] Cp. Dauer's excellent critique of de la Potterie's position (*Passionsgeschichte*, pp. 269-274).
[4] So Hoskyns, *The Fourth Gospel*, p. 524.

hour at which the actual observation of the Passover regulations must begin.[1] The allusion is significant because the Passover observation involved commemoration of God's liberating action in which He demonstrated His sovereign power as King as indicated in the Passover Haggada and the concluding Nismat, the hymn sung after the greater Hallel.[2]

Throughout the trial the theme of Jesus' sovereignty has emerged as the theologically dominant issue. From proclamation to presentation; from investiture to epiphany and acclamation, Jesus' sovereign status is implicitly confirmed and consistently maintained for those who see the events from the standpoint of the believing community. The theme continues through the final scene depicting the crucifixion (19:17-30). In contrast to the preceding, this narrative is more strongly dependent on traditional material although pointed additions by the evangelist, including particularly vs. 20-22, 26, 27, 28a and the τετέλεσται of v. 30, highlight typically Johannine concerns.[3] Here the motif of Jesus' sovereignty is further developed. Attention is centered on the official title[4] attached to the cross. Universally it is proclaimed that Jesus is King of the Jews (v. 20). Offensive to the religious representatives, the chief priests, the title nevertheless stays in place as Pilate refuses to subvert the truth into a lie (v. 22).[5] Nothing can change Jesus' real identity. Even on the cross he reigns as king. The cross is, as it were, his throne, a demonstration of his victory. The supporting details of the scene, as well as the conspicuous absence of others, serve to emphasize the sovereign character of Jesus who exultantly and exaltedly departs to his home in the

---

[1] *Mishnah Pes.* 1,4. Billerbeck, *op. cit.*, II, pp. 812ff.
[2] The decisive accent in the Passover reference does not consist in an allusion to the sacrifice of the Passover lamb as a parallel to the death of Jesus (it is not yet the time of Jesus' death) but in the king motif which is the prevailing theme of the trial scene. Cp. Meeks, *The Prophet-King*, pp. 76f. Dauer, *Passionsgeschichte*, p. 142.
[3] Bultmann (*Ev Joh*, pp. 515-523), Dauer (*Passionsgeschichte*, pp. 165-210), and Fortna (*The Gospel of Signs*, pp. 128-134), all agree, with minor variations, in assigning these verses to the evangelist and in positing a written source for the remaining verses.
[4] Not a charge (αἰτία) as in Mk. 15:26 par, but a τίτλος of proclamation.
[5] Hoskyns, *The Fourth Gospel*, p. 528.

Father's house. In contrast to the Synoptics it is noted that Jesus himself carries his own cross (v. 17). He takes the initiative and is in no need of help from others. The specific mention of the central position of the cross attests to his dominance. Significantly there is no indication that the crucifixion process was an ordeal laden with torment and suffering. There is no cry of dereliction (Mk. 15:34 par), no apocalyptic signs (Mt. 27:51f.), no eerie darkness that covered the land (Mk. 15:33 par), no prayer of commital (Lk. 23:46). With sovereign composure and omniscient knowledge Jesus gives his final instructions. Mary is to be the mother of the disciple whom he loved (v. 26). Because he knew that the end was at hand and that the Scriptures were to be fulfilled he requests a drink.[1] A sponge full of vinegar is raised to him not as to a forsaken man who needs the deliverance of an eschatological Elijah (Mk. 15:35f. par) but as to him who dies freely and of his own accord and who infinitely knows the beginning and end of his work so that he can triumphantly and majestically depart with the victorious "It is finished" (19:30).[2] Thus the cross event is not the mark of condemnation (Lk. 23:40) but reflects throughout the victorious action of a sovereign Jesus who returns to the heavenly world of glory from which he had come.

So unique is John's presentation of the passion account that the question regarding the underlying motivation for these specific accents is of paramount importance. Where else can that motivation derive than from the conviction of Jesus' oneness with the Father? That is John's dominant christological theme. It is his pervading and fundamental dogma. The trial process and the reaction of unbelief are all kindled at the point of confrontation with Jesus as God. Similarly, the royal and sovereign character of his passion action is but the consequent reflection of his oneness with

---

[1] Unwarranted is Wilken's conclusion (*Zeichen und Werke*, p. 75): "Dieses Wort kennzeichnet die ganze Qual des am Kreuz Hängenden." Wilkens overlooks the clear textual context that this word is adduced "to fulfill the Scripture" and not to depict torment.

[2] S. Schulz, *Ev. nach Joh.*, p. 236: "Dieser Gottessohn stirbt friedlich, erhaben und überlegen."

the Father. It is from the standpoint of Jesus' divinity that John's passion account receives its distinctive reorientation and allows Jesus to appear as the heavenly One who determines his own hour and whose death is exaltation because it is a return to the world of glory.[1] Far from being inconsistent with his high christology or appearing as an unintegrated appendix, John's passion narrative appears fundamentally motivated by the theme of Jesus' oneness with the Father and as such is finely interwoven into the overall and dominating conception of the Fourth Gospel.

We are now at the end of our first major section. The cumulative evidence thus far has revealed how deeply the theological implications and consequences of the oneness motif are embedded in the structure and orientation of the Fourth Gospel. In the form and meaning of the reciprocity statements, the direction set in the use of the christological designations, the dialectical presentation of the demonstrative semeia, and in the formation of the passion material, the oneness motif has proved itself to be the constitutive and underlying theme. As such it has appeared pre-eminently as a christological motif, depicting and deriving from an understanding of Jesus as God who fulfills his mission in an epiphany of sovereign and demonstrative power. Jesus' oneness with the Father is the central concern of John's proclamation.[2] It is the content of faith.

If oneness is John's pervading theme, then it remains for us to examine the explicit oneness passages themselves to determine their specific meanings and their further ramifications in relation to the rest of the Fourth Gospel's witness.

---

[1] Haenchen, "Joh. Probleme," *op. cit.*, p. 80 n.1: "Außerdem liegt der Schwerpunkt bei Johannes nicht auf dem Tod Jesu. Es ist kein Evangelium der Passion, sondern...der (vom Tod freilich nicht zu trennenden) Erhöhung und Verherrlichung."

[2] Haenchen ("Vom Wandel," *op. cit.*, p. 12) fails to do justice to this pervasive character of the oneness motif when he restricts its function to a fringe role and insists that it be subordinated to the sending motif: "Die wenigen Stellen, die von Jesu Einssein mit dem Vater sprechen --es kommen neben der Hauptstelle 10,30 noch 17:11,21f. in Frage-- werden vielmehr mißverstanden, wenn man sie nicht von der so unvergleichlich oft im vierten Evangelium vorkommenden Wendung 'der Vater, der mich gesandt hat' aus interpretiert." The result is a failure to recognize the motivating center of the Gospel.

Significantly, each of the three passage complexes occurs at a decisive point in the Gospel's argument and structure. 10:16 and 30 come at the end of the major central section of debates with the Jews during Jesus' public ministry. 11:52 occurs as part of the introduction to the passion. And 17:11, 20-23 come as part of the summary prayer that rehearses the accomplished work of Jesus. Our aim in the second half of this study will be to analyze the literary structure and the source nature of these passages and, secondly, to clarify their theological significance in relation to the Gospel's christology, ecclesiology, and soteriology.

PART II

THE ONENESS PASSAGES

A. LITERARY AND SOURCE ANALYSIS

CHAPTER VI: ASPECTS OF THE COMPOSITIONAL PROBLEM AND ITS HISTORY

A. THE PROBLEM

Differentiation between source and redaction in John is enabled through the recognition that, despite its thematic, stylistic, and linguistic unity, the Fourth Gospel embodies prior, set traditions of the Christian community. As we have already seen in the case of the semeia and passion narrative, an identification of the interacting traditive layers has important consequences for the theological interpretation of the Gospel. To draw these consequences it is necessary to deal with the question of literary structure as well as with the historical situation out of which the Johannine traditions devolved and how or with what intent they were forged into one document. Over the years this has given rise to a profusion of diverse source hypotheses and literary theories. Much less a case of "quot capita, tot sensus," the varying proposals instead reflect the complexity as well as the necessity of literary and source analysis.[1] To be sure, the

---

[1] The terms "literary" and "source" analysis are used here in a broad sense as the endeavor to clarify by means of a variety of considerations (contextual, internal, stylistic, and religio-historical) the structural form and transmission history of given traditions. In a systematic analysis of the various 'Johannine methodologies,' S. Schulz (*Untersuchungen zur Menschensohn Christologie*, pp. 39-95) contests the validity of such an identification and would like to restrict the function of "literary criticism" to the heuristic confines of the method first applied by Wellhausen in 1907 to the Fourth Gospel (*Erweiterungen und Änderungen im 4. Ev.*) and then allegedly for the last time by Blauert in his 1957 Tübinger dissertation (*Die Bedeutung der Zeit in der joh. Theologie.*). Defined in this way, literary criticism is made to appear as one independent methodology among 13 others that have been applied with limited degrees of success to the Fourth Gospel over the years. Although extremely informative,

literary and source problem is in a sense secondary and does not have a claim to priority.¹ Nonetheless, it cannot be denied that theological statements derived from the Gospel are conditioned by an understanding of their origin and place in tradition as well as by the inner-relationship between literary genera as transmitters of certain traditions and the historical situation out of which they arose. As such the literary-critical question is indispensable for exegesis.

B. HISTORICAL DEVELOPMENT

Lest it be understood in an oversimplified way, it is well to view the demands of Johannine literary and source analysis in the light of its presuppositions and historical development. Our purpose here cannot, of course, be to unfold a detailed history of Johannine criticism, but rather to distil significant lines of development that have determined the way in which the exegetical questions of the Fourth Gospel have been placed.

A decisive aspect of the problem to which literary and source analysis seeks to give an answer is already provided with the simple recognition of the uniqueness of the Fourth Gospel over against not only the Synoptic but also the rest of NT tradition. What was the cause and origin of the singularity of John's theological expression and content? What were the motivating factors involved in the composition of a Gospel that manifests so many unparalleled features? Already at an early date in the church the uniqueness of John's Gospel was emphatically noted[2] and its divergency was one of

---

Schulz's distinctions lack a clear objective basis and much too schematic to be really helpful. His own proposal of a methodological approach called "theme history" has, as far as the terminology is concerned, not found acceptance and is essentially no different than motif analysis. Cp. reviews by Käsemann, *V u F* 1963/65, pp. 88-90 and J. Robinson, *JBL*, 78, 1959, pp. 247-252.

[1] Cp. Haenchen, "Jesus vor Pilatus," *op. cit.*, p. 155: "...aber sie (die moderne Exegese) hat erkannt, daß die wichtigste Frage die ist: Was hat der Evangelist seinen Lesern sagen wollen? Was er an Quellen jeder Art (mündlicher und schriftlicher Tradition) dabei benutzt hat, ist zwar nicht ohne Zusammenhang damit, hat aber nicht auf die exegetische Priorität Anspruch."

[2] For Clement of Alexandria the Synoptics were "somatic" while the Fourth

the major causes for its slow acceptance as a normative document.¹ And yet soon after the end of the second century, critical responses to the Gospel receded swiftly into the background. The initial silence on the part of the emerging orthodox church reverted from the end of the second century to a consentient chorus witnessing to the apostolicity of the Fourth Gospel and testifying to its unity and harmony with the rest of the Gospel tradition.

It wasn't until the beginnings of the historical-critical period some 16 centuries later that the composition and origin of the Fourth Gospel once again became problematic. Critical evaluation endeavored to come to terms with the peculiarity of John's witness. From this point on one can appropriately speak of the "Johannine problem." Attacking the problem gave rise to controversial views that sought to examine the text from every conceivable standpoint. And yet treatment of the Johannine literary and source problem fatefully remained under the aegis of the prevailing theological tendency of the day. In fact, it can be said that it was decisively determined by it and as such was never fully motivated by a genuinely historical concern. As a result research on the Johannine problem was essentially caught between two alternatives. It labored, on the one hand, either to

---

Gospel was spiritual or "pneumatic" (Eus. H. E. vi. xiv, 7 - PG 20, 552 BC). The Roman presbyter, Gaius, whom Hippolytus censures for rejecting the Gospel of John and the Apocalypse, (cp. Quasten, Patrology, II, Maryland, 1953, p. 197), based his position on the fundamental difference of John from the Synoptics (Epiphanius. Haer. LI6 - PG 41, 895-900). Characteristic for the Alogoi was the charge that the Fourth Gospel was forged by the Gnostic Cerinthus (Epiphanius, Haer. LI. 3).

¹ Hardly coincidental is the fact that John's Gospel received early circulation among Gnostic circles or that the first extant commentary on John comes from the pen of a Gnostic (Cp. E. Pagels, The Johannine Gospel in Gnostic Exegesis, SBL Monograph Series, Vol. 17, Nashville and New York, 1973.). John's acceptance, on the other hand, into the orthodox church was apparently relatively slow (cp. W. Bauer, Rechtgläubigkeit und Ketzerei im ältesten Christentum, Tübingen, 1964, pp. 207-215). The evidence seems to substantiate the thesis that Irenaeus in his polemic against the Gnostics signaled a significant reversal in the assessment of the Fourth Gospel (so v. Loewenich, Das Johannes-Verständnis im zweiten Jahrhundert, Gießen, 1932, esp. pp. 115-120). This position developed above all by v. Loewenich and W. Bauer may in some points need correction (cp. Haenchen, "Neuere Literatur zu den Johannesbriefen," Theol. Rund., 26, 1960, pp. 274ff.) but still is the best basic explanation for the available evidence.

establish verifiability based on a historically reliable eye-witness account or to establish that which is spiritual, ideal, and eternally true.[1] Challenging the traditional harmonizing attempts which were implicitly motivated by the assumption of apostolic eye-witness authenticity, research during the rationalistic period gave an important thrust and stimulus to the course of Johannine critical investigation. The differences of the Fourth Gospel were placed into sharp relief, and apostolic authorship was called fundamentally into question. The subsequent dilemma created the groundwork for a controversy that dominated Johannine studies for the next century. Marked by wide diversity in the proposed solutions offered, the discussion on both sides, nevertheless, remained well within the confines of dogmatic and apologetic interests.[2]

With the advent of the liberal school, heralded by the pioneer work of F. C. Baur, the historical concerns of critical Johannine research were given a strong impetus. Freed from the domination of the harmonizing approach, the Johannine question became the subject of radical historical criticism. The independency of John's Gospel was tenaciously maintained and the proposition that the authority and value of the Gospel be measured by its factuality and historicity was radically broken. And yet Baur's work as well as that of many in

---

[1] Cp. the historical survey in F. Overbeck (Hrsg. Bernoulli), *Das Johannesevangelium*, Tübingen, 1911, pp. 1-122. W. Kümmel, *Das Neue Testament. Geschichte der Erforschung seiner Probleme*, München, 1958, *passim*. A. Schweitzer, *The Quest of the Historical Jesus*, London, 1956, *passim*.

[2] A classical example of this is illustrated in the respective positions of Bretschneider and Schleiermacher. In his outstanding and for that time revolutionary contribution to clarifying the contrasting relation of John and the Synoptics, C. T. Bretschneider (*Probabilia de Evangelii et Epistolarum Joannis, Apostoli Indole et Origine*, Leipzig, 1820) based his observations on his preference for what he understood to be the synoptic view of Jesus as the popular preacher of genuine piety and morality. The Fourth Gospel appeared, consequently, as fabrication and was accredited secondary value. On the other hand, since his understanding of Christ was not compatible with this view, Schleiermacher impugned Bretschneider's position, and by throwing the aegis of his authority over the whole problem reversed Bretschneider's conclusions and set the course for the ensuing discussion with its emphasis on the historical priority of John's Gospel. (Cp. Schleiermacher, *Einleitung ins neue Testament* (hrsg. v. G. Wolde), Berlin, 1845, pp. 315-326. In both cases *a priori* conceptions were the determining factors.

the generation that followed in his footsteps remained fatefully under the sway of an idealizing and spiritualizing understanding of history,[1] which blunted the effects of their radical criticism. As such the historical nature of the sources could again not really be taken seriously. In fact, the whole discussion regarding the sources was only loosely connected with the process of arriving at theological conclusions, since these conclusions were already fixed in advance by the theological horizon of the day. A parallel situation may be observed in the capricious liberal lives of Jesus that abounded in this period.

Significant developments to emerge out of the liberal school were the varied literary and source analyses and the accompanying trend to investigate the milieu and the religio-historical background of the Fourth Gospel. In regard to the latter development it is important to note the shift in emphasis that took place as the problem progressively crystallized.[2] The earlier attempts to clarify the religious thought world of John were dominated by the attempt to identify a single and unified type of religious phenomena as the decisive background. Vested interests were often the motivating factors.[3] In the later stages of research it became increasingly clear that parallels must be explained on the basis of a plurality of religio-historical traditions. A similar move towards complexity developed in the question of composition. The earliest works remained restricted in their attempts to account for the types of material in John by distinguishing

---

[1] For Baur both "idea" and "spirit" were basic categories of historical interpretation and had constitutive importance for theology. An idea is an actualization of thought. Thought is that process by which Spirit mediates itself with itself in order to become free and self-conscious Spirit. Cp. H. Liebing, "Historisch-kritische Theologie," ZThK, 75, 1960, p. 311: "Der Prozeß der Geschichte läßt als das Nächste eine Fülle von Differenzen, Gegensätzen, Individualitäten erkennen. Aber durch alle Gegensätze und Individualisierungen hindurch...hält sich etwas Identisches, Kontinuierliches durch, das das Ganze bestimmt und erklärt. Dieses Eine, Identische ist das Subjekt der Geschichte. Baur nennt es jetzt im Anschluß an Hegel den "Geist," und zwar den "absoluten Geist" oder "das Absolute."
[2] Cp. S. Schulz, Untersuchungen, pp. 43-48.
[3] Thus, e.g., it was thought that if the Jewish or OT character of the Fourth Gospel could be demonstrated, its integrity would be maintained, or if the Hellenic character could be shown, then its "spiritual" cast would be confirmed.

between original composition and subsequent modification through redaction(s). Basically the endeavors amounted to erecting partitions in which the discourse material was played off against the narrative sections and where one or the other, depending on the theological orientation of the critic, was assigned theological or historical priority. Important though they were in helping to clarify the literary structure and in laying the groundwork for subsequent investigations, these source-critical studies were too schematic and tendentious in their basic orientation to be of lasting value.[1] As source-critical analyses reached their heyday during the first part of this century, considerations of primarily literary and philological factors were used to expose the multiple aporia as a means of verifying different literary strata.[2] Out of the spate of theories that accumulated during this period no one in particular gained ascendency or was to provide an adequate and acceptable explanation for the inner discrepancies and inconsistencies. Instead, a growing chorus of reaction to this kind of source analysis arose,[3] which in turn led to the development of a broader attack based not simply on structural and internal breaks or uneven literary sutures, but on a consideration of stylistic and linguistic characteristics as well.[4] Thus the lines of the discussion were laid for the

---

[1] Cp. Bousset's observation ("Ist das vierte Ev. eine literarische Einheit?" *Theol. Rund.*, 12, 1909, p. 2): "Die hier einsetzende Kritik war also von Anfang dogmatisch tendenziös bestimmt."
[2] Cp. J. Wellhausen, *Das Evangelium Johannis*, Berlin, 1908. E. Schwartz, *Aporien im 4. Evangelium*, Nachrichten von königlichen Gesellschaft der Wissenschaften zu Göttingen, Berlin, 1907, 1908. (It is interesting to note that this work was not included in Schwartz's *Gesammelten Schriften*, V, Berlin, 1963, since, as the editor noted, p.vi, the author had regarded the work as "verunglückt.") F. Spitta, *Das Johannes-Evangelium als Quelle der Geschichte Jesu*, Göttingen, 1910. W. Soltau, *Das 4. Evangelium in seiner Entstehungsgeschichte dargelegt*, Sitzungsberichte der Heidelberger Akad., 6, 1916. For a historical survey of the respective positions see W. F. Howard, *The Fourth Gospel*.
[3] Already Bousset spoke of the "relative justification" of this kind of criticism (*RGG*[1], III, p. 614). In 1927 Bultmann observed ("Das Joh. Ev. in der neuesten Forschung," *Die Christliche Welt*, 41, p. 502: "Quellenkritische Analysen sind heute ohnehin in Mißredit geraten..." Similarly, W. Bauer, *Theol. Rund.*, N.F.1, 1929, p. 138.
[4] Pioneer works in the linguistic area were: A. Schlatter, *Die Sprache und Heimat des 4. Evangelisten*, Gütersloh, 1902. Schlatter sought to demonstrate the Palestinian origin of the diction of the Fourth Gospel by citing rabbinic parallels. C. F. Burney, *The Aramaic Origin of the Fourth*

following generation. The two-strata scheme of original composition or "Grundschrift" (A) and a subsequent redaction (B) increasingly receded[1] and gave way to a more complex understanding of the problem.

C. BULTMANN'S SYNTHESIS

Out of the many Johannine source and literary critical studies to appear in the successive period, R. Bultmann's work, begun with a series of preparatory articles in the 1920's[2] and culminated in his commentary on John, proved to be the most comprehensive and far-reaching.[3] Synthesizing elements of literary theories that to a large extent had already been variously advanced and boldly applying the results of current developments in comparative-religious research, Bultmann programmatically postulated the existence of a written semeia and Gnostic revelation speech source, both of which, together with a Passion source and scattered synoptic-like traditions, formed the core of John's Gospel. In other words, the evangelist was conceived of primarily as an annotator, who commented on and reinterpreted large blocs of given written material which had their separate and respective

---

Gospel, Oxford, 1922. Groundwork for stylistic analysis was laid by E. Abbot's extensive studies, *Johannine Vocabulary*, London, 1905. *Johannine Grammar*, London, 1906.

[1] The "Grundschrift" scheme never did die out but has continued to be represented in a variety of forms. Among its most recent advocates must be mentioned: W. Wilkens, *Die Entstehungsgeschichte des vierten Ev.* C. Dekker, "Grundschrift und Redaktion im Johannesevangelium," NTS, 13, 1966, pp. 66-80. A representative modification is evidenced in Brown's proposals (*The Gospel According to John*). Brown believes to be able to distinguish between five stages of composition in which the latter four redactional stages, products of John's disciples, are developments of and reflections on the eyewitness testimony and historical homiletical reminiscences of the apostle. Thus it is still a question of author - authority. The resulting historicizing attempt does not really proceed beyond the intention of the partition and "Grundschrift" analyses advanced at the turn of the century and as such is subject to the same basic criticism. Cp. the critique by T. Holtz, ThLZ, 93, 1968, pp. 348f.

[2] "Der religionsgeschichtliche Hintergrund des Prologs zum Johannes-Evangelium." (1923); "Die Bedeutung der neuerschlossenen mandäischen und manichäischen Quellen." (1925); "Analyse des ersten Johannesbriefes." (1927). All in *Exegetica*.

[3] For a lucid presentation of Bultmann's literary theory see D. M. Smith, *Composition and Order*. Cp. also "The Sources of the Gospel of John: An Assessment of the Present State of the Problem," NTS, 10, 1964, pp. 336-351.

histories of origin.[1] In order to separate the source material from the composition of the evangelist and a later postulated redactor, Bultmann resorted to theological considerations as well as to contextual and stylistic evidence for criteria, which in turn --and this was an important factor in his analysis-- were reciprocally conditioned by one another.

The theological considerations adduced by Bultmann as criteria derive basically from his interpretation that Jesus appears in John as the Revealer incognito. This interpretation is rooted pre-eminently in an understanding of the incarnation as a manifestation of the revealer's pure humanity. With this as leitmotif, Bultmann finds the justification and motivation for relegating to a more primitive and non-Christian level of tradition any material which does not reflect or is inconsistent with the paradox of God's revelation in purely human form. If, however, it can be demonstrated that there is basic similarity between Bultmann's source sections and the evangelist's intention and that the conceptuality of both is essentially the same, in other words, that John's concern is with the heavenly nature of the Revealer and not with the issues of paradox or Jesus' humanity, then the inner justification for postulating a theologically sophisticated commentator who demythologized non-Christian source material would be substantially removed.[2] Thereby it may be seen that Bultmann's theological criteria are actually contingent on the supposition that the evangelist used a non-Christian Gnostic speech source as well as a crude propaganda document of semeia. Only in this way can he consolidate his case for a cleavage in the interpretation.

The use of contextual evidence as a source-analytical

---

[1] The semeia source is thought of as a non-synoptic tradition of a peripheral Christian group which sought to document Jesus as a θεῖος ἀνήρ by means of a collection of primitive and naive miracle accounts. Bultmann suggests that (*Ev Joh*, p. 76 n.6) this group comprised former Baptist disciples. The speech source, on the other hand, is thought of as having stemmed from a non-Christian Gnostic circle, for which Mandaean-like baptist sects may have been typical (*Ev Joh*, pp. 4f. *RGG*,³ III, p. 842f.

[2] This is the effect of E. Käsemann's critique in "Rudolf Bultmann, Das Ev. des Johannes," *V u F*, 1942/46, München, 1946/47, pp. 182-201. "Neutestamentliche Fragen von heute," *Exegetische Versuche und Besinnungen*, II, p. 24f. Cp. also Haenchen, "Aus der Literatur zum Joh. Ev." *op. cit.*, pp. 326ff.

criterion is one of the surest methods for locating eventual interpolations or textual glosses. Bultmann expanded the consequences of this method by using them to confirm the identification not only of scattered redactional elements but of the larger corporate blocs of his proposed source material. Contextual evidence, when used in isolation, seldom if ever is conclusive and consequently must be used in conjunction with other considerations. Here again theological factors are determinative. For if it could be shown that the evangelist misunderstood his source or was of a contrary theological opinion, then the breaks suggested by contextual evidence would receive decisive confirmation.

Bultmann's use of the criteria of style and speech engendered a lively discussion as well as new perspectives regarding Johannine interpretation and source criticism. Stylistic and philological characteristics provide an indispensable means of separating compositions with divergent origins. If the evangelist is to be understood primarily as one who reformed and reinterpreted already existing written sources, it would be a reasonable assumption to expect differences in style and language in the respective parts. This assumption, however, was seriously challenged by research based on rigorous statistical analysis of stylistic characteristics, which impressively demonstrated the pervasiveness of Johannine stylistic unity.[1] It was shown that characteristics ascribed to the sources appear regularly also in the material alloted to the evangelist and vice versa. The incontrovertible conclusion was that the Fourth Gospel is on the whole a unified work in its present form and is stamped by a single form of language and style. The net result further led to a modified view of the applicability of style criticism.

An initial reaction was to dispute the use of all written sources whatsoever and to posit an original composition consistent with the overarching stylistic unity and the random distribution of philological characteristics.[2] That this was

---

[1] E. Schweizer, *Ego Eimi*, pp. 82-112. J. Jeremias, "Johanneische Literarkritik," *TB*, 20, 1941, pp. 33-46.

[2] So E. Ruckstuhl, *Die literarishce Einheit des Johannesevangelium*,

an extreme and unwarranted position became increasingly clear as the intrinsic limitations of statistical style analysis were exposed. Even in a careful investigation the individuality of certain stylistic characteristics could be infringed upon so that a generalizing conclusion based on a simple statistical listing would by no means be compelling.[1] Furthermore, one could always proceed on the assumption that the evangelist in adopting extensive source material was so influenced by it that he assimilated into his own style the peculiarities characteristic of his source.[2] Where that should be the case, a precise and clear-cut distinction between source and evangelist could not be maintained. Or if the attempt were made, other factors would have to be introduced in support. As long as the discussion remained in the realm of style criteria alone, the argument was locked in a circle.

D. REACTIONS AND SHIFTS

Recognition of the thoroughgoing unity of style and substance in the Fourth Gospel prompted a reaction to Bultmann's proposals[3] and a basic rethinking of the literary and source critical problem that led to some of the following results. The existence of an extensive Gnostic speech source, which the evangelist was to have revamped and incorporated into his Gospel, increasingly lost what plausibility it had.[4] In

---

Freiburg, 1951. Ruckstuhl went so far as to maintain (p. 16): "Sollte es sich herausstellen, daß B. nicht im Recht ist, dann dürfte allein schon diese Tatsache zeigen, daß jede literarkritische Arbeit am vierten Ev. zum Scheitern verurteilt sein muß, daß dessen Einheit und Geschlossenheit jeder zersetzenden Aufteilung widersteht." Cp. also P. Menoud, *L'Evangile de Jean d'après les recherches récentes*, Neuchatel/Paris, 1947.
[1] E. Hirsch, "Stilkritik und Literaranalyse im vierten Evangelium," *ZNW*, 43, 1950/51, pp. 128-143, shows the weaknesses of Schweizer's approach. Similarly E. Haenchen, "Aus der Literatur," *op. cit.*, p. 309.
[2] Already Bultmann, *Ev Joh*, p. 264 n.5; p. 382 n.6. Likewise H. Becker, *Die Reden*, p. 12.
[3] Unexplainably many studies on John took only scant notice of Bultmann's source critical analysis. E.g. Dodd's two volume magnum opus (*Interpretation* and *Historical Tradition*) took no account of them at all.
[4] J. Heise's study (*Bleiben*) is the only recent work to adopt as a working hypothesis Bultmann's source proposals. J. Robinson (*Entwicklungslinien*, p. 219) speaks of "das rasche Verschwinden dieser Quelle aus der wissenschaftlichen Diskussion."

addition to arguments based on the Johannine unity of style
and theology came observations which underscored the improb-
ability of the independent existence of an integral Gnostic
speech source, originally composed in Aramaic,[1] and consisting
primarily of apodictic versification in thetical and antithetical form.[2] Similarly crucial was the question why the
rhythmic concatenation of the Prologue did not extend with
the same stringency throughout the rest of the reconstructed
source.[3] In view of these difficulties the existence and use
of a written Gnostic revelation discourse source could no
longer be convincingly maintained. Although the existence of
a written narrative semeia and a Passion source was likewise
thrown into question, basically because of the stylistic unity of the Gospel, other considerations entered into the picture which left this question an open one. In fact, recent
studies have marshalled cogent evidence in support of the
thesis that the evangelist did use a signs source[4] as well as
a passion account distinct from the synoptic versions.[5] These

---

[1] K. Beyer (*Semitische Syntax im NT. Studien zur Umwelt des NT*, Bd.I, Göttingen, 1962, p. 17 and *passim*) demonstrates the preponderance of Hebraicisms instead of Aramaicisms.
[2] Not only does the proposed source lack an inner coherency, but there are also no compelling parallels for a similar phenomenon in the ancient world. H. Becker's reconstruction (*Die Reden*, pp. 129-136) assumes that the thematically related statements of the discourses at one time formed a literary unity. Apart from its tenuousness, the assumption involves a *non sequitur* when applied to John. Demonstration of an external scheme whose essential elements consist of 1) the self-predication of the revealer; 2) the call to decision; 3) a promise or threat; and whose use is ascribed to Gnostic circles, does not warrant the conclusion that the evangelist used a developed source patterned after the scheme. Already F. Büchsel ("Zu den Johannesbriefen," *ZNW*, 28, 1929, pp. 235-241) observed that the apodictic antithesis which Bultmann assigned to the source, cannot be separated from the intervening material without robbing the antithetical sentences of their real meaning. In other words, they are integrally bound to the context. Furthermore, evidence has not confirmed the assumption that discourses in the form of antithetical distichs are primarily characteristic (so Becker, op. cit., p. 24) of a Gnostic dualistic style as found e.g. in the C.H. (Cp. Haenchen, "Das Johannesevangelium und sein Kommentar," *ThLZ*, 89, 1964, pp.883f.
[3] Cp. Käsemann, *V u F*, 1946/47, p. 188.
[4] Cp. the detailed studies by Fortna, *The Gospel of Signs*; W. Nicol, *Semeia*. For a survey of developmental lines leading to the question of the semeia source as posed in current research see J. Robinson, "Geschichte als Weitergabe von Überlieferungen im Neuen Testament," pp. 49-55 and "Die johanneische Entwicklungslinie," pp. 220-235 --both in *Entwicklungslinien durch die Welt des frühen Christentums*.
[5] Cp. A. Dauer's exhaustive investigation, *Die Passionsgeschichte* and F. Hahn, *Der Prozeß Jesu*.

endeavors have been carried on apart from Bultmann's comprehensive source hypothesis even though many of the individual results delineating the content of a signs and passion source have been strikingly similar.[1] And yet the exact scope and character of the source material remain highly uncertain. Strong cases have been made for identifying the signs source as an original missionary document springing from a Jewish-Christian milieu and having the express intent of giving witness to Jesus as the Christ.[2] But the extent of the original material as a whole and whether or not it was part of a larger document including also a passion account[3] are questions that are still open and require further investigation.

A further significant reaction to Bultmann's source hypotheses developed in the thesis that the evangelist drew exclusively on oral tradition for his material.[4] Bolstered by observations that certain Johannine "logia," though unique in content, were basically similar in structure to logia in the synoptic tradition, plus observations that OT quotations were cited freely and apparently from memory, that large portions

---

[1] Dauer e.g. concludes (*Passionsgeschichte*, p. 226): "so deckt sich unser Ergebnis in vielen Stücken mit den Vorstellungen, die Bultmann in seinem Kommentar bezüglich der joh. Passionsgeschichte entwickelt hat." Dauer's advance over Bultmann consists in the attempt to clarify more precisely the origin of the passion source material. Similar circumstances apply also to current analyses of the semeia.

[2] Bultmann too recognized the missionary character of the semeia material (*Ev Joh*, p. 76, n.6). But in characterizing it as a propaganda document of former baptist disciples, he was able to posit a greater interpretational distance between the evangelist and the source. Insistence, however, that this distance is not all that great (cp. Käsemann, *V u F*, 1946/47, pp. 186f; *RGG*,[3] VI, p. 1836; and Haenchen, "Aus der Literatur," *op. cit.*, p. 303) has led to a re-characterization of the source. Both Fortna (*Signs*, pp. 223f.) and Nicol (*Semeia*, pp. 142f.) are agreed in emphasizing the Jewishness of the source as a missionary tract aimed at potential Jewish converts.

[3] Haenchen ("Joh. Probleme," *op. cit.*, pp. 112f.) envisages a source containing more than just the miracle accounts, viz. a kind of primitive Gospel, a "crude Mark" ("Aus der Literatur," *op. cit.*, p. 303). How this is developed promises to be an important part of his forthcoming commentary on John. Fortna has brought impressive evidence together arguing for a source containing both the semeia and the passion account, thus presenting, along the lines of Haenchen's proposals, a kind of mini-Gospel. (Incorporation of the passion account into an original level was also a basic tenet in Wilken's earlier study, *Die Entstehungsgeschichte*, although with different motivation and consequences.) And yet Fortna's argumentation raises more questions than it answers and the whole construction remains highly problematic. Cp. critiques by D. M. Smith, *JBL*, 89, 1970, pp. 498ff. and J. Robinson, *Entwicklungslinien*, pp. 231-235.

[4] B. Noack, *Zur Johanneischen Tradition*.

of the narrative material were common with the rest of the
Gospel tradition but developed independently of the Synoptics
in their present form, and that the style in many cases appeared to be non-literary and reflective of colloquial speech,
it was concluded that the evangelist was determined wholly by
the oral tradition of the Church without any reference to
written sources and that he wrote down his Gospel account relying on his memory of what he had heard and learned in the
Church. That also this position was one-sided and failed to
do justice to the complexity of the evangelist's relation to
tradition was evidenced in the criticism evoked in response.[1]
Nevertheless, the role of oral Church tradition in the formation of the Fourth Gospel received an importance that remained central in the subsequent discussion.[2]

An overall outcome of the post-Bultmann Johannine source
debate, particularly in regard to the speech material, was to
focus attention on the smaller individual components of tradition. While recognition of John's pervasive unity of style
and substance engendered skepticism about the recovery and
precise delimitation of extensive written sources in the form
of integral wholes, it did not by any means permit a categorical judgment about every passage and individual unit.[3] As a
result it became increasingly clear that the problem must be
attacked by a rigorous analysis of the isolable units and individual segments of tradition.[4] This move toward a segment
analysis, coupled with the search for a variety of traditions
within the context of a development in the Johannine community, was as inevitable as it was necessary and as such characterized a basic shift in the source-critical problem of
John. An inherent danger in this approach, however, was the
tendency to concentrate on the smallest unit at the expense

---

[1] Cp. Haenchen, "Aus der Literatur," *op. cit.*, p. 304. Bultmann, "Zur Johanneischen Tradition," *ThLZ*, 80, 1955, pp. 521-526. D. M. Smith, *Composition and Order*, p. 112.
[2] This is basic to Dodd's (*Historical Tradition*) and Haenchen's approach.
[3] From this standpoint the converse may also be maintained with Haenchen ("Joh. Probleme," *op. cit.*, p. 111): "Das vierte Evangelium ist keine stilistische Einheit."
[4] Cp. S. Schulz, *Untersuchungen*, p. 94; H. Blauert, *Die Bedeutung der Zeit*, pp. 124-132.

of the larger segments which they built. The discourses, for example, are more than simply the summation of originally small composites and disparate elements. They form an organic whole and must be considered as literary genera also from the aspect of their wholeness.[1]

In order to get closer to the root of the origin of Johannine composition it is necessary to develop a working hypothesis with which the material is broken down into its smallest traditional unit and yet at the same time examined in its relation to the whole of which it is a part. What is called for is a multiplicity of approaches based on consideration of theological orientation, contextual aporia, style, form,[2] and religio-historical evidence. Thus the lines of development can be detected in the transmission-history, viz. how specific traditions were shaped and colored by the conditions and needs of the various groups within the early Christian community. Thus also the possibility is given of exploring and classifying the various elements that lay behind the Fourth Gospel --traditions which could hardly be attributed to the free composition of the evangelist.[3] For some this meant the task of trying to establish chronological priority in terms of historical reliability by identifying the earliest

---

[1] Completely warranted in this respect is Bultmann's critique of Noack's position (*ThLZ*, 80, 1955, pp. 521-526).
[2] The charge that "form-criticism" is of little value in Johannine source analysis (so Schulz, *Untersuchungen*, p. 76) or that Bultmann never resorted to this method in his commentary (Schulz, *ibid.*) is a curious misjudgment. Quite apart from Bultmann's endeavor to delineate the discourses form-critically, it must be maintained that form-criticism is of utmost importance as a method of analysis for John. (Consider Dodd's work or Leroy's study in the "*Formgeschichte des Johannesevangeliums*.")
[3] Here three basic distinctions can be made: a) prior tradition; b) evangelist's composition; c) later redaction. Blauert's classification of the Johannine traditive material is useful (*Die Bedeutung der Zeit*, pp. 115-124): 1) synoptisch-verwandte Tradition; 2) nicht-synoptische Erzählungstradition; 3) Gemeinde Hymnen; 4) johanneisches Spruchgut; 5) urchristliche-eschatologische Gemeinde-Tradition. Dodd's (*Historical Trad.*) division into two basic categories --narrative and sayings-- and his further subdivisions according to form-critical principles (e.g. the Sayings are arranged into five categories: a) discourses; b) sayings common to John and the Synoptics; c) parabolic forms; d) sequence of sayings; e) predictions) are useful but fail adequately to account for the tradition-historical movement and development in the redactional phase. Cp. E. Haenchen's critique, *ThLZ*, 93, 1968, pp. 346f.

"attested facts."[1] And yet the recognition that even the reservoir of primitive tradition --oral or written-- had been recast and conditioned by the translation of the earliest witness into varying expressions of christological piety and faith demonstrated how controvertible and problematic such undertakings must be.

Coupled with the attempt to clarify the literary structure and the relation of previously formed tradition to the evangelist's own composition went also the endeavor to illuminate the religio-historical character of the material. Particularly the last two generations of Johannine research made it abundantly clear that the religio-historical background of John could not be explained on the basis of a single and uniform influence or tradition.[2] Simple alternatives in terms of either Palestinian or Hellenistic influence could not be maintained. Subsequent working hypotheses had to take account of the plurality of historical-cultural contexts that left their stamp on the Johannine text. The endeavor to identify these contexts and to label their characteristic traits brought with it the inevitable question of the inner motivation that led to their amalgamation. Inherent in this question was the whole problem of the inner relation of one religio-historical tradition to another and whether one cultural context had priority over the other so that it was responsible in some way for the predisposition of subsequent translations or modifications. Could it be maintained, for example, that the point of departure or the ground-soil of the Johannine tradition in

---

[1] So R. Gyllenberg, "Die Anfänge der johanneischen Tradition," NT Studien für R. Bultmann, Berlin 1957, pp. 144-147. W. F. Albright, "Discoveries in Palestine and the Gospel of John," pp. 170f. and T. W. Manson, "Present-day Research in the Life of Jesus," p. 219 n.2 --both in The Background of the New Testament and Its Eschatology, ed. by W. Davies and D. Daube, Cambridge, 1956. Cp. the observation by F. W. Beare (NTS, 10, 1963/64, p. 521): "British scholarship has an unquenchable longing for brute historical and biographical fact, and there is the perpetual danger that the wish may give birth to the persuasion that the facts are more readily ascertainable than is actually the case."
[2] Cp. O. Michel, "Das Gebet des scheidenden Erlösers," ZST, 18, 1941, p. 522: "Das johanneische Problem kann nicht allein von der palästinensischen Tradition, auch nicht ausschließlich vom hellenistischen Kultstil, auch nicht ausschließlich aus der Verwandtschaft mit gnostischen Parallelen verstanden werden."

its original context was late-Jewish apocalypticism[1] and that this anterior context, without losing its real substance and character, was reshaped and recast in terms of Hellenistic and syncretistic Gnosis of a later period?[2] The intrinsic probability of such a scheme might seem at first entirely plausible. But simply to posit that kind of linear development begs the question. It is a fallacious argument e.g. which maintains that because apocalypticism provides a given concept or theme, this concept or theme is necessarily apocalyptic. This goes to show that a reliable and precise determination of the religio-historical character of various steps in the development and transmission of Johannine tradition cannot rest on the identification of mere word parallels or form equivalents. Part of the problem is also due to the fact that the inherited categories, such as normative Judaism, Hellenistic Judaism, Jewish mysticism, apocalypticism and Gnosis have been subjected to a process of dismantling and reassembling which grew out of the discovery and interpretation of new texts and the realignment of already extent subject matter.

Significant for the subsequent course of the discussion was the new understanding of the essence, scope, and influence of the phenomenon of Gnosis.[3] If Gnosis was indeed a distinctively singular world-and self-view whose syncretistic potentiality permeated a variety of essentially divergent religious phenomena,[4] then it could no longer be permissable to

---

[1] Proposed by K. G. Kuhn in his programmatic essay, "Die in Palästina gefundenen hebräischen Texte und das Neue Testament," ZThK, 47, 1950, pp. 192-211.
[2] So S. Schulz (Untersuchungen, p. 138): "denn die spätjüdische Apokalyptik...scheint als tragender Grund vorzuliegen." p. 142: "Dieser tragende Grund bildete andererseits den Ausgangspunkt für die im vorjoh. Stadium der Überlieferung stattfindende Neuinterpretation, die vor allem mit Hilfe hellenistisch-gnostischer Anschauungen erreicht wurde." Similarly, Komposition und Herkunft, pp. 130, 138.
[3] Instrumental in effecting this understanding was the pioneer work of H. Jonas, Gnosis und spätantiker Geist, FRLANT N.F., 33, Göttingen, 1964. Jonas demonstrated the existential character of a "Gnostic principle" which absorbed a variety of religious forms in giving expression to a radically acosmic self-understanding in which man, a stranger in the world, was called to a realization of his consubstantiality with the light world.
[4] The presence of a metamorphosed "Gnostic principle" in divergent manifestations need not necessitate the conclusion that this principle was

isolate these phenomena with the same finality and exclusiveness as was earlier the case. On the contrary, their innerrelatedness became a subject of increasing importance with far-reaching consequences for the understanding of the religio-historical character of the Fourth Gospel. The basic criterion for the evangelist's witness did not derive from religio-historical factors but from the christological witness of the Christian community. And yet the cultural-historical nature of the situation in which the witness was proclaimed and heard was a decisive factor in conditioning the character of the proclamation made, and as such variously determined the idiom into which the proclamation was translated. The extent to which that would entail a shift in meaning is debatable.[1] In any case it can be maintained that witness and situation or theology and context are correlatives in the process of translation so that the one cannot really be separated from the other without incurring a fatal one-sidedness.

In the light of the above survey of changes and formative lines of development in the history of Johannine source-critical problem the inner necessity for raising the questions as posed in the following analysis becomes apparent. Our subsequent task is to examine those places where the εἷς motif appears as an explicit term and, relying on a multiplicity of approaches, to inquire whether these instances can be reduced to isolable units of tradition, which derive from either previously formed material or from the evangelist's own composition, and to what extent they form integral parts of the larger corporate complexes. Inherent in this latter question is also the problem of whether or not these instances are later redactions deriving from a different level

---

the absolute denominator of the Hellenistic religious thought world. Rightly so: H. M. Schenke, *Die Gnosis, Umwelt des Christentums* I, hrsg. v. J. Leipoldt und W. Grundmann, Berlin, 1965, p. 375: "die Gnosis ist nicht der Geist der Spätantike schlechthin..." Cp. also H. Langerbeck, hrsg. v. H. Dörries, *Aufsätze zur Gnosis*, Göttingen, 1967, p. 21.

[1] Cp. J. Robinson, "Kerygma and History in the New Testament," *The Bible in Modern Scholarship*, ed. by J. P. Hyatt. Nashville/New York 1965, p. 119. Also E. Gräßer, "Kol 3, 1-4 als Beispiel einer Interpretation secundum homines recipientes," *ZThK*, 64, 1967, esp. pp. 142-144.

of traditional-historical material. In each case the question of the diversity or unity of background must be posed as well as the peculiarity of literary form. What this amounts to is the attempt to clarify and to localize the tradition-historical place of the material and to inquire into the religio-historical factors that may help to illuminate its specific character. Once these steps have been taken and the structural and traditive groundwork of the motif is cleared, it will be possible to proceed to a summary theological explication in the final chapter.

CHAPTER VII: ONENESS PASSAGES IN THE DEPARTING PRAYER OF JESUS

A. TEXT STRUCTURE AND SOURCE ANALYSIS

Ch. 17 gives the initial appearance of an integral whole.[1] Even when this unity is granted, the question is not obviated whether embedded in this material there are isolable units of set tradition which the evangelist took over and adapted to his account. The question is particularly acute for vs. 20-23. Consideration of the following structural, stylistic and religio-historical factors could make a prima facie case for the existence of preformed material in these verses. Whether or not that is, in fact, the case must be tested.

1. Structural Considerations

The structural form of the vs. 20-23 is especially striking. It is possible to divide respectively the two sentences, which are coupled in typical Semitic parallelism, into two main clauses, each of which is followed by a series of three ἵνα-clauses. In both cases the initial ἵνα-clauses are expanded by comparative καθώς-clauses, whereas the final ἵνα-clauses are supplemented by complementary ὅτι-clauses. This remarkable parallelism and unique structural form can be clearly seen in the following diagram

vs. 20,21	vs. 22,23
Οὐ περὶ τούτων δὲ ἐρωτῶ μόνον, ἀλλὰ καὶ...	κἀγὼ τὴν δόξαν ἣν δέδωκάς μοι δέδωκα αὐτοῖς
<u>ἵνα</u> πάντες ἓν ὦσιν	<u>ἵνα</u> ὦσιν ἓν
<u>καθὼς</u> σύ πατήρ ἐν ἐμοὶ καγὼ ἐν σοί	<u>καθὼς</u> ἡμεῖς ἕν ἐγὼ ἐν αὐτοῖς καὶ <u>σὺ ἐν ἐμοί</u>
<u>ἵνα</u> καὶ αὐτοὶ ἐν ἡμῖν ὦσιν	<u>ἵνα</u> ὦσιν τετελειωμένοι εἰς ἕν
<u>ἵνα</u> ὁ κόσμος πιστεύῃ	<u>ἵνα</u> γινώσκῃ ὁ κόσμος
<u>ὅτι</u> σύ με ἀπέστειλας	<u>ὅτι</u> σύ με ἀπέστειλας

Nowhere else in the Fourth Gospel does one find a similarly

---

[1] Already J. Wellhausen, *Das Evangelium Johannis*, Berlin, 1908, p. 75: "An der wesentlichen Einheit des Ganzen läßt sich nicht zweifeln."

unified thought sequence expressed in such extended and yet tightly structured and balanced literary form. The parallelism used here is not antithetical or progressive (step-parallelism), both of which are standard forms employed in the Fourth Gospel,[1] but repetitive or synonymous.[2] As such it is particularly characteristic of the Semitic mode of poetic expression[3] as found e.g. in the Odes of Solomon and in the OT Psalms. In vs. 20-23 this scheme of repetitive <u>parallelismus membrorum</u> has undergone a significant modification inasmuch as what is contrasted or paralleled are not two short sentences, each expressing one idea, but a series of secondary anaphoric clauses forming with minimal variation[4] an integral thought. In other words, the basic principle of repetitive parallelism has been retained but the number and sequence of the components have been changed and the format enlarged so that it is no longer a matter of a simple couplet as is usually the case with this kind of expression. The succession of six ἵνα clauses, two καθώς clauses, and two ὅτι clauses, each paralleled by its respective counterpart, leaves the first-hand impression of a carefully devised literary construction, atypic of free composition, and gives the appearance of a stylized form characteristic of fixed tradition.

The parallelism of these verses also raises the question of their corresponding rhythm. Although the rhythmic nature of the Johannine speech material has long been recognized, attempts at demonstrating a unified and continuing metrical

---

[1] Cp. Bultmann, *Ev Joh*, pp. 2, 100 ; B. Noack, *Tradition*, p. 47f. Ruckstuhl, *Lit. Einheit*, pp. 43ff.

[2] This kind of repetition occurs often in John (cp. Abbot, *The Johannine Grammar*, pp. 437-465) as a type of couplet where one sentence, generally gnomic in form, parallels its counterpart in thought and structure (e.g. 6:35; 13:16. See also C.F. Burney, *The Poetry of our Lord*, Oxford, 1925, pp. 63-71). Unique, however, for 17:21-23 is that the repetitive mode of expression spreads out over a series of component clauses in the first sentence which have their corresponding syntactical counterparts in the second sentence.

[3] Cp. Norden, *Agnostos Theos*, pp. 356f.

[4] M. Boismard's ("Critique Textuell et Citations Patrisques," *Revue Biblique*, 57, 1950, p. 396) reconstruction of the original text of 17:21 to read in accordance with Origen and other church fathers: ὡς ἐγὼ καὶ σὺ ἕν ἐσμεν, ἵνα καὶ αὐτοὶ ἐν ἡμῖν ἕν ὦσιν, if correct, would tend to minimize the variation in the passage. Similarly the introduction of ἕν in the second clause by ℵ K Θ. And yet these readings are too weakly attested to be accepted.

pattern have remained forced and unconvincing. In particular, vs. 20-23 do exhibit a loose kind of rhythm, but it is not possible to detect either clearly distinguishable accents of tone or a fixed metrical pattern. At best, the rhythm here is simply a product of the form of parallelism employed.[1] As such it can be termed free rhythm.[2] Attempts have been made on this basis to establish the hymnic character of these verses,[3] and yet there are no real indications to substantiate that the verses were ever part of a strophic unit.

In addition to the features of repetitive parallelism and free rhythm which left their imprint on these verses, the formula character of certain component parts must also be noted. Particularly striking are the two καθώς clauses which express variations on the theme of reciprocity. The expressions are analogous to types of technical religious language which in various Hellenistic syncretistic contexts developed into stereotyped forms. In fact, it is possible to speak of the "formula" of reciprocity which became a technical expression in different strains of Hellenistic syncreticism.[4] The formal language parallel to John's usage is clear. Such expressions could be adopted by him and evidently were deeply rooted in his church community because they eminently reflected central theological concerns. Striking also are the final ὅτι clauses which have the nature of fixed faith statements characteristic for the Johannine church. The formulation "that you (the Father) sent me" occurs with slight variation with such regularity (17x) especially in ch. 17 (6x) as to suggest that it was not only a favorite formula of the evangelist but also indicative of a standard dogmatic statement typical for John's

---

[1] Cp. C. F. Burney, *Poetry*, pp. 100ff. Also M. Black, *An Aramaic Approach to the Gospels and Acts*, Oxford, 1954.
[2] Cp. Ruckstuhl, *Lit. Einheit*, p. 49.
[3] The loose rhythmic structure of ch. 17 is not marked and consistent enough to warrant the conclusion drawn by W. H. Raney (*The Relation of the Fourth Gospel to the Christian Cultus*, Giessen, 1933, p. 12) that the entire chapter was written as prose-hymn to be sung or chanted by a cantor or choir. Raney, who cites the 4th cent. Nonnus, who made a metrical paraphrase of John into Homeric pentameter, tried to demonstrate that the Prologue and the discourses were all originally based on prose-hymns used in worship.
[4] Cp. W. Bauer, *Joh. Ev.*, p. 141.

church. The validity of this supposition is further underscored by the evangelist's use of the circumlocution which identifies the Father with the stereotyped form "he who sent me" 24x in the Fourth Gospel. Thus it becomes increasingly probable that what we are dealing with here are typically Johannine dogmas or confessional statements that had acquired normative character for the Johannine church.[1] It may well be that the statement, ὅτι σύ με ἀπέστειλας, rests on a confessional formulation such as "Jesus is sent from God" which in Johannine circles had the same thrust and weight as did e.g. the confession "Jesus is Lord" in other circles.

Inasmuch as the εις motif in the second half of v. 11 —ἵνα ὦσιν ἕν καθὼς ἡμεῖς— is integrated into a thought unit which displays no peculiar structural moments apart from the loose and irregular rhythmical pattern characteristic for most of the chapter,[2] there is no indication to justify on the basis of form considerations the presence of an isolable or independent unit of tradition.

2. Stylistic Factors

Consideration of stylistic factors in vs. 20-23 present the following picture. Of the 50 stylistic characteristics listed by Ruckstuhl as being peculiar to the Fourth Gospel only one occurs in this passage --the καθὼς-καί clause.[3] And yet it would be misleading to stop at that point. There are other indications that underscore the thoroughly Johannine nature of the passage. The evangelist's marked preference for the ἵνα construction[4] receives no stronger confirmation than in

---

[1] So. G. Wetter, *Der Sohn Gottes*, pp. 62,96.
[2] Bultmann (*Ev Joh*, p. 384) forms a distich (πάτερ...αὐτούς/ἕν...μοι) out of the first two lines of v.11 and attributes the ἵνα clause to the evangelist.
[3] Noack (*Tradition*, p. 53) objects, suggesting that this construction is not due to the propensity to a particular style but is simply the appropriate form for the relational thought that is expressed. And yet that is precisely the point. The nature of the content is a determinative factor for the style that is used.
[4] ἵνα occurs ca. 130 in the Fourth Gospel. Cp. Burney, *Aramaic Origin*, p. 69: "the frequency of ἵνα in Jn is one of the most remarkable phenomena in this Gospel." F. Blass, A. Debrunner, *A Greek Grammar of the NT*, tr. and rev. by R. Funk, Chicago, 1960, p. 388. Radermacher, *Neutestamentliche Grammatik*, pp. 190f.

these verses where it is used 6x (18x in the entire chapter). Whereas the first two ἵνα clauses in v. 21 are used complementarily,[1] the succeeding four in vs. 21-23 are employed in a final or purpose sense. Although the complementary and final usage of ἵνα subordinate clauses is by no means peculiarly Johannine, its usage in discursive material where Jesus speaks in the first person on behalf of the believers and where the main verb (usually a verb of saying, e.g. 5:34; 13:19; 15:11 etc.) is either present or perfect tense, is in fact a unique feature of John. There are no logia in the synoptic tradition formulated in the same way. An analogous usage, however, may be noted in the Johannine Epistles where fundamental elements of Christian teaching or instruction are presented in terms of ἵνα clauses dependent on verbs of hearing, seeing, and writing (e.g. I Jn.1:3; 5:13; 2 Jn.5). In all of NT epistolary literature such usage is unique.[2]

A noted stylistic peculiarity of the Fourth Gospel is asyndeton.[3] Although only asyndeton epicum can be termed specifically Johannine,[4] the paratactic construction in v. 22 where the phrase ἐγὼ ἐν αὐτοῖς καὶ σὺ ἐν ἐμοί is used as an appositional qualifier to the preceding καθώς clause,[5] is typical of the evangelist's asyndetic stylistic tendency and may well be an indication of his formulating hand. Also the οὐκ...ἀλλά construction is stylistically typical for the evangelist who loves to preface a positive thought with its negated contrary (cp. 17:9; 15:15; 11:4 etc). The construction οὐ μόνον and the elliptical ἀλλὰ καί in v. 20 is simply a variation of this tendency.[6] Even though a ἵνα clause follows directly on

---

[1] Blass-Debrunner, op. cit., p. 392. It would also be possible to take them as purpose clauses which has the advantage of strengthening the parallelism in the passage. Cp. Bultmann, Ev Joh, p. 394.
[2] Cp. H. Riesenfeld, "Zu den johanneischen ἵνα-Sätzen," Studia Theologica, 18/19, 1964/65, p. 218.
[3] Blaß-Debrunner, op. cit., p. 462 (1). Burney, Aram. Origin, pp. 49f.
[4] E. Schweizer, Ego Eimi, pp. 91 and 104 (no.10). Bultmann consistently refers to the semiticizing character of asyndetic style as an indicator of source material (Ev Joh, p. 68, n.7; 177, n.4; 250, n.1 etc.) and yet at the same time ascribes this stylistic feature to the evangelist (Ev Joh, p. 301, n.4; 122, n.1; 491).
[5] ἐγὼ ἐν αὐτοῖς etc. is not parallel to κἀγὼ τ. δόξαν (so Bultmann, Ev Joh, p. 395, n.1) but to the corresponding καθώς clause.
[6] Blaß-Debrunner, op. cit., pp. 448, 479 (1).

the heels of the ἀλλά sentence and can be construed formally as a whole, it is not warranted to include this construction under the category of the οὐ...ἀλλ ἵνα usage which is characteristic exclusively of John.[1] Nor is it possible to see in this form an indication of Semitic background. In fact, the non modo - sed etiam construction has no common equivalent in Semitic linguistic usage.[2] Other distinguishing marks of the evangelist's style may be seen in the placement of the verb before the noun (v.23),[3] in the causal comparative usage of καθώς (v.23),[4] in the use of the perfect tense,[5] and in the characteristic terminology (λόγος, κόσμος, δόξα, πιστεύω, γινώσκω) employed. The present participle construction in v. 20 displays no special peculiarities other than a Semitic background. Such a construction is used with great frequency in Aramaic as also in Hebrew as a *futurum instans*.[6]

V. 11 evidences also distinctively Johannine stylistic characteristics. The ἵνα construction is analogous to the occurrence in vs. 20ff. as is also the elliptical καθώς phrase. Likewise the use of the perfect tense (δέδωκας) and the typical terminology all speak for the thoroughly Johannine nature of the unit. Whether the difficult reading ᾧ is based on a mistranslation of the Aramaic particle ךְּ,[7] which could stand for either οὕς, ὅ, or ᾧ, is unlikely. Even if it were a mistranslation, the ambiguity of the particle's meaning would remain.

---

[1] E. Schweizer's (*Ego Eimi*, p. 91) statistical result for this construction: 3 + 1/0. Ruckstuhl's (*Lit Einheit*, p. 194) modification: 5 + 1/0. (From here on Schweizer's formula will be adopted when referring to the comparative statistical occurrences of stylistic characteristics. Thus the first digit refers to the number of occurrences in John's Gospel; the second digit to the Johannine Epistles; the third digit after the diagonal to the rest of the NT with separate reference to the Synoptics in parenthesis ( ).
[2] K. Beyer, *Semitische Syntax*, p. 126, n.4.
[3] This kind of reversal is typically Semitic (cp. Black, *An Aramaic Approach*, p. 33) yet can hardly be used to warrant positing the use of an Aramaic source document. See Ruckstuhl, *Lit. Einheit*, pp. 100f.
[4] Cp. Bultmann, *Ev Joh*, pp. 291, n.3; 362; 376, n.1.
[5] Blauert (*Die Bedeutung der Zeit*, p. 81): "Auch bei der Berücksichtigung der ziemlich gleichmäßigen Verwendung des Partizip Perfekt ist bei Joh. noch eine ausgesprochene Vorliebe für das Perfekt festzustellen, dessen Häufigkeit dann die doppelte Frequenz der Synoptiker erreicht." Cp. Radermacher, *Grammatik*, pp. 177f.
[6] C. F. Burney, *Aramaic Origin*, p. 94.
[7] C. F. Burney, *op. cit.*, p. 102.

One final characteristic needs to be noted, and that is
the construction ἓν ὦσιν. It occurs in these passages (vs.
11, 20-23) a total of four times[1] and apart from this never
again in the NT. Using Schweizer's formula, the results
would be 4+0/0 (considering the proportionate length of the
texts, it would even be 32/0). Regardless of whether the expression is a product of the evangelist or of the tradition
out of which he draws, the expression remains a distinctive
characteristic peculiar to the Fourth Gospel.

3. Excursus: Religio-historical Profile

a) The Greek World

A central impulse motivating the development and interaction of the thought systems and philosophical enquiries of
the Greek world was lodged in the problem of "oneness." The
common abstraction used was the neuter τὸ ἕν.[2] The problem of
oneness runs like a thread through the various philosophical
systems from the Ionians and Eleatics through Plato, Aristotle, and the Stoa, down to the neo-Pythagoreans and the
neo-Platonists. The need to identify an original substance
or cause which would provide intelligibility in the face of
constantly changing phenomena and mutability, harmony in the
face of dissonance, led to a progression of interpretations
conceived in terms of oneness and plurality as ultimate realities. World views emerged in which the One, τὸ ἕν, was understood as the highest principle descriptive not only of absolute being but of the cosmos which it embraced.[3] As a key
philosophical concept the idea of oneness, in addition to
ethical[4] and sociological[5] significance, took on   primarily

---
[1] In v.23 the ὦσιν ἕν is expanded with the participial construction
τετελειωμένοι and the preposition εἰς.
[2] Cp. Andresen, et al., Lexikon der alten Welt, Zürich/Stuttgart, 1965,
p. 1251.
[3] The Milesian School e.g. held that all things derive from a single primal substance. For Heraclitus oneness was the combination of opposites
whereas Parmenides conceived true being as "the One" which is present everywhere, infinite and indivisible. In Platonic thought a split was introduced with the world of ideas constituting the one and the phenomenal
world constituting the many.
[4] Plato e.g. designates the Good as τὸ ἕν.
[5] Aristotle defined the State as an organic unity. It is prior to the
individual and represents the whole of which the individual must be a part.

transcendental and cosmological character and was oriented to a description of reality outside of and beyond man.

b) Hellenistic Trends

In the religious and philosophical trends of the Hellenistic period, on the other hand, there appeared increasing concentration on the search for meaning in human existence as such. Coupled with this was the move toward introspection with the endeavor to find the Absolute in the inner being of man.[1] At this point anthropology and theology became essentially one and resulted in developments that generated corresponding language to comply with respective insights and aspirations. God was sought in man and the essence of man in God. Out of this phenomenon grew a mode of religious speaking which sought to give expression to thoughts of mutual indwelling and the mergence of the divine and human. Although characteristic for a wide variety of religious movements, expressions of reciprocity and the resulting images of oneness became so stereotyped in form that it is possible to speak of set, monotypic formulas.

Indicative of the concern to describe the relation between God and the universe are the cosmic pantheistic formulas of the Stoics as illustrated in classic form in the statement by Marcus Aurelius: ἐκ σοῦ πάντα, ἐν σοὶ πάντα, εἰς σὲ πάντα.[2] Examples of similar formulas and variations of the same, expressing relation between the All and the One, could be multiplied ad libitum.[3] Of course, the exact content and intent of these formulas vary in accordance with their respective contexts. Whether, however, the formulas are used in a

---

[1] Cp. G. Hansen, *Umwelt des Urchristentums*, I, hrsg. v. J. Leipoldt and W. Grundmann, p. 350.

[2] *Marcus Aurelius Antonius*, ed. H. Schenkel, Lipsiae, 1913, IV. 23, (p. 38).

[3] Cp. Chrysippos in Stobaios, *ecl.* I 1, 26: "Δία δὲ αὐτὸν λέγουσιν, ὅτι πάντων ἐστὶν αἴτιος καὶ δι' αὐτὸν πάντα." Ps. Apuleius Asclep. 30: "in eo sunt omnia et in omnibus ipse est solus." In an outstanding analysis of the historical development of this kind of formula, E. Norden (*Agnostos Theos*, pp. 240-250) collected a wide variety of pertinent texts ranging from the pre-Socratics through the Stoic pantheists and rightly concluded that these formulas represent a kind of universal religious expression (246[5]).

genuinely Stoic sense emphasizing the monistic identification of φύσις and θεός as the cause of the grand cosmic harmony in the universe, or whether they occur in Jewish Hellentistic propaganda modified by OT predications (e.g. Philo. De confus. ling. 170; Josephus. Contra Apionem II. 193), or whether they appear in Pauline theological constructions (Rom.11:33f. I Cor.1:16f. Eph.4:5f.),[1] the language is basically identical and demonstrates a common form.

What distinguishes formulas of reciprocity and oneness in a Stoic context is the cosmic concern. God is understood as ἕν and πᾶν. Occurrences of the formula in the multiple contexts of the Hellenistic mystery religions are stamped by a marked personal orientation. No longer is it a matter of cosmic totality in relation to the one God but the relation of the individual believer to the Divine.[2] For the genuine cultic mystic this relationality, expressed in terms of mutual indwelling, was descriptive of the process of one's incorporation into the Divine which ended in complete identification, i.e. deification or apotheosis. The fusion of subject and object, basic to all forms of mysticism, could be described interchangeably with formulations of being in God and of receiving God into one's self.[3] The one implied the other. Only where both terms are specifically identified with each other, however, can one properly speak of a clearly defined formula of reciprocity. Characteristic of this kind of language are the frequent formulations of mutual identification that occur in the Hermes prayers retained in the magical papyri. The formula-like expressions —σὺ γὰρ ἐγὼ καὶ ἐγὼ καὶ ἐγὼ σύ (London Papyrus CXXII) and σὺ γὰρ εἶ ἐγὼ καὶ ἐγὼ σύ (Leyden Papyrus II)--

---

[1] Cp. M. Dibelius, "Die Christianisierung einer hellenistischen Formel," in *Botschaft und Geschichte*, Bd. II, hrsg. v. G. Bornkamm, Tübingen, 1956, pp. 14-29.

[2] And yet it should be remembered that a characteristic feature of the mystery religions was not so much the element of individualism as of community. The mystics understood each other as "fratres" (G. Haufe, "Die Mysterien," *Umwelt des Urchristentums*, I, p.122) and were bound to each other through cultic practices.

[3] R. Reitzenstein, *Die hellenistischen Mysterienreligionen*, Darmstadt,1966, p.73: "Ich stelle zunächst die auffällige Tatsache fest, daß die Vorstellungen "in Gott eingehen," und "Gott oder den Geist oder den hl. Geist in sich aufnehmen" in der heidnischen Literatur, und zwar nicht in der mystischen allein, ebenso beliebig wechseln wie bei Paulus die Vorstellungen "in Christo sein" und 'Christus in sich tragen.'"

are standard features in these mystical prayers. They can also variously appear in terms of reciprocal knowledge (οἶδά σε, Ἑρμῆ καὶ σὺ ἐμέ) or of the reciprocity of names (τ.σὸν ὄνομα ἐμὸν κ.τὸ ἐμὸν σον) hypostatically understood as persons.[1] Analogous to these basic formulas is the wide variety of formulations in Hellenistic liturgical and mystery texts where mutual indwelling or union with the Divine is depicted as a reciprocal relation in sacramental,[2] spatial,[3] and legal[4] terms. Particularly prominent are the relational statements in the Hermetic tractates which represent such a rich cross-fertilization of Greek and Oriental thought in terms of popular mystical piety. Here the worshipper of God can say: σὺ εἶ ὃ ἂν ὦ, σὺ εἶ ὃ ἂν ποιῶ, σὺ εἶ ὃ ἂν λέγω·σὺ γὰρ πάντα εἶ (C.H. V.2). Although common in much of Greek thought, this is a typical statement of the Hermeticists, for whom to know God was in some sense to partake of his nature. Like was thought of as being apprehended by like (C.H. XI.20: ἐὰν οὖν μὴ σεαυτὸν ἐξισάσῃς τῷ θεῷ, τὸν θεὸν νοῆσαι οὐ δύνασαι. τὸ γὰρ ὅμοιον τῷ ὁμοίῳ νοητόν) and consequently the language of reciprocity took on increasingly technical character unique to this kind of religious phenomenology.

c) Gnosis

Although the oneness and reciprocity statements serve as constitutive expressions of basic concerns in the mystery religions, i.e. identification with or absorption into God, still it is significant that the occurrence of these statements spreads out over a much broader range of texts whose essential character is Gnostic. In part that is due to the fluid crossover and interrelation between Gnostic thought currents and the mystery religions as indicated by the discovery of Hermetic tractates in the Gnostic library of Nag

---

[1] Texts in Reitzenstein, *Poimandres*, Darmstadt, 1966, pp. 17, 20f. 28. A. Dieterich, *Eine Mithrasliturgie*, hrsg. v. O. Weinrich, Leipzig und Berlin, 1923, p. 97.
[2] Dieterich, *op. cit.*, pp. 92ff.
[3] H. Hanse, "Gott Haben" in der Antike und im frühen Christentum, Religionsgeschichtliche Versuche und Vorarbeiten, Bd. XXVII, Berlin, 1939, pp. 127ff.
[4] Hanse, *op. cit.*, pp. 119f.

Hammadi.¹ Despite their syncretistic diversity, the mystery
faiths manifest a definite discreteness that precludes a
simple indentification with Gnosis. Nevertheless, there are
points of convergence, as reflected in the utilization of
common speech modes, that betray a process of mutual influence between the two phenomena.² This convergence is notably
apparent in the formulas of reciprocity and oneness. The intentions in the respective contexts may, of course, be different. In the mystery religions the point at issue is man's
transformation or metamorphosis from the terrestial to the
divine by means of external actions, visions, or ecstatic experience. In Gnosis, on the other hand, it is a matter of
the realization of divinity which one had always possessed.³
Here man needs to be awakened out of the stupor of sleep,
hear the call of the revealer, and be directed back to the
point of his real origin which is the basis of his oneness
with the divine world. Since the element of oneness is a
fundamental point of departure in the world view of Gnosis,
it is understandable that statements of reciprocity and unity
would propagate within its context and/or be absorbed from
other contexts such as the mystery faiths and related traditions. The extent to which this may be seen depends in part
on a fuller understanding of the essence and structure of

---

[1] Cp. W. Foerster (Hrsg.), *Die Gnosis I*, Stuttgart/Zürich, 1969, p. 420:
"So stehen Poimandres und der siebte Traktat des Corpus Hermeticum zwar in
der Gnosis, die Erweichung der harten Konturen derselben ist allerdings
deutlich." See further, A. Böhlig, *Mysterion und Wahrheit*, Gesammelte
Beiträge zur spätantiken Religionsgeschichte, Leiden, 1968, p.89. K.W. Tröger,
"Die hermetische Gnosis," in *Gnosis und Neues Testament* (Hrsg. Tröger),
Berlin, 1973, pp. 101f.
[2] Böhlig (*Mysterion und Wahrheit*, p.43) in fact, regards the mysteries as
a source for the development of Gnosis. H.M. Schenke ("Hauptprobleme der
Gnosis," *Kairos*, VII, 1965, p.117) recognizes points of convergence and mutual influence, but emphasizes (against the tendency of Bousset and Reitzenstein to speak primarily of the cultic side of Gnosis as well as against
H.Jonas who tends to identify "the spirit of the time" with Gnosis): "Gnosis
und Mysterienglaube sind nicht identisch, sind wurzelhaft, ursprünglich und
im Wesen verschieden." Similarly, H.Gaffron, *Studien zum koptischen Philippus-
Evangelium*, Dissertation Bonn, 1969, pp. 85ff. P. Pokorny, *Der Epheserbrief
und die Gnosis*, Berlin, 1965, pp. 26-32.
[3] In the mystery religions redemption was a process of becoming what one
previously was not (καί εἰμι νῦν οὐχ ὃ πρίν --C.H. XIII.3) whereas in Gnosis
man became what he originally was (ἵνα πάλιν γένωμαι ὃ ἤμην --Acta Thomae 15).
In both cases the goal was identification with God. The conception of its
realization, however, was fundamentally different.

Gnosis.

In the attempt to introduce terminological order into the extremely complex and conflictive field of Gnosis investigation, the International Congress at Messina in 1966 proposed a working hypothesis which in effect not only established lines for making distinctions but simultaneously also implied a definition of the problem. The proposal was that differentiation be made between the classic second century systems of Gnosticism and the designation Gnosis understood as knowledge of the divine mysteries reserved for an elite.[1] Characteristic for Gnosticism is a twofold movement --the devolution of the Divine whose extreme edge (usually identified with Sophia or Ennoia) fatefully falls victim to a crisis which brings forth the world from which the fallen Pneuma must be retracted and again integrated into the Divine. With this definition it can be noted that not every Gnosis is Gnosticism but only that which contains the idea of the consubstantiality of the fallen Pneuma element with the Divine. In addition it was also suggested that a distinction be made between proto-Gnosticism and pre-Gnosticism. Pre-Gnosticism would involve the recognition and identification of concepts and motifs that prepared the way for Gnosticism proper whereas proto-Gnosticism would embody in embryonic form elements of the Gnosticism that later appeared in the second century. Useful and essential though these differentiations may be, they are not without considerable problems since they tend to give advance answers to the very questions they are designed to raise.[2] It is not at all clear that Gnosis can be thus separated from Gnosticism since both concepts are so integrally related to a broad spectrum of common religious phenomena. Nor can it be maintained that Gnosis simply refers

---

[1] The Messina proposals listed here are given in W. Eltester (Hrsg.), *Christentum und Gnosis*, pp. 129-133. Cp. also R. McL. Wilson, *Gnosis and the New Testament*, Philadelphia, 1968, p. 17.
[2] Cp. the cogent critique by K. Rudolph, "Gnosis und Gnostizismus, ein Forschungsbericht," *Theol. Rund.*, 36, 1, 1971, pp.18f. On the other hand, there is an unavoidable circularity between definition attempts and the construction of original models. Cp. R. Haardt, "Methoden der Ursprungsbestimmung der Gnosis," in *Gnosis und Gnostiziamus*,(Hrsg. v. K. Rudolph), Darmstadt, 1975, pp.654-667.

to an elite knowledge of the elect without obscuring the contours of its much broader function. Finally at stake is a definition of Gnostic religion both from a phenomenological point of view as well as from the perspective of a historical complex that can be geographically and chronologically located.

Research has demonstrated the untenability of postulating an extrapolated model gained by distilling motifs from a wide range of divergent texts and then by placing them together into a constructed myth which is to serve as the measure of the essence of Gnostic religion. Hardest hit has been the "Redeemed Redeemer" formula of the history of religions school.[1] While it is now generally agreed that the formula can no longer be used as the key to understanding the whole of Gnostic soteriology neither can it, on the other hand, be simply dismissed as a modern invention contrived from a variety of diverse texts. The construction does have substantiation in some texts (Od. Sal. 8,22; Gospel of Phil. 119,2f. Hippolytus, Ref. V.2-9; VI17,2-3)[2] but represents only one expression among others in the variety of Gnostic soteriological understanding. That variety is demonstrated e.g. in the fact that there are instances when the Redeemer must first himself be redeemed before he can mediate redemption or, on the other hand, when he is not essentially connected with the salvandi, just as the redemptional act for the salvandi is not always definitive in itself but requires next to the salvational indicative a corresponding imperative.[3] Despite the diversity in soteriological as well as also in cosmological Gnostic interpretation, it is still possible to establish uniform tenets fundamental to Gnostic phenomenology. Here there is general consensus in regarding as an irreducible

---

[1] C. Colpe, *Die religionsgeschichtliche Schule*. FRLANT N.F., 60, Göttingen, 1961, p. 189: "So halte ich die Formel vom Erlösten Erlöser zwar für ein logisch unangreifbares und heuristisch gelegentlich nützliches Interpretament, aber nicht für eine hermeneutisch ergiebige und im letzten sachgemäße Kategorie." Cp. also R. Haardt, *Die Gnosis, Wesen, und Zeugnis*, Salzburg, 1967, p. 27.
[2] K. Rudolph, "Gnosis und Gnostizismus," *op. cit.*, p. 11.
[3] Cp. L. Schottroff, "Heil als innerweltliche Entweltlichung," *op. cit.*, p.309. Also E. Haenchen, *Die Botschaft des Thomasevangeliums*, Berlin, 1961, p. 49.

descriptive minimum the radically acosmic dualism and the consubstantiality of the Divine with the self of the Gnostic whose state of separation is resolved in the realization of the original oneness that takes place in response to the realization of the original oneness that takes place in response to the revelational call from above.[1] As such, Gnosis cannot be understood as a loose syncretistic farrago of mythological elements. Diverse elements, instead, relate to a unifying center. In fact, current research has tended to reinforce the thesis that at center is a "Gnostic principle" which introduced into the ancient world a new understanding of man and cosmos.[2] Important for our investigation is the observation that an inherent and constitutive factor in the Gnostic principle is the concept of consubstantiality.[3] This concept runs like a red thread throughout Gnostic texts and gives form and shape to the Gnostic message. Against this background the formulas of reciprocity and oneness both in Gnostic and Gnosticizing texts become intelligible. They give expression to the fundamental tenet of Gnostic self-understanding: the essential identity between the Salvator and the salvandi or, where there is no redeemer figure involved, between the salvandi and the transcendent world.

As evidence for this phenomenon reference is made to a range of representative texts in which the Gnostic principle of oneness appears in formula expressions of reciprocity and oneness. Irenaeus relates the practice of the Gnostic Marcus who had "great power from the invisible and unspeakable places" (redeemer figure?) and who is said to have preached a type of sacramental marriage[4] by which his followers could be

---

[1] H. Jonas, *Gnosis und spätantiker Geist*, pp.94-140. W.Foerster, (Hrsg.), *Die Gnosis* I, p.17. H.M. Schenke in *Umwelt des Urchristentums*, (hrsg. v. Leipoldt-Grundmann), I, p.374. McL. Wilson, *Gnosis and the NT*, p. 4. S. Schulz, "Die Bedeutung neuer Gnosisfunde für die neutestamentlich Wissenschaft," *Theol. Rund.*, 26,4, 1960, p.332.
[2] Eloquently presented by H. Jonas. Cp. *The Gnostic Religion*, Boston, 1963, p.25.
[3] The salient feature of Gnostic faith is that both man and God have the same essence. Cp. H.M. Schenke, *Der Gott "Mensch" in der Gnosis*, Göttingen, 1962, p. 69. And yet the Gnostic does not gain salvation because of his substance but because of his knowledge.
[4] Cp. Bousset, *Hauptprobleme der Gnosis*, Göttingen, 1907, pp.315ff. The marriage theme is a popularly used aspect of the oneness motif. Cp. *Exegese über die Seele*, 133,5 (Foerster, *Die Gnosis*, II, p.131) and *Philippusev*, 77 (Foerster, II, p.111).

joined to him so that together they could enter the realm of the One (ἵνα σὺν αὐτῷ κατέλθῃ εἰς τὸ ἕν). Accordingly Marcus could admonish his hearers to prepare themselves as a bride prepares for the bridegroom ἵνα ἔσῃ ὃ ἐγὼ καὶ ἐγὼ ὃ σύ. (Iren. Adv. Haer. I. 13,3).[1]

In Hippolytus' rendering of the Megale Apophasis (Refutatio VI.9-18)[2] which contains citations deriving from an earlier source, we find elements of a non-Christian Gnostic salvational plan attributed to the teaching of Simon Magus.[3] Of particular importance is ch.17 where the obscure formula —ἑστώς, στάς, στησόμενος (17,1)— is used to denote three stages of the Gnostic redemption drama (perfect oneness, fall, reintegration) which is then recapitualed in the subsequent formula-like statement (17,2) ἐγὼ καὶ σὺ ἕν, πρὸ ἐμοῦ σύ, τὸ μετὰ σὲ ἐγώ.

Epiphanius (Pararion XXVI. 2,2-3,1)[4] speaks of a Gnostic group that rested its claims on a Gospel of Eve, on the basis of which they testified to having seen "a great man and another small one (procerum hominem et mutilum alium) who spoke the following message: "Ego idem sum ac tu, et tu idem atque ego (ἐγὼ σὺ καὶ σὺ ἐγώ) et ubicunque tu es, illic ego sum, ac per omnia sum dispersus. Et undecunque volueris me colligis, me vero colligendo temetipsum colligis." The message is a concise summary of the Gnostic redemptive scheme spelled out in terms of the identity of the Salvator with the salvandi. Significant is that the scheme is expressed in terms of the characteristic reciprocity formula of oneness.

These formula-like statements appear with regularity also in Gnosticizing interpretations of Jesus and the believers. In the Nag Hammadi Gospel of Truth (42:26-28)[5] it is said of

---

[1] W. Völker, Quellen zur Geschichte der christlichen Gnosis, Tübingen, 1932, p.137.
[2] Völker, op. cit., p.9.
[3] J.H. Frickel, "Die Apophasis Megale, eine Grundschrift der Gnosis?" Studia di storia religiosa della tarda anticita, Messina, 1968, pp.35-49. Also E. Haenchen, "Gab es eine vorchristliche Gnosis?" Gott und Mensch, pp. 265-298, esp. 281f. Schmithals, Die Gnosis in Korinth, FRLANT N.F. 48, Göttingen, 1956, pp.32-44.
[4] Migne, P.G., 41, p.337. Foerster, Die Gnosis, I. p.406.
[5] Cp. also 18,30 and 19:30. The Gospel of Truth., tr. and com. by K. Grobel, London, 1960.

the faithful: "and the Father is in them and they are in the
Father. Similarly in the <u>Unbekanntes altgnostisches Werk</u>[1] the
Gnostic says: "sie wurden alle eins in dem Einzigen Allein-
igen" (351,6). In the <u>Pistis Sophia</u> the believer confesses,
"Wir aber alle mit Dir Selbst, wir sind ein und dasselbe"
(10,30).[2] Here Jesus repeatedly uses the formula of reciprocity in speaking to the redeemed. Regarding the ψυχαί of
the τέλειοι he says, "Jene Menschen bin ich und ich bin sie"
(148,7). To those who have received the inexplicable mystery
which he himself is, the Gnostic Jesus declares: "ich bin
sie and sie sind ich" (148,18). Of Mary Magdalene and John
the maiden (παρθένος) the Savior says, "ich bin sie und sie
sind ich und sie werden mit euch in allen Dingen gleich
sein..." (148,29). The same theme of oneness occurs in the
explanation of the Gnostic redemptive scheme in <u>Excerpta ex
Theodoto</u> (§36)[3] where it is maintained that Jesus was baptized
ἵνα ἡμεῖς, οἱ πολλοὶ ἓν γενόμενοι, [οἱ] πάντες τῷ ἑνὶ τῷ δι' ἡμᾶς
μερισθέντι ἀνακραθῶμεν. The unique assertion here is that the
Revealer himself was divided on account of the believers (δι'
ἡμᾶς) so that the believer could be joined to him and thus be
reintegrated into heavenly oneness.[4] While the emphasis here
is on the unity with Jesus as a means of attaining final oneness, there are other passages which describe the reintegration process as a matter of recognizing one's own self. Thus
in a typically stylized passage in the Syrian <u>Acts of Thomas</u>
the bridegroom (the believer) in response to Jesus, who had
taken the form of Thomas, offers a prayer of thanks in which
it is said: "Ich danke dir, Her... der du... mir gezeigt
hast, mich selbst zu suchen und zu erkennen wer ich war und

---

[1] *Koptisch-Gnostische Schriften*, I, GCS 45, 13, hrsg. v. G. Schmidt, 2nd ed., rev. by W. Till, Berlin, 1954.
[2] Also cited from *Koptisch-Gnostische Schriften* I, (Schmidt). Further cp. the Nag Hammadi *Book of Thomas the Athlete* 145,15, (Foerster, *Die Gnosis*, II, p.148): "indem ihr mit ihm einig seid und er mit euch einig ist von jetzt an bis in alle Ewigkeit."
[3] Völker, *op. cit.*, p. 125. Foerster, *Die Gnosis*, I, p. 294.
[4] Further cp. *Ev. der Wahrheit*, 22,10 (Foerster, II, p.71): "Ihm wird der Name des Einen zuteil." Oneness is the goal of the Gnostic. *Ev. der Wahrheit* 24,25; 25,5-24. *Über die Auferstehung* 49,10 (Foerster, II, p. 190): "Wandle auch nicht nach diesem Fleisch wegen der Einheit, sondern komme aus den Teilungen..." Cp. further E. Haenchen, *Die Botschaft*, pp. 58ff. A. Klijn, "The 'Single One' in the Gospel of Thomas," *JBL*, 81, 1962, p. 272. *Gospel of Thomas*, 4.

wer und wie ich jetzt bin, damit ich wieder würde, was ich war..."[1] Final reference is made to a passage in the Gnosticizing Acts of John (100)[2] where in somewhat broken form the formula-like language of reciprocity is used to describe the revelation of the mystery of the cross. Here the Gnostic Jesus declares:[3] "...and I shall be what I was, when *you* (are) as I am with myself; for from *me* you are <what I am> ...for you must know that I am wholly with the Father, and the Father with me."[4]

In the various instances cited above it may be observed how the language of oneness and reciprocity has taken on a type of formula character. Despite the wide chronological span of the texts involved, there is represented a common phenomenology. These various types of expressions appear as the logical consequence of the view which insists that man is not a part of the cosmos but that his true being is essentially identical with the Transcendent. Statements of reciprocity and oneness are the intrinsically appropriate expressions for the Gnostic self-understanding and world view. Characteristic for their use within Gnostic circles is both the revelational context in which they occur as well as their relational capacity to describe the ontological connection between the Redeemer and the Divine, between the redeemed and the Divine, and between the Redeemer and the redeemed whereby the redeemed are often understood collectively as one. In Greek philosophical texts the language of oneness is used primarily in non-personal cosmic terms and as an abstraction for

---

[1] Foerster, Die Gnosis, I, p.434.
[2] E. Hennecke, (tr. by R. McL. Wilson), New Testament Apocrypha, II, London, 1965, pp.233ff.
[3] The text is rendered with a number of emendations and conjectures. The asterisks indicate an omission from Bonnet's text; () indicate an explanatory edition; <> denotes restoration of a missing word.
[4] Mention might also be made of the passage in the Epistula Apostolorum 18 (Hennecke, op. cit., II, p.201): "I am wholly in my Father and my Father in me." A clear instance of the formula expression is found in the late text of Die Biene of the Metropolitan Solomon of Bosra where Zoroaster says of the Messiah: "He shall descend from my family. I am he and he is I; he is in me and I am in him...he and I are one" E. Böklen, Die Verwandtschaft der jüdisch-christlichen mit der parsischen Eschatologie, Göttingen, 1902, p.98. Cp. also R. Reitzenstein, Das iranische Erlösungsmysterium, Bonn, 1921, p.100.

transcendent being. In the mystical texts the language of oneness receives a characteristic reciprocal orientation but is basically restricted to the idea of transformation and fusion. In the Gnostic context, however, the language of oneness receives its fullest and most specific function as the basic structural element intrinsic to a cosmological and soteriological interpretation of man and the world. Here oneness is explicated not as an abstract principle or in terms of personal transformation but as a soteriological state of being in separation from the world and in awareness of a given identity with the transcendent world. It is not at all surprising then that formula-like statements of oneness and reciprocity occur typically within the phenomenology of specifically Gnostic thought patterns, for it is here that they have their most appropriate home.

d) Old Testament

A comparison with the Old Testament will further help to clarify the contours specific to the development of reciprocal and oneness language. Any idea of self-identification with God was foreign to the Hebrew mentality. To make one's self equal to or a part of God was blasphemy and was consistently anathematized as the deepest and most heinous offense. Consequently, the language of oneness and reciprocity, as evidenced in the Gnostic formulas and in the Johannine expressions, does not at all develop within the framework of Hebrew thought. This, of course, does not mean that the terms of oneness are not used in a theological sense. They are, but the direction is decidedly different. In the OT oneness is not a relational term but a denominator for the exclusiveness and absoluteness of God. God is not understood in a philosophical abstract sense as a first cause, as a harmony in cosmic diversity, or as cosmological consubstantiality or as a principle of immanent order but rather in a historical dynamic and eschatological sense as the only One who acts for his people.[1] Oneness here is synonymous with

---

[1] Cp. G.F. Moore, *Judaism*, I, Cambridge, 1958, pp.115, 361.

exclusiveness. The prophet who gives some of the clearest
expressions to this absoluteness is Deutero-Isaiah: "I am
Jahweh and there is no other" (Is.45:5f.); "Before me no god
was formed nor shall there be any after me. I, I am the Lord"
(Is.43:10). As a summary of faith the Israelite would recite:
שמע ישראל יהוה אלהינו יהוה אחד (Deut. 6:4). Relationships to
Jahweh who is God alone consist in following His will alone
and in obeying His statutes. The resulting covenant relationship (ברית שלום) is not one of parity or natural association, but rather derives from the right of Jahweh who is
God alone.[1] The covenant people are one people set off as a
group distinct from others. Failure to keep Jahweh's will
results in a breaking of the covenant bonds. From this
standpoint the OT oneness theme takes on eschatological significance. The day of the Lord will see final realization of
Jahweh's will. "And the Lord will become king over all the
earth; on that day the Lord will be one and his name one"
(Zech. 14:9). The character of Israel's anointed one can
variously be understood in terms of a filial relationship
with Jahweh (Ps. 2:7) depicted as a legal act of adoption,[2] or
in terms of the eschatological emissary (Is. 61:1ff.) who has
been given a charge to fulfill. But never is the relationship described in terms of oneness and reciprocity. The
identity expressed is at best one of representation[3] but not
of parity.

e) Judaism

A strictly monotheistic confession is maintained and in
fact increased in the various and complex developments within
Judaism.[4] "God is forever one" (Sir.42:21). Recitation of
the Schema is a rabbinic requirement as a daily reminder that
Jahweh is one Lord. "The One" can be substituted for the
name of God.[5] R. Akiba is reported to have been martyred

---
[1] Cp. G. V. Rad, *Old Testament Theology*, I, Edinburgh and London, 1963, p. 130.
[2] G. V. Rad, *op. cit.*, p. 320.
[3] S. Hanson, *The Unity of the Church*, p. 19.
[4] Cp. Bousset, *Die Religion des Judentums*, HzNT, 21, Tübingen, 1966, p.302.
[5] E. Dietrich, *RGG*³, II, p. 1713. Also Billerbeck, *op. cit.*, II, p. 28 (Mk. 12:29).

uttering his last word אחד (Ber. 61b). Josephus writes that all the Hebrews know that God is one (Jos. Ant. 5,112), therefore the Hebrew nation is but one (Jos. Ant. 4,201). Similarly, there is only one Law given by the one Lord (Syr. Baruch 48:24; 85:14). Since God is one, there can also be only one temple (Philo, De spec. leg. 1:67). The theme of oneness in Judaism moves basically within these confines. It is motivated by a strictly monotheistic faith. The language of oneness and reciprocity is not used to describe relationships to God. As a descriptive term oneness is not relational but static. Thus there is one God, one Law, one temple, one people. Where the communal aspect of the one people is reflected on, the unity is conceived of either in tribal terms (XII Patr. Jud. 22:1; Zeb. 8:4-6; Neph. 8:2)[1] or in moral and legal terms as the consequence of fidelity to the Law and obedience to God's commands. The language used here is distinctly not relational and reciprocal. In texts where an eschatological messianic figure appears, his relationship to God is similarly not described in terms of oneness even when the figure has been mythicized and projected into pre-existence.[2] In short, it may be said that language suggesting mutual immanence between God and anyone else is scrupulously avoided. Philo may indeed be able to say that to know God is to be a son of God (De conf. 145), but even for Philo, who represents such a rich cross-fertilization between Hellenistic and Jewish thought,[3] the son remains at best an adopted person (De Sobr. 56) consistent with OT tradition. Within Judaism an absolute separation between God and any other being is consistently maintained. Here the rabbinic dictum is representative: "Wenn dir ein Mensch sagt, 'Ich bin Gott,'

---

[1] Randall, *The Theme of Unity*, pp.68-79, draws the far-fetched conclusion that these expressions of tribal unity are typical "Johannisms." Closer examination reveals that there is no real contact at all.
[2] Bousset, *Die Religion des Judentums*, pp. 259-268.
[3] Philo betrays his Greek influence when he speaks of the unity of God in a metaphysical sense: "God is singular and one (ἕν), not composite, a simple nature, while everyone of us and of all other created things is many (πολλά)..." (*leg. alleg.* 2:1. Cp. also *De opif. mundi* 61 §170; *De conf. ling.* 33, 170) Philo can also adopt language of the mystery religions in regarding ecstasy as a means of relating to God (*q. rer. div. her.* 69; *Leg. alleg.* 1,82).

so lügt er: 'Ich bin der Menschensohn' (=Messias), so wird
er es schließlich bereuen; 'Ich steige zum Himmel empor', so
hat er es gesagt, wird es aber nicht ausführen."[1]

f) Wisdom Traditions

Despite its pervasive unity, Judaism manifests a tremendous
diversity.[2] Some of that diversity may be seen in the new impulses that can be detected in the emergence and development
of the wisdom (חָכְמָה, σοφία) traditions in Israel. Within
these wisdom circles theological reflection became less concerned with the dimension of covenant history and prophetic
action as with the question of creation and nature and with
the practical knowledge of the laws of life and experience.
This can be seen in the development of a distinct wisdom tradition, which in its later stages reflected thought patterns
similar to those that generated the oneness terminology in
Gnostic contexts. Although the language of reciprocity and
oneness is itself not formally characteristic for the wisdom
literature, nevertheless Jewish theological reflections on
wisdom offer significant points of contact with the underlying content and direction of the oneness statements of
identity so typical for Gnostic views. In fact, it has
rightly been suggested that Jewish wisdom traditions and their
antecedent roots of skepticism provide an important bridge
between Judaism and Gnosis.[3]

In pre-exilic Israel wisdom was primarily understood in ex-
periential terms expressed in maxims and gnomic sayings

---

[1] Billerbeck, op. cit., II, p. 542.
[2] The lines between orthodox and heterodox Judaism are not always easily
drawn. Similarly, the lines between palestinian and hellenistic Judaism
can, as H.-F. Weiss has shown, be very fluid (Untersuchungen zur Kosmologie
des hellenistischen und palästinischen Judentums, TU, 97, Berlin, 1966).
[3] K. Rudolph ("Randerscheinungen des Judentums und des Gnostizismus,"
Gnosis und Gnostizismus, Darmstadt, 1975, p.790) speaks here e.g. of an
"entscheidende Nahtstelle zwischen Gnosis und Judentum." Of course, it
would not be warranted to speak of a developed Gnostic myth underlying
Jewish wisdom speculation (cp. H. Conzelmann, "Die Mutter der Weisheit,"
Zeit und Geschichte, p. 226). And yet a mythological character and background of these speculations can hardly be denied (M. Hengel, Judentum
und Hellenismus, 2 Aufl., Tübingen, 1973, p. 347f.

designed to provide insight into life situations.[1] Such proverbs and sayings had a marked empirical character. They were the products of past experience and mature understanding. Their goal was to disclose underlying principles of behavior which regulate relationships and which lead to the greatest happiness for the individual. These maxims were made to serve the interests of OT faith. "No wisdom can avail against the Lord" (Prov.21:30). It must always be an understanding and insight subject to him. This is determinative for the tradition in Israel. Here it is repeatedly maintained that the beginning of wisdom is the fear of the Lord.

In post-exilic times a major change becomes apparent in the understanding of wisdom. The older empirical wisdom teaching, due to inner shifts and under pressure from syncretistic inroads and a different question of God, gives way to a new theological development in which wisdom is personified and viewed as a pre-existent entity.[2] She is not just an abstract principle but a heavenly person, a hypostasized being, who speaks to the world and who appears as a heavenly mediator of divine revelation. Thus σοφία addresses the world: "To you, O men, I call, and my cry is to the sons of men" (Prov.8:4; cp. also Sirach 24). True to OT Jewish concerns, however, wisdom is not reciprocally equated with God. Rather she is God's creation, the first of his acts (Prov.8:22; Sirach 1:4,9).

Although subordinate to God, Wisdom is placed in order before all the rest of creation. She was παρ' αὐτῷ when he marked out the foundation of the earth (Prov.8:30). She was like a child playing in his presence continually, playing on the earth when he had finished it (Prov.8:30).

Despite the diversity in the tradition in its various levels of development, there is a marked tendency, reflective of

---

[1] Cp. G. von Rad, *op. cit.*, I, pp. 418-441. Also H. Gese, "Weisheit," *RGG*³, VI, p. 1576.
[2] The tendency to hypostatize ideas and abstractions can be documented throughout the post-classical world particularly in Egypt, to some extent in Greece, and also in post-biblical Judaism (Cp. Hengel, *op. cit.*, pp. 278f. Also Bousset, *Die Religion des Judentums*, p. 347f.

the mythological background,[1] to expand on the identification of wisdom with God. In the poetic descriptions in Job 28 an understanding shines through which depicts wisdom as an individual entity, separate from God, and yet related only to him. Wisdom is inaccessible for man. "Man does not know the way to it, and it is not found in the land of the living" (Job 28:13). It is concealed from creation. Only "God understands the way to it, and he knows its place" (Job 28:23). The hiddenness of wisdom reflects not only the skepticism[2] which despairs of being able to know God, but it also underscores and reinforces the transcendent character of wisdom. There is a kind of unity between σοφία and God.[3] She is wedded to him and has συμβίωσιν θεοῦ (Sap. Sal. 8:3). In fact, she decides for him what he is to do (αἱρετὶς τῶν ἔργων αὐτοῦ Sap. Sal. 8:4). She is but one (μία οὖσα), yet can do everything (Sap. Sal. 7:27). She is eternal (Sirach 1:9), omnipotent, unchanging, spans the world in power from end to end, and orders all things benignly (Sap. Sal. 7:27-30). She has all the attributes of God and in this sense can be said to be one with him.

Even though one level of the tradition reflects primarily the absolute transcendence of wisdom, its most common depiction recounts its nearness and accessibility to the world. In ben Sirach 24 that accessibility is narrowed down to Israel (v.4). Wisdom is equated with the Torah (24:23) and is received by learning and studying the Law of Moses. Elsewhere wisdom can be universalized and pictured as having cosmic scope.[4] In any case it is understood as the revelational medium. In fact, wisdom itself is the way to God. It is the form in which God wishes to be sought by man. "Whoever finds me, find life" (Prov.8:35). Only God can speak that way. And yet wisdom is differentiated from him and understood as

---
[1] For the relation to the Isis-Osiris myth see B.L. Mack, *Logos und Sophia*, SUNT 10, Göttingen, 1973, pp. 61ff. Conzelmann, "Die Mutter der Weisheit, *op. cit.*, p. 227.
[2] Cp. G. von Rad, *op. cit.*, I, pp. 453f. B.L. Mack, *op. cit.*, pp.184f.
[3] U. Wilckens, σοφία, *ThWB*, VII, p. 508, speaks of Wisdom's "Synusie mit Gott und Menschen."
[4] Wisdom is identified with Pneuma (Sap. Sal. 1:6; 9:17) and Pneuma fills the whole earth and holds it together (Sap. Sal. 1:7).

being under his direction (Sap. Sal. 7:15). Although she is παρὰ κυρίου καὶ μετ' αὐτοῦ εἰς τὸν αἰῶνα (Sirach 1:1), she is infused into all his works and in some measure given to all mankind (Sirach 1:9,10). Wisdom here is pictured as a kind of "world soul."[1] Nonetheless not everyone desires her, and wisdom will not make her home in a body mortgaged to sin (Sap. Sal. 1:4). Therefore she must be sent (Sap. Sal. 9:10) and issue a summons to the sons of men (Prov. 8:4). Those who accept her and make their home with her have a "life together with" her (συμβίωσιν Sap. Sal. 8:3). With wisdom there is immortality (Sap. Sal. 8:17), peace and health (Sirach 1:7). Acceptance of her means salvation and life (Prov. 3:18). The soteriological process of man's finding and identifying with wisdom is the complement of wisdom's identification with God.

Herein lies the significance for a clarification of the religio-historical background out of which patterns emerge that generate expressions of the oneness motif. Although reciprocity statements and the term "oneness" are not used in these traditions, wisdom in its hypostatized form is described in a way that suggests parallelism and oneness with God. God has a complementary, depicted not as a principle or thing but as a heavenly person who serves as the medium of divine revelation. People who respond to and identify with wisdom receive her blessings and the blessings of God. It is significant that this structural pattern which involves a process of mutual identification between God and wisdom and wisdom and man is the same pattern underlying the development of explicit statements of oneness that thrive later in specifically Gnostic contexts.

g) Esoteric Rabbinic Tradition

Fringe developments within Judaism point to variations that have significant implications for the further characterization of the oneness motif. Of importance here are early traces of esoteric rabbinic traditions and the problem of

---

[1] In Philo Logos takes the place of Sophia in the world (references in B.L. Mack, *op. cit.*, pp. 181f.) and is represented by figures like Moses, Abraham, Isaac, and Jacob-Israel. Israel is spiritualized and takes on cosmic proportions.

their relation to Jewish mysticism, Merkaba and Hekaloth speculations. For our purposes a significant case in point is the variation on the אֲנִי הוּא and שֵׁם הַמְפֹרָשׁ traditions, where the altered form of "I and He" (וְהוּא אֲנִי) appears. The traditional אֲנִי הוּא form is typically OT (e.g. Deut. 32:39) and Is. 43:11) and in rabbinic Judaism is used occasionally as an equivalent for the Divine name.[1] Although the context is essentially the same, the alteration from אֲנִי הוּא to וְהוּא אֲנִי introduces an important new factor. According to the oft-cited tradition in the Mishnah tractate (M. Sukkah IV, 5b:

רַבִּי יְהוּדָה אוֹמֵר אֲנִי וְהוּא וְהוֹשִׁיעָה נָּא אֲנִי וְהוּא וְהוֹשִׁיעָה נָּא[2]

"Rabbi Judah used to say, 'I and he deliver now.'"

This tradition has reference to the Sukka festival where the priests encircle the altar and chant the prayer of Ps. 118:25 "Oh Lord, deliver!" But in the variation of R. Judah the "I and He" phrase is used as an equivalent term for God, suggesting some element of duality. Formally there is an affinity here to the phenomenology inherent in the Gnostic formulas of reciprocity. Odeberg surmises that the underlying meaning of R. Judah's words, although obscured by the rabbinical tradition, is based on the mystical belief that salvation was to be brought about through the union of the Holy One and his Shekinah hypostatized in the temple.[3] Dodd, citing further passages from R. Akiba and Abba Shaul,[4] refers the "I and He" expression to the community character between God and Israel. In any case, the אֲנִי וְהוּא expression suggests an incipient reciprocity form, foreign to orthodox Judaism and thus repressed, but reminiscent of standard Gnostic formulations and consonant with the character of the קוֹמָה שִׁעוּר and שֵׁם הַמְפֹרָשׁ traditions in Jewish esoteric circles where convergence with syncretistic Gnostic elements is particularly noticeable.[5]

---

[1] Cp. passages cited by Dodd, *Interpretation*, pp. 93ff.
[2] *Die Mischna* (hrsg. v. H. Bornhäuser), Berlin, 1935, pp. 116f.
[3] Odeberg, *The Fourth Gospel*, p. 332.
[4] Dodd, *Interpretation*, p. 95.
[5] Cp. the outstanding study of points of contact between early talmudic tradition, Jewish Merkabah mysticism, Gnostic speculations, and theurgic elements in the Hekaloth literature and mystical texts by G. Scholem, *Jewish Gnosticism, Merkabah Mysticism, and Talmudic Tradition*, New York,

h) Qumran

The sectarians at Qumran provide us with further material for the characterization of the oneness motif. Too orthodox to adopt explicit reciprocity formulas and expressions of oneness describing faith relationships, these heterodox Jews nonetheless understood themselves as a whole in terms of oneness, i.e. as a unity.¹ In fact, they called themselves the יחד, literally "the togetherness" or the unity. Appearing almost always in the substantive form, this designation in Qumran takes on the character of a terminus technicus and is simply the substitute name for the community. The term evidently experienced its own history of development within the Qumran circles since it appears profusely in the Manual of Discipline (ca. 66x substantively and 4x verbally) but then only in scattered form in the remaining texts (cp. 16x in 1QH; 9x in 1QSa and QSb; 1x in QHab.). In the War Scroll the term occurs both adverbially (5x) and substantively (2x) but always in a general sense and never as a fixed designation for the community. In the Damascus Document the יחד term is used only in XX, 1, 14, 32 and gives way to the more frequent ברית designation. The typically OT designations עם אל, קהל אל, קהל, עדה and מועד אל, are either consciously avoided in Qumran or diminished in meaning.² The characteristic Qumranitic designation of יחד, on the other hand, has its roots neither in the OT nor in rabbinic tradition.³

1965, esp. pp. 36ff. and 81ff. Further, H. Fischel, "Jewish Gnosticism in the Fourth Gospel," *JBL*, 65, 1946, p.172. G. Quispel, "Gnosticism and the New Testament," *The Bible in Modern Scholarship*, pp.252-271. H. Jonas, in his reply to Quispel's essay, emphasizes "the anti-Jewish animus" of Gnosticism (*The Bible in Modern Scholarship*, p.292). And yet the interaction of Jewish elements in the emergence of Gnosis is so broad that it is questionable whether its part can be termed as only catalytic (so Jonas). Cp. K.Rudolph, "Gnosis und Gnostizismus," *Theol.Rund.*, 2, 1971, pp.89-119.

¹ Cp. K. Kuhn, "Die in Palästina gefundenen hebr. Texte und das NT," *op. cit.*, p.198, n.1: "Der genaue Sinn des Nomens יחד ist 'Einheit' und von da aus 'Gemeinschaft', 'Gemeinde'." Dupont-Sommer, *The Essene Writings from Qumran*, (tr. by G. Vermes), Oxford, 1961, p.44, maintains that the term is "the exact equivalent of the Greek κοινωνία employed by Philo and Josephus."

² G. Baumbach, *Qumran und das Johannes-Evangelium*, Berlin, 1957, p.23⁴³.

³ S. Talmon, "The Sectarian יחד --a Biblical Noun," *Vetus Testamentum*, 3, 1953, pp.133-144, argued for an OT background. Similarly A. Neher ("Echos de la secte de Qumran dans la littérature talmudique," *Les manuscrits de*

As a substantive the term יחד appears only once in the OT
(I Chr.12:17 "I will have a heart toward you for united-
ness."), three times in verbal form[1] (Gn.49:6; Is.14:20; and
Ps.86:11), and frequently as an adverb. Thus the OT usage
clearly offers no point of contact with the stereotyped substantive designation in Qumran. The distance at this point
between Qumran and the OT is analogous to the distance between Qumran and the Judaism represented in the Jerusalem temple. In opposition to the rest of Judaism the Qumran sectarians understood themselves as the real representatives of Israel, the elect, who in total obedience to the Law fulfill
the stipulations for the final apocalyptic coming of eschatological salvation. As has often been pointed out, the double (polaric) meaning of the semitic root יחד, --together
one/alone--[2] gives expression to the essential character of
the community in its tight covenant fellowship and in its
separation from the rest of Judaism as well as in its isolation from the world. And yet the actual pre-history of the
term and its development leading to the level of usage manifested in Qumran remain obscure. Some studies have attempted
to establish parallels with Hellenistic ideas suggesting e.g.
that the Qumran community represents a mystery group based on
a common life shaped after the Greek πόλις pattern.[3] But the
dominant ritual-cultic aspects of the term, together with its
association with Temple symbolism as well as its pointed absence in other eschatological texts apart from Qumran, in-
crease the likelihood of locating the specific background
within Jewish priestly traditions. This, of course, does not
exclude the possibility of syncretistic influences.

The יחד is variously described as "the unity (community) of

---

la Mer Morte colloque de Strasbourg, 1957, pp. 44-60) who points out in addition rabbinical parallels. And yet these positions have not been able
to be maintained. Cp. the cogent critical reaction by J.C. de Moor, "Lexical Remarks Concerning yaḥad and yaḥdaw," Vetus Testamentum, 7, 1957, pp.
350-355. J. Maier, Zum Begriff יחד in den Texten von Qumran," ZAW, 72,
1960, pp. 148f.
[1] Other instances such as the oft cited Deut.33:5 have adverbial meaning.
Cp. Brown, Driver, Briggs, Hebrew and English Lexicon of the Old Testament, Oxford, 1957, p. 403.
[2] J.C. de Moor, op. cit. J. Maier, op. cit., p. 149.
[3] So B. Dombrowski, "היחד in 1QS and τὸ κοινόν. An Instance of Early Greek
and Jewish Synthesis," Harvard Theol. Rev., July, 1966, pp. 293-307.

God" (1QS I,12; II,22), "the unity of truth (1QS II,24,26), "the holy unity" (1QS IX,2), "the unity of his council" (1QS III,6), "the unity of the everlasting Covenant" (1QS V,6), and a "unity in the Law" (1QS V,2). The place of the Tora in the יחד was central; in fact, the Tora was the integrating center.[1] Every initiate took an oath of obligation to be converted to the Law of Moses (1QS V,8). And if anyone through slackness or deliberation should sin against the Law of Moses, he would be expelled from the community and would not be allowed to return (1QS VIII,22,23). Entrance into the יחד was an act of the free will. Indeed, the novitiates as well as the members were simply called נדבים, the volunteers (1QS I, 7,11; V,21,22). And yet only the elect, the predestined ones who walk in the way of light (1QS III,19f.), were members of the community.[2] All those outside of the יחד stood under God's wrath and curse (1QS II,17; V,12) and were subject to the dominion of the Angel of darkness (1QS III,20). Consequently the יחד stood in strict antithesis to the world. Radical separation was demanded from anyone who was not a part of the community (1QS V,1,10; VIII,13; IX,9,20). Here there was no neutrality. Those outside of the community merit only hate and reproach (1QS I,10; IX,21) while the command to live in love and charity applies only to the members of the יחד. This rigorous application of love and hate is but a reflection of God's own action as He loves everlastingly and delights in his own works (1QS III,26) but loathes the counsel of "the other" and hates his ways forever (1QS IV,1).[3]

Further characteristic for the יחד is a rigid organizational pattern in which the priests occupied the highest rank (1QS I,18f. II,19f. VI,8), followed by the Levites and the lay (1QS II). The superior rank of the priests was not only indicative of the structured nature of the community but gave the יחד its marked cultic character. Lustral washings, cultic

---

[1] H. Braun, *Spätjüdisch-häretischer und frühchristlicher Radikalismus*, I, Beitr. z. Hist. Theol, 24, Tübingen, 1957, pp. 15-32.
[2] Qumran maintained the paradox between predestination and human freedom. Cp. H. Braun, *Qumran und das Neue Testament*, II, Tübingen, 1966, pp. 125f. 243-245.
[3] Baumbach, *op. cit.*, p. 34.

meals, and ritual purity distinguished life within the יחד from the unconverted ways of those on the outside. טהרה was one of the gifts of the Spirit (1QS IV,5) and although ritual lustrations themselves did not remove impurity as long as the person did not subject himself to the ordinances of God (1QS III,4-6), still ritual impurity was considered as a cause of contamination (1QS VI,16; VII,19,20).[1] On the one hand, ritual stipulations were placed with exacting rigor. And yet, on the other hand, true purity was not ritually constituted but was effected only through conversion to the יחד in total obedience to the Tora.

A further characteristic of the oneness life in the Qumran community was a mutual sharing and possession of goods (1QS VI,19). This communality of possessions was not the result of a monastic ideal of poverty. Rather it was a stipulation progressively exacted in correspondence with the degree of integration into the community (1QS VI,17,21). Full membership meant common ownership of goods and wages. Thus the community could be referred to simply as the יחד in חון (1QS V,2).

A final feature of importance in the יחד terminology is its symbolic correspondence with the temple. That is particularly significant since the community had separated itself from the official temple service in Jerusalem. Nonetheless, temple nomenclature is used to describe the יחד as "a foundation of truth for Israel" (1QS V,5), "the house of truth in Israel" (1QS V,6), "the house of holiness for Israel" (1QS VIII,5), "the Dwelling of infinite holiness for Aaron" (1QS VIII,8f.), "the tried wall, the precious cornerstone; its foundations shall not tremble" (1QS VIII,7). The temple allusions present an important aspect of the community's self-understanding and demonstrate once again its cultic priestly character.[2]

It should also be noted that for Qumran expressions of oneness and reciprocity are never used to describe the Messiah figures --the priestly messiah of Aaron, the royal Davidic

---

[1] Cp. Braun, *Radikalismus*, I, p. 29, n.5; p. 35.
[2] J. Maier, *op. cit.*, pp. 160f.

messiah of Israel, and the prophet or the Teacher of Righteousness.[1] Nor are their relations either to God or to the sectaries identified in terms of mutual immanence or oneness. Use of oneness language is reserved for a description of the community alone. In summary it may be said that as a motif "oneness" characterizes the Qumran sectaries as a single body joined together in covenant by a radicalized understanding of and obedience to the Tora and set off from others in strict antithesis to all outsiders. The oneness of the sectaries is further characterized by a tight organizational structure, ritual priestly practice, and by common ownership of goods. While the structural and jurisdictional aspects of this oneness are evident, its essence is conceived of as consisting not in participation in organizational community but in a converted life totally regulated by absolute obedience to the Law.

i) Mandaean Gnosis

We turn now to a final complex of literature, the Mandaean texts whose substratum has with increasing probability been identified with a heretical Jewish sectarian movement which already in its Syrian-Palestinian place of origin was thoroughly imbued with Gnostic thought.[2] The terminology and nomenclature developed in these texts is peculiarly Mandaean but the underlying phenomenology of the mythology and of the Mandaean self-understanding follows distinct Gnostic patterns. Of significance for our investigation is the basic pattern of soteriology in which relationships between the light world, its messengers, and the believers are described in terms of a oneness of mutuality and togetherness.

A key concept at work is that of Laufā or communion,[3] a designation by means of which expression is given to a type of oneness motif characteristic for Mandaean faith and cultic

---

[1] Braun, *Qumran*, II, pp. 54-84.
[2] Cp. K. Rudolph, *Die Mandäer I: Prolegomena, Das Mandäerproblem*, Göttingen, 1960. Foerster, *Die Gnosis*, II, p. 182. Leipoldt-Grundmann, *Umwelt*, I, pp.396-401. S. Schulz, "Die Bedeutung," *op. cit.*, pp.316-329.
[3] E. Drower, R. Macuch, *A Mandaic Dictionary*, Oxford, 1963, p. 227. E. Drower, *The Mandaeans of Iraq and Iran*, Oxford, 1937, p. 180.

practice. This may be seen, first of all, in the understanding of the nature of the heavenly envoys. For the Mandaeans there are numerous revealer figures, pre-eminent among whom is Manda d'Haije and next to whom are the three Uthras, Hibil, Shitil, and Enosh.[1] Since these messengers are understood as transcendent beings whose origin is in the world of light, their relation to the Great God (mar a d̲rabuta) can be described in terms of a oneness of togetherness. They are bound through Laufā. Thus the Great God can say to Shitil: "Deine Rede sei unsere Rede; sei mit uns verbunden (verbunden durch unsere Laufā) and werde nicht abgeschnitten (G̲.R̲. 146, 9f.).[2] The Great Life commissions Enosh and declares: "Wenn Angst dich befällt, werden wir alle bei dir sein." (G̲.R̲. 296, 38f.). The envoy is not alone but is in constant communion with the Transcendent: "Aber ich habe eine Stütze darin, daß ich weiß, daß ich nicht allein stehe" (Johannes Buch 39,15f.).[3] The reciprocity formulas so typical for the Hellenistic mysteries and Gnostic movements do not appear here. That may be due not only to the Semitic character but to the isolated development experienced by the Mandaeans. What is significant, however, is the central role of revealer figures and, common to Gnostic thought, their identification of essence and origin with the transcendent world.

This mutuality in identification is characteristic also for the relation of the believers to the heavenly world. Thus the divine messenger can speak to the soul: "Dir sind wir (zu eigen). Wir sind bei dir und deine Gestalt (oder: dein Abbild) leuchtet durch uns" (G̲.L̲.II,7).[4] The lack of communion (Laufā) with the divine world is the cause of evil.[5] "Die Bösen wollen sie (die Seele) in einzelne Teile spalten" (G̲.R̲.3, 103).[6] Laufā is therefore no possession of the world

---

[1] Cp. Foerster, *Die Gnosis*, II, p. 188. Also Dodd, *Interpretation*, p.127.
[2] Unless otherwise indicated, references to both the right (G.R.) and to the left (G.L.) parts of the *Ginza* are cited by page number in M. Lidzbarski's translation, *Ginza, Der Schatz oder Das Große Buch der Mandäer*, Göttingen, 1925.
[3] *Das Johannes-Buch der Mandäer*, (Lidzbarski), Gießen, 1915.
[4] Foerster, *Die Gnosis*, II, p. 331.
[5] Cp. Rudolph, *Die Mandäer*, II, p. 237: "Die Hauptsünde ist...die Aufhebung der 'Laufa' mit der Lichtwelt."
[6] Foerster, *Die Gnosis*, II, p. 254.

(G̲.L̲. 65,11). It is a transcendent reality proleptically received through cultic experience and sealed in the beyond after death.[1] Laufā is the final goal of the soul, i.e. reintegration into its original state of being ("ihre Skina sei im Hause des Lebens" G̲.R̲. 241,34). Accordingly, the believer can say, "ich kam und fand das Leben meiner selbst" (Mand. Lit. Qol. 30).[2] And yet this self-discovery is contingent on the function of the heavenly messenger. "Als ich kam, ich der Gesandte des Lichtes... (da) kam ich Laufā und Glanz in meiner Hand" (G̲.R̲. 57,33). Oneness is initiated by the Great God of Life. "Das Leben streckte (seine Hand) aus, schloß Gemeinschaft (Laufā) mit ihr, (so) wie die Auserwählten am Lichtort Gemeinschaft (Laufā) schließen" (G̲.L̲. III,5).[3]

For the Mandaean union can be realized through ritual practice. Baptism (masbūtā)[4] brings Laufā. "Mit der großen Taufe tauft er sie und verbindet sie (auf diese Weise) mit der großen Laufā..." (Joh. Buch 74).[5] Just as the baptismal act so also accompanying actions involving sacramental bread (Pihtā) and water (mambūhā)[6] mediate union with the Transcendent. "Glanz kam aus dem Pihtā heraus... Als er (Glanz) über dem Tanna (creative potency) loderte, entstanden die Mambuhas, entstand die Gemeinschaftlichkeit (Laufā), die ohne Unterbrechung (Psaqtā) ist. Es entstand die Gemeinschaft mit dem Leben ...das Leben stellte sich in den Quellen des Wassers auf" (G̲.R̲.240,3ff.). Next to the baptismal practices the ceremony for the dead (mas(a)iqta) is the most important ritual action.[7] It is, in fact, one of the essential marks of Mandaean religion. Coupled with the Masiqta are numerous related ritual actions.[8] Purpose of the ceremonies is to assist the soul in its migration to complete Laufā with the world of light. (Mand. Lit. 115,3ff.). Complete union with the Transcendent, i.e. reintegration into the world of light, is

---

[1] Rudolph, Die Mandäer, II, p. 153.
[2] Foerster, Die Gnosis, II, p. 360. Cp. further p. 375.
[3] Foerster, Die Gnosis, II, p. 339. See also p. 210.
[4] Rudolph, Die Mandäer, II, pp. 74ff.
[5] Foerster, Die Gnosis, II, p. 290.
[6] Lidzbarski, Ginza, p. 19 n.7.
[7] Rudolph, Die Mandäer, II, pp. 259ff.
[8] E. Drower, The Mandaeans, pp. 210ff.

achieved only after death.

Just as Laufā or oneness is the essential character of heavenly reality (all the Uthras are bound together through Laufā (G.R. 302,16) so the Mandaean community, in earthly reflection of heavenly reality, is characterized by Laufā (G.R. 283,20; 284,2; 285,15,17). An important ritual action symbolizing this oneness was the Kusta handshake.[1] "Kusta" conveys the meaning both of faithfulness and truthfulness as well as also the soteriological meaning of redemptive power. As such it can be hypostatized as the redeemer. In its immanent sense, however, Kusta characterizes the nature of the community. Accordingly the Mandaean community can be designated as "Brüder in Kustā" (G.R. 20,14), "Diener der Kustā" (G.R. 58,13), "Kinder der Kustā" (G.L. 591,1) etc. The Kustā handshake, in turn, demonstrates the self-understanding of the Mandaean community. They are bound together in a communion that is a projection of the communion of the transcendent world. "Reichet einander die Rechte und machet euren Treuschwur (Kustā) nicht zur Lüge. Denn die Uthras und Könige des Lichtes gewähren einander Bündnis (Laufā) und Treuschwur (Kustā) (G.R. 22,6).

j) Summary

Sorting through the contours and lines of development displayed in the various religio-historical areas discussed above, we may briefly summarize our findings as they relate to the Johannine oneness motif. From a formal language perspective the reciprocity formulas that occur in the Hellenistic mysteries provide an initial point of contact with the Johannine expression of mutual immanence. But since these mystery formulas are restricted in their use to a description of the relation between God and the mystic believer who through cultic, esoteric experience is absorbed into the Divine, they are too narrow in scope to provide a cogent analogy with the Johannine use of the oneness motif. In the broad phenomenon of Gnosis, on the other hand, the motif of

---

[1] Rudolph, *Die Mandäer*, II, p. 145.

oneness receives a much more extensive base. In fact, it is a constitutive factor in the structure and substance of the Gnostic self-understanding, soteriology, and world view.

For the Gnostic the state of oneness is descriptive of the transcendent world per se; division is the mark of evil and fallenness. Redeemer figures, variously described, are essentially one with the heavenly world from which they were sent in order to bring divine revelation.[1] The essence of the believers and their destiny is also understood in terms of oneness. In response to the awakening call of the heavenly envoy, the individual soul can be re-established in a relationship of oneness to its transcendent origin and in projection of that heavenly oneness be joined in earthly communion with fellow Gnostics. It is within this context that the language of oneness developed a distinctly theological significance and as a motif experienced its broadest ramifications. The Johannine mise-en-scène and its predilection for the language of oneness and reciprocity reflect interaction with these developments. John's christology was such that the Gnostic oneness terminology could be readily adopted. This is not to say that the evangelist borrowed from a fixed Gnostic system. Rather it would seem that he was exposed to a fluid cross-movement of varying Gnostic traditions, which contributed as catalyzers in the formation of the character of the structures and language he uses to convey his unique Gospel witness. As has often and rightly been pointed out, the typically Gnostic idea of the pre-existent consubstantiality between the Divine and the redeemed, the prolix mythological descriptions of cosmology, the ascent of the soul, and the transcendent scenes are all absent in the Fourth Gospel. And yet the Johannine oneness language, which describes the relation of solidarity between Father and Son, between the believer and God, and among the believers, has its closest parallel to the language of Gnostic phenomenology.

---

[1] E. Percy's objection (*Untersuchungen*, p. 206) that "der Gedanke bei Joh. der einzigartigen absoluten Gemeinschaft zwischen Vater und Sohn... in den mandäischen Schriften kein Gegenstück (hat)" can hardly invalidate the broader formal affinities that consist in the heavenly nature of the revealer.

SUMMARY

A similar parallel to OT or orthodox Jewish traditions cannot be maintained. There the relational character of the oneness motif is singularly absent. The extent to which oneness appears as a motif at all in the OT is to express the exclusiveness and absoluteness of God. This aspect of oneness is also included in the Johannine conception as when Jesus in x.16 declares that there will be one Shepherd. But in John this exclusivistic aspect is contingent on the relational. There is and can be only one Shepherd because Jesus and the Father are one. The relational aspects of the oneness theme are basically foreign to the OT as well as to Judaism and begin to appear only in peripheral esoteric and sectarian movements. A notable exception within the perimeters of traditional Judaism can be seen in the wisdom traditions which incorporate some basically non-Israelitic tendencies that describe a hypostatized and personal wisdom in a oneness relationship with God and man. The underlying structure in this scheme closely parallels the revelational structure that develops in specifically Gnostic circles.

In Jewish apocalyptic traditions the movement represented at Qumran offers initially another point of contact. Although the יחד terminology of Qumran was at first heralded to be the closest parallel to John's oneness motif,[1] the contention has since lost its plausibility. True, there are lines of analogy between Qumran and the Fourth Gospel as e.g. in the strict antithesis to the world and in the absence of the command to love one's neighbor. But real analogies cease when it comes to the use of oneness terminology. In Qumran oneness applies only to an exclusive community which is priestly oriented and dominated by Tora obedience. In John, on the other hand, oneness describes not only the inter-relationship among the believers but above all the believer's oneness relation to the Son who in turn is one with the Father.

---

[1] F.M. Cross, *The Ancient Library of Qumran and Modern Biblical Studies*, New York, 1958, p. 156: "The Johannine phrases, 'that they may be one,' 'become perfectly one'...use typical Essene diction." R. Brown (*John*, II, 777) has tried to further this thesis in maintaining that the religious vocabulary of Qumran is the best parallel to John's oneness motif. "It is not impossible that the Johannine hen, 'one,' literally translates the concept yaḥad."

Results of Section A: When the results of our findings thus far in section A are summarized, the following picture emerges. Because of its tightly structured form bearing the distinctive marks of extended repetitive parallelism embracing a series of 10 (12) separate and mutually balanced parts, the passage in vs.20-23 gives the first hand appearance of an isolable unit of pre-formed tradition. The preponderance of the reciprocity phrases and the relational statements expressing oneness reveal such a striking affinity to the phenomenology of fundamental Gnostic thought patterns and speech modes that these must be considered as constitutive elements in the formation of the tradition in its original context.

Although strictly speaking only one stylistic factor (καθώς ...καί) can be specifically claimed for the evangelist, the presence of such other accompanying factors as the ἵνα constructions, the asyndetic phrase in v.22, the οὐ μόνον...ἀλλὰ καί usage in v.20, as well as the placement of the verb before the noun (v.23), the casual comparative use of καθώς (v.23), the preference shown the perfect tense, and the terminology used are all so thoroughly Johannine in character that it is not possible to make a definitive separation between an original layer of tradition and the evangelist's own composition.

The evidence points to a highly stylized passage permeated with Johannine literary and terminological characteristics and reminiscent of Gnostic speech modes. Beyond that it may be said that the confessional kerygmatic nature of the two ὅτι clauses suggest formative levels of tradition within the Johannine church. It is within the stream of that tradition that the entire passage with its typical oneness and reciprocal expressions may well have received the elements of a fixed form before adaptation by the evangelist, although the exact extent of these inner relationships can no longer be precisely determined.

The problem of pre-formed material is much less acute in v.11 where the εἷς motif appears in a single clause closely woven into the fabric of the surrounding thoughts and demonstrating similar stylistic and religio-historical characteristics as those discussed for vs.20-23. It remains for us to examine the relation of these passages to the larger context in which they are embedded and to consider their place in the prayer as a whole.

B. THE LITERARY CHARACTER OF CHAPTER 17

Ever since David Chytraeus (1531-1600) spoke of the 17th chapter as a "praecatio summi sacerdotis," it has been customary to refer to this chapter as Jesus' high priestly prayer. The designation took its cue from v.19 where Jesus declares: "And for their sakes I consecrate myself." The words ὑπὲρ αὐτῶν and ἁγιάζω have obvious sacrificial tones in NT tradition. Within the context of the letter to the Hebrews or to the Corinthians (cp. Hebr.2:11; I Cor.1:30), their connection with the work of atonement is clear. But the picture is different in the Fourth Gospel. While it is true that scattered references are made to Jesus' expiatory death (10:15,17; 11:50; 15:13), it must be noted that these occur in traditional statements and are not developed as such as part of the evangelist's general theme. In fact, the motif of sacrifice is clearly peripheral to his Gospel's orientation.

Apart from the occurrence in 17:17,19, ἁγιάζω appears only in 10:36. In both instances it has a primary reference to sending and mission. In 10:36 Jesus identifies himself as "the one whom the Father consecrated and sent into the world." Here ἡγίασεν καὶ ἀπέστειλεν form a hendiadys and are mutually complementary in meaning. Jesus was sent even as he was set aside (ἁγιάζω) for the specific works which the Father gave him to do. He was consecrated even as the Father sent him into the world.[1] The force of ἁγιάζω here is to emphasize reciprocity with the Father. That is further underscored by the context. The Jews do not take offense because Jesus is identified in terms of the priest who will offer himself as a sacrifice. Instead, they are offended because of the oneness he claims with the Father.[2]

---

[1] Significant here is the aorist tense in words spoken before the passion. The consecration is a point of action already in the past.
[2] In 6:69 Peter makes the confession, "You are ὁ ἅγιος τοῦ θεοῦ" —the only occurrence of ἅγιος, a cognate of ἁγιάζειν, applied to Jesus. Also here the connection with Jesus' oneness relationship with the Father is basic. Peter recognizes who Jesus is, namely he who has the words of eternal life. Therefore he is the Holy One of God. But only he whom God has sent utters the words of God (3:34).

Similarly in 17:17,19 ἁγιάζω is distinctly qualified through the added interpretations of the sending and the culminating expression of oneness. Jesus prays for his disciples, the church, (v.17) and asks that they be set apart from the world, that is, made distinctive through exposure to God's presence, which is truth mediated through the Word. The manifestation of this consecration consists in their being sent into the world even as the Father sent the Son (v.18). The Son then states that for the sake of the disciples he consecrates himself, that is, he so fully shares in the holiness of the holy Father (v.11) that the Father is in him and he is in the Father (v.21). His consecration consists in his coming from and returning to the Father with the express purpose that his disciples be thus consecrated and so act as instruments of the Word for those who are yet to believe (v.20). Here the themes of sending, consecration, and oneness are tightly interwoven. There is no intimation of sacrifice. Despite the fact that many interpreters insist on reading this into v.19 as its primary orientation and on interpreting the entire chapter accordingly,[1] an examination of the verses in context reveals that there is nothing in the usage of ἁγιάζω in vs.17 and 19 to make necessary and explicit a reference to the death of Jesus in sacrificial terms. To refer then to the prayer as Jesus' "high priestly prayer" is clearly a misnomer.

A related problem is the oft proposed relation of ch.17 to the Eucharist. Much of the same argumentation is involved here as that discussed for v.19 with, however, the additional consideration of the general context which is taken to be that of the Upper Room and the celebration of the Last Supper. Accordingly Jesus is understood as consecrating himself unto death and declaring that his disciples should participate in that consecration by remembering his death in the Eucharist. In this light v.19 would then not only be a direct reference to the Eucharist but would help to color the entire chapter

---

[1] Pre-eminently E. Hoskyns (*The Fourth Gospel*, p. 502) who sees in v.19 the key to the entire chapter and interprets the ἁγιάζω as "Jesus dedication of himself as an effective sacrifice."

as a eucharistic prayer of the church.¹ Convincing textual evidence for this interpretation, however, is lacking. A. Greiff attempted to establish the eucharistic character of ch.17 by proposing a relation to the eucharistic prayers in Didache 9 and 10 and by citing as parallels the following occurrences: "life and knowledge" (Did.9:3); "the broken and scattered bread become one" (Did.9:4); prayer addressed to "our Father" and the "making known" theme in Did.9:2; and finally the "deliverance from evil, the perfection in love and the gathering" themes (Did.5:5).² The conclusion is drawn that Jn.17 is based on a eucharistic liturgy similar to the type represented in the Didache, and further that the evangelist used the Didache text as a kind of model or pattern. The thesis never did gain support. Closer examination reveals that the proposed parallels are at best only formal word parallels without inner correspondence and that the respective contexts are vastly different with divergent eschatologies and ecclesiologies so that no real relationship could be maintained. Didache 9 and 10 are clearly Eucharistic prayers. The same cannot be held for Jn.17.

There are intrinsic reasons for wanting to think of the Eucharist at this point inasmuch as the prayer in ch.17 appears at a place where an account of the Lord's Supper may well have been included or where at least reference to its occurrence could have been made. It has long been noted that the prayer comes as a kind of substitute. Added to this is the fact that Johannine terminology tends to lend itself easily to sacramental explication. But against these considerations are the following factors. The prayer is considerably separated from the supper mentioned in ch.13 and is further

---

[1] So O.Cullmann, *Early Christian Worship*, Studies in Biblical Theology, 10, London, 1962, p.111: "The so-called high-priestly prayer is a typical Eucharistic prayer." Similarly W.Wilkens (*Die Entstehungsgeschichte*, p.165) speaks of the Eucharist in chs. 13,14, and 17. J. Betz (*Die Eucharistie in der Zeit der griechischen Väter*, Vol.2, pt.1, Wien, 1961) describes v.19 as a paraphrase of the institution.
[2] A. Greiff, *Das älteste Pascharituale der Kirche, Didache 1-10 und das Johannesevangelium*, Schöningh-Paderborn, 1929, pp. 166f. and 182f. Similarly W. von Loewenich, *op. cit.*, p. 21. Cp. critique by J. Jeremias, *ThLZ*, 55, 1930, pp. 350f.

disconnected by the troublesome 14:31.¹ Moreover, the inner
motivation for the celebration of a Passover meal prior to
the day of crucifixion is removed within the Johannine time
scheme where the evening before is understood as the Day of
Preparation instead of the Passover day itself. Finally,
there is nothing in the text itself which makes reference to
the Eucharist a necessity. To assume that a Christian writing at the end of the first century would not have been acquainted with the Eucharist is, of course, an impossible assumption. It is all the more startling then that the evangelist should not include similar to the Synoptics an account
of the words of institution and the Last Supper. The cumulative evidence, however, compels us to conclude that there is
no warrant in stamping ch.17 as a eucharistic prayer or as
part of a sacramental liturgy of the Johannine church.²

If ch.17 contains neither a high priestly nor a eucharistic
or eucharistically-oriented prayer, then the question of its
basic character remains open for other considerations. These
will be discussed here. While it is true that homiletic-like
expansions occur in this chapter, as e.g. in vs.2,3, it is
hardly possible to categorize the whole as a sermon³ or to
make this its major orientation without failing to recognize
the intimate contemplative tones as well as the rhythmic parallelism that pervade the whole. The material has less the
character of public proclamation than that of extended reflection. For the same reason the proposal that the essential

---

¹ Bultmann (among others) helps himself by rearranging the text and by
placing ch.17 adjacent to 13:1-30 thus strengthening his claim that Jesus'
prayer is in fact the evangelist's substitute for the Eucharist (*Ev Joh,*
p. 370, n.4). His claim, however, that the prayer of Jesus appears with
"unverkennbarer Beziehung auf das Sakrament der Eucharistie" (*Ev Joh,* p.
371) is unwarranted. It is not supportable that 17:19 should be an explicit reference to the Eucharist (so Bultmann, *Ev Joh,* p. 391, n.3) and
even less so that for John "beginnt die Passion schon mit der Fleisch-
werdung."
² So also W. Thüsing, *Herrlichkeit und Einheit,* p. 125.
³ So e.g. W. Oehler, *Das Johannesevangelium eine Missionsschrift für die
Welt,* Gütersloh, 1936, who contends that chs. 15-17 originally comprised
sermon material inserted into a missionary tract. Wikenhauser (*Das Ev.
nach Johannes,* p. 36) stresses the homiletic nature of the discourse material. Cp. also Bousset, *RGG¹,* III, p. 615 or more recently Barrett (*St.
John,* p. 379) who entertains the possibility that at least the last discourses were originally eucharistic sermons.

character is that of a teaching lecture which the evangelist was accustomed to hold[1] is also inadequate. There is no indication that the setting was determined by school-like circumstances which left their didactic imprint on the formation of the material.[2] Certainly there are elements of instruction that are characteristic for the chapter. And yet the category of instruction can hardly apply to the whole. There are other characteristic elements as well, such as prophecy (v. 20), confirmation (v.6), comfort (v.20), confession (v.3), and petition (v.17). Furthermore, unlike e.g. the Sermon on the Mount or a public exposition, the material of ch.17 has an arcane and exclusivistic character. The once popular interpretation describing Jesus as the mystagogue, the supreme and representative initiate, who provides instruction for his own, leading them into mystical union through the vision of God,[3] gives at least expression to the important recognition that the orientation of ch.17 is not to the world. The words spoken there are aimed, as it were, at the initiate few who are qualified by a relationship of solidarity with God. They receive what the world cannot see and hear. Nevertheless, the category of mysticism is much too misleading to be retained.[4] Ch.17, as well as for that matter the entire Fourth Gospel, is anything but mystical.

---

[1] P. Gächter, "Der formale Aufbau der Abschiedsrede Jesu," ZKTh, 58, 1934, p. 203f.: "die Abschiedsrede kann...nur die Wiedergabe von Lehrvorträgen sein, die Joh. mit wesentlich gleichem Inhalt und in gleicher Form...zu halten pflegte.

[2] K. Stehdahl (*The School of St. Matthew*, Philadelphia, 1968, p. 163) contends that the Fourth Gospel developed within the school of St.John "where the Scriptures were studied and meditated upon in the light of preaching, teaching, and debating in which the church was involved." Stendahl adopts theses here developed earlier by W. Heitmüller, "Zur Johannes-Tradition," ZNW, 15, 1914, p. 207 and W. Bousset, *Jüdisch-christlicher Schulbetrieb in Alexandria und Rom*, FRLANT N.F. 6, Göttingen, 1915. Schlatter's objection is still (p.x) apropos "daß die Formel 'johanneische Schule' für mein Auge völlig phantastisch wird." Instead of a Johannine school it is more appropriate to speak of the Johannine church community which served as the context for the development of a specifically Johannine theology.

[3] Typical here is W.Bousset (*Kyrios Christos*, p.164) with the classic caption "Vergottung durch Gottesschau." Cp. Also Mußner, $Z\Omega H$, p.145: "bei Joh handelt es sich um innere religiöse Wirklichkeiten, die unter dem Ausdruck 'Mystik' am besten zusammengefaßt werden kann."

[4] Constitutive elements of mysticism as the gradated ascent in spirituality, the visio Dei, and apotheosis are totally absent.

THE LITERARY CHARACTER OF CHAPTER 17   199

The observation that ch.17 reflects liturgical practices of the church (cf. the address, "O holy Father") touches on an important insight. While it is clear that the chapter is not simply a collection or summary of liturgical forms and usages,[1] still it may be recognized that elements of the prayer had their home within the worship context of the Johannine community. As was shown in the analysis of vs.11,20-23, formulations were incorporated which reflected earlier formation within the worshipping community. Ch.17 is not simply the literary creation and product of the evangelist.[2] Rather we find here an illustration of the sovereign manner in which he used resources from the stream of tradition and worship experiences to which he had been exposed. John did not live in a vacuum. Even though he was substantially more than a collection or redactor, his material in ch.17 does not simply represent reflections and confessions of an individual but is intimately tied into the theological growth process of the worshipping community and moulded by the problems and conditions peculiar to situations of that community. It is within this context that the formation and crystallizytion of the material will have taken place.

The church was convinced that Jesus did not stop speaking after the ascension but that the voice of the Shepherd continued to be heard afresh and anew in speech moved by the Spirit who takes what is Christ's and declares it to the disciples (16:15). The prayer of ch.17 has an inner connection with the worship experiences of the Johannine church and in reflecting a segment of Jesus' life reflects simultaneously the life and faith of the congregation. It is not altogether impossible that parts of ch.17 constituted actual prayers of the congregation.[3] Although the rhythmic parallelism of the chapter gives some merit to the claim that the material is a "prayer-hymn,"[4] the hymnic properties are not consistent and

---
[1] Käsemann, *RGG*³, IV, p.403: "Phantastisch erscheinen die Versuche...aus den joh. Abschiedsreden liturgische Summarien ...zu erheben."
[2] Against W. Bauer (*Joh. Ev.*, p.207) who maintains for ch.17: "Wir haben es also mit einem schriftstellerischen Produkt des Evangelisten zu tun..."
[3] So also G. Wetter, *Der Sohn Gottes*, p. 61.
[4] O. Michel, "Das Gebet d. scheidenden Erlösers," *op. cit.*, p. 522, speaks of a "Gebetshymnus."

pervasive enough to justify that kind of caption. Despite the analogy to what may be a hymnic unit in 13:31,32,[1] it should be noted that ch.17 is considerably longer and by contrast much more complex and fluid in form and content.

Another category to be mentioned is one suggested by parallels with the Testament literature of late Judaism. Accordingly Jesus' words here have been referred to as his last will and testament.[2] But as a general category for the chapter, the designation is not wholly adequate because it tends to blur the evangelist's concern that Jesus' will is always contemporary. Jesus does not leave behind a "last" will or a "final" legacy as though he were a religious founder or a patriarchal progenitor passing on his last wishes or a code of instructions and teachings. Furthermore, the suggestion of a last will is nowhere given in the text. This brings us after a rather long and circuitous route back to the statement that despite the variety of its inherent elements, ch.17 is preeminently and foremost a prayer --the prayer of the departing Jesus[3] or the farewell prayer of the Revealer.

Jesus' prayer is typically Johannine in nature and bears characteristics that are unique to the Fourth Gospel. This may be seen by a comparison with the form of prayer as it otherwise appears in OT and NT and related texts. Two basic component parts which regularly characterize the form of prayer in the OT are lamentation and petition. Added to these are frequently expressions of praise and thanksgiving and also confessions of sin. In post-exilic times the confession of sin appears with even greater regularity (cp. Ezra 9 and Dn.9). Coupled with the confession is the plea

---

[1] Because of their unified rhythmic form with five balanced parts, devoid of Johannine stylistic characteristics, Blauert (*Die Bedeutung der Zeit*, p. 33) identified these two verses as a pre-Johannine (Joh.=evgst.) hymn reminiscent of the Prologue. Similarly S.Schulz, *Untersuchungen*, p.120f.
[2] Cp. Käsemann's title, *Jesu Letzter Wille Nach Johannes 17*, Bultmann (*Ev Joh*, p. 401, n.1): "In Kap.17 bringt sich die Gemeinde vielmehr das Vermächtnis Jesu zum Bewußtsein."
[3] Barrett (*St. John.*, p.416) formulates simply: "the prayer of Jesus." Bultmann (*Ev Joh*, p. 371): "the farewell prayer." O. Michel's formulation, "Das Gebet des scheidenden Erlösers" (*op. cit.*) introduces a category foreign to John, i.e. the Redeemer, and therefore is not acceptable.

for forgiveness and for God's intervention in the affairs of
his people. Particularly in the Psalm prayers we find in addition to the elements already mentioned (lamentation, petition, thanks, praise, and confession) also the forms of retrospect of God's saving acts, requests for retribution, and
vows for future action. The language is noticeably stylized.
Even the wholly personal prayers of lamentation employ phraseology typical for conventionalized formulations.[1] In the earlier period of the OT the concerns of the individuals tend to
merge more readily into those of the larger group whereas in
later times prayers of specific individuals play an increasing
prominent role.

The prayer of the mediator has in many respects its own
history. The intercessor speaks on behalf of others as e.g.
Abraham prays for Sodom (Gen.18) or Moses for Pharaoh (Ex.7f.).
Here prayer has more the nature of dialogue or conversation.
In the days of the prophets intercessary prayer appears as a
prophetic function even when for a time this is interdicted.
(Jer.7:16). In the post-exilic period the intercessary
prayer shifts more into the sphere of distinctly priestly
tasks. A further development may be noted in the elevation
of the intercessor to a heavenly figure (Zech.3). This is a
development especially prominent in apocalyptic contexts
where the pious can no longer approach God directly but need
an intermediary in the person of a heavenly Enoch, Noah, or
Moses who intercedes before the heavenly throne in view of
the impending judgment. Structural elements in these intercessory prayers are praise, retrospect, and petition.[2]

In Judaism the tendency to regulate prayer forms and to use
fixed expressions with stereotyped introductions, closings,
and responses receives significant impulses. Times and
places for prayer are stipulated including also the mode and
content of praying itself. The Shemoneh 'Esreh (the Eighteen), the table prayers, the Kaddish prayer, the travel

---

[1] Cp. G. v. Rad, *Old Testament Theology*, I, p. 398f.
[2] Cp. O. Betz (*Das Paraklet*, p. 86) who observes in regard to the intercessory prayers of late Judaism: "Lobpreis, Erinnern, und Bitte sind die drei Teile jeder Fürbitte."

prayers, and other prayers of the synagogue become standard forms.[1] A significant variation may be noted in heterodox Judaism. The Hodayot texts of Qumran preserve a prayer form which includes typically OT elements and a hymn-like lyricism but which in addition is pervaded by a meditative, at times abstract, or speculative tone.[2] Their formation and content are further characteristically colored by the community's strict separation from the world and by the representative first person speech of the Teacher in whose words the community prayerfully participates.

Although the NT contains numerous references to the practice of prayer in the life of Jesus and in the life of the church, there are relatively few places where actual prayers are retained in the text apart from brief sentences (e.g. the cross words) and fragmentary formulation as e.g. acclamations and doxological elements. Where prayers do occur, as in the eschatological Psalm-like responses of Mary (Lk.1:47ff.), or Zechariah (Lk.1:68ff.), and Simeon (Lk.2:29ff.) or in the prayer of the church after the release of Peter and John (Acts 4:24ff.) or in the Lord's Prayer, relationships with OT forms are apparent. The situation is markedly different with the prayer of Jesus in Jn.17.

The very length of Jesus' farewell prayer is already in itself a unique feature and sets it apart in the NT tradition. Doxological elements of praise and thanksgiving are absent. Traces of lamentation or confession, or expressions of doubt as implicitly noted in Jesus' Gethsemane prayer (Mt.26:36ff. par.) are nowhere to be found. Other typical categories as promise or the threat of retribution common above all to the Psalm prayers are not represented here. On the other hand, the presence of the following features is characteristic for the prayer of Jn.17. There is, first of all, the address

---

[1] Cp. W. Bousset, *Die Religion des Judentums*, pp. 367ff. G. F. Moore, *Judaism*, I, pp. 291ff. and II, p. 212f.
[2] Consider the reflective, lofty character, the frequent references to "mystery" (25x) and "knowledge" (24x), and the use of speculative imagery. Dupont-Sommer, *The Essene Writings*, p. 200, maintains that the hymns "constantly betray new ideas which are obviously connected with the religious world of Zoroastrianism and Hellenistic Gnosis."

form. The forceful directness of the simple vocatives in
vs. 1,5,11,21,24, and 25 (πάτερ (ἧρ) (4x), πάτερ ἅγιε, πατὴρ
δίκαιε)[1] without any further descriptions (cp. Mt.11:25; Mt.6:9)
or without any of the embellishments typical of the stylized
forms of prayer testify to an immediacy and closeness of
speech between Jesus and the Father. Then there is the reflective, meditative tone of the style which appears more
distant to OT forms and yet closer to the form-development of
prayer represented in the Qumranitic Hodayot prayer-canticles
marked by their antithesis to the world and by the representative first person speech in which the elect of the community
participate. Two constitutive categories of OT prayer forms
do appear in ch.17. They are the intecessory petition and
the retrospect or review of past works. Both, however, receive essential modifications in John.

We will consider the latter category first. OT prayer-
forms often embody the element of retrospect in which reference is made to past redemptive works and events determinative for Israel's salvation history. The person praying
enumerates either a single salvific event as the Exodus or he
expands over a larger range of events rehearsing highlights
from the patriarchs to the prophets. Such reviews appear as
assurances of God's faithfulness that just as he acted in the
past so he is at work in the present. It should also be noted that these reminiscences are decidedly theocentric in orientation pertaining to the works that God has wrought. Whenever, on the other hand, the works are of the one who is
praying or of the community in which he stands, then the orientation is toward confession, i.e. works which demand forgiveness and redress.

Jesus' prayer in Jn.17 also makes use of the form of retrospect but the orientation here is unique. In constantly revolving themes Jesus points to the accomplished work which he

---

[1] The fact that the first three occurrences use the form πάτερ and the last three the form πατήρ, although initially striking because of the uniformity in sequence, has no special significance. As the corrective variations in the manuscripts help to show, the use of πατήρ without the article for the vocative may be regarded as a scribal slip. Cp. Blaß-Debr., op. cit., §147,3.

has done. He has glorified the Father (v.4) and manifested his name to them whom the Father has given him (v.6). Indeed, they kept the Father's word, for Jesus gave them those words and they believed (vs.6-8). Having kept the believers in the Father's name (v.12), Jesus sent them into the world (v.18) and gave them the glory of the Father (v.22). He made the Father's name known to them (v.26) because he himself knew the Father (v.25). Here the form of retrospect is entirely personalized. It deals not with the works of another but with the work and person of the one who is praying. In place of the normative salvation-history perspective of Israel, of which there is no mention here, stands the cumulative work of the Son. Significantly, however, the Son's work is the work of the Father. Consequently there is no qualitative difference between the one who is praying and the one to whom the prayer is directed. The obvious further inference is that the Father and the Son are one.[1] In short, the reoriented use of this prayer category falls in line with the underlying theme of the oneness motif. It remains for us now to examine the other category used --that of petition.

It is clear that the form of petition provides an essential framework for Jesus' prayer in ch.17. Here Jesus makes petition for himself that he be glorified with the glory which he had from the beginning (vs.1-3,5). He makes petition for those who had been given him out of the world, and he asks that they be kept in the Father's name and that they may be one (vs.9-11). He asks further that they may be kept from the evil one (v.15) and be sanctified in the truth (v.17). Jesus also makes petition for those who are yet to believe and asks that they likewise may all be one (vs.20f.) and that they may be where he is (v.24). Even though these petitions provide the framework for Jesus' prayer, it should also be noted that the framework is at best only an outer construction. The inner motivation for these petitions has in a sense been removed since Jesus' prayers are always heard. He

---

[1] It is impossible then for the prayer to be a sign of Jesus' humiliation as e.g. G. Behler (*Die Abschiedsworte*, p. 262) maintains: "Christus kann nur beten weil er Mensch ist."

knows that the Father always hears him (11:42) because he
speaks what he has heard from the Father (8:26). His words
are not his own but the Father's who sent him (14:24). Properly construed, a petition is a request that anticipates an
answer. But for Jesus the answer is already given.[1] There is
no anticipation, no conditionality because he and the Father
are one.[2] One must ask, then, why the form of petition is
used at all? Doesn't that create an inner conflict or present at least an open redundancy?

To answer that question we must consider the witness to
Jesus' pre-passion prayer which appears to have been an integral part of the primitive Gospel tradition. That witness is
preserved variously in the Synoptic tradition as well as also
in Hebrews 5:7-8 and Jn.12:27,28. In the synoptic versions
the theme of the Passion as a "cup" that is to be drunk and
Jesus' compliance to the Father's will in drinking this cup
(of wrath) are the dominating motifs respectively developed
in each of the Synoptics. In the Epistle to the Hebrews this
prayer tradition finds further expression. The cup motif is
not mentioned nor as such is compliance to the Father's will.
Despite the lack of these verbal parallels to the Synoptics,
the basic thoughts remain similar. The synoptic motifs of
περίλυπος (Mt.22:38; Mk.14:34) and the ἐν ἀγωνίᾳ (Lk.22:44) are
echoed and equivalently expressed with the μετὰ κραυγῆς ἰσχυρᾶς
καὶ δακρύων in Heb.5:7. The counterpart to "not my will but
thine be done" is found in the Son's learning obedience
through what he suffered. Nor does the writer hesitate to
identify the reason why Jesus' prayers are answered. It is
due, to his εὐλάβεια.

In the Johannine passage (12:27,28) similar notes are
sounded but with substantial revision in meaning. The familiar theme of anguish and stress finds formal expression in

---

[1] It is therefore in a sense correct to say with W. Bauer (*Joh. Ev.*, p.154) that "der joh. Christus überhaupt nicht wirklich beten kann." This is not to say then that his praying is only a pretext or an accommodation. Much rather it is a sign of his indissoluble relationship with the Father.
[2] Unwarranted is the introduction of the category of paradox or e.g. the statement by Bultmann (*Ev Joh*, p. 374) that "der Offenbarer, gerade um seine Vollendung als Offenbarer zu gewinnen, sich in den Schranken des Menschen hält."

the Johannine τετάρακται (v.27). And yet the orientation is
different. Regardless of the possible allusion to the language of Ps.41:6,7 (LXX), it can hardly be maintained that
the evangelist deliberately makes this reference in order to
characterize Jesus as the Righteous Sufferer of the Psalm
since this motif is nowhere developed in his Gospel.[1] Furthermore, the τετάρακται of v.27 cannot be understood as an
equivalent to the Hebrew Epistle sense of "loud cries and
tears" nor to the Mt./Mk. sense of "deathly sorrow and distress" or to the Lk. accent on agony with the implication
that Jesus needs personal strengthening[2] because of the an-
guishing weight of the impending events of the Passion.[3]
These accents are all singularly absent in the Johannine account, as is underscored by the qualifying question which immediately follows with its deliberative subjunctive: καὶ τί
εἴπω. Whether or not Jesus' answer ("Father, save me from
this hour?") is an extension of the question καὶ τί εἴπω or,
reminiscent of the Synoptic petition that the cup be removed,
a precative imperative is finally immaterial since the reply
of the voice from heaven is explicitly stated as an answer
given not for the sake of Jesus, intended as a strengthening
or given because of his εὐλάβεια (Heb.5:8), but as given for
the sake of the bystanders. In failing to understand that
word, the bystanders give expression to the judgment that is
spoken against them as the world. Thus Jesus' prayer is not
really petition at all but rather serves to illustrate his
continuing communion with the heavenly world, the rejection
of which results in judgment and darkness.

The evidence is clear that the tradition of Jesus' prayer
before his Passion was deeply rooted in a broad stream of

---

[1] C.H. Dodd (*Tradition*, p. 69) maintains that this Psalm verse underlies
both the Marcan and Johannine versions and that in both Gospels Jesus is
conceived of as speaking in the character of the Righteous Sufferer. He
then draws the untenable conclusion that both Gospels therefore give expression to the same conception of the Passion.
[2] R. Brown's attempt (*John*, I, p. 476) to harmonize the Johannine version
by speaking of "Jesus' submission to God's plan...met with a reassuring
answer from the Father" cannot be substantiated. Just the opposite is
the point of John's account: Jesus himself needs no reassurance.
[3] So also Bultmann (*Ev Joh*, p. 328): "Nicht sein Seelenkampf soll sichtbar werden..."

Gospel witness. This prayer tradition was variously transmitted and given unique accents and expansions in accordance with the aims and idiosyncracies of the respective theological contexts in which it appears.[1] Thus it seems reasonable to assume that also the prayer of ch.17 received its basic impulse from this stratum of tradition. To be sure, the departing prayer of Jesus in ch.17 has no content parallel with any of the non-Johannine forms already discussed, apart from the isolated affinity between the announcement in 17:4 that the hour has come and Jesus' similar post-prayer announcement to the disciples in Mt.26:45 that the hour has drawn near or in Mk.14:41 that the hour has come (ἦλθεν). On the other hand, the connection between the prayer of ch.17 and the Johannine version of the pre-Passion prayer in 12:27,28 is so compelling that the likelihood of Jesus' farewell prayer being an independent expansion within the lines of this same general tradition is substantially secured. This, of course, is not to say that ch.17 is simply a dublette to the passage in 12:27,28. Rather it is to say that the origin and formation of the material in ch.17 received its inner justification and formative impulse from the same tradition represented in 12:27,28.

Consideration of the relationship of these two "prayers" will help to sustain the argument. The constitutive elements of the statements in 12:27,28 center around the motifs of ὥρα, ὄνομα, and δοξάζω. Jesus points to the cross in saying, "For this purpose I have come to this <u>hour</u>." Then he asks, "Father, <u>glorify</u> your <u>name</u>."[2] The voice in reply states: "I have glorified it and I will glorify it again." These same themes are central to the expansion and interpretation found

---

[1] Dodd (*Hist. Tradition*, p. 71) holds that this pre-Passion prayer tradition was one of the most strongly attested elements in the Gospel story and that this tradition was preserved in as many as four variant forms.
[2] There is no reason to suppose with R. Brown (*John*, I, p.476) or J.H. Bernard (*A Critical and Exegetical Commentary on the Gospel according to St. John*, ICC, Edinburg, 1928, p. 559) that this verse presents the Johannine version of the petition in the Lord's Prayer: "Hallowed be thy name." Similarly W.Gericke, "Zur Entdeckung des Johannes-Evangeliums," *ThLZ*, 90, 1965, p.815. Unwarranted is Barrett's interpretation (*St. John*, p. 354): "God is glorified in the complete obedience of his servant..."

in ch.17. There Jesus likewise speaks of the impending hour (v.1). The request in 12:28 that the Father glorify his name is in effect the request that the Father himself be glorified. But how does that transpire? The Father is glorified to the extent that the Son is glorified (v.1). The Son gives glory to the Father by accomplishing the work which the Father gave him to do. This work is further explicated as a manifestation of the Father's name (v.6). The Father's name is glorified (12:27) even as his name is manifested and made known. This manifestation is evidenced by the fact that those whom Jesus received receive and keep the Father's word (vs.6,7) in believing that Jesus is sent from him.

The Father's manifestation and corresponding glorification are closely related to the response of faith that characterizes the believer. Therefore the line of thought in ch.17 shifts to those who have received the word (vs.8,14) i.e. those in whom the Father's name is manifested. The request is made that they be kept in this name. While Jesus was with them, he kept them in the Father's name. Now that he is leaving, he asks that they continue to be kept. That introduces a future motif, which in summary fashion is repeated in the closing verse (v.26): "I made known to them thy name, and I will make it known." Note the correspondence between 12:28 and 17:26. Just as the Father said that he has glorified his name and will glorify it again (12:28) so the Son may say that he has made the Father's name known to the believers and he will make it known." (17:26). At the heart of this reciprocal exchange of actions and descriptions lies the witness that the Father and the Son are one. It is the oneness motif that generates the accents peculiar to the "prayer" in 12:27,28 and gives it a unique and divergent cast in comparison to the parallel traditions in the Synoptics and in the Epistle to the Hebrews. Ch.17 is an extension of the line of development begun in 12:27,28. It is a typically Johannine expansion on the pre-Passion prayer tradition of Jesus.

If these observations hold true, we may conclude that the prayer form of ch.17 is not simply an independent literary device or an artificial creation designed e.g. to facilitate spiritual dialogue[1] or to establish a solemn atmosphere for the scene.[2] Nor is it necessary to postulate derivational factors for the prayer scheme in a convergence of intertestamental trends[3] or for that matter in Gnostic mythological

---

[1] This is the implication given by Dodd (*Interpretation*, p. 419): "It is that spiritual ascent to God which is the inward reality of all true prayer." Or (p. 422): "They (the farewell discourses) are a dialogue on initiation into eternal life through the knowledge of God, ending with a prayer or hymn which is itself the final stage of initiation." Cp. Barrett (*St. John*, p. 417): "The effect of putting this summary into the form of prayer is to consummate the movement of Christ to God..."
[2] So W. Bauer, *Joh. Ev.*, p. 207.
[3] Formal resemblances between Jn. 13-17 and examples of farewell speeches in, above all, the late Jewish Testament Literature, where the dying patriarch speaks a departing discourse, have long been noted (cp. *Reallexikon für Antike und Christentum*, Bd. I, pp. 29-35. J. Munck, *Discours d'adieu dans le Noveau Testament et dans la Litterature biblique*, Neuchatel-Paris, 1950, pp. 150-170.). And yet the analogies do little to explicate the Johannine material except in a very formal sense. In an unpublished doctoral dissertation previously cited (*The Theme of Unity in John XVIII. 20-23, Its Background and Meaning*) and a subsequent summarizing essay ("The Theme of Unity in John 17:20-23," *Ephemerides Theologicae*, Louvanienses, Fasciculus 3, 1965, pp. 373-394), J.F. Randall proposes to demonstrate an evolutionary growth process for the literary genus of farewell discourses. Citing lists of OT, late Jewish, and NT passages previously compiled by Stauffer, Munck, and Schnackenburg, his study gives the initial impression of a tedious réchauffé. The main characteristics which he established for the OT and late Jewish farewell discourses are: 1) departing person says farewell to assembled family or disciples; 2) he recalls the past; 3) exhortation to be faithful to the Law; 4) predictions about the last days; 5) appoints a successor; 6) before dying he blesses or prays for them. For the NT genus Randall maintains (p.58) essentially the same characteristics with minor modifications inherent in the growth process. Then in a characteristic tour de force he cites (p.85) four final prayers (*Ps. Philo* 19:8ff. 24:3; *Jos. Ant.* II. 8; *Apoc. Bar.* 48) on the basis of which he concludes that the idea of a farewell prayer was forming a sort of literary genus as an integral part of the larger discourse genus. Randall further maintains that coupled with this literary evolution was the integration of the concept of unity. Referring to passages in *Jubilees, Syr. Baruch*, and the Testament literature (*Job, Isaac,* and the *XII Patriarchs*) which deal in general terms with the themes of unity, love, and division among the people or which refer in typically OT fashion to the one God or the one Law or the one people, Randall would like to demonstrate that beginning with the late Jewish writings the concept of unity steadily grew in importance as an integral part of the farewell discourse genus. The final implication is that John 17 has its home in this development and must be understood, particularly in reference to vs. 20-23, against this background. Randall's argument, marked by serious methodological failings and non-sequiturs, is too generalizing and too imprecise in analysis to be convincing. The Johannine oneness motif, expressed in reciprocal language and referring pre-eminently to the relation of the Revealer to God, has nothing in common with the scattered unity references that randomly appear in the Testament literature. Nor is it at all evident that the

discourse-prayer sequences.[1] On the other hand, the contention is not warranted that the evangelist was motivated by the desire to reflect a model worship pattern of the church whereby teaching and exhortation are followed by prayer.[2] There is simply no evidence to substantiate the claim that it was the evangelist's concern to preserve liturgical practices and, as it were, to camouflage these as a framework for his Gospel. Similarly untenable is the contention that the prayer of ch.17 emanates from a concern to reconstruct the

---

prayer form and, for that matter, the unity theme were organic and integral elements of the broad literary genus of farewell discourses in whose stream the evangelist was purportedly to have stood.

[1] Cp. parallels listed by W. Bauer, *Joh. Ev.*, *ad loc.* and Bultmann (*Exegetica*, pp. 87ff. and *Ev Joh*, *ad loc.* Consequently Bultmann can speak of "das von der Mythologie fast ganz gereinigte, durchgeistigte Gebet Joh.17." (*Exegetica*, p.88, n.66). Evidence, however, is too tenuous to be able to speak of a farewell prayer tradition within Gnostic texts. Of the three passages listed by Dodd (*Interpretation*, p. 420, n.1) as parallels (*C.H.* 1:31-32; V:10b-11; XIII:17-20) the following points should be noted. In I:31,32 the libellus closes with a prayer of praise to Poimandres who has imparted teaching to the initiate. It is Poimandres who departs and returns to the Powers and not the one who has spoken the prayer. In V.10b,11, after a discourse with his son Tat, Hermes concludes with a psalm-like prayer of praise which repeats the pantheistic theme of the libellus that God has created all things and all things are in him. The prayer is not characterized by any particular situation. XIII:17-20 is not a prayer at all but is specifically designated as a "hymn of rebirth" which the Powers sing to God in the Eighth Sphere. Clearly the literary relation of these passages to Jn.17 is at best remote. Similarly the prayer of λόγος τέλειος in the *Papyrus Mimaut* (cited by Reitzenstein, *Hellenistische Mysterienreligionen*, p. 285 and W. Bauer, *Joh. Ev.*, p. 208) can hardly be said to offer a pertinent parallel. Also Bultmann's reference to the *Odes of Solomon* 17:12-14 (*Exegetica*, p. 88)is anything but compelling. The passage is not a prayer, and the reference to "Fürbitte" in v.12 is too general to draw an analogy to Jn.17. In the Mandaean passages (cited by Bultmann, *Ev Joh*, p.374, n.2 and *Exegetica*, p. 87f.) where Anos-Uthra in dialogue form prays for his disciples (*Johannes-Buch*, 236-239) or where the Mandaeans pray to Manda d'Haije (*Mand. Lit.*, 140), or the individual soul laments its exile in the world (*Mand. Lit.*, 208), or the emissary reflects on his past work and asks that the faithful do not fall asleep (*Mand. Lit.*, 190-192), the situation is not that of a departing prayer.

[2] This is the suggestion advanced by Hoskyns (*The Fourth Gospel*, p.495): "it may be that the structure of chs.xiii-xvii corresponds with the structure of Christian worship at the time when the Gospel was written... If this be so, the author does intend to describe that perfect conjunction of teaching, exhortation, and prayer..." Cp. further the unsuccessful attempt by A. Guilding, *The Fourth Gospel and Jewish Worship*, Oxford, 1960, to read the Fourth Gospel against the background of a reconstructed Jewish lectionary system. Cogent critique by E. Haenchen, *ThLZ*, 86, 1961, pp.670-672.

historia of the Upper Room events.¹ Nowhere does the evangelist evidence that kind of interest. Instead we have here an independent theological expansion on the pre-Passion prayer tradition represented variously in the NT. It was this tradition which provided the inner motivation and justification for the adoption of a form which in itself presented a certain inconsistency with the Johannine description of Christ and which consequently was subject to a process of reinterpretation.

In summary we may state that our investigation has led to the following conclusions. The material and form of ch.17 appears neither as a homiletic or didactic nor as a hymnic or liturgic adaptation. It was not conceived of as the instruction of a mystagogue or as the final legacy of a great religious figure. Instead it was formed pre-eminently as a prayer, a prayer, however, which is neither sacrificial, high priestly, nor eucharistic in nature and which, furthermore, is decidedly different from the genus of prayer as otherwise found in OT and NT. Only two familiar prayer categories are employed --that of retrospect and of petition. Both are characteristically recast along lines consistent with the Johannine conception. Although the prayer form in its traditional sense appears tautologous as a medium of expression for the Johannine Jesus, still the form is used not as a literary device or as a church liturgical expression or as the reenactment of a mythological sequence analogous to other religious texts of the day, but rather as the outgrowth of the pre-Passion prayer tradition of Jesus. The net theological result is that the Johannine prayer form for the departing Jesus appears as another witness to the formative impact of the underlying motif of oneness between the son and the Father.

---

¹ So e.g. Hoskyns (*The Fourth Gospel*, p. 495): "the origin and prime significance of the prayer lie in the historic situation in the Upper Room, and its content in the words and actions of the Lord in the Upper Room..." Similarly Bernard (*Commentary*, p. 557): "We have not here a shorthand report taken down at the time, but rather the substance of sacred intercessions preserved for a half century in the memory of a disciple"

C. PROBLEMS OF INTERNAL STRUCTURE AND THEOLOGICAL VARIANCE

Now that the general character of Jn.17 has been delineated, the further problem needs to be investigated regarding the chapter's internal structure and also the related question of whether or not its contents introduce theological accents at variance with the evangelist's conception. In that case, the chapter would have to be viewed as a secondary addition and the product of a changed or changing theological point of view. Admittedly this question is a very complex one and entails consideration of the larger context of the Farewell Discourses of which the closing prayer is a part.

In the heyday of the partition hypotheses at the turn of the century with their spate of theories inspired by the wish to recover a historically reliable "Grundschrift" was the recognition that Jn.13-17 were marked by numerous aporiae and were consequently not a unified composition. The most apparent difficulties were triggered by recognition of the disjunctive conclusion to ch.14, where right in the middle of the discourses Jesus says, "Rise, let us go hence" and also by the recognition that chs.15-17, as far as their internal evidence is concerned, are not tied to any specific situation. They are, as has often been noted, "situationless." Historicizing resolutions of the problem have insisted that the remaining discourses and prayer after ch.14 were spoken along the way on the streets of Jerusalem.[1] Other proposals were either to excise the objectionable part of v.31[2] or to interpret it abstractly or spiritually.[3] None of these has proved to be an acceptable working hypothesis.

J. Wellhausen was among the first to draw incisive consequences from the aporiae. In addition to the disjuncture at 14:31, conceptual inconsistencies were pointed to as well.[4]

---

[1] So e.g. B. Westcott, *The Gospel According to St. John*, London, 1958, p. 216.
[2] So P. Corssen, "Die Abschiedsreden Jesu im vierten Evangelium," *ZNW*, 8, 1907, p. 137.
[3] Illustrations in Barrett (*St. John*, p. 379). Cp. also H. Zimmermann, "Struktur und Aussageabsicht der joh. Abschiedsreden (Joh.13-17)," *Bibel und Leben*, 8, 1967, p. 289.
[4] J. Wellhausen, *Erweiterungen und Änderungen*, pp.7-15. Also *Das Evangelium Johannis*, pp. 78f.

Thus it was claimed that chs.15-17 represent a different eschatology by remaining with the witness of the parusia, which in ch.14 had been declared superfluous. The difference in the description of the Paraclete was also noted. In 14:16,26 Jesus says that the Father will send the Paraclete. In chs. 15-17 Jesus does the sending. Another inconsistency was seen in the promised dispersal of the disciples and yet their unified appearance in 18:8 and in ch.20. Furthermore, it was maintained that the use of κόσμος, χαρά, and ἀγάπη in chs.15-17 demonstrate closer conceptual proximity to the Johannine Epistles than to the rest of the Gospel. Consequently Wellhausen was able to conclude that chs.15-17 are not organically connected with the rest of the Gospel and that their origin was due not to the Evangelist but to a supplementer who was theologically closer to the changed position represented in the Epistles. Wellhausen's cogent and concise argumentation had a logical rigor and textual consistency that were not soon to be forgotten. His essential position is maintained today and further developed in two well organized and carefully detailed studies by J. Becker.[1]

Whether or not the dismissal of chs.15-17 as literarily secondary and as theologically modified does justice to the text is open to serious question. Bearing in mind that the peculiar Johannine literary style may be the product not simply of the evangelist but characteristic for his church community, one cannot maintain that the stylistic unity of chs. 15-17 be the final index for the chapters' compositional unity. Stylistic factors can at best be an adjunct and are most aptly employed in identifying smaller isolable units of tradition but not larger complexes. Here the final decisions lie in the area of contextual and theological questions. And it is precisely at this point that the debate is most acute. The theological unity of these chapters has been variously maintained.[2] One view is to regard chs.15 and 16 as literary

---

[1] "Die Abschiedsreden Jesu im Johannesevangelium," *ZNW*, 61, 1970, pp. 215-246. "Aufbau, Schichtung und theologiegeschichtliche Stellung des Gebetes im Joh. 17," *ZNW*, 60, 1969, pp. 56-83.
[2] Cp. Corssen, "Die Abschiedsreden," *op. cit.*, p. 127. M. Dibelius, "Johannesevangelium" *RGG*², III, pp. 354f. Bultmann, *Ev Joh*, p. 349.

dublettes to ch.14, and then to see ch.17 as a kind of commentary on the whole without denying the essential theological consistency of the entire unit.[1]

Another approach is to refer the difficulties back to the process of transmission whereby chs.15-17, as composites of levels of tradition, were incorporated into the Gospel at some final point by a writer other than the evangelist. Thus, although the material retained a common theological orientation due either originally to the evangelist's own hand or to composition formed by others in intimate association with the intention represented by the evangelist, the literary breaks were never fully resolved with the result that the Fourth Gospel entered the canon without achieving a smooth contexture and without reaching a final contiguous form.[2] Still another attempt at explaining the disjunctures in these chapters without sacrificing a prevailing theological unity was to postulate a rearrangement scheme.[3] Bultmann's endeavors have been pre-eminent in this regard but have served perhaps better than any other in demonstrating that as many questions are raised in rearranging the material as are solved so that finally nothing is really gained in the process.[4] The rearrangement theories, apart from helping to delineate clearer inner textual relationships, contributed the least to resolving the problems of internal textual aporiae.

To enter the problems of internal structure and theological orientation as they pertain to the entire farewell discourse complex would take us beyond the limits of this study. Here we will have to restrict our further considerations to ch.17 alone. It is surprising that in the pertinent literature little has been devoted to ch.17 as such. Most interpreters have contented themselves to give a summary of the contents

---

[1] Thus Käsemann (*V u F*, 1942/46, p. 184): "...und c.14 und 15-16 offensichtlich lit. Dubletten darstellen, die c.17 in gewisser Weise kommentieren." Further (*ThLZ*, 64, 1939, p. 411) this relation "kann nicht aus verschiedenen Tendenzen erklärt werden."
[2] Cp. Schnackenburg, *Joh. Ev.*, I, pp. 46ff. R. Brown, *John, I*, pp. xxxii ff.
[3] For an overview of various possibilities that have been postulated cf. Bultmann, *Ev Joh*, p. 350, n.2.
[4] Cp. critique by D.M. Smith, *The Composition and Order*, pp. 116ff.

without raising the form and source critical questions and
subjecting the whole to a literary critical analysis. There
have been representative exceptions along the way. Bultmann
e.g. sought to resolve the problems by locating differences
on the level of prior tradition. Accordingly, vs.1,4-6, 9-14,[1]
16, 17, and 20-23[2] were assigned to an originally non-Christian
Gnostic revelation speech source which the evangelist demythologized, annotated with the remaining verses, and adapted
for his own purposes. This proposed source material for
ch.17 was understood as part of a larger coherent Gnostic
text which served as the basis for all of the discourse material. Bultmann's argumentation, however, has not been sustained by the evidence.[3]

Prior to and concurrent with his proposals were attempts to
explain the aporiae of ch.17 not on the basis of prior tradition but on the basis of subsequent additions to the composition of the evangelist. Here representative hypotheses may
illustrate the point. F. Spitta e.g. reduced the prayer of
ch.17 to about 1/3 of its present size, claiming the detruncated version as the historical original and assigning the
remaining verses to a later church redactor.[4] Operating with
a different set of criteria, H. Preisker exercised considerably more restraint with his proposed excisions. For him vs.
13, 21b, 23a, 24, and 26c were later interpolations designed
to change the eschatological character of the original.[5] The
parusia was delayed; the Second Coming did not appear. Consequently, Preisker maintained, the original apocalyptic orientation of the Fourth Gospel ("eine ganz apokalyptische
Schrift mit aller eschatologischen Glut urchristlicher Anfangszeit") had to be modified. The above changes were part of

---

[1] v. 9b οὐ περὶ etc. does not belong to the source (*Ev Joh*, p. 382, n.4).
v.10 is uncertain (p.382,n.6). The second part of v.13 καὶ ταῦτα λαλῶ
etc. is a rephrasing by the evangelist of what originally in the source
may have been identical with v.11 αὐτοὶ ἐν τῷ κόσμῳ (p.386,n.3).
[2] Whether or not vs.20-23 were part of the source or the composition of the
evangelist is left uncertain (*Ev Joh*, pp. 392, n.4; 392, n.6; 390, n.4).
[3] The reasons for the unacceptability of Bultmann's source hypothesis
have already been discussed. Cp. pp. 142, 144f.
[4] F. Spitta, *Das Johannes-Evangelium*, pp. 328-338.
[5] H. Preisker, "Das Evangelium des Johannes als erster Teil eines
apokalyptischen Doppelwerkes," *Theol. Blätter*, 15, 1936, pp. 189f.

the general overhaul.

E. Hirsch also proposed substantial later redaction.[1] His criteria were derived from a reconstructed Jewish-Christian church situation in Palestine during 70 - 100 A.D. (characteristic for the original form of the Fourth Gospel) and a later catholicizing situation in Asia Minor 130 - 140 A.D. (characteristic for the church redaction). Thus the redactor, intent on saving a Gospel tradition otherwise doomed to extinction, profusely annotated and modified the original to make it acceptable for the church of his time. According to Hirsch vs.2 (the last two words), 3, 11b, 12, 13a, 20, 21, and most of 22 and 23 are ascribed to the later redactional level.[2] A final example is cited with the analysis given by W. Hardtke.[3] His working criteria were gained from the contention (formed in association with Blumhardt's social concern theses) that the oldest level of tradition in the NT Scriptures (= 4. Gospel) was marked by a positive orientation to the world. This orientation became blurred and muddled through the increasingly dominant world-hostile and world-denying tendencies taking hold in the emerging church. Thus Hardtke can divide the Fourth Gospel into three strata: $\underline{Z}$ for the signs strata (1:19 - 12:42); $\underline{V}$ for the original unpublished composition of the evangelist; and $\underline{H}$ for the church redaction. $\underline{H}$ who had a basically sectarian and world inimical bias was made responsible for the addition in ch.17 of the following verses: 1a,c, 4-6a, 8b, 11a,c, 12a, 18, 21-23, and 26b.

It may be noted that in each of the four latter analyses precisely those passages in which the oneness motif is embedded were viewed as problematic and were consequently either emended or identified as interpolative additions. Other verses as well fell into the same category depending on

---

[1] E. Hirsch, *Das 4. Evangelium in seiner ursprünglichen Gestalt verdeutscht und erklärt*, Tübingen, 1936, p. 63. Also *Studien zum 4. Evangelium*, Tübingen, 1936, pp. 116f.

[2] Hirsch's time scheme assigning the redactional stage to 130-140 A.D. received a fatal blow with the discovery of Papyrus 52.

[3] *Vier urchristliche Partien und ihre Vereinigung zur apostolischen Kirche* I, Deutsche Akademie der Wissenschaften zu Berlin, Berlin, 1961, pp. 99ff.

the criteria of the critic. These criteria varied. In one
instance they were determined by the search for historia
(Spitta). In another instance they were conditioned by the
tension between apocalyptic and delayed parusia (Preisker).
Then it was a Pauline-like conflict between a liberating
faith in the Word and a Judaizing bondage (Hirsch) and finally a changing approach to an understanding of the world
(Hardtke). Ch.17 was dissected accordingly --and understandably with varying results. The results, however, were more
demonstrations of the respective critic's presuppositions
than they were clarifications of the prayer's inner structure
and theological orientation. Such analytical procedures,
operating with outside criteria not delivered by the Gospel
itself, are methodologically invalid.

In marked contrast to these analyses and signaling a significant procedural advance in the analysis of ch.17 is the
previously mentioned study by J. Becker.[1] Recognizing the
questionableness not only of those analytic attempts determined by a pre-programmed scheme but also seeing the limitations of the traditional summary approaches oriented around
the customary threefold division of the prayer,[2] Becker isolates ch.17 and undertakes an analysis of the chapter first
of all on its own terms. Accordingly four separate literary
categories (Gattungen) are distinguished, which are said to
follow without variation in a set sequence constituting five
isolable segments each conditioned by (a) dominant theological motif(s).[3] Becker detects in this sequence a line of development beginning with the introductory petition for δόξα

---

[1] "Aufbau" ZNW, 60, 1969, pp. 56-83.
[2] Jesus prays for himself, for his disciples, for the future church.
Variations on this basic scheme deal mostly with vs. 6-8 which can be
aligned either (a) with the first segment (1-8) thus providing motivation
for Jesus' petition, or (b) with the second segment (6-19) thus providing
an introduction for the subsequent petition, or (c) which can be regarded
as an independent unit reviewing the ministry of Jesus. Another frequent
subdivision is between 20-23 and 24-26. The other basic divisional option is to partition the prayer into two major sections --Jesus' petition
for himself (1-5) and for the church (6-24). Here also multiple subdivisions are possible.
[3] 1) vs.1b-2: glory and eternal life; 2) vs.4-5: glory; 3) vs.6-13: the
name (of God); 4) vs.14-19: Word and truth; 5) vs.22-26: glory and love.
--"Aufbau" op. cit., p. 69.

in 1b and culminating in the final segment which again speaks of δόξα but which, above all, ends on the motif of ἀγάπη. The ἀγάπη motif is accorded a central position in the progressively developed plan of the prayer which divides into two major sections. In fact, ἀγάπη is understood as illuminating the inner coherency of the various other motifs and as such becomes an interpretational key for the entire prayer.[1]

On the basis of these five very tightly structured and closed units, which are to constitute the essential construction of the prayer, Becker is able to regard vs.3, 12b, 16, and 20, 21 as interpolative additions. Further excised --although only in a contingent sense and not with the same finality as with the preceding verses-- are vs.8, 10a, and 11a. In answer to the question whether or not the evangelist created the matrix of the prayer without the anonymously added supplements, Becker responds evasively with a further reference to contextual problems. It is in the area of these contextual and internal problems --the place of the prayer in the larger context of ch.15 - 17 and the alleged appearance of significant theological shifts-- that he is able to conclude, fortified by his literary finding, that all of ch.17 is an interpolative supplement and, à la Wellhausen, is representative for a changed theological position in the proclamation-history of the Johannine church. Thus it is maintained as final outcome that the themes of dualism, christology, and eschatology have been so substantially modified in ch.17 that the prayer stands closer to the theology of the Johannine pastoral epistles with their specific paranetic and ecclesiological concerns than it does to the theology of the evangelist.

So far-reaching are the implications of this conclusion for an understanding of the Johannine oneness motif that the thesis of Becker must be examined in greater detail. Crucial to the entire argument is the contention that it is possible to distinguish four literary categories on the basis of which noncompatible verses are to be excised from the original.

---

[1] Similarly Bultmann (*Ev Joh*, p. 373) who can refer to ch.17 as "ein Gebet der Liebe." Bultmann's rearrangement of the text to follow 13:1-30 helps to provide the inner motivation for this kind of identification.

Should this original contention prove to be untenable, then the corresponding theological implications that are drawn would also be invalid. We must now examine in detail the literary proposals. Becker's first literary category is what he calls "a statement of accounts" (Rechenschaftsbericht) which is said to appear in four of the five segments, i.e. in a) v.4; b) vs.6-8; c) v.14; d) vs.22f. To this category are assigned the following characteristics: 1) the passage always begins with a main sentence whose verb is in the <u>aorist first person singular</u>. 2) This principal sentence, with one exception in v.6, is said to manifest the same four following elements: a) an introductory ἐγώ; b) <u>a verb of revelation</u>; c) an <u>accusative object</u> describing what is revealed; d) a <u>dative object</u> designating the recipient of the revelation. This construction is said to be peculiar to these four passages mentioned and is otherwise not used in ch.17. 3) Purpose of the category is to provide expression for a <u>retrospect</u> of Jesus' completed earthly work.[1]

Do Becker's criteria hold true? Examination reveals the following inconsistencies. In vs.14 and 22f. the perfect tense is used instead of the aorist. In v.4 the dative object is not present.[2] The absence of ἐγώ in v.6 had already been conceded. More devastating than these inconsistencies, however, is the appearance of the same four structural elements and their intentional orientation in other verses of the chapter as well. 1) v.12 has also the character of retrospect recalling the completed work of Jesus. Here the principal sentence likewise begins with an emphatic ἐγώ. The tense of the verb is imperfect instead of aorist, but as evidenced above, the tense is not a constant feature. Even at that it should be noted that the imperfect ἐτήρουν is balanced in typical Johannine synonymous parallelism with the aorist

---

[1] Becker, "Aufbau" *op. cit.*, pp. 61f.
[2] The logic of Becker's contention ("Aufbau," p.62, n.38) that the prepositional phrase ἐπὶ τῆς γῆς is equivalent to the force of the dative object and that "diese Ortsangabe ist... nur eine andere Art, die Offenbarungsempfänger anzugeben" may be granted. But then the same argumentation is valid for v.18 as well.

ἐφύλαξα.[1] The accusative object appears in the αὐτούς, and the absence of a dative object may be compensated for in the accompanying dative adverbial phrase which refers not to the recipients of the revelation (here transferred to the accusative) but to the mode of revelation. While the verb τηρέω may not seem to have the immediate force of a verb of revelation, still its implications in the Johannine usage suggest this accent. The Father's revelation is manifested to the extent that the Son engaged in keeping the disciples in the Father's name. 2) Becker's criteria appear with some variation also in v.18. Introduced with a καθώς comparative clause similar to the introductory clausal expansion in v.22, the principal sentence here is marked by the use of an emphatic ἐγώ (κἀγὼ tantamount to the κἀγὼ in v.22), the aorist verb, and an accusative object.[2] Similar to the construction in v.4 as discussed below in n.1, the prepositional phrase εἰς τὸν κόσμον may be taken as an equivalent for the dative object. The place of revelation describes in effect the revelation recipients. Finally, the verb ἀποστέλλω has an obvious revelational connotation and embraces a description of the work of Christ. 3) These distinguishing characteristics appear also in v.26. The verb is an aorist in the first person singular similar to the construction in v.6 where an explicit ἐγώ is likewise missing but included in the introductory verb form. Ἐγνώρισα is clearly revelational in thrust, has an accusative object describing what is revealed and a dative object referring to the recipients of the revelation. Similar elements may also be found in the second half of the compound sentence in v.25 which includes an introductory ἐγώ, an aorist first person singular verb with revelational character, and an accusative object describing what is revealed.

---

[1] Barrett e.g. speaks here of "synonymous variation in John's style" (*St. John*, p. 424).
[2] The object here denotes those whom Jesus sends. To the extent that they are in the Father and the Son (v.21) the believers are in an extended sense understood as the revelation; it is through their word (v.20) that others are yet to believe. While the accusative object in Becker's four segments refers either to the Father's name (v.6) or to his word (v.14) or to his glory (v.22), it can also be expressed in terms of a personal pronoun as in v.4 and likewise in vs.12 and 18.

The missing dative object here finds equivalent expression in the subsequent καὶ οὗτοι clause designating those who received the revelation. In conclusion it may be seen that the evidence does not support Becker's thesis regarding a "Rechenschaftsberich" category since the distinguishing characteristics are much too broad and apply to other verses in addition to the four segments originally cited.

The second literary category which Becker establishes as a distinct and structural form of the prayer is what he terms "the introduction to the petition ("die Einleitung zur Bitte"). This category is said to appear in vs.9-11a and 15f. i.e. in only two of the five possible segments. Its purpose is to remove any eventual misunderstanding in the subsequent petition. The fact that this category has no particular literary characteristics apart from the usage of the verb ἐρωτάω, which however also appears in v.20,[1] gives it the weakest attestation of all. In fact, it appears an an extremely artificial and contrived construction which can hardly be said to reflect a set and crystallized or a distinct form.

The third category proposed is the "petition." Together with the retrospect form it is the best attested. Two characteristics are noted as constants: a) the address form of "Father" and b) the imperative verb form.[2] But also here the inconsistencies are considerable and the distinguishing marks are evidenced in other verses as well. The address form of πάτερ indeed appears in vs.1b, 5 (not, however, at the beginning), 11b (πάτερ ἅγιε), and in 24, but it is notably absent in v.17. What is more, πατήρ also is used in v.21 and πατὴρ δίκαιε in v.25, verses not reckoned as petitions by Becker.[3] Although the imperative does occur consistently in the first four passages cited, it is absent in the last one.

---

[1] To claim as Becker does ("Aufbau," p. 63) that the use of ἐρωτάω in v.20 is an interpolative imitation of the style in vs.9f. and 15f. is without substantiation. It is begging the question to excise a passage so that theological consequences can be drawn which presuppose its omission.
[2] Becker, "Aufbau," pp. 63,64.
[3] Becker recognizes the occurrence of πατήρ in these two verses but helps himself out of the dilemma by regarding v.21 as a later redaction and by explaining the usage in v.25 as a natural occurrence for the closing of a prayer that began with the same address form.

In order to save his hypothetical construction, Becker must give the first person singular θέλω of v.24 a function equivalent to the imperatives in the preceding verses. On the one hand, this substitution is thoroughly legitimate since the force of the sentence is essentially the same as the meaning connoted by the precative imperatives. If, on the other hand, this be granted, then the same concession may be made for the ἐρωτάω forms in vs.9, 15, and 20. In fact, there is nothing to hinder placing these latter verses into the category, not of the "introduction to the petition," but of the petition itself. What could be clearer when the Johannine Christ explicitly says, "I am praying for..." or "I am making petition for..." As was already noted, the evidence for an "introduction" category was so lacking that its existence could not be convincingly established. It would seem best then to identify these passages (vs.9-11a and 15f.) simply with the category of petition.

The fourth and final category proposed is what is termed "the subsequent motivation given for the prayer" ("die nachgestellte Begründung zur Bitte"), a kind of afterthought explaining the prayer's raison d'etre. This category is to include the following verses: 2, 12f. 18f. and 25f.[1] By his own admission Becker regards this category as the most fluid and the least structured of all. Indeed, a closer look reveals that there is no evidence at all to regard these passages as constituting a separate and distinct literary category. The fact that all four passages end with a final ἵνα clause is hardly convincing when one considers that the ἵνα construction occurs 18 x in this chapter alone, 12 times of which it is employed in a final sense. The only really connecting and cohesive element in these passages consists not in formal structural factors but rather in the general orientation of the content, which in each case, apart from v.2, deals with a review of the work of Jesus. A more compelling partition then would be to align v.2 to the petition in v.1 and to regard vs.12f. 18f. and 25f. as expansions within the

---

[1] "Aufbau," pp. 64,65

literary category of retrospect and review. The only real variation in these passages is the difference in tense between the present (vs.13, 19) and future (v.26) themes. And yet inasmuch as each demonstrates an organic connection to its respective preceding verse in which Jesus details aspects of his accomplished work, they cannot be said to disrupt the lines of that larger context especially since time demarcations in the Fourth Gospel are notably fluid.

Despite the sharp-witted analysis, Becker's literary proposals fail to stand the weight of textual evidence. The internal inconsistencies, the occurrence in other passages of the same characteristics that should be peculiar only to the one category, and the lack of regularly occurring syntactical forms that would normally distinguish one literary category from another all demonstrate that the proposals are not tenable and that revision is necessary. As our examination has shown, there is no reason to maintain separate literary categories for a so-called "introduction to the prayer" and a "subsequent motivation given to the prayer." As separate constructions they are not distinct enough and are better understood as parts of the review and petition categories. This is further substantiated by the haphazard sequence of appearance of all four proposed categories in the respective five segments. An ideal sequence --the accounting statement, the introduction, the petition, and the subsequent motivation-- appears in only two of the units (vs.6-13 and 14-19).[1] In the first unit (1b-2) the accounting and the introduction are missing. In the second unit the introduction and subsequent motivation are absent. And in the fifth unit the introduction is missing. With such irregularities in addition to the inconsistencies already noted it would seem best to scrap the entire scheme and not to force the chapter into a literary Procrustean bed.

If any literary principle at all is apparent in the

---

[1] Even here further inner adjustments must be made to make the pattern plausible. v.8 is excised because it does not follow the unit theme of ὄνομα signaled in v.6 ("Aufbau," p. 75/. Thus the larger segment (6-13), otherwise atypical because of its disproportionate length (p.67) is reduced in size. Also v.10a is excised because it appears superfluous.

construction of ch.17, then it is the constant exchange between retrospect or review on the one hand and petition on the other.[1] This construction, though consistent, is nevertheless loose and flexible, totally in keeping with the 4. Gospel's characteristically fluid style determined more by theological concern than by structural form. A review of the chapter's contents makes this plain. Vs.1,2 begin with <u>petition</u>. Unique for these verses is speech in the third person instead of the characteristic first person otherwise used in the chapter. This significant variation leaves the way open for the addition of the appositional expansion in v.3.[2] Glory and eternal life are the dominant themes here.[3] V.4 shifts to <u>review</u> as Jesus recalls his accomplished work. In v.5 the <u>petition</u> is again resumed and Jesus asks that he be glorified with his pre-existent glory. The thought then reverts to <u>review</u> in vs.6-8[4] where Jesus rehearses what he has accomplished. Two themes stand out, signaled by the use of ὄνομα and λόγος. Jesus has successfully manifested the Father's name to those who were given him and to whom the Father's words have been imparted. They believed and knew that Jesus was sent from

---

[1] These two categories --review and petition-- were discussed in the previous section (pp. 203-205) as the two forms constitutive to the character of ch.17.

[2] Admittedly the character of v.3 as a definitional sentence sets it apart from the rest of the chapter. The hapax legomena ἡ αἰώνιος ζωή (the article is otherwise missing) and μόνος ἀληθινὸς θεός also underscore its uniqueness. The designation Ἰησοῦς Χριστός has its only parallel in 1:17. The relation, however, is significant. Just as 1:17 most likely had its roots in the confessional tradition of the Johannine church (cp. C. Demke, "Der sogenannte Logos-Hymnus," *op. cit.*, p. 63) so every indication is that v.3 represents a piece of pre-formed Johannine confessional or prayer tradition which the evangelist incorporated, perhaps because of its familiarity, but in any case because it helps to advance the thought of the prayer not only by explaining the essence of eternal life (v.2) and the intention of the glorification (v.1) --both the Father and His revealer are the object of the γινώσκειν (so also Bultmann, *Ev Joh*, p.378)-- but also by anticipating the "knowing" theme of v.7 and the conclusion in vs.25f.

[3] Unwarranted is Thüsing's claim (*Herrlichkeit und Einheit*, p.21) that δόξα is the theme of the whole prayer or when O.Michel ("Das Gebet," *op.cit.* p.522) insists that the culminating point is v.24f. The prayer is not marked by an evolving progression of thought or dominated by a singular theme. It is rather circular in nature touching in summary fashion on key themes.

[4] J. Becker's ("Aufbau," p.75) excision of v.8 as an unnecessary dublette is unsubstantiated. The τὰ ῥήματα theme of v.8 is an important, organically consistent complement to the τὸν λόγον reference in v.6. The complementary usage of λόγος and ῥῆμα is typically Johannine. Cp. 12:48.

the Father. Vs.9-11 shift back to petition.[1] Here Jesus prays for those whom he received because they belong to both himself and the Father. But since he is leaving the world, Jesus asks that those whom he has received be kept in the Father's name so that they may be one even as he and the Father are one. The petition leads over again into review in vs.12-14,[2] where echoes of the ὄνομα and λόγος themes from the previous review segment (vs.6-8) are sounded again and further detailed. Jesus points out that he has kept his own in the Father's name so that none was lost except, as announced in 13:18, the betrayer. Jesus has given them the Father's word with the result that they do not belong to the world even as he who is about to depart to the Father is not of the world. Thus the disciples' joy may be complete in the knowledge that they have been kept and are not possessed by the world.

---

[1] Unwarranted is J. Becker's suggestion that 10a and 11a be regarded as secondary additions ("Aufbau," p.75). Since 10a has appositional character as was the case with v.3, it is tempting to regard it as an independent unit (cp. also Dibelius, RGG^2, III, p.356). Indeed, it is so characteristically stamped by the formula-like reciprocity language so typical for stereotyped Gnostic expressions that it may well have been lifted from such a context. To regard the clause in its present context as redundant is hardly called for. The verse segment does not blindly repeat but carefully qualifies the preceding by underscoring that the Father's possessions are also the Son's. Thus the underlying motif on oneness is strengthened in anticipation of further explication in vs.11 and 20-23. The neuter plural designation for the disciples can hardly be said to be a foreign element (against Becker) in the light of similar usage (neuter singular) in v.2. In regard to 11a it should be remembered that repetition is typically Johannine (cp. Abbot, Johannine Grammar, pp.437ff.). When 11a then appears as a kind of doublet to 13a, this does not necessitate regarding one or the other as a later addition.

[2] It is not necessary to regard v.12b as a later corrective insertion (against Becker, "Aufbau," p.74). The fact that ἐτήρουν is paralleled by the essentially synonymous ἐφύλαξα is not a strange redundancy, but, as has already been noted, a typical feature of the constantly recurring Johannine parallelism (e.g. in ch.17: λόγος - ῥῆμα; ἐρωτάω - θέλω; ἔγνωσαν - ἐπίστευσαν and the regular use of doublets as e.g. vs.11a and 13a; 14b and 16a; 20f. and 22f.). Neither surprising nor out of context is the reference to the person of Judas since the larger context presupposes the eleven (τοῖς ἀνθρώποις v.6) as representatives of all believers. While the ἵνα ἡ γραφὴ πληρωθῇ has implicit salvation-history overtones of promise and fulfillment, these aspects are not developed here. Rather the accent is on God's Scripturally revealed will (cp. W. Bauer, Joh.Ev., p.204) consistent with the prayer's emphatic use of δίδωμι (16 x) and contiguous with the 13:18 reference. Although the term ὁ υἱὸς τῆς ἀπωλείας has apocalyptic character (cp.II Thess.2:3), it is not apocalyptically understood (contra Barrett, St. John, p. 424).

Vs.15-17[1] swing back to <u>petition</u> as Jesus asks not that his own be taken out of the world but that they be kept from the evil one and not fall prey to the world but be set apart in the truth of the word. The subsequent <u>review</u> segment (vs.18, 19) which recalls Jesus' sending and his consecration prepares the way for the next <u>petition</u> in vs.20,21[2] where Jesus prays not just for those who have believed but for the future church as well that they all be one in order that the world may believe. From petition the line of thought returns again to <u>review</u> in vs.22,23 where Jesus recalls that the glory he received he has given to the believers in order that they may be perfectly one and in order that the world may know that he is sent from the Father and that the Father has loved the believers. V.24 moves back to <u>petition</u> as Jesus asks that the believers be with him to behold his glory. The closing vs. 25,26 then revert to <u>review</u> once again as Jesus recapitulates by declaring that even though the world has not known the

---

[1] To label v.16 as an inept interpolation because it is a repetition of v.14b is not warranted (against Becker, "Aufbau," p.74). Stylistically such repetition and analogous forms of parallelism are typically Johannine. Furthermore, v.16 is well motivated by the preceding (since they are not taken out of the world, again the reminder: they are not of the world) and leads logically into the petition of v.17.

[2] Becker's most crucial deletion, and yet strangely enough his least documented, is the excision of vs.20,21. His prime reason for regarding these verses as later interpolations is because they disrupt his proposed literary scheme. As supporting evidence he cites that no other verse in ch.17 employs the differentiation between disciples of first and second hand. In rebuttal it should be noted that not the matter of first and second hand discipleship is at issue in v.20 but rather a future orientation that is constitutive for the remaining verses of the prayer. Furthermore, there is no qualitative difference between disciples of the first hand and τῶν πιστευόντων διὰ τοῦ λόγου αὐτῶν εἰς ἐμέ as long as that word leads directly to Jesus. (Cp. the implicit critique against the Samaritan woman in 4:42 (contra R. Walker, "Jüngerwort und Herrenwort," *ZNW*, 57, 1966, pp.49-54) and the possible distinction between διὰ τὸν λόγον (4:39) and διὰ τοῦ λόγου (17:20) --Schlatter, *Evangelist Joh.*, p.324). From a literary structural standpoint the break suggested in Becker's construction between v.21 and vs.22,23 can likewise not be maintained. As our analysis of these passages demonstrated (pp. 157ff.), the striking synonymous parallelism of forms between the respective parts suggests a tightly integrated and coherent unit. With what justification e.g. Becker in imitation of E. Hirsch (*Studien*, p.117) can regard v.21 as the more pallid and stereotyped of the formulations is not clear. Finally, it must be noted that the use of the reciprocity formula in reference to the disciples is hardly evidence for secondary redaction (against G. Richter,"Zur Formgeschichte," *op. cit.*, p.40) but rather is fundamentally characteristic for the evangelist's language modes and consistent with his theological intent.

Father, he has known him and has made his name known to the believers so that love may be in them and he in them.

The results of our overview reveal a surprising consistency in the structural form of ch.17. In all, there are six petition units and six review units. They follow without exception in a constantly rotating pattern: petition, review, petition, review etc. This is the literary principle governing the arrangement of the prayer. The essence of the petition category consists in requests which are variously expanded with qualifying explanations or motivations. The essence of the review category consists in the rehearsal of past accomplishments and circumstances complemented with present and future themes. None of these category-units is rigidly independent; nor are they distinguished by stringent structural features.[1] Their form instead is determined by the interplay of theological motifs which weave back and forth in alternating fashion giving the entire chapter a unified and interconnected appearance.[2]

A final question remains to be discussed. Does ch.17 represent a theology different from the rest of the Fourth Gospel? The question is best seen against the background of the Johannine Epistles. These epistles demonstrate a different orientation than the Fourth Gospel. They give evidence of theological shifts and a changed situation within the Johannine community. Whereas the Fourth Gospel speaks against the non-christian "world" represented by the Jews, the epistles are distinguished by their struggle with Christian heretics. In the epistles the place of fixed church tradition takes on an increasing importance and assumes the role of serving as a criterion for distinguishing between orthodoxy and heterodoxy.[3] Emphasis shifts from the person of Jesus to the salvation

---

[1] The only exception are vs.20-23 which demonstrate a series of carefully balanced and stylized literary features. According to the above scheme these passages comprise a complete unit of petition and review.
[2] Cp. again Wellhausen's conclusion regarding the literary structure (*Ev. Joh.*, p.75): "An der wesentlichen Einheit läßt sich nicht zweifeln."
[3] Cp. H. Conzelmann, "Was am Anfang war," *Neutestamentliche Studien für R. Bultmann*, Beih. ZNW 21, Berlin, 1954, pp. 194-200.

which he brings.¹ In the Gospel Jesus' relation to the Father is the central issue, repeatedly described, and quintessentially expressed in terms of oneness. In John's epistles, on the other hand, it is the believer's relation to God that occupies the limelight. Εἷς never appears as a designation for Jesus' relation to the Father. Christological explications are replaced by ecclesiological ones and paranetic appeals move into the central position. There is a further tendency to formalize dualistic concepts² as well as a marked development in the direction of future eschatology. In short, every indication points to a history of theology within the Johannine Corpus.

John's epistles reflect theological accents and a historical situation well along the way in the development of early catholicism.³ The question here is whether ch.17 has its real roots in this same level of tradition and whether as such it evidences inconsistencies with the rest of the Fourth Gospel.⁴ The abundance of statements in the prayer describing not the person of Jesus but the accomplished work which he has been given may seem initially to point in this direction. Jesus imparts eternal life (v.2), manifests the Father's name (v.6), presents the Father's words (v.8), keeps the disciples in the Father's name (v.12), and gives them the Father's glory (v. 22). Thus far Jesus' role appears as that of the mediator, the middle man who negotiates for another. He is not the word himself but --in fashion reminiscent of the epistles-- the one who brings the word. And yet to stop at this point

---

[1] The introductory neuter ὅ in I Jn.1:1 is in this respect significant. Cp. Bultmann, *Die Johannesbriefe*. Kritisch-exeget. Kommentar über das NT, Göttingen, 1969, pp. 13ff. Similarly, H. Braun, "Literar-Analyse im ersten Johannesbrief," *Gesammelte Studien zum NT und seiner Umwelt*, Tübingen, 1962, p. 232: "Es handelt sich nicht um eine Person an und für sich sondern um die mit dieser Person verknüpfte Sache."

[2] R. Bergmeyer, "Zum Verfasserproblem des II und III Johannesbriefes," *ZNW*, 57, 1966, pp. 93-100, demonstrates this convincingly for II and III Jn. Bergmeyer's conclusions, however, do not apply to I Jn. as J. Becker ("Aufbau" p. 79) mistakenly implies.

[3] So E. Haenchen, "Neuere Literatur zu den Johannesbriefen," *Theol.Rund.*, N.F. 26, 1960, p. 39: "I Joh...gehört tatsächlich viel tiefer in den Frühkatholizismus hinein als die paulinischen Pastoralbriefe."

[4] J. Becker, "Aufbau," *op. cit.*, pp. 77ff. maintains that it does together with chs. 15 and 16.

would be a fatal short-circuiting. For who else is it who is so solidary with the Father that it can be said --in the present tense!-- he is one with God. Who except Jesus? Jesus manifests God's name (v.6). It is the very name which he himself has received (vs.11f.).[1] He keeps the disciples in the Father's name (v.12) but what belongs to the Father is also the Son's (v.10a). Jesus gives the disciples the words he received (v.8) but through the word people believe in Jesus (v.20). Likewise he gives the believers the Father's glory (v.22) in order that he (Jesus) may be in them (v.23). And finally it is noted that when the love with which the Father loved the Son is in the believers, then it is Jesus who is in them (v.26). The meaning of these reciprocal identifications is obvious. Jesus is not simply a mediator, i.e. one who points beyond himself to a greater reality. Rather he himself is the ultimate, the final point of revelation. Thus in manifesting the name of the Father, he manifests his own name. When he keeps the Father's own, he preserves his own. He doesn't give the truth; he is the truth through which the believers are consecrated. The word of the Father points only to Jesus because that word is Jesus. When the Father's love and glory dwell within the believers, then it is Jesus who is within them. Lest the point still be missed, all of these reciprocally conditioned statements are capped off with the indelibly clear oneness motif in vs.11,20-23 where Jesus is explicitly declared to be one with the Father.

If the descriptions of Jesus' works seem to lodge initially only on the level of mediation, then their further qualifications must be considered. It is in the light of the prayer's overriding intention to give witness to the unity of Father and Son that the full picture is gained. Here Jesus' divinity overshadows every further consideration. That is seen first of all in the use of the δόξα theme. Jesus prays that he be glorified with his pre-existent glory (17:5). That glory had already been singularly manifested at the incarnation so that those who saw the Incarnate One could respond

---

[1] ᾧ must refer to ὄνομα and it is doubtless the preferred reading over against the corrections of ὅ and οὕς. (cp. p. 162).

that they had seen the glory of the only begotten Son of the Father (1:14). That same glory was made known in demonstrative epiphanies of power through Jesus' ministry. Now in the impending hour of the cross, it receives further expression. Not even Jesus' death disrupts his oneness with the Father. His death is rather the hour of glorification and return to the Father. For Jesus there is no abdication of pre-existent glory which is then resumed at a later point. Jesus' glorification on the cross is with the same glory that had always been his. There is no qualitative difference, no change in essence. The Incarnate One, the Crucified One, is the Glorified One because Jesus was and always is one with the Father. Clearly, here is a theologia crucis that is a theologia gloriae.[1] Further it should be noted that Jesus' glorification has explicit future implications. The effects of his glorious presence continue to permeate the ongoing church and point to the final gathering when Jesus' own will be fully in his presence and behold his eternal glory. It is also this theme which ties ch.17 in with the preceding.[2] In his farewell discourse Jesus speaks of the greater works which he will accomplish through the disciples in order that the Father be glorified in the glorification of the Son (14:13). The disciples' "fruit" will effect this (15:8), and the work of the Spirit, in declaring the things of Jesus, will ensure the glorification of the Son (16:14). It is thoroughly in keeping with this line of thought when in 17:10 Jesus speaks of his glorification through the disciples (v.10), and then

---

[1] G. Bornkamm ("Zur Interpretation," *op. cit.*, pp. 113f.) objects to this and refers to what he calls "the paradox of the cross event." Bornkamm insists that the faith of the Johannine church is rooted primarily in the retrospective view of the cross. But it is precisely here that the lines are blurred. To be sure, the Johannine church unfolds its witness of Christ from the perspective of retrospect. But the point of orientation is not so much the cross as it is Easter. Admittedly, resurrection terminology is not used, but, nevertheless, it is the exalted eternally living and powerful Christ who everywhere makes his appearance. Therefore it is not warranted, as Bornkamm does, to play out the earthly ministry of Jesus against the cross as though one or the other should receive priority. Both are qualified and distinguished by eternal glory. Johannine faith is based not in the first instance on "den am Kreuz Vollendeten" (p. 114) but on the exalted and risen Son.

[2] Against Becker ("Aufbau," p.82) who maintains that the evangelist has no interest in making statements about the pre-existent and end-time glorification existence of Christ.

in v.24 speaks of the final gathering when they will behold his glory which is affected neither by the beginning nor the end of time.[1]

It is also from this standpoint that the dualism of the chapter must be understood. Johannine dualism is not metaphysical. While it may be said that light and darkness, truth and lie, above and below, etc. are strictly opposed, their character is not understood as deriving from primeval circumstances that immutably fixed all ensuing destiny. Heaven and earth do not face each other as a priori and unalterably opposing entities.[2] Their antithesis and character are created instead by response to the Word who is Jesus. His centrality and dominance evoke hostile reaction and create the lines of separation which set those who are his own apart from those who are of the world. Because the disciples have received the word (17:14), they can no longer be of the world. But since they remain in the world, Jesus prays that they be kept from the evil one (17:15) who is the personal embodiment of the hostile cosmos. The reference to τοῦ πονηροῦ can hardly be said to be only incidental and on the fringe of the thought expressed in v.15.[3] Although the mythology of the designation has been removed,[4] it is clear that the role of "the evil one," in typically dualistic orientation characteristic for the whole of the 4.Gospel, receives a constitutive function in its opposition to the word.

Relation to the word is also determinative for the use of ἀλήθεια in vs.17-19. Simply because its dualistic counterparts —ψεῦδος or πλάνη— do not appear here, which, however, is hardly surprising since ψεῦδος occurs only once in the

---

[1] The final consummation or union of believers in heaven is the end point of an eschatological event that begins in the present. Thüsing (Erhöhung und Verherrlichung, pp. 107ff.) has carefully worked out the future aspects of Jesus' glorification although, as previously noted, his imposition of a two-stage developmental process is foreign to John's intention.
[2] Cp. Käsemann, Letzter Wille, p. 131.
[3] J. Becker, ("Aufbau," p. 79) contends that the mention of the evil one is only "nebensächlich." While it is true that the term occurs only here, the use of ὁ τοῦ κόσμου ἄρχων in 12:31; 14:30; 16:11 underscores the constitutive role which the analogous ὁ πονηρός (masc. and not neuter, cp. W. Bauer, Joh. Ev., p. 205) plays here.
[4] Cp. Bultmann, Theology of the NT, II, p. 17.

cp. also vs. 8, 21, 23, and 25). He is sent to manifest the Father's name (v.6) and to speak his word (v.14) so that those who "hear" and "see," who know and believe may be recognized as "his own" i.e. as the chosen ones whom the Father has given him. Jesus' sending has paradigmatic value for the believers. They too are sent into the world (v.18) to speak and live the word (v.20) in confrontation with the world. Church is mission! Therefore the oneness of Father and Son together with the oneness of the believers in the unity of Father and Son is expressed with the sole intention --that the world may believe (v.21) and that the world may know (v.23).[1] Separated from the world, the believers still relate to the world because it is the arena for confrontation and proclamation. The thrust of these passages is not to indicate passive, isolationist waiting for the heavenly vision of glory (v.24) but projection into the world and active witnessing in the word (v.20).

It is from this standpoint that the predestinatory accents must be understood. The fact that the διδόναι motif is used with greater frequency in ch.17 than in any other place in the Fourth Gospel calls for special comment. Its orientation is definitely predestinatory in indicating that only those are believers whom the Father has given to the Son (vs. 2, 6, 9, 24). This thought is, however, by no means new. It is deeply embedded in Johannine theology (cp. 6:37, 39, 44, 65; 8:47; 10:26; 18:37). To claim that its use in ch.17 is one-sided and rigidly deterministic[2] is to muddle the dialectic that is consistently maintained. Throughout the 4. Gospel the thrust of the predestinatory formulations is to reinforce the fundamental Johannine concern that faith is not merely the result of a choice between inner-worldly possibilities. Believing existence is not the product of one's own self-

---

[1] These passages argue against J. Becker's ("Aufbau," p. 80) one-sided contention that the predestinatory statements of ch.17 are not qualified and that the Joh. church is therefore motivated by an insular withdrawal from any contact with the world.
[2] So. Becker ("Aufbau," p. 80f.): "Demgegenüber kennt Joh.17 keine Korrektur der prädestinatianischen Theologie. Vielmehr tritt sie hier sogar besonders massiv als starre theologische Vorstellung auf."

discovery but of God's working. The centrality and efficacious power of the word is the motivating and qualifying context for those statements which declare that only those receive life whom the Father has given to the Son. He who hears the words of God is of God; but only he who is of God hear his words. The dialectic is never resolved. This is also the orientation for ch.17.

Divine election is inseparably tied to response to and preservation in the word. On the one hand, the Father's name has been manifested only to those who have been given to Jesus out of the world. If that were to be understood in terms of a rigid determinism, then of course it would not be necessary that prayer be made for them nor would it be conceivable how through their words the possibility would be given for others to come to faith. Therefore the two lines of thought run parallel to each other. Although only those receive the gift of eternal life who have been given to Jesus (v.2), the essence of their "givenness" or "chosenness" is constituted by their relation to the word. Consequently Jesus prays that they be sanctified in the truth which is the Father's word (v.17). Similarly he prays for the believers of future generations. How will they come to faith? It is not said "because they too have been given (although that also is implied) but rather διὰ τοῦ λόγου αὐτῶν (v.20).

SUMMARY: Just as little as ch.17 betrays major literary breaks and sutures which support the excision of selected verses, so little does it evidence theological shifts that are basically inconsistent with the rest of the Fourth Gospel. Instead of being a later unit addition somewhat awkwardly grafted into a larger complex and requiring still further harmonizing emendations and smaller interpolations to comply with the changing accents of the day, the prayer reflects a carefully integrated theological plan rephrasing in summary fashion the same witness to the work and person of Jesus as is developed in the rest of the Gospel.[1] Particularly

---

[1] Germane is Thüsing's conclusion (*Herrlichkeit und Einheit*, p. 5): "Tatsächlich ist dieses 17. Kap. wie ein Spiegel, in dem sich der ganze Gehalt des Evangeliums noch einmal reflektiert..."

significant are these results for an understanding of the oneness passages in vs.11, 20-23. They appear not as modified additions or corrective interpolations but as the evangelist's own choice and as the quintessential expressions of his Gospel's deepest concerns.

Chapter VIII: The Oneness Passage in a Prophetic Statement

The oneness motif receives explicit usage also in the interpretive statement added to the prophecy of Caiaphas. The statement is embedded in a larger unit of tradition (11:47-53) which gives the first hand impression of being an independent narrative segment. In its present position the unit serves to heighten the dramatic imminence of the approaching Passion[1] and, in typically Johannine fashion, sets the theological contrasts of life and death into bold relief. Jesus' most demonstrative miracle, the raising of Lazarus from the dead, not only has powerful effects on those who saw what he had done (v. 45) but also sets the context for the witness that Jesus himself is the Resurrection and the Life (v. 25). The impact of what took place, in addition to awakening faith (v. 45), hardens the front of the opposition. In the face of life death is decreed. The Sanhedrin convenes and officially resolves to take action against Jesus. From that day on they counsel how to put Jesus to death (v. 53). In turn, the action triggers the ironic and prophetic response of Caiaphas (vs. 49-50).

A. STRUCTURAL CONSIDERATIONS

The form of the pericope in vs. 47-53 is distinguished by noticeable structural peculiarities. A prima facie case could be made for its resemblance to the apophthegmata of the Synoptics where a pregnant saying of Jesus is enclosed within a concise and contextually complete framework so that the component parts give an integrated appearance as an independent segment.[2] Although there is no synoptic counterpart to the narration in the Johannine pericope,[3] it may well be that

---

[1] F. Hahn (*Der Prozeß Jesu*, pp. 26f.), in fact, identifies elements of this pericope as the original introduction to the Johannine passion source. And yet it is a question whether the synoptic model should predominate.
[2] Cp. Bultmann, *Die Geschichte der synoptischen Tradition*, pp. 8f.
[3] Mk. gives no account of the actual decision to put Jesus to death but rather variously alludes to it (11:18; 12:17; 14:1). Mt. 26:3f., on the

dynamics similar to those at work in the synoptic apophthegmata were also instrumental in the structural formation of vs. 47-53. The one decisive difference, as C. H. Dodd has pointed out,[1] is that the motivating center in the Johannine passage comprises words spoken not by Jesus, as is always the case in the synoptic forms, but by Caiaphas, an opponent of the Gospel. Apart from this divergency, which has no real parallel, the construction is basically similar. A pointed statement or question[2] builds the center (here: vs. 49, 50). This central statement not only motivates the clarifying expansion in vs. 51, 52 but also complies with the preceding decision to convoke the Sanhedrin and with the subsequent dialogue of the constituents (vs. 47, 48) as well as with the summary statement in v. 53. The independent character of the whole passage is reinforced by absence of any specific reference to place and, apart from the general pre-Passion implications, to time. Further it should be noted that within 7 verses there is a total of 5 hapax legomena: συνέδριον (v.47); λογίζεσθαι (v. 50); λαός (v.50);[3] προφητεύειν (v.51); and διασκορπίζειν (v.52).[4] Coupled with these observations is also the fact that the construction τί ποιοῦμεν (v.47), a present indicative used in a deliberative sense in place of the future, is a rare NT occurrence otherwise never employed in John.[5] The overall impact of these considerations is to

---

other hand, mentions a specific gathering in the palace of Caiaphas at which time counsel was taken to arrest and kill Jesus. Significantly, all of the further expansion in Jn. (no specification of the place) is peculiar to Jn.

[1] "The Prophecy of Caiaphas," *Neotestamentica et Patristica, Suppl. Nov. Test.*, Vol. VI. Brill, 1962, pp. 135f. Using V. Taylor's classification, Dodd designates this pericope a "pronouncement story."

[2] Taking the two sentences in v.49 (beginning with ὑμεῖς οὐκ) and v.50 as questions has merit (contra Barrett, *St. John*, p. 339). It has the effect of softening the tone of the charge in v.49 and of obviating pedantic considerations about "boorish behavior" (so Bernard, *Commentary*, p.404) as well as providing in v.50 a tighter integration with the preceding verses (cp. Bultmann, *Die Geschichte d. syn. Tradition*, p. 9, on the place of the question in the apophthegmata.

[3] λαός also appears in the repetition of this verse in 18:14 as well as in 8:2 in a narrative not originally part of the Gospel.

[4] It should also be noted that ἔθνος which occurs 4 times (vs.48, 50, 51, 52) in this passage is used only once again in 18:35. Similarly, συμφέρειν (v.50), which is repeated in the duplication in 18:14, occurs otherwise only once again in 16:7.

[5] Cp. Blaß-Debrunner (Funk), *op. cit.*, §366.4.

suggest that what we have before us is a pre-Johannine unit of tradition in the form of an organically structured apophthegma.

B. STYLISTIC FACTORS AND INTERNAL PROBLEMS

And yet the argument is precarious as further investigation will show. The entire unit is so permeated with typically Johannine stylistic characteristics that the question of their distribution and their implications for the composition of the evangelist must now be considered. The οὖν historicum in vs. 47,53 is a favorite connecting link.[1] While not a specifically Johannine characteristic, the causal conjunctive use of ὅτι in v.47 to introduce an explanatory notation reflects a typical pattern used elsewhere in the 4. Gospel.[2] The reference to Jesus' works and miracles as σημεῖα (v.47), though rooted in prior tradition, is a standard Johannine feature. Similarly characteristic for John are the following usages: the use of ἄνθρωπος as a designation for Jesus in v.47;[3] the expression πιστεύσουσιν εἰς αὐτόν in v.48;[4] τις with the partitive ἐκ in v.49;[5] the present participle ὤν as an adjectival modifier in vs.49,51;[6] the τοῦτο δέ...εἶπεν

---

[1] The relational and frequency figures are impressive: 146+0/8+0 (formula explanation on p. 156 n.6). Here I am using Nicol's (Semeia, p.17) revision of E. Schweizer's calculation. Nicol, however, does not include the οὖν of v.53. His reasoning is not clear. The force of οὖν in v.53 is more resumptive after the interpretive interlude of vs.51,52 than it is inferential. The use of οὖν in v.47 is, on the other hand, not as clear. It could have inferential meaning (Bauer/Arndt-Gingrich, Lexicon, ad loc. 1) introducing the consequence from the report given to the Pharisees (v.45). It could also be used in a hist. sense in providing transition to a new theme (Bauer, Lexicon, 2b).
[2] Cp. Bultmann, Ev Joh, p.313, n.2. The 7:35 reference is unclear.
[3] Cp. Nicol (Semeia, p.24; no.73). Results: 15/[7+3].
[4] First cited by Jeremias as a characteristic feature ("Joh.Lit.Kritik," Theol. Blätter, 1941, p.35) and since repeated in subsequent lists. Results: 38+3/8(9).
[5] Fortna (The Gospel of Signs, p.209f.) has refined the usage of this characteristic more sharply than earlier classifications. The resulting frequency figures for the partitive ἐκ after τις (or τινές, πολλοί, and οὐδείς) are an impressive 25(26)/[1]0. The uniqueness of the τις ἐκ construction together with εἷς in v.49 (only occurrence in NT) does not alter its inclusion in this category.
[6] Bultmann, Ev Joh, p. 313, n.1.

construction in v.51;[1] ἀφ ἑαυτοῦ in v.51;[2] the οὐκ...ἀλλ' ἵνα construction in v.52;[3] and finally the use of ἕν as a description of the goal of those who belong to God. It may be noted that Johannine stylistic characteristics are uniformly distributed in all of the verses with the exception of v.50 where none at all are represented. Of further significance is the fact that two of the hapax legomena listed above are lodged in this verse.

Consideration of internal content problems strengthen the indication that v.50 represents an isolable unit of tradition. Couched in Caiaphas' maxim of political expediency is the textually well attested,[4] yet thoroughly unexpected phrase, ὑπὲρ τοῦ λαοῦ implying an expiatory death. The implication, however, so contrasts with what follows that an inner tension between these two parts is unavoidably created. Apparently the theme of expiation was not congenial with the intention of the writer since in the subsequent interpretive comment a new and unrelated twist is given to the statement. One would expect comment on the meaning of expiation but instead a different accent is introduced. Jesus was not to die ὑπὲρ τοῦ ἔθνους μόνον but in order to gather into one the children of God who are scattered abroad (v.52). The inference seems compelling, and wholly consistent with our stylistic findings, that the composition of v.50 was not the work of the writer responsible for the following verses. In view of the above observations, it would seem unwarranted to conclude either with Bultmann that the entire pericope is the composition of

---

[1] Nicol (*Semeia*, p.24; no.71) lists this characteristic, although its uniqueness is thrown into question by fairly frequent use in Lk. Cp. also Bultmann, *Ev Joh*, p. 157, no.1.
[2] E. Schweizer's results remain unchanged (*Ego Eimi*, p.104; no.21): 13+0/1(2)+0. (Critical: Schulz, *Untersuchungen*, p.128, no.14.).
[3] Cp. Nicol's revision (*Semeia*, p.17; no.13): 10+1/1. Ruckstuhl's remark (*Lit. Einheit*, p. 194; no.8) regarding 11:52 that the ellipsis is strongly weakened by the connection with ἀποθνῄσκειν in v.51 is hardly a serious objection. There is no substantial difference between the occurrence in v.52 and similar construction in 1:8; 1:31; 3:17 etc.
[4] There are no manuscript variants or emendations for the phrase. Boismard (*Revue Biblique*, 60, 1953, pp. 350-353) refers favorably to variants by Chrysostom, Augustine, Theodoret etc. where the phrase ὑπὲρ τοῦ λαοῦ is omitted thereby excluding the possibility of Caiaphas speaking of atoning death. Similarly R. Brown (*John*, I, p.440) would like to regard the phrase as a gloss. And yet there is no textual justification for excision.

the evangelist[1] or with Dodd that the whole pericope represents a closed unit of preformed tradition, a "pronouncement story," which was slightly emended by the evangelist who added the corollary in v.52 together with other scattered locutions.[2] The extent of the evangelist's own composition appears to be substantially greater than the hypothesis of Dodd or the suggestion of a closed apophthegma would allow.

This is further underscored by other noteworthy content features within the pericope. The initial reference in v.47 to the Pharisees' and high priests' convening the Sanhedrin is historically confusing. Allegiance to the Pharisaic party, which was a voluntary association, cut across the lines of the established ruling bodies. Properly speaking, the chief priests, the elders, and the scholars (scribes) constituted the membership of the Sanhedrin,[3] and although any one of these could belong to the movement of the Pharisees, the Pharisees themselves as a body had no right to convoke the Sanhedrin. Since the Sanhedrin met under the presidency of the ruling high priest, the whole council could at times be referred to with the shorthand designation "the chief priests" (e.g. Acts 9:14). The standard expressions, however, were "the chief priests and scribes" (Mt.2:4; 20:18; Mk.11:18 etc.) or "the chief priests and the elders" (Mt.21:23; 26:3; 27:1 etc.) or all three (Mt. 16:21; Mk.15:1; Lk.20:1 etc.). But the Fourth Gospel never uses the designations γραμματεῖς and/or πρεσβύτεροι. When referring to the Sanhedrin with a combination term, it is always as in v.47 ἀρχιερεῖς καὶ οἱ Φαρισαῖοι (7:32,45; 11:57 and 18:3). The imprecision in this usage may perhaps be best understood from the perspective of the distance between the time of composition and the actual historical situation.[4] In the evangelist's own day hostile Jewish

---
[1] Bultmann, Ev Joh, p.313, no.2.
[2] Dodd ("Prophecy" op. cit., p. 141) credits the evangelist with the following expressions: ποιεῖν σημεῖα, πιστεύειν εἰς, ἀφ ἑαυτοῦ, ἀρχιερεὺς τοῦ ἐνιαυτοῦ ἐκείνου, and the use of Φαρισαῖοι collateral with ἀρχιερεῖς. Dodd, however, concludes that "...the Johannine stamp on the language of this passage is not in any case deep." On the basis of parallel language with Mt.26:3f., Fortna (The Gospel of Signs, p. 148) contends that v.47a and 53 were pre-Johannine units of Passion tradition.
[3] Bauer (Arndt-Gingrich), Lexicon, p. 793.
[4] Cp. Martyn, History and Theology, p.72. Also Bultmann, Ev Joh, p.231, no.7.

authority (9:22; 12:42; 16:2) had consolidated on the local scene into the party of the Pharisees. This situation is transposed back into the Gospel account and may well serve as an index for the evangelist's part in the composition of the pericope.

A further indication for the evangelist's hand in the composition may be seen in the troublesome phrase in v.49, ἀρχιερεὺς ὢν τοῦ ἐνιαυτοῦ ἐκείνου, reiterated in v.51. The implication, as has often been noted, is that the high priest changed office from year to year. Appointment to the Jewish high priesthood, however, was not an annual affair but was for lifetime. Attempts to resolve the conflict by interpreting the genitive construction in a temporal sense ("in that year")[1] are not only forced[2] but, in the light of similar imprecision with the ἀρχιερεῖς καὶ οἱ Φαρισαῖοι combination, not convincing. When one bears in mind the custom in Asia Minor and Syria among non-Jewish high priests whose office was changed on a yearly basis,[3] it is not unlikely that similar syncretistic factors were at work in coloring the evangelist's understanding of the priesthood in Jerusalem particularly since he is considerably separated from the actual proceedings there. Again, distance from the inner relationships and conditions of the governing bodies before the destruction of the Temple seems to be a determinative factor.

Related considerations are also involved in v.52 in the interpretation of Caiaphas' words as prophecy. Whereas in pre-exilic times prophecy and high priestly function were closely connected (Ex.28:30; Lev.8:8; Nu.27:21), it appears that during the captivity the high priestly power of divination was lost (Ezra 2:63; Neh.7:65). The trend in Judaism was to disassociate the priestly office from prophetic inspiration. Thus e.g. Josephus could regard the connection as a thing of the past (Ant.,III, 8,9). Or when Hyrcanus I receives the gift of prophecy, it is not specifically connected with his office

---

[1] So Barrett (*St. John*, p. 339), Schnackenburg (*Joh. Ev.*, II, p. 449) and R. Brown (*John*, I, p. 440). Schlatter (*Evangelist Joh.*, p. 258) attempts an unconvincing distinction between ἐνιαυτὸς (12 months) and ἔτος (a series of years).
[2] Cp. Blaß-Debrunner (Funk), *op. cit.*, p. 186.2. See also W. Bauer, *Joh. Ev.*, p. 156.
[3] Bauer (Arndt-Gingrich), *Lexicon*, p. 365. W. Bauer, *Joh. Ev.*, p. 156.

as high priest (Josephus, *Bell.*, I, 68f.). It appears that in first century Judaism it was no longer a self-evident matter that the high priest should have the gift of prophecy simply by virtue of his office as high priest.[1] The connection in the Hellenistic world, on the other hand, between priestly and prophetic function appears significantly stronger.[2] It is this kind of context which may well have provided the interacting impulses in facilitating the interpretation of Caiaphas' words as prophecy because he was the high priest. Should these observations be applicable, we would have another indication of the influence of the evangelist's contemporary scene on his choice of formulations in expounding a piece of transmitted tradition.

C. RELIGIO-HISTORICAL COMPARISONS

One final point needs still to be discussed in this section and that is the religio-historical background of the central statement in v.52: ἀλλ' ἵνα καὶ τὰ τέκνα τοῦ θεοῦ τὰ διεσκορπισμένα συναγάγῃ εἰς ἕν. The eschatological theme of the gathering of those scattered abroad is richly represented in the OT. "The Lord will assemble the outcasts of Israel and gather the dispersed of Judah" (Is.11:12). In varied form the theme is repeated (Is.43:5; 60:4; Micah 2:12; Jer.23:3; Ez.34:12, 13 etc.) and gives expression to the hopes and prayers of Israel (IV Ezra 13:8; Shemoneh Esre 10). But always the object of the gathering is Israel,[3] the reconstitution of the 12 Tribes. Precisely this accent, however, is absent in John. Had the

---

[1] The passages listed by Schlatter (*Evangelist Joh.*, p. 259) and reiterated in part by R. Brown (*John*, I, p. 444) are not actually germane since they do not speak to the issue of the high priest prophesying because he holds the office of high priest.

[2] Cp. W. Bauer, *Joh. Ev.*, p. 32 --Exkurs zu der Frage nach den Propheten. Also p. 157.

[3] O. Hofius ("Die Sammlung der Heiden zur Herde Israels," *ZNW*, 58, 1967, pp. 289f.) recognizes that the OT references refer only to Israel. He then cites Is.56:3-8 as the lone exception which speaks of the foreigners who will be brought to the holy mountain. They will be gathered in addition to those already gathered (v.8). But since the gathering is contingent on keeping the Sabbath and holding to the Covenant (v.6) and offering sacrifice (v.7), the "foreigners" are really only an extension of Israel and are viewed as a kind of final addition. As such the passage offers no real analogy to the Joh. text.

idiomatic formation of the passage received its essential motivation from the OT, one would have expected an expression like "my people," "sheep," "remnant," etc. The OT speaks of the "children of Israel" but never of the "children of God." Τέκνα τοῦ θεοῦ does, on the other hand, bear resemblance to expressions in the Hellenistically influenced Jewish Wisdom Literature (Sap.2:13,16,18),[1] but its real roots lie in the syncretistic sphere of the mystery religions[2] and Gnosis[3] where themes of rebirth and birth from beyond play central roles. Indeed, here are decisive elements in the formation of the contextual background for the typically Johannine expressions of "birth from above" (3:3), "birth of the Spirit" (3:6), and "birth of God" (1:13), and "becoming the children of God" (1:12), a consistent extension of which is the τέκνα τοῦ θεοῦ in 11:52. Furthermore, the gathering theme played a constitutive role in the phenomenology of Gnosis.[4] The plight of a lost mankind was described in terms of its dispersal from the point of its origin. Thus the soteriological goal could be verbalized as a gathering of the scattered into one as illustrated in the statements: "The seeds (children) of God are gathered" (*Exc. e Theod.* 49, 1). "Wiederum wird man sie zu dem Offenbaren versammeln" (*Thomasbuch* 141, 5).[5] "Daher versammelt sich die Menge und sie kommen zu einer Einheit" (*Eugnostosbrief* 86, 20).[6] Similar expressions are frequent in Gnostic texts.[7] The gathering of those who have been born from above, i.e. the children of God who are now dispersed —this typically Gnostic thought offers the clearest analogy to the idiom and formulation of the Johannine passage in v.52.

SUMMARY: The cumulative internal and stylistic evidence

---

[1] Cp. the Wisdom background for the Q Logion in Lk.7:35 and the τέκνα θεοῦ designation in the Prolog. Further, Bultmann, "Die religionsgeschichtliche Hintergrund des Prologs," *Exegetica*, pp. 19, 23.
[2] Leipoldt-Grundmann, *Umwelt*, I, p.126. Reitzenstein, *Mysterienreligionen*, pp.262f. Dieterich, *Mithrasliturgie*, pp.134-156. *Theologisches Begriffslexikon zum NT*, Bd. II, Wuppertal, 1972, p. 780.
[3] Bultmann, *Johannesbriefe*, p. 50; *Ev Joh*, p. 96, n.5.
[4] H. Jonas, *Gnosis und spätantiker Geist*, pp. 139f.
[5] Foerster, *Die Gnosis*, II, p. 143.
[6] Foerster, *Die Gnosis*, II, p. 44.
[7] Bultmann, "Die Bedeutung d. mand. und manich. Quellen," *Exegetica*, pp. 74f., lists numerous further parallels.

fails to support the conclusion that the pericope of 11:47-53 was originally an intact pronouncement story or apophthegma slightly emended by the writer or that it was a coherent and intact unit of a prior passion source. Apart from the stylized passion fragments in vs. 53 and 47a (hapax: συνέδριον), the only segment which allows itself to be isolated with a reasonable amount of surety is v.50 which may well have been an independent unit of tradition (it appears again independently in an abbreviated form in 18:14) preserved because of its aphoristic character and its ironic overtones --a kind of political maxim on the one hand and yet on the other a succinct testimony to the salvific and redemptive nature of Jesus' death. As such the saying may originally have been part of a complex of material relating to the passion account. In any case the tradition is adopted and significantly reinterpreted by the evangelist in the interest of the oneness motif and expanded with language and formulations consistent with the rest of his Gospel. Thus a maxim of political expediency with an underlying significance of redemptive expiation becomes a piece of unconscious prophecy explained in the Gnostically colored terms of a "scattered and gathering of God's children" theme and incorporated into a pre-passion sequence consistent with the evangelist's overarching theme of oneness.

Chapter IX: Oneness Passages in a Discourse

The explicit terminology of John's oneness motif occurs again in two separate passages in 10:16 and in 10:30, each bearing a unique and yet related theological orientation. Both passages are embedded in two larger, formally separate yet essentially contiguous complexes of material which comprise chapter 10. The overall character of the chapter breathes an atmosphere of polemic and struggle. It is not the quiet pastoral scene that it is often made out to be, designed for peaceful contemplation and inspiring edification. Sharp sounds of antithesis and exclusive claims loom up behind the bucolic imagery and give expression to the crisis and division as well as to the security and unity that follow confrontation with the Revealer.[1] Tied together by a pervading and continuous christological concern, the material is nevertheless marked by a literary disparity that has been a chronic problem for interpreters.

A. CONTEXTUAL PROBLEMS

Hardly another chapter in the Fourth Gospel presents such crass literary breaks and surface inconsistencies. The manuscript variations in themselves already give an indication of the problem involved. These include, above all, the following. Motivated by the difficulty of the sudden introduction of the door predication in v.7, pap.75 and the Sahidic give instead the smoother reading of ὁ ποιμήν. The change, however, is obviously a correction and not the original.[2] Similarly the troublesome πρὸ ἐμοῦ of v.8, which, literally taken, would include a negative judgment against the OT prophets and righteous men as well, is conveniently deleted by pap. 45, 75, ℵ*,

---

[1] Cp. Wetter, *Der Sohn Gottes*, p. 164: "diese Sätze (atmen) Kampf und Streit." Similarly Bousset, *Kyrios Christos*, p. 182.
[2] Wellhausen (*Erweiterungen und Änderungen*, p. 35), however, accepts the gloss as original and thus finds additional support for regarding v.9 as a secondary insertion.

the Koine texts, lat. and the Syriac versions.¹ The offence
of the phrase is clear and makes its deletion obviously a
secondary reading. The superior attested aorist ἦρεν in v.18
presents a chronological break in the present context (Jesus
has not yet given his life)² and its difficulty explains the
emendation of αἴρει. These relatively minor textual variations are only the beginning of a whole series of further
problems lodged in this chapter.

The transition from chapter 9 with its theme of blindness
and light to chapter 10 which begins with an unrelated parable without any introduction is so abrupt that the two complexes can hardly be said to fit together. A reference to
the opening of the eyes of the blind does, to be sure, occur
in v.21, but it is at a place and in a manner that makes for
anything but smooth and integrated composition. The chronological references are also problematic. As the material now
stands, ch.10:1-21 appears as a part of the discourse spoken
in the general context of the Feast of Tabernacles mentioned
in 7:2. But the continuation of the discourse as a dispute
with the Jews in 10:22-39 is located at the Feast of Dedica-
tion³ so that the scene, apparently intended to be continuous
in view of the resumption of the Shepherd theme in vs.26-29,
is interrupted by a span of some 2 - 3 months.⁴

Not only do the contextual and chronological breaks reflect
a disordered structure but also the following internal

---

¹ The negative judgment against the OT figures was a favorite theme in
Gnostic interpretation.   Cp. examples cited by W. Bauer, *Joh. Ev.*, p.
139.
² Torrey's suggestion (*Our Translated Gospels*, New York and London, 1936,
p. 114) that the past tense is due to a translational error (Aramaic to
Greek) is unlikely. The same motivation which prompted the substitution
of αἴρει for ἦρεν would have prevented such an error. A further point may
be noted. The passage provides a good example, typical for the whole 4.
Gospel, of an event yet to occur in Jesus' life and yet viewed as already
past from the evangelist's own time perspective.
³ Tabernacles was celebrated in October; the Feast of Dedication in December.   Cp. Billerbeck, *op. cit., ad loc.*   Schlatter, *Evangelist Joh.*,
p. 240.
⁴ R. Brown's harmonizing attempt (*John*, I, p. 389) suggesting that Dedication was another Tabernacles (II Macc. 1:9) or that the incident of ch.
9 and the discourse of 10:1-21 may have taken place between Tabernacles
and Dedication (implying that the time gap is not so great) is both forced
and unconvincing.

sequences. The opening verses begin with the antithesis between the shepherd who enters the sheepfold through the door and the thief and robber who climb in by another way. Then, unexpectedly, the metaphor is mixed and Jesus, the shepherd, is identified as the door <u>to</u> the sheep. A different accent is introduced in v.9 where Jesus is identified simply as the door. The implication here is that he is the door <u>for</u> or on behalf of the sheep, i.e. through him as point of entry the sheep will find pasture, viz. receive salvation. Again the metaphor is modified in v.11 where Jesus declares himself to be not just the shepherd, or the door to or for the sheep, but in an absolute sense, the one and only good shepherd who lays down his life for the sheep. A similarly disconnected mixture appears in the antithesis. The thieves and robbers of v.1 are replaced by the stranger in v.5 only to reappear again in v.8 but then to be reduced to a singular thief in v.9. A totally new picture emerges in v.12 with the hired man, who leaves the sheep, and with the wolf who scatters the sheep. The initial impression here is that of a farrago of metaphors and word pictures.

The impression of a mixture is reinforced through the variously made contentions that the first discourse contains contrasting literary forms. Thus the first 5 verses seem to be a parable[1] or a fusion of two originally separate parables,[2] whereas vs. 7-10 are said to shift over to allegory. Accordingly vs.11-13 resume the parable form and vs.14ff. revert again to allegory.[3] Furthermore, the line of thought does not provide a continuous thread. Just as vs.7 and 9 have intrusive character with their introduction of different symbolic forms not immediately consistent with the shepherd theme, so it may also be said that v.16 disrupts an otherwise continuous

---

[1] Cp. Bultmann, *Ev Joh*, p. 273. Also Jeremias, ποιμήν, *ThWB*, VI, p. 494, no.30.
[2] J.A.T.Robinson, "The Parable of the Shepherd," *ZNW*, 46, 1955, pp. 233-240.
[3] Bultmann (*Ev Joh*, p. 273) speaks of vs.1-5 and vs.11-13 as parables. Jeremias (*ThWB*, VI, 494) identifies vs.1-5(6) as a parable and the rest of the discourse as allegorizing interpretation. R. Brown (*John*, I, pp.391f.) speaks of two parables in vs.1-5, allegory in vs.7-10, parable in vs.11-13, and allegory in vs.14-18.

thought pattern between vs.15 and 17.¹ Also if vs.1-8 are parabolic and allegorical speech, then the charge of demon possession hardly seems appropriate in v.20. Other marks of unevenness may be noted in the dispute scene in vs.24-39. The discourse is tied together by the ἔργα theme which sets the direction in Jesus' opening response in v.25, which is then carried through in the reiteration in vs.32f., and which concludes the discourse in v.38. The insertion of the sheep reference in vs.26-29 introduces a new element and can hardly be said to be a smooth integration. Similar unevenness may be noted with v.30. Although thoughtwise the revelatory declaration in v.30 is well prepared for and thoroughly consistent, its structural brevity and literary form suggest independent and formula character.² Further literary dissonance may be noted in the scriptural argumentation in vs.34-36. While the passage evidences a relationship with substantiating arguments as in 7:23 and 8:17, as well as with rabbinical a minori ad maius arguments,³ its expanded use in vs.34-36 is unique for the 4. Gospel and may, in fact, be said to be un-Johannine.⁴ What is more, the passage is not tightly fitted into the context since it neither provides an accurate answer to the charge of the Jews nor does it repeat the provocative statement of v.30 as, strictly speaking, would have been called for in v.36. In summary, we have seen that chapter 10 is marked by continual breaks and by a literary unevenness that characterizes its entire structure.

The proposals advanced in past studies to explain, minimize, or to resolve the structural disorder of the chapter have been basically threefold. One such approach has been to suggest that the original pages of the manuscript somehow became so badly jumbled that the original order can now be established only through rearrangement. Numerous proposals have been

---

¹ So e.g. Wellhausen (*Erweiterungen u. Änderungen*, p. 35): "10:16 sprengt den logisch strengen Connex zwischen 10:15 und 17 und gehört inhaltlich in eine Reihe mit 11:52 und 17:20.
² Cp. Norden, *Agnostos Theos*, pp. 177f.
³ Cp. Billerbeck, *op. cit.*, ad loc.
⁴ Thus e.g. Odeberg, *The Fourth Gospel*, p. 332: "vs.34, 35 are, indeed, scarcely Johannine in character."

given.¹ Typical is Bernard's proposal for the following original order: ch. 9; 10:19-29; 1-18; 30-39.² Bultmann's rearrangement sequence is considerably more complex: 10:22-26; 11-13; 1-10; 14-18; 27-39 with vs. 19-21 forming the conclusion to a preceding "light of the world" complex consisting of 8:12; 12:44-50; 8:21-29; and 12:34-36.³ Apart from disclosing inner connections and thought patterns, the value and validity of the rearrangement hypotheses remain, as previously noted, highly questionable. Granted that the intrinsic possibility of major paginal disorder cannot be wholly excluded, its probability is however minute.⁴ Moreover, the re-ordering hypotheses are so weighted with tacit assumptions that it would be better to seek out other less tenuous alternatives.

A second approach has been to reckon with the insertion of glosses and later redactional emendations. Thus vs. 7 and 9 have been most frequently regarded as secondary additions.⁵ The same has also been most often maintained for v. 16⁶ and with less frequency for vs. such as 26-28⁷ and 34,35⁸ as well as others⁹ depending on the presuppositions of the critic. The case for redactional additions and interpolations, however, bears weight only when it can be demonstrated that the passages in question evidence theological motives and possibly stylistic peculiarities (although here the factor of imitation must be taken into account) at variance with the context. It is precisely at this point that the oft cited glosses for ch. 10 become problematic. Bultmann in a sense

---

¹ See the discussion in Howard, *The Fourth Gospel*, p. 264. Also E. Schweizer, *Ego Eimi*, pp. 108f.
² *Commentary*, p. 341. Cp. also Bd. I, xxiv f.
³ *Ev Joh*, pp. 236f. and 274.
⁴ A positive assessment of the possibilities is given by E. Schweizer, *Ego Eimi*, pp. 109f. Skeptical, Jeremias, *ThWB*, VI, p. 494. Excellent critique by D. M. Smith, *The Composition and Order*, pp. 119-179. See also Fortna, *The Gospel of Signs*, p. 7.
⁵ So E. Schweizer, *Ego Eimi*, p. 148. S. Schulz, *Komposition und Herkunft*, p. 77.
⁶ Originally Wellhausen, *Erweiterungen und Änderungen*, p. 35. Similarly Bultmann, *Ev Joh*, p. 292. E. Schweizer, *Ego Eimi*, p. 150. J. Becker, "Aufbau" *op. cit.*, p. 75.
⁷ So R. Schütz, "Ev. Joh. 10:25-29," *ZNW*, 10, 1909, p. 324f.
⁸ So E. Hirsch, *Studien z. vierten Evangelium*, p. 86.
⁹ E.g. F. Spitta, *Joh. Ev.*, pp. 209ff. Also Hirsch, *Studien*, ad loc.

recognized this already in regard to vs. 7 and 9 which he ascribed as a gloss attributed not to a redactor but to the evangelist because neither verse betrays any specific interests of a later redaction[1] as e.g. would be the case with ch. 21. A similar argument may also be maintained not only for vs. 26-28 and 34,35 but also for v.16. There is nothing compelling in the content of these verses which makes the assumption of interpolation a necessity.

A third approach in trying to explain the uneven structure of ch. 10 has been to posit the use of pre-formed Johannine traditions. Indeed, this remains the most viable option. Thus it is conceivable that the evangelist incorporated units of tradition which had been transmitted and further developed within the context of the Johannine church. Because, however, many of the formulations had already received a set character, their integration into a continuous speech and narrative scene, despite recasting and adaptation by the evangelist, became more difficult and helped to contribute to the chapter's lack of structural smoothness and order.[2] Although numerous source analyses have been undertaken a precise division between prior tradition and the evangelist's own composition for ch. 10 remains highly uncertain. Bultmann's source hypothesis has merit in isolating verses which may indeed represent earlier tradition (8, 10, 11-13, 14-15a, 27-30). But as part of a larger written, literarily unified and rhythmically structured, non-Christian Gnostic speech source, the hypothesis has, as we have seen elsewhere, little credibility. In his reconstruction of Bultmann's proposed source, H. Becker himself concedes in regard to this chapter that the rhythmic contrasts (vs. 14f. and 27f. are substantially more rhythmically structured than the prosaic vs. 1-5) and the stylistic unity pose such problems that an exact delimitation of underlying source material is virtually precluded.[3] The nature of

---

[1] *Ev Joh*, p. 286, no. 2.
[2] Cp. Bornkamm ("Zur Interpretation," *op. cit.*, p. 115): "Die Vielschichtigkeit und Schwierigkeit der Fragen...sind offensichtlich dadurch bedingt, daß der Evangelist...Traditionen weitergibt, aber sie zugleich selbständig und kritisch verarbeitet."
[3] H. Becker, *Die Reden d. Johannesevangeliums.*, pp. 88f.: "Sicheres ist...

the problem may be further seen in the sheer variety of the proposals advanced. S. Schulz e.g. speaks of vs. 1-5, 8, 10, 12-13, and 15 as parts of earlier tradition.[1] Blauert reduces this to vs. 1-4.[2] Jeremias identifies vs. 1-6 as primitive Palestinian tradition and regards the remaining portion of vs. 1-18 as periphrastic interpretation.[3] The uncertainty at this point is reinforced by the wide and even distribution of Johannine stylistic characteristics. The following compilation will help to make this clear.

B. STYLISTIC FACTORS

In v.1 the ἀμὴν ἀμήν, though easily imitated,[4] is a typically Johannine feature as is also the casus pendens in this same verse.[5] In v.2 the separation of the genitive form from its nomens regens is also characteristic for John.[6] Further stylistic idiosyncracies may be seen in the chiastic pattern in v.4f.;[7] the genitive before the article in v.5;[8] the use of the term παροιμία in v.6;[9] ἀμὴν ἀμήν in v.7 (cp. v.1); the ἐάν τις construction in v.9;[10] τιθέναι ψυχήν in v.11;[11] the grammatical parataxis for logical hypotaxis in v.12;[12] the chiasmus in v.14f.[13] τιθέναι ψυχήν in vs.15 and 17 (cp. v.11); the διὰ τοῦτο...

---

nicht auszumachen. Möglich ist ja auch, daß der Evgst. hier mit seiner Vorlage noch freier umgegangen ist, als er sonst schon tut und daß infolgedessen unsere Logik den Text allzu sehr belastet."
[1] *Komposition und Herkunft*, p. 79.
[2] *Die Bedeutung der Zeit*, p. 121.
[3] *ThWB*, VI, p. 494.
[4] Cp. Ruckstuhl's warning against attaching too much value to this characteristic (*Lit. Einheit*, p. 198). The occurrence ratio is nevertheless an impressive 25/0.
[5] Cp. Burney, *Aram. Origin*, p. 64. Frequency ratio (Nicol, *Semeia*, p. 24, no. 79): 27/|28|.
[6] E. Schweizer, *Ego Eimi*, p. 94. Frequency ratio: 30/[25+3].
[7] E. Schweizer, *ibid*, (p. 97).
[8] E. Schweizer, *ibid*, Frequency ratio: 5/[1+0].
[9] Ruckstuhl, *Lit. Einheit*, p. 196. Ratio: 4/0.
[10] Fortna (*The Gospel of Signs*, p. 207, no.47) provides a helpful listing of the Joh. passages for Schweizer's figures: 24+4/19+2.
[11] Cp. Ruckstuhl's revised figures (*Lit. Einheit*, p. 196) for the ratio: 8+2/0.
[12] A standard feature of John and a Semitic characteristic of his Greek. Cp. K. Beyer, *Semitische Syntax*, p. 280.
[13] Cf. v.4.

ὅτι construction in v.17;[1] ἀπ' ἐμαυτοῦ and τιθέναι αὐτήν in v.18;[2] the οἱ Ἰουδαῖοι in v.19;[3] πολλοὶ ἐκ in v.20;[4] the asyndeton epicum in v.22;[5] the οὖν historicum[6] and οἱ Ἰουδαῖοι (cp. v.19) and παρρησία in v.24;[7] ἔργον for the Messianic works of Christ[8] and the casus pendens (cp. v.1) in v.25; ἐμός in the second attributive position in vs. 26,27;[9] the εἰς τὸν αἰῶνα phrase in v.28;[10] the collective neuter singular ὅ in v.29;[11] οἱ Ἰουδαῖοι in v.31 (cp. v.19); the unusual word separation (ἔργα...καλά),[12] ἀπεκρίθη + direct speech;[13] and the use of ἔργα (cp. v.25) in <u>v.32</u>; ἄνθρωπος used for Jesus;[14] the use of ἔργον (cp. v.25) and οἱ Ἰουδαῖος (cp. v.19) and ἀπεκρίθη + direct speech in v.34 (cp. v.32), and the τινα λέγειν construction[15] in vs. 35,36, plus the occurrence of κόσμος[16] in v.36; and finally the use of ἔργα in vs. 37,38 (cp. v.25). Considering the cumulative effect of such distribution plus the fact that in none of the verses from 1-39 in which no specific characteristics were listed (vs. 3, 8, 10, 13, 16, 21, 23, 30, 35, and 39) can any un-Johannine stylistic features be noted,[17] the overall stylistic

---

[1] One of Nicol's additions (*Semeia*, p. 23, n.51) to Ruckstuhl's list. Frequency ratio: 6+1/3.
[2] For the ἀπ' ἐμαυτοῦ construction, see Schweizer (*Ego Eimi*, p. 93) and the ratio: 13+0/1(2)+0. For τιθέναι αὐτήν v.11.
[3] Cp. Nicol (*Semeia*, p. 23 no.55) and the ratio: 67/[10+6].
[4] Fortna's revised figures for this usage (*The Gospel of Signs*, p. 209 no.45): 25(26)/[1]0.
[5] E. Schweizer, *Ego Eimi*, pp. 91f. Ratio: 39/5.
[6] Cp. Nichol's revised figures (*Semeia*, p. 17): 146/8.
[7] Ratio: 7/1.
[8] Cp. Nicol's listing (*Semeia*, p. 23 no.54): 20/2.
[9] E. Schweizer, *Ego Eimi*, pp. 88f. Ratio: 29+1/0.
[10] Ruckstuhl (*Lit. Einheit*, p. 198): 12+2/11+1.
[11] Nicol (*Semeia*, p. 17): 4/0.
[12] E. Schweizer, *Ego Eimi*, p. 96.
[13] Nicol (*Semeia*, p. 23 no.62): 45/12.
[14] Nicol, *ibid.* (no.73): 15/7+3.
[15] Nicol, *ibid.* (no.77): 6/1.
[16] Nicol, *ibid.* (no.66): 78+24/83.
[17] E. Schweizer (*Ego Eimi*, p. 142; cp. also S. Schulz, *Komposition und Herkunft*, p. 77) maintains that the genetive τῶν προβάτων of v. 7 is linguistically irregular. That judgment, however, is theological and not grammatical. Similarly the claim is made (Schweizer, *ibid.*) that the ὅτι recitativum in v. 7 is "un-Johannine." While it is true that the ὅτι before an accentuated ἐγώ is not frequent in John, still it does occur (1:20, 8:24; 9:9 and 18:8) and can therefore be hardly termed un-Johannine. There is only one hapax legomenon in the chapter: ἀλλαχόθεν in v.1. The irregular use of οὐκ with the participle in v. 12, occurring only here in the 4. Gospel, is likely due to the preference for καὶ οὐ instead of καὶ μή (cp. Blaß-Debrunner (Funk), *op. cit.*, p. 430, 1.).

unity of the chapter appears substantially secured.

C. THEOLOGICAL ARGUMENT

Our findings lead to what at first glance seems to be a contradictory result. On the one hand, ch. 10 is marked by repeated literary breaks, and yet on the other hand it is characterized by an essential stylistic unity. It remains for us to ask whether or not there is any discernible plan or continuous line of theological thought which may help to clarify the problem. Various proposals have been advanced. J. Schneider contends that the integrating center of the chapter is to be found in vs.1-5 which are followed by three interpretive explanations. In vs.7-10 the gate is explained; in vs.11-18 the shepherd is explained; and in vs.26-30 the sheep are explained.[1] The proposal is, however, not acceptable for the following reasons. The first explanatory section (vs.7-10) can hardly be said to be an interpretation of the door reference in vs.1f. If the mark of the true shepherd is his entry through the door of the sheepfold, then it is not clear how in the interest of explanation the shepherd can then simply be identified with the door. Obviously a connecting link is missing as long as one operates within the framework of parable - interpretation. Coupled with this is also the fact that vs.7-10 speak of the sheep, as does for that matter section vs.11-18, so that Schneider's proposed outline sequence of "door, shepherd, sheep" is not consistent. Similarly there is a problem with the third section in vs.27-30. This section is at best repetition, not interpretation. The only new thought is that the sheep shall not be snatched out of the shepherd's or the Father's hand. Furthermore, this thought is not prompted by the alleged original parable in vs. 1-5, but is rather motivated by a new scene and comes as the antithesis to the unbelief of the Jews expressed in v.24f. In short, it is not possible to understand the chapter as an interpretive expansion on the first five verses.

For similar reasons the proposal advanced by J. Jeremias is

---

[1] "Zur Komposition von Joh. 10," *Coniectanea Neotestamentica*, XI, Fridrichsen Festschrift, Lund, 1947, pp. 220-225.

also inadequate. Maintaining a unified development of thought for the chapter, Jeremias contends that vs.7-18 follow a literary technique of parable interpretation whereby both sections (vs.7-10 and 11-18) are constructed according to the following fourfold scheme: 1) interpretive statement; 2) its antithesis; 3) repetition of the statement; 4) its qualifying explication.[1] Here again the implication is that vs.7-18 represent an organic outgrowth of the first five verses and that a definite compositional plan was used in the exegesis of a basal unit. But again the evidence fails to support the hypothesis. Vs. 7 and 9 can hardly be interpretation of v.1. V. 10a, which should be part of the explication, is also an antithesis thus removing the consistency of the proposed category. The final category (14b - 18) of the second section is conspicuously irregular because of its length and disproportionate elaboration in comparison with its corresponding part in v.9b.f. Then too, it must be noted that it revolves around a theme, the laying down of one's life for the sheep, which is nowhere even suggested in the first five verses. Finally, Jeremias' proposed construction does not help to explain the extension of the discourse in vs.26-29. Clearly another way must be found.

What our analysis thus far has shown is that vs.1-5 cannot be viewed as the point of orientation in the sense that everything which follows is interpretation or allegorizing paraphrase of the same. In other words, the parable - allegorizing interpretation scheme cannot be the guiding compositional principle underlying the structure of the chapter. In fact, it would be best not even to use the categories of parable and allegory for this chapter since the metaphoric speech modes here are not equivalent to the parable forms (e.g. synoptic) with a tertium comparationis or to allegory with a series of comparative points.[2] Neither category properly applies

---

[1] *ThWB*, VI, p. 494f.
[2] Cp. E. Schweizer (*Ego Eimi*, p. 122): "Es geht also genau um das, worum es im Gleichnis oder in der Allegorie niemals gehen darf, um den Nachweis, daß dieser Jesus ("die Sache") mit Recht den Titel des 'Hirten' ...in Anspruch nimmt." Cp. further the pertinent critique of Jülicher's rigorous separation between parable and allegory by E. Jüngel, *Paulus und Jesus*, Tübingen, 1964, pp. 137f.

to the speech employed in ch. 10. This is not to say that the speech is not metaphoric. It is. Jesus himself calls it παροιμία in v.6. But it is metaphoric in a singular and unique fashion. The figures of speech[1] used receive their inner motivation from a christological concern. It is the concern to give witness to the absolute uniqueness and singularity of Jesus and the exclusiveness of his person and mission. Using this concern as his governing compositional principle, the evangelist is able to recast and to join independent units of tradition which do not form a smooth literary coherency in their present sequence. Instead they are all tied together by an inner christological motivation meant to detail and to authenticate the person of the Revealer as well as to express not only the faith but also the opposition which his words and works evoke. The language used here is not a conglomeration of pictures only but is actual speech characterized by statements that have revelational force. If this be granted, then it becomes clear how the argumentation of the chapter unfolds. Less a basis for subsequent interpretation, the initial verses instead serve as cues for the addition of thematically similar, in part independently preformed material, which is to reinforce the christological center. It is not a literary principle at work but rather a christological one. Thus it may be said, e.g., that the mention of the door in v. 1 paves the way by virtue of a formal word parallel for vs.7 and 9 which were added for no other reason than for their testimony to the centricity of Jesus.

This helps to clarify not only the formal unevenness of the chapter but also the inner relation of its parts and thus provides the clue for understanding the chapter's basic structure. The evangelist's method of composition does not result in a progressive line of literarily continuous and smoothly integrated thought. He can mix traditions and metaphors and formulations as long as they serve the purpose of giving witness to the absoluteness of Jesus and his divine status.

---

[1] Searching for a more neutral designation, Barrett with some justification (*St. John*, p. 304) uses the term "symbolic discourse." Cp. Schweizer's critique of this term (*Ego Eimi*, p. 121).

Likewise chronological and geographical references, though deeply embedded in the Gospel tradition,[1] are utilized by the evangelist not for the sake of accurate historical recording but as the scenery and backdrop for a display of the Revealer's glory in his confrontation with the world. Thus the references can shift and change in accordance with the theological design and without apparent regard for inner inconsistencies of time and place and for literary breaks in the composition.[2] Jesus moves about and speaks at will. He supercedes the restrictions of historical sequence which are but framework and buttress for the christological witness. The discourse accordingly is not structured on the basis of a logical, unbroken progression of thought but rather in relation to a variety of interwoven themes whose singular characteristic is their witness to who Jesus is.

From this standpoint we are able to turn our attention back to vs.16 and 30. Ever since Wellhausen's pronouncement that v.16 must be an interpolation since it breaks the otherwise logically consistent connection between vs.15 and 17,[3] most critical studies have followed suit in striking the verse as an essentially foreign element. The reason for doing this, however, is highly suspect since, as we have seen, logical consistency is not a characteristic of Johannine compositional technique. Further it must be noted that in the verse there are no linguistic or stylistic peculiarities which could be termed un-Johannine or suggest that it originated from a different hand. In fact, the asyndetic formula at the end of the verse μία ποίμνη, εἷς ποιμήν betrays a typically Johannine preference for paratactic constructions.[4] In the light of our

---

[1] The portico of Solomon e.g. was a gathering place for the early church (Acts 5:12), and the area may well have retained sacral significance for the evangelist's generation after the destruction of Jerusalem because of the tradition associated with the place where Jesus appeared in open opposition to his hostile contemporaries. Cp. K. Kundsin, *Topologische Überlieferungsstoffe im Johannes-Evangelium*, FRLANT, N.F. 22, Göttingen, 1925, pp. 39, 76.
[2] Cp. F. C. Baur, *Kritische Untersuchungen über die kanonischen Evangelien*, Tübingen, 1847, pp. 283ff.
[3] See p. 249 n.1.
[4] There is strong manuscript evidence for the variant reading giving the plural form of the verb (γενήσονται) instead of the generally accepted singular. (Cp. Barrett, *St. John*, p. 312 and Hoskyns, *The Fourth Gospel*,

previous observations it is also clear that there is no need to interpret the verse allegorically so that the αὐλή must refer to Israel and the ἄλλα πρόβατα to the Gentiles.[1] This favorite approach of the commentators has no real justification.[2] Jesus simply speaks of those sheep who are not yet in the fold but who will be led to hear his voice and be thus incorporated into the oneness of the Shepherd and the flock.[3] The verse introduces a future orientation totally consistent with the future aspects of the oneness motif in 11:52 and 17:20ff. The future is also contiguous with the force of the future tense in 10:5[4] where it is noted that the sheep will not follow strangers. Emphasis on the one shepherd in v.16 furthermore comes as the antithetical counterpart to the many strangers, robbers, and thieves whose dissentive voices are countered by the one voice of the one Shepherd. As such, v. 16 builds a culminating point in the first half of the discourse[5] and appears in a structurally integral position because of its christologically centered orientation. Here it serves a key function in the explication of the oneness motif.

Closely connected to and yet formally separated from this part of the discourse which ends initially with v.18 is the next section of the chapter which extends through v.39. The resumption of the shepherd theme in vs.26ff. evidences the evangelist's desire to connect the following episode with the previous shepherd dicta. The pervading aim of the metaphoric

---

p. 378, both of whom accept the future plural.) If accepted (and the manuscript evidence plus the *ardua lectio potior* principle are compelling), then the force of the asyndetic construction is increased.

[1] So Bultmann, *Ev Joh*, p. 292. W. Bauer, *Joh.Ev.*, p. 141. E. Schweizer, *Ego Eimi*, p. 150. Hoskyns, *The Fourth Gospel*, p. 378 *et al*.

[2] H. Odeberg, *The Fourth Gospel*, p. 330. "10:16 is an instance of such passages where one particular interpretation has got a hypnotical hold of the reader. It seems impossible to explain 'the fold' otherwise than as referring to (the disciples within) Israel and 'other sheep' as referring to the Gentile Christians to be. But this interpretation is not by incessity (*sic!*) implied by the wordings of the verse."

[3] The passage is not allegory. Thus Bultmann's objection (*Ev Joh*, p. 292 n.6) based on the ἐκ and the ταύτης is not tenable.

[4] The gnomic character of the future tense in v.5 does not exhaust its significance and does not, contrary to Schweizer (*Ego Eimi*, p. 150), preclude a relation to the function of the future in v.16.

[5] So also Jeremias, *ThWB*, VI, p. 495: "Ihren Höhepunkt erreicht die Hirtenrede in v.16." Similarly Bousset, *RGG*[1], III, p. 625.

speech in the first 18 verses was to give witness to the absoluteness and exclusiveness of Jesus. This now becomes explicit in the following scene and above all in the central declaration of 10:30. A first-hand impression of vs.22-30 is that they form a self-contained unit prompted and motivated by the pregnant saying in 10:30, thus reminiscent of the pronouncement story category discussed in relation to 11:47-53.[1] The structure, however, is too diverse to admit that kind of classification. What we do have before us is, including vs. 31ff., a loosely constructed unit built along the same compositional lines governing the formation of the first 18 verses, i.e. along christological lines. The formal diversity is held together by the christological witness which climaxes in the statement that Jesus and the Father are one.[2] V.30 forms the center of the unit and explicates the christological standard which is constitutive not only for the discourse of ch. 10 but for the entire Gospel. Its brevity and independent syntactical character, similar to the formula-like statement in v.16 (μία ποίμνη, εἷς ποιμήν), may indicate a set pre-Johannine formulation, although precise differentiation from the composition of the writer at this point can at best be only conjecture.

D. RELIGIO-HISTORICAL CHARACTER

A final word needs to be said about the religio-historical character of the terminology employed in these two verses. As noted in the Excursus in ch. 7,[3] OT and orthodox Jewish thought despite its "enormous diversity"[4] offers no real parallels to the mutual identity formula of 10:30. Here language is used which has its closest affinity to idioms peculiar to Hellenistic syncretism and Gnostic thought. The religio-historical coloring of the oneness and shepherd terminology used in 10:16, on the other hand, has broader potential affinities. The

---
[1] Cp. V. Taylor, *The Formation of the Gospel Tradition*, London, 1960, p. 82.
[2] Against Hoskyns (*The Fourth Gospel*, p. 382) et al. who lay the accent on the Dedication of the Temple and analogously stress the point of Jesus' consecration.
[3] See pp. 163-193.
[4] F. Hahn, "Methodenprobleme," *op. cit.*, p. 13.

exclusive implications of the oneness term here evidence
clear lines of correspondence with the OT and its central concern of an exclusively monotheistic faith. Although the OT
shepherd tradition (cp. Ps.23; 95:7; Is.40:11; Micah 2:12;
Jer.31:10 etc. and especially Ez.34) shows undeniable lines
of correspondence with the shepherd motif in ch. 10,[1] it is
nevertheless not broad enough to parallel the characteristically new accents introduced in that chapter.[2] In John the
shepherd is not a king nor are the sheep a new Israel. Instead the shepherd is the revealer[3] and the sheep are "his own"
who hear his voice and whose relationship to the shepherd is
characterized by mutual knowledge.[4] Here are accents reminiscent of expressions peculiar to distinctly Gnostic traditions.[5]
This is reinforced further by use of the door motif which was
similarly a favorite term in Gnostic speculation.[6] It may also
be noted that the distinctly Christian expression of the "shepherd laying down his life for the sheep" is not understood in
terms of the OT Suffering Servant motif but in terms of the
divine Shepherd who is Lord over life and death and who laid
down his life freely and of his own accord that he may take it
again. The formulation in v.16 of "one shepherd, one flock"
echoes the theme expressed in Ez.34:23 and 37:24 and yet the
context and orientation of the Johannine verse is so unique
that derivation from the OT passage can hardly be maintained.[7]

---

[1] Cp. W. Bauer, *Joh. Ev.*, p. 143. R. Schnackenburg, *Joh. Ev.*, II, p. 371.
Schlatter, *Evangelist Joh.*, pp. 233f. Dodd, *Interpretation*, pp. 358f.
[2] Cp. Bultmann, *Ev Joh*, p. 279.
[3] Consider the implicit equation between revealer and shepherd suggested
by the name "Poimandres" in the first Hermetic tractate.
[4] Jeremias' contention (*ThWB*, VI, p. 495 n.106) that the expression of
mutual knowledge in v.14 is a Semiticism and does not reflect the language of Gnostic usage lacks convincing documentation.
[5] So also H. Preisker/ S. Schulz, *ThWB*, VI, p. 601: "Wenn auch einige
Züge im Hirtenbild der altestamentlichen Tradition entsprechen, so finden
sich die meisten Gedankenanalogien und Sachparallelen in außerjüdischen,
gnostisch-hellenistischen Aussagenkreis. Cp. also Schulz, *Komposition
und Herkunft*. p. 103.
[6] Cp. Bultmann, "Die Bedeutung der mand und manich. Quellen," *Exegetica*,
p. 92.
[7] Unwarranted is Barrett's contention (*St. John*, p.23) that v.16 represents a direct quotation of Ez.34:23 and 37:24.

B. Theology of the Oneness Passages

Chapter X: Theological Explication

The foregoing analysis has demonstrated how deeply the oneness motif is embedded in the Fourth Gospel. In fact, it may be said that John's Gospel is conceived and developed from the standpoint of Jesus' oneness with the Father. To testify to this oneness is the evangelist's most basic concern and appears as his Gospel's most distinguishing and pervasive characteristic. It is the determining factor in the interpretation of Jesus' words and works, his life and his death,[1] and results in what has often and legitimately been referred to as "high christology." Since the heart and the core of this proclamation consists in the witness to the Son's oneness with the Father, the oneness motif in John is pre-eminently a christological motif. That is unique in the whole of NT tradition. Consistent with the groundwork and basic orientation provided throughout the Fourth Gospel are the explicit statements giving expression to Jesus' oneness with God (10:30; 17:11; 20-23). Nowhere else in the NT is the terminology of oneness explicitly used to describe Jesus' relation to the Father.

The christological character of the oneness motif, however,

---

[1] There is a tendency among interpreters to restrict John's high christology by associating it only with the miraculous semeia, i.e. only with one particular interpretation of Jesus' works. Thus E. Haenchen ("Vom Wandel," *op. cit.*, pp. 10ff.), by contending that the Fourth Gospel, similar to Matthew and Luke, is the product of two evangelists with differing theological orientations, can insist that the emphasis on Jesus' divinity is more compatible with the Gospel writer whom John corrects as evidenced in the adoption and redaction of the semeia works of Jesus. Haenchen thereby, however, fails to respect the weight given to Jesus' divinity in the development of the rest of the Fourth Gospel as evinced in the reinterpretation of the Passion account, in the reorientation given to the christological designations, and in the prominent role of the reciprocity statements. Here, as well as in the ascending and the descending motifs, and in the emphasis on Jesus' pre-existence the function and testimony of Jesus' oneness with the Father appear substantially more central than would be the case had it been associated only with the semeia.

is not its only orientation. John's ecclesiology and soteriology are also developed along analogous lines and derive their distinctive explications from the underlying pervasiveness of his oneness christology. This too finds explicit expression in the oneness passages (10:16; 11:52; 17:11,20-23). What is enlarged upon in constantly varying forms and modes throughout the whole of John's Gospel is put into definitive and summary expression in these oneness passages. As our literary and source analysis of these passages demonstrated, they cannot be regarded as secondary additions, corrective interpolations, or as the results of a theological shift that reflects basic variance with the evangelist's original intention. Instead they are wholly congruous with the major orientation of the Fourth Gospel. As integral parts of the composition they provide climactic expression to the development of the corresponding themes. Here the oneness motif appears as a theological abbreviation for the evangelist's deepest concerns. Our purpose in this final chapter will be to examine in greater detail the theological implications of these respective passages and to explore the aspects of their meaning relationships.

A. CHRISTOLOGY AND ECCLESIOLOGY OF THE ONENESS MOTIF

Far from being an extraneous addition, v.16 appears as an integral, coherent expansion within the context of the shepherd discourse. The future orientation pointing to the goal of the believers who will be led into one flock gives the verse climactic force. Emphasis on the one Shepherd underscores its compendious character by summarizing in a concise formula-like phrase a major theme of the Fourth Gospel. The dual orientation of the formulation -- μία ποίμνη, εἷς ποιμήν is both ecclesiological and christological and details these two aspects of the usage of the oneness motif. The formulation sharply reflects a major aspect of the faith of John's community[1]

---

[1] R. Brown's strained considerations (*John*, I, p. 396) on whether v.16 represents a theme of Jesus' ministry or of later Christian theologians misses the point. His implication that the words must be *ipsissima verba* of the historical Jesus in order to be "a directive...from Jesus himself" obscures one of the most fundamental tenets of the Fourth Gospel, namely that Jesus continues to speak after the cross.

by giving expression, on the one hand, to the absoluteness of
the Revealer and, on the other hand, to the exclusive character of "his own." The virtual unanimity among commentators
that the v.16 reference to the "other sheep which are not of
this fold" must be seen within a Jewish-Gentile context[1] is,
however, not warranted. The problem in John is not how a
Jewish Christian church can incorporate those of Gentile extraction, nor is Jesus understood as he who makes Jew and
Gentile one by breaking down the dividing wall of hostility
(Eph.2:14).[2] A salvation-history perspective for an understanding of the church is singularly absent in John. Here
church is not seen as a continuation of OT Israel, a reconstitution of the people of God,[3] to which must now be added
those who were "afar off," the Gentiles who had been excluded
from God's covenant plan. Nowhere is there indication that
John thought in terms of a salvation-history priority of Israel. The terminology for such a conception is absent. Accordingly, the issue in John is not the Gentile mission seen
against a Jewish background and the problem of how Jews and
Gentiles could be united into one. It is therefore unclear
with what justification commentators repeatedly insist that
the αὐλή of v.16 must be allegorically identified with Israel
so that the intention of the statement is equivalent to saying,
that Jesus has some sheep who are of the αὐλή of Judaism and
others who are not, i.e. the Gentiles,[4] who must now be led

---

[1] So S. Schulz, *Johannes*, p. 151. Barrett, *St. John*, p. 312. W. Bauer, *Joh. Ev.*, p. 141. Bultmann, *Ev Joh*, p. 292. Schnackenburg, *Joh. Ev.*, II, p. 376. Dodd, *Hist. Trad.*, p. 380.
[2] This e.g. is the orientation given to v.16 by A. Corell, *Consummatum est. Eschatology and Church in the Gospel of St. John*, SPCK, London, 1958, p. 99. Similarly K. Haacker, *Stiftung*, p. 100.
[3] In an exegetical *tour de force* S. Pancaro ("'People of God' in St. John's Gospel?" *NTS*, 16, 1970, p. 122) introduces this meaning as a constitutively Johannine thought expressed in xi.50 and xviii.14. He claims that the sparse usage of the term (only in these two places) indicates that for John λαός had a highly technical meaning and in context must be interpreted as "the new people," "the people of God." In disregarding the tradition-historical problem of these verses, Pancaro overlooks the fact that the two λαός usages derive from an earlier tradition which otherwise plays no significant role in John and which in fact is given a radically new orientation (cp. our analysis pp. 237-245). To determine the character of John's ecclesiology on the basis of the two λαός occurrences in continuity with corresponding OT themes is simply not tenable.
[4] The problem is even further obscured when L. van Hartingsveld (*Eschatologie*, pp. 95f.) claims that the other sheep is a reference to the Jews

into the one flock. That kind of distinction is not at all called for. Instead, when Jesus speaks of "this fold," referral is made to the present believers regardless of background. Those not of this fold is a future reference to those who are yet to believe. The fact that they are already designated as sheep before their incorporation into the flock is consistent with the strong predestinatory theme that determines the Fourth Gospel's depiction of the church. Although already sheep, they have not yet been manifested as sheep. That is what takes place with incorporation into the flock. The basic distinction then in v.16 is between present believers manifestly identified with the existing community and those who, though chosen, are yet to manifest response to the Shepherd's voice and to be integrated into his own flock. Here the view of the gathered congregation is directed beyond its own confines to a broader scope of the future church that needs still to be manifested and realized.

There is scarcely another book in the NT where the presence and role of the church is so strongly exerted and felt as in the Fourth Gospel. And yet traditional church terminology is absent. Just as the salvation-history perspective is missing, as noted previously, so also any reference to structured order, ranks, and offices within the church. In John there are no special ministries, no variety of gifts expressed in formalized areas of service, no distribution of function. Of course, the twelve disciples appear (6:67,70; 20:24), but their positions are not elevated to particular roles of leadership or distinguished by outstanding actions. Peter and the Beloved Disciple play prominent parts in the account,[1] but their position as well as that of the other nine is essentially

---

of the Diaspora. Nor is it warranted to hold with J. Jeremias (*Jesu Verheißung für die Völker*, Stuttgart, 1959, p. 55) that 10:16 is equivalent in orientation to Mt.25:32 which speaks of the gathering of the nations for judgment.

[1] These roles receive thoroughly exaggerated and untenable proportions when A. Kragerud (*Der Lieblingsjünger im Johannes-Evangelium*, Oslo, 1959, pp. 63f. 82) maintains that Peter is to be understood representatively as the "Exponent des Amtes...Hirte der von Jesus gestifteten Gemeinde, successor und vicarius Christi" and this in tension with the position of the Beloved Disciple who is to be "Repräsentant eines kirchlichen Dienstes und zwar eines pneumatischen." Kragerud's synthesis between "office" and "Spirit" hardly represents the Johannine intention.

no different than that of all believers of succeeding generations. Sacramental references and allusions are frequent but nowhere is there any indication that the sacraments were validated ecclesiastically or identified with institutionalized clerical function. In fact, the characteristic signs of institutionalizing church development associated with early catholicism are not at all present in John. That is indeed surprising considering the time when John's Gospel was composed--a time when the development of the organizational patterns and institutional forms within the church were well underway. The approach represented in John appears in sharp contrast to these developments. Here is an understanding of the church rooted in the presence of Christ alone and distinguished by charismatic features. The activity of the Spirit is identical with the effectiveness of the church. Membership in the church is determined by one's integration into the oneness of Father and Son. Church is not conceived of structurally but eschatologically. It is the event through which the call to faith is realized and the voice of the Shepherd heard. It is the point at which a new creation takes place, where one is drawn to Christ and kept in Him. The presence of Jesus is the one central and determinative factor. In his presence faith and unbelief divide. Only in his presence is church at all possible. He who knows and hears Jesus has life.

The consequences are obvious. Church in John is, as a result, understood first of all from the point of view of the individual. While it can be said that whole groups responded in faith to Jesus (2:23; 8:30), it is nevertheless the decision of the individual in confrontation with God's presence in Christ that is constitutive. And yet the new relationship established in the birth of faith has clear horizontal consequences. Church in John is not simply the summation of separate believing individuals but is rather a tightly knit

---

Thoroughly unsubstantiated is Blank's conclusion (*Krisis*, p. 349): "Wenn theologiegeschichtlich und dogmengeschichtlich eine Schrift des Neuen Testaments als Dokument des 'Frühkatholizismus' angesehen werden muß, dann ist es das Johannesevangelium."

Sharply seen and developed in D. Faulhaber's superb little study, *Das Johannes-Evangelium und die Kirche*, Kassel, 1938.

community, a brotherhood whose distinctive characteristics are marked by an intimacy and closeness modelled after the integrating oneness of Father and Son.[1] Jesus knows those who belong to him and therefore he can call them "his own," those who have been given to him, his friends and his sheep[2] --all designations which reflect the basic character of the Johannine understanding of church. The conceptuality not only underscores the <u>closeness</u> descriptive of the inner relationships involved but also implicitly gives expression to one of the most dominant features of the Johannine community --its <u>closedness</u> to the world. Here there is no positive relation to the world, no command, as in the Synoptics, to love one's enemy, no mission commissions or grand outreach plans in the sense of either conversion efforts or contributions to the ordering of the world. Witness, of course, is public confession "in order that the world may know..." but the world always remains an antithetical, hostile force with which the Johannine brotherhood has nothing in common. Thus church for John is fellowship in a close and exclusive sense. It is set apart and marked by a strong consciousness of its self-understanding in the radicalized awareness of the presence of Christ.

It is within this larger context that the ecclesiological oneness formulation of v.16 becomes clear. There are the sheep of "this fold" and "other sheep." The fact that they will be "one flock" gives expression, first of all, to the claim of absoluteness and exclusiveness which is coextensive with the emphasis on the one Shepherd. The believers will constitute not many flocks but one. Such exclusiveness is the outgrowth of the community's insistence that the only criterion for its existence is the reality of the presence of

---

[1] E. Schweizer ("Kirchenbegriff," *op. cit.*, pp. 261f.) tends to emphasize the role of the individual at the expense of the group. If, however, the community were not central to John's thinking, then the oneness theme would not be an issue. Cp. on the other hand, D. Faulhaber (*Kirche*, p. 60): "Das Wesen der Kirche muß notwendig von dieser Paradoxie zwischen dem Einzelnen und dem Gesamten bestimmt sein."

[2] The other prominent ecclesiological designation in John is that of the vine and the branch (ch.15). The picture given is consistent with the other categories, namely the inseparable relation between Jesus and the believers.

Christ. In any area where that presence is either absent or diminished and no longer central there is critique and separation. Such is the underlying motivation for the community's sharp antithesis to the world in its representation for any sphere not dominated by the one Shepherd.

The world is concretized in terms of specific groupings represented in "the voice of stranger." The text's reference to robbers and thieves, strangers and hirelings leaves open the suggestion that specific empirical persons and groups are being pointed to which represent the kinds of opposition with which the Johannine fellowship had to contend. Various attempts at a more precise definition have raised possibilities ranging from contemporary messianic pretenders,[1] or Hellenistic savior figures[2] to Jamnia loyalists[3] or Gnosticizing Jews expelled from the synagogue.[4] And yet an exact historical localization and delimitation of the opponents seems precluded by the metaphorical nature of the references which are open-ended and, evidently with purpose, only generally oriented. The interest of the text is not so much the description of the circumstances of one particular situation as it is presentation of the broader ongoing issues of faith and unbelief kindled in confrontation with the presence of Jesus. It has already been established that the characterization of unbelief must be seen against the background of its identification with unbelieving Jews as a model for the rejecting response of the world and against the background of John's debate with the synagogue. Within this larger context of hostile Jewish opposition the forces contrary to the one flock may summarily be understood. This is further the point at

---
[1] Cp. R. Meyer, προφήτης, ThWB, VI, pp. 826f.
[2] So G. Wetter, Der Sohn Gottes, p. 164. Also Bultmann, Ev Joh, p. 286.
[3] J. L. Martyn (History and Theology, pp. 104ff.) identifies the opposition in terms of Jamnia loyalists who are to have dominated the local Gerousia in John's city and who accordingly were the instigators of the hostile reaction. Somewhat similarly Kragerud (Lieblingsjünger, p. 78): "Die Hirtenrede hat eine Abwehrfront gegen die jüdischen Leiter." Most commentators simply refer to the Pharisees.
[4] Cp. N. A. Dahl, "Der Erstgeborene Satans und der Vater des Teufels," Apophoreta, Festschrift für E. Haenchen, ZNW, Beih. 30, Berlin, 1964, pp. 70-84. Hanson (Unity of the Church, p. 162) maintains that the one Shepherd designation is intended as polemic against the pluralistic doctrine of salvation among the Gnostics.

which emphasis on the exclusiveness of the flock takes on an apologetic-polemical character. Whereas in the changed situation of the Johannine Epistles this aspect of polemic and exclusiveness moves more within the realm of an inner Christian conflict, in the Gospel the opponents are always understood as being on the outside and not originally part of the community (cp. I Jn.2:19). Here the lines are differently drawn.[1] The sheep do not follow strangers in the first place. They don't heed the voice of another (10:5).

Another aspect of the "one flock" formulation is shown in the make-up of the existing fold. Not all of the sheep are the same. The differences and the peculiarities remain but shift into a new light because all the sheep hear and know the Shepherd. This hearing and knowing is the essence of their oneness which consists not in uniformity or in the mergence of that which is peculiar to each. Instead they are qualified by a solidarity which derives from their relation to the Word alone. Therefore the oneness of the sheep is not a static quality or an acquired possession but the result of a relation that is to be realized and renewed in confrontation with the presence of Christ. This is underscored by the future orientation given to the verse "they will be one flock." The oneness of the church is not commanded or enjoined as though it were an achievable inner-worldly possibility dependent on the proper initiative and guidelines. The oneness of the church is rather a promise, an eschatological reality.

Since oneness among the sheep derives from the heavenly world, such oneness always comes from beyond. It is a gift from above and not the product of manipulations from below. As a result, ecclesiological unity for John always appears with a future orientation. It is a goal to be reached; it is

---

[1] Because W. Wilkens (*Zeichen und Werke*, p. 163) indiscriminately presupposes the same situation for both the Johannine Epistles and the Gospel he is able to maintain that the emphasis on oneness in the Gospel derives from an inner church conflict in which the opponents are characterized by docetic tendencies. And yet such a supposition fatally obsucres the character not only of the evangelist's oneness christology but also the orientation of the exclusiveness of the church which is set off not by opposition to docetists who refuse to accept the humanity of Jesus but to an unbelieving world which analogous to the Jews fails to accept the divinity of Jesus.

promised and must be prayed for. Though indeed present, it is never absolutized as a fully present reality. This is particularly noteworthy and striking for the evangelist who otherwise so freely moves within the enthusiastic traditions of the church and whose Gospel is so pronouncedly marked by the emphasis on the present reality of resurrection life.[1] But here a qualifying future orientation is introduced which not only characterizes the hope of the believers but describes their final goal free from the assailments of the world. From this perspective the popular term of present or realized eschatology is not wholly adequate to describe John's intention. Although it is done in a comparatively limited way, he too speaks in terms of future eschatology. The essential motivation for this future orientation lies within the sphere of anthropology and as such has nothing to do with the objectified form of an apocalyptic future. The gift of heavenly oneness is tied inextricably to the response of faith through which oneness becomes present reality. But since faith is incomplete[2] and in the earthly context is always under assault by a hostile world, faith is always in danger of losing the projection of heavenly oneness. Therefore faith most constantly be renewed and continued. Consequently also the gift of oneness retains its futuristic character descriptive of

---

[1] Unsubstantiated is J. Becker's claim ("Die Abschiedsreden Jesu," *op. cit.*, p. 228) that John's Gospel belongs to the "'unenthusiastischen' Büchern des NT!" While it is true that the Lucan scheme and terminology are notably absent (cp. E. Schweizer, πνεῦμα, *ThWB,* VI, pp. 436-443), still John's emphasis on limitless prayer promise (14:13; 16:23), on the measureless gift of the Spirit (3:34) through whom one is born again (3:5-8) emphasizing the resurrection as present reality (3:18f. 5:24; 11:25; Cp. Käsemann, *Letzter Wille*, pp. 39f; also *Der Ruf der Freiheit*, 5. Aufl., Tübingen, 1972, pp. 244f.) and the powerful presence of Christ as the sphere of believing life, all associate John with enthusiastic strains of the faith. To circumscribe the gift of the Spirit by an "apostolic teaching office" is certainly not the intention of the evangelist. So to interpret him can only be the result of an arbitrary exegesis as e.g. with F. Mußner ("Die johanneischen Parakletsprüche und die apostolische Tradition," *Praesentia Salutis*, Düsseldorf, 1967, p. 156) who concludes: "In diesem Sinne ist die Geistgabe also an das apostolische Amt gebunden... Insofern sind die joh. Parakletsprüche ein Zeugnis des sogenannten Frühkatholizismus im NT."

[2] Thus the disciples must always experience faith anew —2:11; 11:15; 13:19; 14:29; 16:27,31.

the ultimate realization in heaven.[1]

Thus far we have observed that the aspects of ecclesiological oneness as indicated by the "one flock" formula of v.16 include an absolute-exclusive and an apologetic-polemical character as well as a future orientation that qualifies the solidarity of the sheep. But most important is the underlying motivation and cause for this oneness of the church. With unmistakable clarity that is climactically expressed in the complementary formula "one Shepherd." Expressed is a dominant theme of the christological aspect of oneness. Oneness here underscores the absolute and exclusive character of the Shepherd. There are not many shepherds but only one. It is for this reason that the flock receives the same character. The Shepherd knows, calls, and gathers the sheep and makes them into a flock. Their existence and the nature of their togetherness is contingent on the one Shepherd.[2] The fact that the one Shepherd is not everywhere recognized and that there are others who raise contrary claims is inherent in the future orientation of the statement and reflects the involvement of faith in the recognition of the exclusive claims of the one Shepherd. This futuristic character, however, does not diminish or deter from the fact that those who hear his voice now are constituted by his word into a present solidarity of one flock. Again the distinctive feature of the sheep's existence is that they are "his own" (10:4). The one Shepherd determines the course and the character of the flock. What this means is that ecclesiology for John is determined by christology. The church must be seen against the background of christology from which it derives and unfolds. The church does not determine the meaning of Jesus. Rather Jesus determines the meaning of the church. Correspondingly the oneness of the church is not its own creation but derives from hearing and knowing Jesus only. The voice of Jesus, equated with the work of the Spirit, is a contemporary reality which not only limits and qualifies the transmitted words of

---

[1] E. Schweizer's conclusion ("Der Kirchenbegriff," *op. cit.*, p. 264) "Für diese Kirche gibt es eigentlich...keinen Kampf zu bestehen, kein Ziel zu erreichen" is therefore not wholly adequate.

[2] Cp. Faulhaber, *Kirche*, p. 50.

tradition but serves as the only criterion for what constitutes that which is called church.[1]

What is the causative motivation in John for this centrality of christology with its exclusive claims? Frequent attempts have been made in the exegesis of this passage to understand the character and intent of the "one Shepherd" formulation against the background of OT analogies[2] or a Moses[3] or even Joshua[4] figure. Despite formal language parallels with the common shepherd terminology as well as correspondence with the prominent OT concern of exclusiveness, it is clear that John leaves this context and thinks of the "one Shepherd" theme along different lines. First of all, there is only one shepherd because the good shepherd lays down his life for the sheep. This life-giving action is not a superfluous addendum but is the constitutive mark of the shepherd who goes the extreme limit for his own. Significantly his death is not understood here in terms of a vicarious sacrifice but as a demonstration of who he is --one who so knows and cares for the sheep that he lays down his life for them. Furthermore, it is a life which he lays down of his own accord and which he takes up again (10:18). This is a determinative factor in John's understanding of the life-giving action of the Shepherd. Jesus' death is in itself not seen as the central point which explains the exclusiveness of the one Shepherd. Instead, the laying down of life is placed within the larger context of Jesus' sovereign and divine nature, and it is from this standpoint that the meaning of the life-giving action is interpreted.[5]

---

[1] Schnackenburg (Joh. Ev., I, p. 32) in effect reverses this and gives ecclesiology the priority when he declares: "Der Geist aber wird...von der Kirche vermittelt..."
[2] Cp. Barrett, St. John, pp. 23 and 313. Schnackenburg, Joh. Ev., II, p. 371. B. Gerhardsson, "The Good Samaritan - The Good Shepherd," Coniectanea Neotestamentica, XVI, Lund, 1958, pp. 1-31, contends that Jn.10: 1-16 is a messianic midrash on Ez.34. Stauffer (ThWB, II, p. 238 n.26) attempts to see parallels with 4 Ez.8,7 and Syr. Bar.30,2; 85;14.
[3] So Meeks, The Prophet-King, pp. 98 and 318, n.2.
[4] H. Sahlin (Zur Typologie des Johannes Evangeliums, Uppsala, 1950) maintains that Jn. 10 must be seen against the background of Numbers 27:16f.
[5] Cp. the analysis on pp. 29-33 and 135f.

For John the exclusive and absolute character of Jesus as the one Shepherd derives not primarily from the significance of Jesus' death, although this of course must be part of the total picture, but from Jesus' oneness with the Father. This is the direction reinforced in the complementary scene (10:22-39) where in resumption of the preceding shepherd theme and in response to the Jew's hostile challenge the declaration is made, "I and the Father are one" (10:30). This climactic sentence reflects the core confession of the Johannine church and may well be regarded as a concise summary of the evangelist's theology and the distinguishing mark of his christology. Here the nature of Jesus' oneness with the Father is not reflected on. What is presupposed and implicitly developed throughout the Fourth Gospel is here presented in point-blank terms. The attempts of the commentators to detail this oneness as moral or metaphysical are fundamentally inadequate. The oneness cannot be understood morally because it is pre-existent and not contingent on acts of obedience and love. Nor is it metaphysical because it is seen and perceived although not in a simple transparent sense since there are those who see and who still do not believe. Nor should the later philosophical categories of the Trinitarian controversies be brought in at this point since they introduce factors not present in John's conception. Here the status of Jesus is simply understood as equivalent to that of the Father's. Both Father and Son are bound in a solidary oneness in which each is definitely distinct and yet in which both are mutually qualified so that it can be said that the Father is in Jesus and Jesus is in the Father (10:38). Further aspects of this relation will be considered in the chapter 17 passages.

B. SOTERIOLOGY AND ECCLESIOLOGY OF THE ONENESS MOTIF

A decisive passage in the explication of Johannine soteriology is the 11:47-53 pericope, where Caiaphas's statement before the council is interpreted by the evangelist as an ironic prophecy explaining the purpose of Jesus' death and preparing the way for the ensuing Passion. With unmistakable clarity v.50 speaks of Jesus' death in expiatory terms as sacrificial action for (ὑπέρ) the people. And yet, as was demonstrated in our literary and source analysis,[1] the cumulative evidence demands that this passage be regarded not as composition by the evangelist[2] but as a segment of his given tradition. This is significant not only because the sacrificial orientation of the verse is not further developed, but in the interpretation by the evangelist is given a decidedly different twist by its incorporation into the oneness theme. Thus the evangelist repeats the words of Caiaphas that Jesus is to die for the nation but qualifies the meaning by adding "and not for the nation only but that the children of God who are scattered abroad be gathered into one."

What are the consequences of this development? First of all it may be noted that the evangelist was indeed acquainted with the pre-Pauline tradition of Jesus' death understood as a vicarious sacrifice. As has already been observed, this thought occurs not only in 11:50 but in 1:29; 10:11,15,17; and implicitly in 17:19 as well. By the same token, it is a thought which is not further developed and which plays no central role in John's proclamation.[3] Attempts to expand this thought into major proportions for the Fourth Gospel[4] appear not only forced and contrived but are fundamentally inconsistent with the evangelist's basic intention. On the other hand, Jesus' death is indeed constitutively related to the soteriology of the Fourth Gospel. But death here is understood as departure. Jesus' departure, in turn, causes κρίσις, final κρίσις, for the Jews and an ongoing κρίσις for the world. As such, Jesus' death has causative function in exposing the face of unbelief and in laying bare the roots of one's origin, whether of God or of the devil (8:44,47). Jesus' death brings about the realization of judgment and confirms the failure to

---

[1] See pp. 237-245.
[2] Against Wilkens (Zeichen und Werke, p. 72) who has no doubts about the composition of the verse: "Denn wenn irgendwo, so besteht hier Eindeutigkeit, daß der Evangelist sie konzipiert und wiederholt unterstreicht."
[3] Cp. Bultmann, NT Theology, II, p. 54. S. Schulz, Johannes, p. 162. Absurd is Corell's contention (Consummatum est, p. 50) that John saw Jesus' death as fulfillment of the Jewish cult.
[4] So e.g. T. Müller, Heilsgeschehen, pp. 59f. G. Delling, Wort und Werk Jesu im Johannes-Evangelium, Berlin, 1966, p. 74.

respond to him as separation from God. Simultaneously, however, his death has a fundamental and intentionally prior life-giving function (12:47). The final goal is not to establish separation but to lead to oneness. Jesus' death has causative function in establishing that oneness. Here soteriology is explicated in terms of the oneness motif. This is the explicit orientation expressed in the evangelist's interpretation given in v.52.

In v.52 Jesus' death is not further described in the terms given by the evangelist's adopted tradition. In other words, it is not said that Jesus died in order to atone for the children of God but rather --consistent with the rest of the Gospel's orientation-- in order that the children of God be gathered into one (εἰς ἕν). By bringing the issues of faith and unbelief to a head, Jesus' departure effects this oneness (cp. also 12:32). While the nature of the oneness is not further described at this point, its component lines are clear. On the one hand, Jesus' death is understood as a departure which evokes a κρίσις-filled realization of either faith or unbelief, light or darkness, truth or lie. On the other hand, his death is depicted as a demonstration of who he really is. The crucifixion, as we have seen, has the character of exaltation and glorification, a manifestation of sovereignty and kingly power. The singularly most unique feature of John's understanding of the cross event centers on the one who is there exalted and glorified, i.e. on him who comes from and returns to God, on him who is one with the Father. It is this oneness between Father and Son which is the basis for authentic oneness among the believers. Because Jesus shares equivalent status with the Father and manifests this relation even in his death, it is possible for those who are to believe to be gathered into one. Here Jesus' oneness has functional priority in effecting the soteriological goal of the gathering into one. His inseparable relation with the Father represents heavenly reality. Projection of that reality into the earthly sphere is manifested in the mission and work of Jesus. Integration into this oneness effects believing existence and results in solidarity among the believers.¹

The effect of the priority of Jesus' oneness is implicitly reinforced in v.52 on two counts. First of all, those who are gathered are designated as being already the "children of God." Their status as God's children is presupposed.² In the only other reference using this designation, 1:12 makes clear that those who receive the true light are given power <u>to become</u> the children of God. Correspondingly, 3:3,5 speak of the necessity of new birth --through water and the Spirit. 11:52, on the other hand, expresses none of these contingencies and instead reflects a pronounced predestinatory strain. Those who are scattered abroad <u>are already</u> the children of God. Analogous to "the other sheep not of this fold" reference in 10:16 (cp. also 10:26), those who are to believe are understood as the chosen ones, the elect who have always been God's own.³ As God's children they need only to be gathered.

Emphasis on the predestined character of believing existence is thoroughly consistent with the lines of Johannine soteriology. Because Jesus' oneness with the Father is a preexistent given, so the believer's integration into that oneness and his status as a child of God must be understood as deriving from God's work alone. This status, which consists of a relationship, has the character of a "given" because the source of believing existence emanates from heavenly reality and is not a human creation. In the presence of God the believer cannot rely on his own faith but only on God's work on him. To express the omnipotence of the Word and the

---

¹ S. Hanson's formulation (*Unity*, p. 163) is typical for the blurring that recurs at this point: "By his vicarious and atoning death Jesus gathers them together (συναγάγῃ) so that the New Race forms a unity (εἰς ἕν)."
² Against Barrett (*St. John*, p. 339) who tends to resolve the tension in favor of the thought expressed in 1:12. Similarly D'Aragon "La notion joh. de l'unite," *op. cit.*, p. 115,no.8: "qui deviendront enfants de Dieu." Schnackenburg (*Joh. Ev.*, II, p. 452) is much closer to the point in maintaining the predestinatory character of the designation.
³ Note the formal correspondence to Gnostic thought where the *salvandi's* inherence in the transcendent world is likewise presupposed. As such they constitute a potential unity which is realized when the Revealer gathers them to himself.

centrality of God's presence in Jesus is the purpose of John's predestinatory formulations. Here (v.52) they underscore the absolute priority of the heavenly world in its impact on man's existence. Consequently, oneness is always understood as transcendent reality in antithesis to the fictions and illusions of the world.

The extent, then, to which oneness among the believers is present in the sphere of the world is always and necessarily characterized by a future factor. This is the second point expressed in this verse. Consistent with the direction expressed in 10:16, "the gathering into one" of 11:52 appears with futuristic orientation. It is the goal to be fulfilled. Future generations will encounter the same basic issues of faith and unbelief where those whose birth is from above will be encompassed by a solidarity that reflects a oneness that is from above. Moreover, since the present realization of the believers' oneness among themselves and with Jesus is always threatened by the disruptive forces of a hostile world and must therefore be prayed for, kept, and continued, its final completion lies in the future, its consummation in heaven.

Against this background the ecclesiological concerns of the evangelist as expressed in this verse also become clear. Of decisive significance for an understanding of these concerns is the fact that the ecclesially loaded term λαός in Caiaphas' original statement (v.50) is not repeated in the evangelist's interpretation in v.52 (it occurs in its unaltered traditional form in 18:14) and as such is not further reflected on or developed. In fact, in repeating Caiaphas' statement, the evangelist substitutes the broader and theologically more fluid term of ἔθνος for λαός. Whereas John is otherwise known for his play on words and for usages with a double meaning, that hardly seems to be the case here, where his use of ἔθνος (v.52), suggested by the second term in the traditional unit of Caiaphas' statement (v.50), appears as a loosely synonymous equivalent for the Jews. In its original context, perhaps as part of a Passion source, the tradition represented in v.50 may indeed have inferred a distinction, with λαός

meant ambivalently to designate not only the Jewish nation
(from Caiaphas' point of view) but also "the people of God"
(from a Christian point of view) and ἔθνος intended as the
standard unequivocal designation for the Jewish nation without its theocratic overtones.[1] But the distinction is clearly
of no interest to the evangelist who not only does not continue the differentiation in his commentary on the statement
but radically departs from this whole frame of reference and
its implications by deleting the term λαός altogether and by
introducing the decidedly non-OT/Jewish designation of τέκνα
τοῦ θεοῦ,[2] thus giving the passage an emphatically new orientation.

Without denying the broader intention of the adopted tradi-
tion (v.50), namely, that Jesus' death has meaning for the
Jews,[3] the evangelist makes it clear that he is not thinking in
terms of a salvation-history perspective where the OT people of
God foreshadow a new Israel with the inclusion of the Gentiles.
In fact, the Jewish-Gentile antithesis is not at all an issue

---

[1] The distinction between λαός and ἔθνος, though not always noted by the commentators, is nevertheless an important detail of which the evangelist must have been aware (Cp. Hoskyns, *The Fourth Gospel*, p. 412). Further, Strathmann, λαός *ThWB*, IV, p. 52.

[2] S. Pancaro ("People of God," *op. cit.*) builds an elaborate case for understanding the τέκνα τοῦ θεοῦ designation as an extension in meaning of
the λαός term which he understands as the evangelist's own choice formulation for v.50. Thus he concludes that the ecclesial connotations of λαός
are also those of τέκνα τοῦ θεοῦ which accordingly is to be understood as
"the new People of God." Pancaro's argumentation, however, breaks at two
decisive points. He fails to recognize the traditional character of v.50
(cp. our critique p. 263 n.2) and without justification asserts that the
traditional sense of τέκνα τοῦ θεοῦ refers to the Jews of the dispersion
(p.127). His supporting references to Is.60:4 and Baruch 5:5, however,
speak only of τέκνα and not of τέκνα τοῦ θεοῦ which is a decidedly non-
Jewish designation and is never used for the Jews whether of Palestine or
of the dispersion. Nor is it warranted to adduce the Jew's claim of Jn.
viii.41 which is intended strictly within the context of OT monotheism
and gives rise to the misunderstanding (Jesus speaks indeed of origin)
which is developed in the following verses.

[3] Although, on one level, the cross signals final and irrevocable judgment for the Jews, on the second level the conversation between the church
and the synagogue continues so that even after the cross the possibility
of faith among the Jews is given. Thus the pre-cross report that "many of
the Jews believed in him" (11:45) "even many of the authorities" (12:42)
reflects the post-cross experience of the church (cp. Martyn, *History and
Theology*, pp. 21, 74f. 79) and provides inner motivation for John's affirmation of the statement in v.50.

here.¹ There are no grounds for interpreting the τέκνα τοῦ θεοῦ designation from the standpoint of the ἔθνος as though the evangelist were interested in further development of the designation in terms of its counterpart so that the "scattered children of God" would correspondingly have to be understood as the Gentiles. For John the τέκνα τοῦ θεοῦ refer neither exclusively to the Jews² nor to the Gentiles³ but rather to all those who believe. It is a designation eminently suited for his understanding of the church which is constituted not by those characterized by salvation-history priorities and continuity but rather by those who have been given to Him who has been sent, i.e. by those whose birth is from above and whose origin is to be manifested in the solidarity of the believing community.

What is the nature of this community which for John is the church? It is, first of all, a gathering. As has already been pointed out,⁴ it is popularly maintained that the gathering theme expressed in this verse has its roots in the OT prophetic and/or apocalyptic tradition of the eschatological gathering of the dispersed tribes of Israel. Should that be the case, then the tradition in 11:52 is radically spiritualized and developed along decidedly different lines. More striking is the analogy to the Gnostic conceptuality of the Revealer who gathers those, who though now scattered, still belong to the spiritual world. This is the pattern followed in John's verse even though the inner motivation and connection with Jesus' death are distinctly Christian. Here, similar to the Gnostic scheme, the gathering has a twofold orientation. The believers (1) are gathered to the Revealer (cp. 12:32) and insofar as they are joined with Jesus in a bond of relationality they (2) are tied to each other in a bond of

---

[1] Contra Haacker, *Stiftung*, p. 100. Rightly seen by S. Pancaro ("People of God," *op. cit.*, p. 126): "this explanation leads right up a blind alley."
[2] Against Hartingsveld (*Eschatologie*, p. 96) and J.A.T. Robinson ("The Destination and Purpose of St. John's Gospel," *NTS*, 6, 1960, pp. 117-131) who maintain that the designation is a reference to the Jews of the dispersion.
[3] This is the interpretation most popularly found in the commentaries.
[4] See pp. 243f.

relational oneness. Secondly, the gathering of the believers is a gathering of "the children of God." That, as we have seen, emphasizes their predestined character and their solidarity not with the cosmos but with the heavenly world which marks their point of origin and circumscribes their real home. Thirdly, the believers, being gathered as the children of God, come from scattered[1] locations. They are not predicated by any one particular historical development or line of circumstances. Their locations are diverse and universal. Fourthly, the gathering of the church is characterized pre-eminently by the reality and goal of oneness. This oneness, prefigured in Jesus' relation to the Father, is John's most comprehensive description of the church.[2] The picture is not that of harmony, or of an organism, or of the body of Christ[3] but of a faith event in which one's relation to the heavenly reality demonstrated in Jesus' oneness with the Father establishes an equivalent relation among the believers, gears them to the consummation in heaven, and sets them in antithesis to opposing forces represented by the world.[4] Further aspects of this oneness relation are expressed in the final section to which our attention is now turned.

---

[1] Far-fetched and untenable are the attempts (cp. A. Greiff, Das älteste Pascharitual, p. 170 and v. Loewenich, Das Johannes-Verständnis, p. 19) to interpret the gathering theme of 11:52 against the background of the bread miracle in Jn. 6:12 and the eucharistic tradition of Didache 9:4 as again recently suggested by Meeks, The Prophet-King, pp. 94ff. or R. Brown (John, I, p. 443). Brown goes on confidently to conclude that "the related themes of Johannine ecclesiology and sacramentalism are no figments of the modern imagination."

[2] F.-M. Braun ("Quatre 'signes' johannique de l'unité chrétienne," NTS, 9, 1963, pp. 147-155) misinterprets the character of this oneness when he allegorizes it against the background of his proposed signs: 1) the gathering of the fragments (6:12f.) understood as sacramental bread which achieves unity in Christ; 2) fulfillment of the sign of the Temple (2:18-22) in 11:47-52 where Jesus appears as the new center of the community of the redeemed; 3) the seamless robe (19:23f.) symbolizing the priesthood of Jesus and the unity of the church threatened by schism; 4) the unbroken net (21:1-11) representing the unity of the church and the mission of the apostolate.

[3] Against Barrett, St. John, p. 339, who maintains that John here is speaking of "the one body Christ." The organism and body terminology, characteristic of Paul, is singularly absent in John.

[4] This separatistic aspect of the Johannine understanding of the church bears a close resemblance to the Qumranitic יחד and yet because of its broader relational qualities, Johannine church oneness moves along different lines. In its total context it is clearly closest to the forms of Gnostic phenomenology.

C. ONENESS: A THEOLOGICAL ABBREVIATION

An overall result of our investigation has been the disclosure of the centrality of the Johannine oneness motif. Even where the oneness terminology is not specifically used, it is consistently presupposed and developed. In constantly varying approaches and modulations the motif of oneness emerges as the most prominent and pervasive qualifying characteristic of the Fourth Gospel's theological concerns. As such, the motif has the function of a theological abbreviation. The confession that Jesus and the Father are one is John's christological abbreviation. It is the premise from which his whole Gospel is conceived. It is the fundamental article of faith by which everything stands or falls, the point at which belief or unbelief is ignited, light or darkness confirmed. From here the lines of development are drawn for the understanding of soteriology and ecclesiology. Again the mark of oneness serves as the shorthand expression for the characteristic accents. In no other passages are these lines more clearly and quintessentially expressed than in 17:11, 20-23. Just as the whole of ch. 17 has summary character in reflecting the content and direction of the Gospel, so these verses have the effect of summarizing the implicit aspects of the oneness motif as developed in the rest of the 4. Gospel as well as of the explicit oneness passages already discussed. Their location at the close of Jesus' farewell lends climactic force to their witness and underscores their pivotal importance in the thematic structure of the Fourth Gospel.[1]

In repeated and balanced alternation between review and petition Jesus renders an account of his work and prays for those who have been given to him asking that they be kept and guarded that they may be one and finally behold his eternal glory in heaven. Although the accent in the first 19 verses lies on Jesus' present disciples and in the succeeding verses on those yet to believe, mutually exclusive lines of separation are not maintained between the two. For when Jesus

---

[1] Both from a structural (cp. our analysis on pp.224-236) and theological-content point of view, vs. 11, 20-23 form integral units tightly fitted into the argument and development of John's Gospel.

prays for his present disciples, they proleptically include
all disciples, and when he prays for the future believers and
asks that they be present, where he is, he includes those of
the past as well. Here the themes constantly interweave and
form finally an integral unity. Of central importance is the
fact that when Jesus prays for the oneness of those who have
been given to him, he asks that this relation be patterned
after his own relation to the Father. The καθώς of v. 11 and
23 has both comparative and causative force. In both instances, similar to 10:30, it is explicitly stated that Jesus
and the Father are one. This oneness has not only paradigmatic value in providing the perfect model for the believers'
appropriation of oneness, but it is also represented as establishing that oneness among the believers. Thus Jesus'
oneness relation with the Father is conceived of as having
motivating power. How that is to be understood is contingent on the understanding of the meaning and nature of Jesus'
relation to the Father.

Significantly, the evangelist nowhere attempts to work out
an explanation for the Father - Son relation. His witness is
simply spoken from the point of view which sees the earthly
Jesus wholly from the standpoint of post-Easter exaltation
and pre-existent glory. It is a witness characterized not by
definition and analysis but by faith reflection and by a repetitive description of given confessions.[1] Here the given,
perceived by the post-Easter faith of the believing community,
is the divine origin and presence of Jesus. The description
is expressed pre-eminently in terms of the reciprocity statements, although the description underlies, as we have seen,
the orientation given to the entire Gospel. As was discussed
in chapter 2, the reciprocity statements offer varying terms
and turns that express the relationality between Jesus and
God in such a way as to make it clear that God is never thought
of apart from Jesus and Jesus never apart from God. Therefore

---

[1] The context of John's Gospel is confessional and anything but philosophical. Hence it is thoroughly unwarranted to speak of "the religious
philosophy of St. John" (so R. Lightfoot, *St. John's Gospel, A Commentary*
(ed. by C. Evans), Oxford, 1956, p. 23) or of "the Johannine philosophy"
(so Dodd, *Interpretation*, p. 384).

it can be said that Jesus is in the Father (17:21) and conversely that the Father is in Jesus (17:21,23). Both are bound in an indissoluable relation so that the one cannot be had without the other. Therefore also the terms of knowledge, glory, love, witness, and work can be mutually descriptive both of the Father and the Son. They reach their logical climax in the proclamation that Jesus and God are one because it is from this premise that they emanate. The circularity of the witness underscores the self-authenticating nature of Jesus and gives expression to his divinity.

Against this larger background the specific character of Jesus' oneness relation moves into focus. It is a relation neither contingent nor dependent on circumstantial developments for fulfillment. Jesus does not achieve or acquire oneness with God. He prays for the unity of the church but not for his relation to the Father since that oneness is presupposed, eternally secured, pre-existently present and never relinquished.[1] And yet, although the Father and Son are one, John never speaks of the relation in terms of mergence. The Father remains the Father and the Son remains the Son. The differences are distinct and do not merge into a homogeneous kind of unity. Oneness in John does not mean the erasure of differences. By the same token, the relation entails more than the terms of solidarity or representation would imply. Jesus' oneness with the Father is more than a relation arising from common responsibilities and interests. It is rather a pre-existent identification which transcends time and which is prior to the effects which it causes. Similarly, Jesus is more than the representative[2] or emissary who obeys and fulfills the will of another, in this case, the Father. Jesus does not take the place of the Father and represent his cause

---

[1] Consequently it is not adequate to speak, as is so often done, simply of the "unity of will and love" (cp. the analysis on pp. 18-34) since these are only derivative aspects of a more comprehensive and prior relationship.

[2] S. Hanson (*Unity*, pp. 163-170; esp. p. 169) comes close to expressing the Johannine conception by using the category of "the identity of representation" but betrays the inherent misorientation of the terminology and its implicit background when he concludes: "Then it is evident that, as to the superior one, it is a matter of sending and giving, whereas concerning the representative it is above all a question of obedience and fidelity."

in the Father's absence; otherwise John could not say that
Jesus is in the Father and the Father in Jesus. Nor is the
relation described in terms of rank as though the emissary or
representative had implicitly a subordinal role. In Johannine christology there is no room for subordinationism. Jesus
has equal status with the Father.

There is only one basic qualification introduced in the understanding of Jesus' historical appearance as God -- and that
is a faith factor. Although his demonstrative miracles move
even observers to recognize that Jesus is more than human and
that he must be an eschatological figure of heavenly dimensions, the evangelist always indicates the inadequacy of such
responses. They do not constitute real faith since they do
not penetrate through to an authentic recognition of who Jesus
is. In other words, Jesus' oneness with the Father is not
wrapped in clear plastic and marked by a simple transparency
fully open to empirical vision. It can only be grapsed
through faith perception. That for John is essentially an
anthropological problem and not a christological one. The
interrelation between the two is not further reflected on
--both are maintained side by side in an unresolved dialectic.
From the perspective of the heavenly world Jesus' oneness is
not conditioned by contingencies. From the perspective of
the earthly sphere it is revelation predicated by faith perception. Consequently, Jesus' oneness with the Father must
be spoken of in both relational and revelational terms. Since
it is a oneness of equivalent relationality, there is no area
in which the Father can be excluded from the Son or the Son
from the Father. This togetherness and mutual correspondence
is an expression of God's reality and can be had only within
his dimensions. The projection of this oneness in the person
of Jesus into the earthly sphere constitutes its revelational
aspect. Thus the Father's oneness with Jesus is presented in
terms of his sending the Son and the Son's oneness with the
Father in terms of his coming as the manifestation of God
among men. The manifestation forces a disclosure of the
world's nature as darkness and hostility and through encounter with the Word offers the possibility of faith which

confirms the whence of one's origin.

Man's integration into this projection of heavenly oneness constitutes the saving event. Thus Jesus prays even as he is in the Father and Father in him that, "they may also be in us" (17:21). Again the oneness motif provides a theological abbreviation, this time for soteriology. The purpose of the revelation is to initiate confrontation between God and man and to provide the possibility of believing existence. The goal is incorporation into God's reality, into truth, into glory, into the presence of Christ. In short, to be bound in a relation of oneness with Jesus ("they in us" 17:21; "I in them" 17:23) is for John the essence of salvation. That is not effected through mystical union or through responses of love and charity as products of human accomplishment. That is brought about only in response to the word (17:20) and in belief that Jesus is sent from the Father (17:21,23) i.e. that he is one with God. That, moreover, is a belief which needs continually to be realized. For this reason Jesus prays that the believers be kept (17:11,15) and be set apart in truth (17:19). Faith is not a one-time event but must continually recognize who Jesus is. The process character of faith, however, does not alter the character of its object. John's confessional statements of Jesus' oneness with the Father remain the fides quae creditur of the church.[1]

Concomitant with the given nature of these faith statements is also the emphasis on the predestined and given character of the believers. When Jesus prays "that they also may be in us" (17:21), viz. that they be integrated into the oneness of Father and Son, he is praying for the believers, for those who have already been given to him. Similar to the function of the predestinatory orientation of 10:16 and 11:52 so also here the thrust is to reinforce the priority of God's work and the omnipotence of the word in the salvation event. The believers are God's elect, and yet they must be manifested as such in response to the Word without which they are nothing. The word offers the possibility of believing existence as life

---

[1] Cp. Käsemann, *Letzter Wille*, p. 60.

in the presence of Christ. Realization of that possibility
is not dependent on an independent subjective choice made as
a free inner-wordly resolve but rather on one's origin. One's
origin, in turn, is determined by hearing and accepting the
Word.

The resulting oneness relation with the Revealer is not
just a spiritual or an internal relation invisible to others
around.[1] It has instead concrete, perceivable manifestations,
central among which is the corresponding oneness among the
believers. The picture here is not so much that of a vertical-
horizontal dimension[2] but rather that of an emanative sequence
or a chain of action whereby oneness describes, as point of
origin, the relational/revelational correspondence of Father
and Son, and then successively but interconnectedly the relation of Revealer and believer, and also believer and believer.
Thus the line leads from christology to soteriology to ecclesiology, and oneness serves as the theological abbreviation
for the constitutive aspects of all three. With unmistakable
clarity this is the pattern followed in Jesus' prayer. Using
his own oneness with the Father as the paradigm ("even as
thou, Father, art in me, and I in thee" 17:21; "even as we
are one" 17:11,23), Jesus asks that the believers be integrated into this relation ("they...in us" 17:21; "I in them"
17:23) so that they may be one (17:11,21,22,23). The fourfold repetition of the request that the believers be one underscores the fact that oneness is the distinctive feature of
the Johannine church. It is a oneness, however, which can
only be understood within the context of Jesus' oneness with
the believers and his prior oneness with the Father. Divorced

---

[1] Bultmann tends to go too far in stressing the invisibility of the relation ("Unsichtbar ist sie, da sie überhaupt kein weltliches Phänomen ist."
Ev Joh, p. 394). The relation is indeed an eschatological event but nevertheless has clear, visible results.
[2] R. Brown's (*John*, II, p. 776) use of the vertical-horizontal categories
to describe Johannine unity is consistent with his failure to recognize
the place and importance of the prior relation of Father and Son. Thus he
maintains that the Johannine statements about unity are constituted by
the relation of the believers to Father and Son (vertical) and the relation of
the believers among themselves (horizontal) ignoring the fact that in
John both of these relations are dependent on the perfect unity between
Jesus and God.

from that context, ecclesiological oneness becomes not only innocuous and harmless but is fundamentally misdirected.

Ecclesiological oneness in John is a relational quality which receives its intrinsic meaning from the believer's inclusion into the presence of Christ. Just as Father and Son remain distinct so the individual believers retain their discreteness.[1] Therefore oneness does not imply uniformity or the absence of diversity but rather a togetherness whose decisive bond is the integration into heavenly reality, the presence of Christ. This gives the oneness of the church its distinctive character. Just as Jesus' oneness with the Father is not established through moral action so the oneness of the church cannot be a human creation accomplished through the works of man. For oneness is always a heavenly reality, and its presence in the church can only be had as an extension of Jesus himself. This is not the picture of archetypes and reflections[2] but rather of equipresence and equipollence. The church's goal is to realize the full presence of the divine Jesus. Therefore the church's oneness for John is not expressed pre-eminently in terms of humiliation, poverty, and suffering but rather in terms of glory, manifestation, and demonstration.[3] It is in this sense that Jesus can say, "The glory which thou hast given me I have given to them that they may be one" (17?22). Here are the marks of an enthusiastic Christianity living in the present power of the real presence of Jesus. That presence is their only authority, the mark of the work of the Spirit, and the only criterion of their life in community.

---

[1] T. E. Pollard's extension of this point ("That they may all be one," *op. cit.*) as a blanket justification for denominational diversity, introduces tacit factors not present in this passage and thus amounts to a considerable oversimplification.
[2] Against Dodd (*Interpretation, passim.*) who consistently uses the platonic categories of timeless realities and their earthly reflection. Even S. Schulz (*Johannes*, p. 218) resorts to the "Urbild-Abbild" terminology.
[3] Against Barrett (*St. John*, p. 428) who maintains that "the church expresses (its unity) in obedience, and pre-eminently in humiliation, poverty, and suffering." Of course, the Johannine church knows persecution (16:2) and tribulation (16:33). But, although Jesus can say, "In the world you have tribulation," he goes on to say, "I have overcome the world" (16:33). So the characteristic mark of the Johannine church is not the suffering of the cross but its glory.

The unity of the church is also expressed in terms of its mission. Since a constitutive element of Jesus' oneness with the Father consists in his being sent into the world, the purpose of the church's oneness is to bring the world into confrontation with judgment and life as the outcome of an encounter with the presence of Christ. Its mission is that the world may know and believe that Jesus is sent from God (17:21, 23). And yet Jesus does not pray for the world as such.[1] The lines between church and world are rigorously maintained. Although it is the time of world-wide mission for the church at large, the Johannine community does not regard the world in itself as its mission object. Oneness as a heavenly reality is always understood dualistically in John in antithesis to the alienage of the world. Just as Jesus moves as a stranger through the world, so the church's relation to the world is not marked by continuity and acceptance. Instead the world retains its hostile and alien character and as such provides the scene and the backdrop against which the mission of the church is realized. In correspondence with Jesus' oneness the Johannine community is aware of its own revelational task and knows that it too is sent[2]--sent not to create a new world or to ensconce itself in the sphere of the world, but to be instrumentally manifest for the gathering into one of those who have been given to Jesus out of the world. They are in the world but not of the world (17:14) since integration into Jesus' oneness confirms their heavenly origin in antithesis to worldly derivation.

Despite stringently separative lines, the Johannine mission is not understood as esoteric activity or as the

---

[1] Cp. 17:9. Bultmann rightly notes (*Ev Joh*, p. 394 n.4) that the third ἵνα of v.21 is, unlike the first two ἵνα clauses, not dependent on the ἐρωτάω of v.20 but is rather the purpose of the oneness of the church (the third ἵνα is dependent on the second ἵνα). Thus Jesus does not pray directly for the world.
[2] Cp. Faulhaber, *Kirche*, p. 57. In his Tübinger dissertation J. Miranda (*Der Vater, der mich gesandt hat*, Europäische Hochschulschriften, Reihe xxiii, Bd. 7, Bern/Frankfurt M., 1972) has assembled a veritable wealth of material in his analysis of the sending formulae but arrives at vague and imprecise conclusions. His extensive treatment of religio-historical traditions lead to few concrete results for a clearer understanding of John. Fatal to the entire study is the failure to recognize the specific character of Johannine christology.

promulgation of recondite doctrine or even as a retreat from the world. Its character, analogous to Jesus' sending, is rather demonstrative and ostensive. Its orientation is not inward but outward. Its doctrine is disturbingly simple, straightforward, and offensive. In short, the Johannine mission is the public proclamation of Jesus' oneness with the Father confessed before the opposition of the world.[1] Since this proclamation is accepted only by those who have been given to Jesus, the resulting oneness of the church is not universal and ecumenical in an unqualified sense. Indeed the world is the field of the church's activity, but the inclusiveness suggested by the term "world" in its neutral sense is decidedly qualified by the exclusiveness of believing existence. That must be understood against the background of the evangelist's dialectic. World ceases to be world when the opposition of unbelief is overcome. At that point the world receives its true character as God's creation. But since in a sense only the believers represent God's creation, as those who have been born again and who have acquired a new past, the lines of separation remain and the goal of the Johannine mission appears predisposed.

A further mark of ecclesiological oneness is, similar to the accent in 10:16 and 11:52, its future orientation. Although the believers' integration into heavenly oneness is present and real ("he who hears my word and believes him who sent me, has eternal life" 5:24) and the corresponding interrelation among the believers is likewise present reality within the world, still the relations are qualified by a future goal. It is not the world objectified and absolutized in an apocalyptic way but rather the relations of faith and love without the framework of traditional apocalyptic expectation.[2] These relations in the earthly sphere are not marked by a final completeness. Therefore Jesus must pray for the oneness of the believers and, because their relations are

---

[1] Cp. Conzelmann, *Outline*, pp. 355f. Bornkamm, "Zur Interpretation," *op. cit.*, 120: "Auch die johanneische Esoterik hat einen proklamatorischen Sinn."
[2] Cp. Käsemann, *Letzter Wille*, p. 149. S. Schulz, *Johannes*, p. 219: "Diese Zukunft des Heils hat der vierte Evangelist nie preisgegeben, nur hat er sie eben nicht apokalyptisch, sondern gnostisierend ausgearbeitet."

not fully perfected, ask that they may become completely one. The emphasis on completeness underscores the eschatological heavenly nature of oneness. The same orientation is reinforced when Jesus asks that the believers may be with him where he is to behold his glory (17:24). This future direction given to the understanding of believing existence derives from the evangelist's emphasis on the priority and centrality of christology. Were the relationships of faith and love to be understood as only anthropological phenomena without further qualification,[1] then the place of the future manifestation would have lost its essential meaning. But since the believer's oneness relations are reflexes of heavenly oneness, as long as the earthly context remains and the assailments of the world continue, despite the church's fundamental separation from the world, the believer's intimate relations of faith and love will be marked by the ultimate goal of final completion corresponding to the perfect relation between Father and Son.

D. UNIQUENESS OF THE JOHANNINE ONENESS MOTIF

The Fourth Gospel's oneness motif with its relational/revelational character and threefold orientation stands out as singularly unique in the NT. The contrast is apparent even within the Johannine Corpus which itself evidences a tradition-historical development with noticeable accent shifts. Significantly, the epistles no longer use the oneness motif. The characteristic Father - Son terminology consistently appears, but in the epistles it approaches a more formalized usage, suggesting set designations without further expansion on the implied relations. Although reciprocity statements do occur, and it still can be said that no one who denies the Son has

---

[1] This is essentially the direction taken by L. Schottroff ("Heil als innerweltliche Entweltlichung," *op. cit.*, p. 294) who maintains "Das Heil, das der Glaubende innerweltlich...hat, ist definitives Heil...nicht eine Vorstufe des Heils, die postmortal eine...Vollendung erfährt." Such a supposition is in line with the thesis which says, "Die Anthropologie ist...die Konstante; die Christologie dagegen ist die Variable" (so H. Braun, "Der Sinn der neutestamentlich Christologie," *Gesammelte Studien*, p. 272) —a thesis which, in any case with John, has nothing in common.

the Father (I Jn.2:23), these statements otherwise never describe the relation between Father and Son but always between the believer and God or Jesus (I Jn. 2:24; 3:24; 4:13f.). The accent now is on paranetic appeals and the problems of faith and love.

In the Gospel the relational statements describing believing existence were developed within the explicit context of Jesus' relation to the Father. In the Epistles that context is not explicated and the statements appear in their own right. The christological concentration so typical for the Gospel is not maintained with the same force in the epistles. Here the central concern is no longer who Jesus is, but what he brings --expiation for sins. It is not he who denies that Jesus and God are one who is a liar but rather he who denies that Jesus is the Christ (I Jn.2:22), a term which in the Gospel, though accepted, is not regarded as a totally adequate title.[1] True, the epistles speak of Jesus as the Son of God (5:10,20) but here again the designation has more formal character than deliberate theological plan. Whereas the overriding and consistent emphasis on Jesus' divinity in the Gospel could hardly allow for its character to be described as anti-docetic,[2] the same can no longer be maintained for the epistles. Here the denial of Jesus coming in the flesh is the cardinal issue. Thus the christological implications of the oneness motif must recede into the background.

In the Synoptics there is no use or development of the theme of oneness as a theological motif. There are scattered instances of the oneness term in its traditional sense indicating exclusiveness (e.g. Mt.23:9f.) but never is oneness used relationally as in John. Similarly, the isolated occurrences of reciprocity formulation in the so-called "Johannine logion" in Mt.10:40 and 11:27 (par.) are not understood within the context of oneness but rather representation.

---

[1] Cp. the analysis on pp. 64-69.
[2] Against W. Wilkens (*Zeichen und Semeia,* p. 160) who represents a popular approach in maintaining that "der kerygmatisch-heilsgeschichtliche Entwurf des Evangeliums einen ausgesprochen anti-doketischen Akzent (enthält)."

Also in Paul the term of oneness never appears in a relational sense as a christological motif. The "one man" formulations and the "one-many" contrast of Rom.5:12ff. are not developed from the standpoint of oneness but rather from the Adam-Christ parallel as designations for spheres of power with universal scope describing the nature of sin and the saving action of Christ.[1] Against the background of nomistic-enthusiastic tensions and the related emergence of divisions within the church, the problem of church unity takes on increasing significance in Paul and gives rise to scattered oneness statements emphasizing the believers' common base. In other words, Paul's oneness expressions are motivated and developed primarily in response to hereticizing tendencies and to conflicting claims of lordship. Against the domination attempts by "many lords," Paul, using traditional formulations, emphasizes that "there is one God, the Father... and one Lord Jesus Christ" (I Cor.8:6). In view of the diversity of gifts and their potential splintering effect, he likewise stresses that "all were made to drink of the one Spirit" (I Cor.12:13). Integrally associated with the understanding of the meaning of oneness for the church is Paul's use of the terms "body," "body of Christ," and the parallel "in Christ" phrase (I Cor.12:12ff. Rom.12:4f. Gal.3:28). Adoption of the terminology and its application to Christ allowed the apostle to maintain his central concern for establishing the priority of christology. For it is not the members that constitute the body but Christ[2] into whose dominion as a comprehensive sphere the members are incorporated.

Similarly the "in Christ" phrase underscores the objective foundation of Christian existence.[3] It is rooted not in subjective experience but in the extra nos. Although at this point both Paul and John coincide in their aims, the conceptualities and lines of development in the explication of oneness are clearly separate. Above all, there is a

---

[1] Cp. E. Brandenburger, *Adam und Christus*, WMANT 7, Neukirchen, 1962, esp. pp. 255-264.
[2] Bultmann, R., *New Testament Theology*, I, p. 310. Cp. also the excellent summary by H. Conzelmann, *Outline*, p. 262.
[3] Cp. W. Kümmel, *Die Theologie des NT*, p. 195.

fundamentally different approach to the understanding of the world. For Paul the unity of the church has cosmic dimensions and is seen as the sphere of communication in which Christ as the Exalted One bodily (realiter) comes to all those whose bodies are incorporated as members into his.[1] That incorporation is sacramentally oriented, established through baptism (Gal.3:27f.) and the Eucharist (I Cor.10:16). Its scope is the scope of world-wide mission.[2] Significantly the expressions of membership in the one body in Christ are located in paranetic contexts. Participation in the body of Christ as the realization of oneness must be lived and expressed in mutual service, in the acts of concrete everyday living and giving, obedience and love.

The Epistle to the Ephesians represents a significant further development in the understanding of the oneness theme. Here the problem of church unity emerges with central importance. The extensive mission efforts of the church resulting in the incorporation of large numbers of Gentile Christians who increasingly gain numerical ascendency allow for the unity of the church to be described as the integration of two peoples. "The dividing wall of hostility" is broken down so that instead of Jew and Gentile "one new man in place of two" may be created (2:14ff.). The simultaneous growth of divisive movements necessitates the appeal "to maintain the unity of the Spirit in the bond of peace" with the reminder that there is only "one body and one Spirit" just as the Christian's calling rests on "one Lord, one faith, one baptism, one God and Father of us all"(4:3-6). In some respects there is a marked correspondence to John. In Ephesians too the church is understood as a heavenly reality whose members have been chosen in eternity (Eph.1:4f. 11; 2:10). But the conception in Ephesians that the church stretches right into

---

[1] Käsemann, *Paulinische Perspektiven*, Tübingen, 1969, p. 199: "Nur so, daß unsere Leiber Glieder seiner Herrschaft werden, kann er, der Erhöhte, irdisch zu allen kommen."
[2] Cp. E. Schweizer, "The Church as the Missionary Body of Christ," *Neotestamentica*, pp. 317-329. Schweizer's recourse, however, to the category of "corporate personality" deriving from the Jewish idea of the patriarch determining the destiny of the tribe and also the Stoic idea of body as an organism obscures the nature of Jesus' position in relation to the members of the body.

the ἐπουράνια is designed more to express its cosmic dimensions and its world-wide unity. Although the church is seen here as a heavenly and completed entity, it is still understood as developing, "growing into a holy temple in the Lord" (2:21) and "attaining to the unity of the faith" (4:13). Coupled with this are subtle shifts in the orientation. Christ is, to be sure, the head of the church (4:15) but more and more the church itself becomes an important object of faith.[1] Christology loses its intensity and its centrality and instead serves more to provide for the ordered growth of the universal church which is now viewed as the central concern itself and whose essential mark is unity in the bond of peace.

The line of development may be further traced in Ignatius. Here too the theme of oneness is of paramount importance. Ignatius never tires of speaking of the unity, oneness, and harmony of the church. These categories form basic concepts in his letters.[2] The church is conceived of by him as union with the living Lord, as oneness with the flesh and spirit of Jesus Christ (Magn. 1,2). Although there is a high regard for the free working of the spirit, the place of order and office emerge with overriding significance.[3] This is above all evidenced in the understanding of the bishop. Here the bishop receives ranking authority not because of his function but because of his position as bishop.[4] He is the representative of the Father of Jesus Christ, the bishop of all (Magn. III,1). In fact Ignatius can demand "that we

---

[1] Cp. E. Schweizer, *Church Order in the New Testament*, Studies in Biblical Theology, 32, (trans. by F. Clarke), London, 1961, p. 107. E. Käsemann, *Perspektiven*, p. 209: "Wo die Ekklesiologie in den Vordergrund rückt, aus welchen noch so berechtigen Gründen das geschehen mag, wird die Christologie ihre ausschlaggebende Bedeutung verlieren..."
[2] Cp. H. Schlier, *Religionsgeschichtliche Untersuchungen zu den Ignatiusbriefen*, Beiheft z. ZNW 8, Gießen, 1929, p. 99.
[3] J. von Walter, "Ignatius von Antiochien und die Entstehung des Frühkatholizismus," *Reinhold Seeberg Festschrift*, II, Leipzig, 1929, p. 106: "Es gibt keinen Schriftsteller der apostolischen Zeit wie der nachapostolischen Zeit der so stark von der Notwendigkeit des kirchlichen Amtes überzeugt wäre. Aber Ignatius fühlt sich zugleich dabei als Pneumatiker."
[4] Cp. H. V. Campenhausen, *Kirchliches Amt und geistliche Vollmacht in den ersten drei Jahrhunderten*, 2. Aufl., 1963, pp. 109-115. Also E. Schweizer, *Church Order*, p. 153.

must regard the bishop as the Lord himself" (Eph. VI,1).
"It is good to know God and the bishop" (Smyrn. IX,1). Consequently a significant development crystallizes at this point. The oneness of the church is determined by obedience and subjection to the bishop (Eph. II,2 - IV; Magn. VII). The Lord forgives if one's repentance leads to the unity of God and the council (συνέδριον) of the bishop (Phil. VIII,1). Ignatius can insist that "as many as belong to God and Jesus Christ --these are with the bishop. And as many as repent and come to the unity of the church --these also shall be of God." (Phil. III,2). Thus the church receives a preponderantly episcopal character. Its oneness cannot be effected without the bishop since he represents the pivotal point of its spiritual mystery.

Against the background of this developmental line the uniqueness of the Fourth Gospel's oneness motif becomes indelibly clear. Its use in John reflects an unparalleled christological concentration and provides the most distinctive mark of the vehicle through which the ground, content, and object of faith are presented. The evangelist's one concern is to know Jesus only and to give witness to him who in oneness with the Father creates believing existence and the oneness of the church.

BIBLIOGRAPHY

Abbott, E., *Johannine Vocabulary*, London, 1905.

_____, *Johannine Grammar*, London, 1906.

Aland, K., "Eine Untersuchung zu Joh.1:3,4. Über die Bedeutung eines Punktes," *Zeitschrift für die neutestamentliche Wissenschaft*, 59, 1968, pp. 174-209.

Albright, W.F., "Recent Discoveries in Palestine and the Gospel of John," *The Background of the New Testament and its Eschatology*, (ed. by W. Davies and D. Daube.), Cambridge, 1956, pp. 153-171.

Andresen, C., Erbse, H., Gigon, O., Sehefold, K., Stroheker, K., Zinn, E., (Hrsg.), *Lexikon der alten Welt*, Zürich/Stuttgart, 1965.

Balz, H., *Methodische Probleme der neutestamentlichen Christologie*, Neukirchen, 1967.

Barrett, C.K., *The Gospel According to St. John*, London, 1962.

_____, "The Lamb of God," *New Testament Studies*, 1954/55, pp. 210-218.

Bauer, W., *Rechtgläubigkeit und Ketzerei im ältesten Christentum*, 2. Aufl., Tübingen, 1964.

_____, "Johannesevangelium und Johannesbriefe," *Theologische Rundschau*, N.F. 1, 1929, pp. 135-160.

_____, (trans. and adaptation by W. Arndt and F. Gingrich), *A Greek-English Lexicon of the New Testament*, Chicago, 1957.

_____, *Das Johannesevangelium*. Handbuch zum Neuen Testament, 6, 3. Aufl., Tübingen, 1933.

Baumbach, G., *Qumran und das Johannes-Evangelium*, Berlin, 1957.

Baur, F.C., *Kritische Untersuchungen über die kanonischen Evangelien*, Tübingen, 1847.

Beare, F.W., "Review of C.H. Dodd, Historical Tradition," *New Testament Studies*, 10, 1963/64, pp. 517-522.

Becker, H., *Die Reden des Johannesevangeliums und der Stil der gnostischen Offenbarungsreden*. FRLANT N.F. 50, Göttingen, 1956.

Becker, J., "Aufbau, Schichtung und theologiegeschichtliche Stellung des Gebetes im Joh 17," *Zeitschrift für die neutestamentliche Wissenschaft*, 60, 1969, pp. 56-83.

_____, "Die Abschiedsreden im Johannesevangelium," *Zeitschrift für die neutestamentliche Wissenschaft*, 61, 1970, pp. 215-246.

———, "Wunder und Christologie," *New Testament Studies*, 16, 1970, pp. 130-148.

Behler, G., *Die Abschiedsworte des Herrn. Johannesevangelium Kapitel 13-17*, Salzburg, 1962.

Bergmeyer, R., "Zum Verfasserproblem des II und III Johannesbriefes," *Zeitschrift für die neutestamentliche Wissenschaft*, 57, 1966, pp. 93-100.

Bernard, J.H., *A Critical and Exegetical Commentary on the Gospel according to St. John*, 2 Vols, ICC, Edinburg, 1928.

Bertram, G., art. ἔργον, *Theologisches Wörterbuch zum Neuen Testament*, Vol. II, 1935, pp. 631-649.

———, art. ὑψόω *Theologisches Wörterbuch zum Neuen Testament*, Vol. VIII, 1969, pp. 604-611.

Betz, J., *Die Eucharistie in der Zeit der griechischen Väter*, Vol. II, pt. 1, Wien, 1961.

Betz, O., *Der Paraklet. Fürsprecher im häretischen Judentum, im Johannes-Evangelium und in neugefundenen gnostischen Schriften*, Leiden, 1963.

Beyer, K., *Semitische Syntax im Neuen Testament*, Studien zur Umwelt des Neuen Testaments, Bd. I, Göttingen, 1962.

Beyschlag, K., "Zur Simon-Magus Frage," *Zeitschrift für Theologie und Kirche*, 68/4, 1971, pp. 395-426.

Bieler, L., ΘΕΙΟΣ ΑΝΗΡ, Darmstadt, 1967.

Billerbeck, P., *Kommentar zum Neuen Testament aus Talmud und Midrasch*, 4 Bde, 3.Aufl., München, 1961.

Black, M., *An Aramaic Approach to the Gospels and Acts*, Oxford, 1954.

Blank, J., "Die Verhandlung vor Pilatus Joh 18, 28-19, 16 im Lichte johanneischer Theologie," *Biblische Zeitschrift*, N.F. 3, 1959, pp. 60-81.

———, *Krisis. Untersuchungen zur johanneischen Christologie und Eschatologie*, Freiburg im Breisgau, 1964.

Blaß, F., and Debrunner, A., (tr. and revised by R. Funk), *A Greek Grammar of the New Testament*, Chicago, 1960.

Blauert, H., *Die Bedeutung der Zeit in der johanneischen Theologie*, Eine Untersuchung an Hand von Joh. 1-17 unter besonderer Berücksichtigung des literarischen Problems, Dissertation-Tübingen, 1957.

Böcher, O., *Der johanneische Dualismus im Zusammenhang des nachbiblischen Judentums*, Gütersloh, 1965.

Böhlig, A., "Christentum und Gnosis im Ägypterevangelium," *Christentum und Gnosis*, hrsg. v. W. Eltester, ZNW Beiheft 37, Berlin, 1969, pp. 1-18.

_____, *Mysterion und Wahrheit*, Gesammelte Beiträge zur spätantiken Religionsgeschichte, Leiden, 1968.

_____, "Vom 'Knecht' zum 'Sohn'," *Wissenschaftliche Zeitschrift der Martin Luther-Universität*, Reihe 6, 1957.

Böklen, E., *Die Verwandtschaft der jüdisch-christlichen mit der parsischen Eschatologie*, Göttingen, 1902.

Boismard, M., "Problèmes de critique textuelle concernant le quatrième évangile," *Revue Biblique*, 60, 1953, pp. 347-371.

_____, "Critique Textuell et Citations Patristques," *Revue Biblique*, 57, 1950, pp. 396-397.

Borgen, P., *Bread From Heaven. An Exegetical Study of the Conception of Manna in the Gospel of John and the Writings of Philo*, Supplements to Novum Testamentum, X, Leiden, 1965.

_____, "Observations on the Midrashic Character of John 6," *Zeitschrift für die neutestamentliche Wissenschaft*, 54, 1963, pp.232-240.

_____, "God's Agent in the Fourth Gospel," *Religions in Antiquity. Essays in Memory of E.R. Goodenough*, Leiden, 1968, pp. 137-148.

Borig, R., *Der wahre Weinstock. Untersuchungen zu Jo 15, 1-10*, Studien zum Alten und Neuen Testament, XVI, München, 1967.

Bornhäuser, H., (Hrsg.), *Die Mischna*, Berlin, 1935.

Bornkamm, G., "Der Paraklet im Johannes-Evangelium," *Geschichte und Glaube, Gesammelte Aufsätze III*, Beiträge zur evangelischen Theologie, 48, München, 1968, pp. 68-89.

_____, "Die eucharistische Rede im Johannes-Evangelium," *Gesammelte Aufsätze III*, pp. 60-67.

_____, "Zur Interpretation des Johannes-Evangeliums," *Gesammelte Aufsätze III*, pp. 104-121.

Bousset, W., *Die Religion des Judentums*. Handbuch zum Neuen Testament 21, 4. Aufl., Tübingen, 1966.

_____, *Hauptprobleme der Gnosis*, Göttingen, 1907.

_____, "Ist das vierte Evangelium eine literarische Einheit?" *Theologische Rundschau*, 12, 1909, pp. 1-12; 39-64.

_____, "Johannesevangelium," *RGG*, 1912, III, pp. 608-636.

_____, *Jüdisch-christlicher Schulbetrieb in Alexandria und Rom*, FRLANT N.F. 6, Göttingen, 1915.

_____, *Kyrios Christos*, 5. Aufl., Göttingen, 1965.

Brandenburger, E., *Adam und Christus. Exegetisch-religionsgeschictliche Untersuchung zu Römer 5,12-21*, WMANT 7, Neukirchen, 1962.

Braun, F.-M., *Jean le Théologion II. Les grandes traditions d'Israel et l'accord des écritures selon le quatrieme Evangile*, Paris, 1964.

_____, "Quatre 'signes' johannique de l'unité chrétienne," *New Testament Studies*, 9, 1963, pp. 147-155.

Braun, H., "Der Sinn der neutestamentlichen Christologie," *Gesammelte Studien zum Neuen Testament und seiner Umwelt*, Tübingen, 1962, pp. 243-281.

_____, "Literar-Analyse im ersten Johannesbrief," *Gesammelte Studien*, pp. 210-242.

_____, *Spätjüdisch-häretischer und frühchristlicher Radikalismus*, Beiträge zur historischen Theologie 24, 2 Bde, Tübingen, 1957.

_____, *Qumran und das Neue Testament*, 2 Bde, Tübingen, 1966.

Bretschneider, C.T., *Probabilia de Evangelii et Epistolarum Joannis, Apostoli Indole et Origine*, Leipzig, 1820.

Brown, Driver, and Briggs, *Hebrew and English Lexicon of the Old Testament*, Oxford, 1957.

Brown, R., *The Gospel According to John I-XIII*, The Anchor Bible, Vol.29, New York, 1966.

_____, *The Gospel According to John XIII-XXI*, The Anchor Bible, Vol.29a, New York, 1970.

Büchsel, F., *Das Evangelium nach Johannes*, Das Neue Testament Deutsch 4, Göttingen, 1946.

_____, "Zu den Johannesbriefen," *Zeitschrift für die neutestamentliche Wissenschaft*, 28, 1929, pp. 235-241.

Bultmann, R., art. ἀλήθεια, *Theologisches Wörterbuch zum Neuen Testament*, Vol. I, 1933, pp. 237-251.

_____, "Analyse des ersten Johannesbriefes," *Exegetica. Aufsätze zur Erforschung des Neuen Testaments*, hrsg. v. E. Dinkler, Tübingen, 1967, pp. 105-123.

_____, *Das Evangelium des Johannes*, Kritisch-exegetischer Kommentar über das Neue Testament, 17. Aufl., Göttingen, 1962.

_____, *Das Evangelium des Johannes Ergänzungsheft*, Göttingen, 1957.

_____, Das Johannes-Evangelium in der neuesten Forschung," *Die christliche Welt*, 41, 1927, pp. 502-511.

_____, "Die Bedeutung der neuerschlossenen mandäischen und manichäischen Quellen für das Verständnis des Johannesevangeliums," *Exegetica*, pp. 55-104.

_____, *Die Geschichte der synoptischen Tradition*. FRLANT N.F. 12, 5. Aufl., Göttingen, 1961.

_____, *Die Johannesbriefe*, Kritisch-exegetischer Kommentar über das Neue Testament, 8. Aufl., Göttingen, 1969.

_____, "Johannesevangelium," *RGG*, 1959, III, pp. 840-850.

_____, *Theology of the New Testament*, Vols. I & II, (Trans. by K.Grobel), New York, c. 1951 (I) and 1955 (II).

_____, "Zur Interpretation des Johannesevangeliums," *Theologische Literaturzeitung*, 87, 1962, pp. 1-8.

_____, "Zur johanneischen Tradition," *Theologische Literaturzeitung*, 80, 1955, pp. 521-526.

Burger, C., *Jesus als Davidsohn, Eine traditionsgeschichtliche Untersuchung*, FRLANT 98, Göttingen, 1970.

Burney, C. F., *The Aramaic Origin of the Fourth Gospel*, Oxford, 1922.

_____, *The Poetry of our Lord*, Oxford, 1925.

Cassem, H.M., "A Grammatical and Contextual Inventory of the Use of κόσμος in the Johannine Corpus," *New Testament Studies*, 19, 1972, pp.81-91.

Charlier, J.P., "La notion de signe dans le IV évangile," *Revue des Sciences Philosophiques et Theologiques*, 43, 1959, pp. 434-448.

Coenen, L., Beyreuther, E., Bietenhard, H., (Hrsg.), *Theologisches Begriffslexikon zum Neuen Testament*, Bd. II, Wuppertal, 1972.

Colpe, C., *Die religionsgeschichtliche Schule. Deutung und Kritik ihres Bildes vom gnostischen Erlösermythus*, FRLANT N.F. 60, Göttingen, 1961.

_____, art. ὁ υἱὸς τοῦ ἀνθρώπου *Theologisches Wörterbuch zum Neuen Testament*, Vol. VIII, 1969, pp. 403-481.

Colson, F.H. and Whitaker, G.H., *Philo with an English Translation*, 1-X, The Loeb Classical Library, London, 1929-1962.

Conzelmann, H., *An Outline of the Theology of the New Testament*, New York/ Evanston, 1969.

_____, "Was am Anfang war," *Neutestamentliche Studien für R.Bultmann*, Beiheft z. ZNW 21, Berlin, 1954, pp. 194-200.

_____, "Die Mutter der Weisheit," *Zeit und Geschichte*, Dankausgabe an Rudolf Bultmann, Tübingen, 1964.

Correll, A., *Consummatum est. Eschatology and Church in the Gospel of St. John*, SPCK, London, 1958.

Corssen, P., "Die Abschiedsreden Jesu im vierten Evangelium," *Zeitschrift für die neutestamentliche Wissenschaft*, 8, 1907, pp. 125-142.

Cross, F.M., *The Ancient Library of Qumran and Modern Biblical Studies*, New York, 1958.

Cullmann, O., *Early Christian Worship*, Studies in Biblical Theology 10, London, 1962.

Dahl, N., "Der Erstgeborene Satans and der Vater des Teufels," *Apophoreta* (Festschrift für E. Haenchen), ZNW Beiheft 30, Berlin, 1964, pp.70-84.

D'Aragon, J.L., "La notion johannique de l'unité," *Sciences Ecclesiastique*, 11,1, 1959, pp. 111-119.

Dauer, A., *Die Passionsgeschichte im Johannesevangelium*, Studien zum Alten und Neuen Testament XXX, München, 1972.

De Jonge, M., "Jewish Expectations about the 'Messiah' according to the Fourth Gospel," *New Testament Studies*, 19/3, 1973, pp. 246-270.

Dekker, C., "Grundschrift und Redaktion im Johannesevangelium," *New Testament Studies*, 13, 1966, pp. 66-80.

De Kruijf, "The Glory of the Only Son," *Studies in John*, Supplements to Novum Testamentum 24, Leiden, 1970, pp. 111-123.

De la Potterie, I., "Jesus, roi et juge d'apres Jn.19,13: Ἐκάθισεν ἐπὶ βήματος," *Biblica*, 41, 1960, pp. 117-147.

Delling, G., *Wort und Werk Jesu im Johannes-Evangelium*, Berlin, 1966.

Demke, Chr., "Der sogenannte Logos-Hymnus im Johannes-Prolog," *Zeitschrift für die neutestamentliche Wissenschaft*, 58, 1967, pp. 45-68.

De Moor, J.C., "Lexical Remarks Concerning yaḥad and yaḥdaw," *Vetus Testamentum*, 7, 1957, pp. 350-355.

Dibelius, M., "Die altestamentlichen Motive in der Leidensgeschichte des Petrus and des Johannes-Evangeliums," *Botschaft und Geschichte I*, Tübingen, 1953, pp. 221-247.

_____, "Die Christianisierung einer hellenistischen Formel," *Botschaft und Geschichte II*, Tübingen, 1956, pp. 14-29.

_____, *Die Formgeschichte des Evangeliums*, 4. Aufl., Tübingen, 1961.

_____, "Johannesevangelium," *RGG*, 1929, III, pp. 349-363.

Dieterich, A., *Eine Mithrasliturgie*, hrsg. v. O. Weinreich, Leipzig/Berlin, 1923.

Dietrich, E., art. "Gott im nachbiblischen Judentum," *RGG*, 1958, II, pp. 1713-1715.

Dodd, C.H., *The Interpretation of the Fourth Gospel*, Cambridge, 1963.

_____, *Historical Tradition in the Fourth Gospel*, Cambridge, 1963.

_____, "The Prophecy of Caiaphas," *Neotestamentica et Patristica*, Supplements to Novum Testamentum 6, Leiden, 1962.

Dombrowski, B., "היחד in IQS and τὸ κοινόν. An Instance of Early Greek and Jewish Synthesis," *Harvard Theological Review*, July 1966, pp.293-307.

Dörries, H., *Aufsätze zur Gnosis*, Göttingen, 1967.

Drower, E., *The Mandaeans of Iraq and Iran*, Oxford, 1937.

Dupont-Sommer, A., *The Essene Writings from Qumran*, (tr. by G. Vermes), Oxford, 1961.

Eltester, W., (Hrsg.), *Christentum und Gnosis*, ZNW Beiheft 37, Berlin, 1969.

Fascher, E., "Christologie und Gnosis im vierten Evangelium," *Theologische Literaturzeitung*, 93, 1968, pp. 722-730.

_____, ΠΡΟΦΗΤΗΣ, Gießen, 1927.

Faulhaber, D., *Das Johannes-Evangelium und die Kirche*, Kassel, 1938.

Fischel, H., "Jewish Gnosticism in the Fourth Gospel," *Journal of Biblical Literature*, 65, 1946, pp. 157-174.

Foerster, W., (Hrsg.), *Die Gnosis*, Bd. I, Zeugnisse der Kirchenväter, Zürich, 1969. Bd.II. Koptische und Mandäische Quellen, Zürich, 1971.

Formesyn, R., "Le sèmeion johannique et le sèmeion hellénistique," *Ephemerides Theologicae Louvanienses*, 38, 1962, pp. 856-894.

Fortna, R., *The Gospel of Signs*, Society for New Testament Studies Monograph Series 11, Cambridge, 1970.

_____, "Source and Redaction in the Fourth Gospel's Portrayal of Jesus' Signs," *Journal of Biblical Literature*, 89, 1970, pp. 151-166.

_____, "W. Wilken's Further Contribution to Johannine Studies," *Journal of Biblical Literature*, 89, 1970, pp. 457-462.

Freed, E., "The Son of Man in the Fourth Gospel," *Journal of Biblical Literature*, 86, 1967, pp. 402-409.

Frickel, J.H., *"Die Apophasis Megale, eine Grundschrift der Gnosis?"* Studia di storia religiosa della tarda anticita, Messina, 1968, pp. 35-49.

Friedrich, G., art. προθήτης, *Theologisches Wörterbuch zum Neuen Testament*, Vol. VI, 1959, pp. 829-863.

Gächter, P., "Der formale Aufbau der Abschiedsrede Jesu," *Zeitschrift für katholische Theologie*, 58, 1934, pp. 155-207.

Gaffron, H., *Studien zum koptischen Philippus-Evangelium*, Dissertation-Bonn, 1969.

Georgi, D., "Der vorpaulinische Hymnus Phil.2:6-11," *Zeit und Geschichte*, (Dankesgabe an Rudolf Bultmann zum 80. Geburtstag. hrsg. v. E. Dinkler.) Tübingen, 1964, pp. 263-294.

_____, *Die Gegner des Paulus im 2. Korintherbrief*, Wissenschaftliche Monographien zum Alten und Neuen Testament 11, Neukirchen-Vluyn, 1964.

Gerhardsson, B., "The Good Samaritan - The Good Shepherd," *Coniectanea Neotestamentica XVI*, Lund, 1958.

Gericke, W., "Zur Entdeckung des Johannes-Evangeliums," *Theologische Literaturzeitung*, 90, 1965, pp. 807-820.

Gese, H.,"Weisheit," *RGG*³, VI, Tübingen, 1962, pp. 1574-1581.

Giblet, J., "La Sainte Trinité selon l'Evangile de saint Jean," *Lumiere et Vie*, 29, 1956, pp. 98-106.

Goppelt, L., art. τρώγω, *Theologisches Wörterbuch zum Neuen Testament*, Vol. VIII, 1969, pp. 236-237.

Gräßer, E., "Der Hebräerbrief 1938-1963," *Theologische Rundschau*, 30, 1964, pp. 138-236.

_____, "Die anti-jüdische Polemik im Johannesevangelium," *New Testament Studies*, 11, 1964/65, pp. 74-90.

_____, "Kol 3,1-4 als Beispiel einer Interpretation secundum homines recipientes," *Zeitschrift für Theologie und Kirche*, 64, 1967, pp. 139-168.

Greiff, A., *Das älteste Pascharituale der Kirche, Didache 1-10 und das Johannesevangelium*, Schöningh-Paderborn, 1929.

Grobel, K., *The Gospel of Truth*, (Translation and Commentary), London,1960.

Grundmann, W., "Mt.11:27 und die johanneischen 'Der Vater - der Sohn' Stellen," *New Testament Studies*, 12, 1965/66, pp. 42-49.

Guilding, A., *The Fourth Gospel and Jewish Worship*, Oxford, 1960.

Gutbrod, W., art. Ἰσραήλ, *Theologisches Wörterbuch zum Neuen Testament*, Vol III, 1938, pp. 360-394.

Gyllenberg, R., "Die Anfänge der johanneischen Tradition," *Neutestamentliche Studien für R. Bultmann*, Berlin, 1957, pp.144-147.

Haacker, K., *Die Stiftung des Heils*, Dissertation-Mainz, 1970.

Haardt, R., *Die Gnosis, Wesen, und Zeugnis*, Salzburg, 1967.

Haenchen, E., "Aus der Literatur zum Johannes-Evangelium 1929-1956," *Theologische Rundschau*, 23/4, 1956, pp. 295-335.

_____, Besprechung von A. Guilding, The Fourth Gospel and Jewish Worship, *Theologische Literaturzeitung*, 86, 1961, pp. 670-672.

_____, Besprechung von Dodd's Historical Tradition, *Theologische Literaturzeitung*, 93, 1968, pp. 346-348.

_____, "Das Johannesevangelium und sein Kommentar," *Theologische Literaturzeitung*, 89, 1964, pp. 881-898.

_____, "Der Vater, der mich gesandt hat," *Gott und Mensch. Gesammelte Aufsätze*, Tübingen, 1965, pp. 68-77.

_____, *Die Botschaft des Thomas-Evangeliums*, Theologische Bibliothek Töpelmann 6, Berlin, 1961.

_____, "Gab es eine vorchristliche Gnosis?" *Gott und Mensch,* pp.265-298.

_____, "Historie und Geschichte in den johanneischen Passionsberichten" *Zur Bedeutung des Todes Jesu,* Gütersloh, 1967, pp. 55-78.

_____, "Jesus vor Pilatus (Joh 18,28 - 19:15)," *Gott und Mensch,* pp.144-156.

_____, "Johanneische Probleme," *Gott und Mensch,* pp. 78-113.

_____, "Neuere Literatur zu den Johannesbriefen," *Theologische Rundschau,* 26, 1960, pp. 1-43 and 267-291.

_____, "Probleme des johanneischen Prologs," *Gott und Mensch,* pp. 114-143.

_____, "Vom Wandel des Jesusbildes in der frühen Gemeinde," *Verborum Veritas,* (Festschrift für G. Stählin), Wuppertal, 1970, pp. 3-14.

Hahn, F., *Christologische Hoheitstitel,* FRLANT 86, Göttingen, 1963.

_____, "Der Prozeß Jesu nach dem Johannesevangelium, *Evangelisch-Katholischer Kommentar zum Neuen Testament,* Vorarbeiten Heft 2, Zürich, 1970, pp. 23-96.

_____, "Methodenprobleme einer Christologie des Neuen Testaments," *Verkündigung und Forschung,* 2/1970, pp. 3-41.

Hanhart, K., "The Structure of John 1:35 - IV:54," *Studies in John,* Supplements to Novum Testamentum 24, Leiden, 1970.

Hanse, H., *"Gott Haben" in der Antike und im frühen Christentum,* Religionsgeschichtliche Versuche und Vorarbeiten, Bd. XXVII, Berlin, 1939.

Hansen, G., "Philosophie," *Umwelt des Urchristentums I.,* hrsg. v. J. Leipoldt und W. Grundmann, Berlin, 1965, pp. 346-363.

Hanson, S., *The Unity of the Church in the New Testament,* Acta Seminarii Neotestamentici Upsaliensis 14, Uppsala, 1946.

Hardtke, W., *Vier urchristliche Partien und ihre Vereinigung zur apostolischen Kirche,* Bd. I, Deutsche Akademie der Wissenschaften zu Berlin, 1961.

Haufe, G., "Die Mysterien," *Umwelt des Urchristentums I,* hrsg. v.J. Leipoldt und W. Grundmann, Berlin, 1965, pp. 101-121.

Hegermann, H., "Er kam in sein Eigentum," *Der Ruf Jesu und die Antwort der Gemeinde,* (Festschrift für J. Jeremias), Göttingen,1970, pp.112-131.

Heise, J., *Bleiben,* Hermeneutische Untersuchungen zur Theologie 8, Tübingen, 1967.

Heitmüller, W., *Das Johannesevangelium,* Die Schriften des NT 4, 3. Aufl., Göttingen, 1918.

_____, "Zur Johannes Tradition," *Zeitschrift für die neutestamentliche Wissenschaft,* 15, 1914, pp. 189-209.

Hengel, M., *Judentum und Hellenismus,* WUNT 10, 2 Aufl., Tübingen, 1973.

Hennecke, E., (ed. by W. Schneemelcher), *New Testament Apocrypha*, (tr. by McL Wilson), Vols. I & II, London, 1965.

Hirsch, E., *Das 4. Evangelium in seiner ursprünglichen Gestalt verdeutscht und erklärt*, Tübingen, 1936.

_____, "Stilkritik und Literaranalyse im vierten Evangelium," *Zeitschrift für die neutestamentliche Wissenschaft*, 43, 1950/51, pp.128-143.

_____, *Studien zum 4. Evangelium*, Tübingen, 1936.

Hofius, O., "Die Sammlung der Heiden zur Herde Israels," *Zeitschrift für die neutestamentliche Wissenschaft*, 58, 1967, pp. 289-291.

Holtz, T., Review of R. Brown's Commentary. *Theologische Literaturzeitung*, 93, 1968, pp. 348-350.

Holtzmann, H., *Lehrbuch der neutestamentlichen Theologie II*, 2 Aufl., Tübingen, 1911.

Holwerda, H., *The Holy Spirit and Eschatology in the Gospel of John. A critique of R. Bultmann's Eschatology*, Kampen, 1959.

Hoskyns, E., (ed. by F.N. Davey), *The Fourth Gospel*, London, 1947.

Howard, W., *The Fourth Gospel in Recent Criticism and Interpretation*. (Revised by C. K. Barrett), 4. ed., London, 1955.

Iber, G., *Überlieferungsgeschichtliche Untersuchungen zum Begriff des Menschensohnes im Neuen Testament*, Heidelberg-Dissertation, 1953.

Jeremias, J., art ἀμνός, *Theologisches Wörterbuch zum Neuen Testament*, Vol I, 1933, pp. 342-345.

_____, art. Μωυσῆς, *Theologisches Wörterbuch zum Neuen Testament*, Vol. IV, 1942, pp. 852-878.

_____, art. ποιμήν, *Theologisches Wörterbuch zum Neuen Testament*, Vol. VI, 1959, pp. 484-501.

_____, Besprechung von A. Greiff, Das älteste Pascharituale, *Theologische Literaturzeitung*, 50, 1930, pp. 350f.

_____, *Jesu Verheißung für die Völker*, Stuttgart, 1959.

_____, "Johanneische Literarkritik," *Theologische Blätter*, 20, 1941, pp. 33-46.

_____, "Joh. 6:51c - 58 --redaktionell?" *Zeitschrift für die neutestamentliche Wissenschaft*, 44, 1952/53, pp. 256-257.

Jonas, H., *Gnosis und spätantiker Geist*, I, FRLANT N.F. 33, Göttingen, 1966.

_____, *The Gnostic Religion*, Boston, 1963.

_____, "Response to G. Quispel's 'Gnosticism and the New Testament,'" *The Bible in Modern Scholarship*, ed. by J. Hyatt, Nashville/New York, 1965.

Jüngel, E., *Paulus und Jesus*, Tübingen, 1964.

Käsemann, E., "Aufbau und Anliegen des johanneischen Prologs," *Exegetische Versuche und Besinnungen*, Bd. II, Göttingen, 1964, pp. 155-180.

_____, Besprechung von R. Bultmann, Das Evangelium des Johannes, *Verkündigung und Forschung 3*, Theologischer Jahresbericht, 1942/46, pp. 182-201.

_____, Besprechung von W. Oehler, Das Wort des Johannes an die Gemeinde, *Theologische Literaturzeitung*, 64, 1939, p. 411.

_____, *Das Wandernde Gottesvolk*, FRLANT N.F. 37, 4. Aufl., Göttingen, 1961.

_____, *Der Ruf der Freiheit*, 5. Aufl., Tübingen, 1972.

_____, *Jesu Letzter Wille nach Johannes*, 3. Aufl., Tübingen, 1971.

_____, art. "Liturgie im NT," *RGG*, 1960, IV, p. 403.

_____, "Neutestamentliche Fragen von heute," *Exegetische Versuche und Besinnungen II*, pp. 11-30.

_____, *Paulinische Perspektiven*, Tübingen, 1969.

_____, Review of publications by S. Schulz and W. Wilkens, *Verkündigung und Forschung*, 1960/62 (1963/65), pp. 88-90.

_____, art. "Wunder im NT," *RGG*, 1962, VI, pp. 1835-1837.

_____, "Zur Johannes-Interpretation in England," *Exegetische Versuche und Besinnungen II*, pp. 131-155.

Kippenberg, H.G., *Garizim und Synagoge. Traditionsgeschichtliche Untersuchungen zur samaritanischen Religion der aramäischen Periode*, Religionsgeschichtliche Versuche und Vorarbeiten 30, Berlin/New York, 1971, pp. 276-305.

Klijn, A., "The 'Single One' in the Gospel of Thomas," *Journal of Biblical Literature*, 81, 1962, pp. 271-278.

Koester, H., "Geschichte und Kultus im Johannes-evangelium und bei Ignatius von Antiochien," *Zeitschrift für Theologie und Kirche*, 54, 1957, pp. 56-69.

Kragerud, A., *Der Lieblingsjünger im Johannes-Evangelium*, Oslo, 1959.

Kramer, W., *Christos, Kyrios, Gottessohn*, Zürich-Stuttgart, 1963.

Kuhn, K.G., "Die in Palästina gefundenen hebräischen Texte und das Neue Testament," *Zeitschrift für Theologie und Kirche*, 47, 1950, pp. 192-211.

Kümmel, W., *Das Neue Testament. Geschichte der Erforschung seiner Probleme*, München, 1958.

_____, *Die Theologie des Neuen Testaments*, Das Neue Testament Deutsch, Ergänzungsreihe 3, Göttingen, 1969.

_____, *Einleitung in das Neue Testament*, begr. von P. Feine und J. Behm, völlig neu bearbeitet von W. Kümmel, 13. Aufl., Heidelberg, 1964.

Kundsin, K., *Topologische Überlieferungsstoffe im Johannes-Evangelium*, FRLANT N.F. 22, Göttingen, 1925.

Lake, Kirsopp (transl.), *The Apostolic Fathers*, The Loeb Classical Library, Vol I, London, 1919.

Leroy, H., *Rätsel und Missverständnis*, Ein Beitrag zur Formgeschichte des Johannesevangeliums, Dissertation-Tübingen, 1968.

Lidzbarski, M., (Hrsg.), *Das Johannes-Buch der Mandäer*, Gießen, 1915.

_____, *Ginza, Der Schatz oder Das Große Buch der Mandäer*, Göttingen, 1925.

_____, *Mandäische Liturgien*, Berlin, 1920.

Liebing, H., "Historisch-kritische Theologie," *Zeitschrift für Theologie und Kirche*, 75, 1960, pp. 302-317.

Lightfoot, R., *St. John's Gospel. A Commentary*, (ed. by C. Evans), Oxford, 1956.

Loewenich, W. V., *Das Johannes-Verständnis im 2. Jahrhundert*, ZNW Beiheft 13, Gießen, 1932.

Lohse, E., (Hrsg.), *Qumran: Die Texte aus Qumran, Hebräisch und deutsch*, Darmstadt, 1964.

Macdonald, J., *The Theology of the Samaritans*, London, 1964.

Mack, B.L., *Logos und Sophia. Untersuchungen zur Weisheitstheologie im hellenistischen Judentum*, Studien zur Umwelt des Neuen Testaments, Bd. 10, Göttingen, 1973.

Macuch, R., Drower, E., *A Mandaic Dictionary*, Oxford, 1963.

Maier, J., "Zum Begriff יחד in den Texten von Qumran," *Zeitschrift für die alttestamentliche Wissenschaft*, 72, 1960, pp. 148-166.

Manson, T.W., "The Life of Jesus: Some Tendencies in Present-day Research," *The Background of the New Testament and its Eschatology*, ed. by W. Davies and D. Daube, Cambridge, 1956, pp. 211-221.

Martyn, L.J., *History and Theology in the Fourth Gospel*, New York, 1968.

Maurer, Chr., "Der Exclusivanspruch des Christus nach Johannes," *Studies in John*, Supplements to Novum Testamentum 24, Leiden, 1970, pp.143-153.

McL Wilson, R., *Gnosis and the New Testament*, Philadelphia, 1968.

Meeks, W., *The Prophet-King. Moses Traditions and the Johannine Christology*, Supplements to Novum Testamentum XIV, Leiden, 1967.

Menoud, P., *L'Evangile de Jean d'après les recherches récentes*, Neuchatel/Paris, 1947.

Metzger, H., "Neuere Johannes Forschung," *Verkündigung und Forschung*, 12, 2/1967, pp. 12-29.

Meyer, R., art. προφήτης, *Theologisches Wörterbuch zum Neuen Testament*, Vol VI, 1959, pp. 813-828.

Michel, O., "Das Gebet des scheidenden Erlösers," *Zeitschrift für systematische Theologie*, 18, 1941, pp. 521-534.

———, "Der Anfang der Zeichen Jesu," *Die Leibhaftigkeit des Wortes*, (Festgabe für Köberle), Hamburg, 1958, pp. 15-22.

———, art. ὁμολογέω, *Theologisches Wörterbuch zum Neuen Testament*, Vol. V, 1954, pp. 199-220.

Miranda, J., *Der Vater, der mich gesandt hat*, Europäische Hochschulschriften, Reihe XXIII, Bd. 7, Bern/Frankfurt M., 1972.

Moore, G.F., *Judaism in the First Centuries of the Christian Era*, Vols. I & II, Cambridge, 1958.

Moule, C.F.D., "The Individualism of the Fourth Gospel," *Novum Testamentum*, Vol. 5, 1962, pp. 171-190.

Müller, Theophil, *Das Heilsgeschehen im Johannesevangelium*, Eine exegetische Studie, zugleich der Versuch einer Antwort an Rudolf Bultmann, Zürich/Frankfurt a. M., 1961.

Munck, J., *Discours d'adieu dans le Noveau Testament et dans la Litterature biblique*, Neuchatel/Paris, 1950.

Mußner, F., "Die johanneischen Parakletsprüche und die apostolische Tradition," *Praesentia Salutis. Studien zu Fragen und Themen des Neuen Testamentes*, Düsseldorf, 1967, 146-158.

———, ΖΩΗ *Die Anschauung vom "Leben im vierten Evangelium,"* München, 1952.

Neher, A., "Echos de la secte de Qumran dans la litterature talmudique," *Les manuscrits de la Mer Morte colloque de Strasbourg*, 1957, pp.44-60.

Nichol, W., *The Semeia in the Fourth Gospel*, Supplements to Novum Testamentum XXXII, Leiden, 1972.

Noack, B., *Zur johanneischen Tradition*, København, 1954.

Noetzel, H., *Christos und Dionysos*, Arbeiten zur Theologie, Stuttgart, 1960.

Norden, E., *Agnostos Theos*, 3. Aufl., Darmstadt, 1956.

Odeberg, H., *The Fourth Gospel*, 2 ed., Amsterdam, 1968.

Oehler, W., *Das Johannesevangelium eine Missionsschrift für die Welt*, Gütersloh, 1936.

Overbeck, F., *Das Johannesevangelium*, (Hrsg. v. Bernoulli), Tübingen, 1911, pp. 1-122.

Pagels, E.H., *The Johannine Gospel in Gnostic Exegesis*, SBL Monograph Series 17, Nashville-New York, 1973.

Percy, E., *Untersuchungen über den Ursprung der johanneischen Theologie*, Lund, 1939.

Pokorny, P., *Der Epheserbrief und die Gnosis*, Berlin, 1965.

Pollard, T.E., *Johannine Christology and the Early Church*, Cambridge, 1970.

_____, "The Exegesis of John X:30 in the Early Trinitarian Controversies," *New Testament Studies*, 3, 1956/57, pp. 334-349.

_____, "That They All May Be One (John xvii.21) and the Unity of the Church," *Expository Times, 70,5, 1959*, pp. 149-150.

Preisker, H., Schulz, S., art. πρόβατον, *Theologisches Wörterbuch zum Neuen Testament*, Vol VI, 1959, pp. 688-692.

Preisker, H., "Das Evangelium des Johannes als erster Teil eines apokalyptischen Doppelwerkes," *Theologische Blätter*, 15, 1936, pp.185-192.

Quasten, J., *Patrology*, Vols. I & II, Utrecht-Antwerp, 1966.

Radermacher, L., *Neutestamentliche Grammatik*, Handbuch zum Neuen Testament I, Tübingen, 1925.

Randall, J.F., *The Theme of Unity in John XVII. 20-23. Its Background and Meaning*, Université Catholique de Louvain, 1962.

_____, "The Theme of Unity in John 17:20-23," *Ephemerides Theologicae, Louvanienses*, Fasciculus 3, 1965, pp. 373-394.

Raney, W.H., *The Relation of the Fourth Gospel to the Christian Cultus*, Gießen, 1933.

Reitzenstein, *Die hellenistischen Mysterienreligionen*, Nachdruck der 3. Aufl., Darmstadt, 1966.

_____, *Das iranische Erlösungsmysterium*, Bonn, 1921.

_____, *Poimandres. Studien zur griechisch-ägyptischen und frühchristlichen Literatur*, Nachdruck der Ausgabe Leipzig, 1904, Darmstadt, 1966.

Rengstorf, K.H., art. ἀπόστολος, *Theologisches Wörterbuch zum Neuen Testament*, Vol I, 1933, pp. 406-448.

_____, art. δοῦλος, *Theologisches Wörterbuch zum Neuen Testament*, Vol II, 1935, pp. 264-283.

_____, art. σημεῖον, *Theologisches Wörterbuch zum Neuen Testament*, Vol. VII, 1964, pp. 199-264.

Ricca, R., *Die Eschatologie des Vierten Evangeliums*, Frankfurt/Zürich, 1966.

Richter, G., *Die Fußwaschung im Johannesevangelium*, Regensburg, 1967.

____, "Zur Formgeschichte und literarischen Einheit von Joh. 6:31-58," Zeitschrift für die neutestamentliche Wissenschaft, 60, 1969, pp. 21-55.

Riesenfeld, H., art. τηρέω, Theologisches Wörterbuch zum Neuen Testament, Vol VIII, 1969, pp. 141-145.

____, "Zu den johanneischen ἵνα-Sätzen," Studia Theologica, 18/19, 1964/65, pp. 213-220.

Robinson, J.A.T., "The Destination and Purpose of St. John's Gospel," New Testament Studies, 6, 1960, pp. 117-131.

____, "The Parable of the Shepherd," Zeitschrift für die neutestamentliche Wissenschaft, 46, 1955, pp. 233-240.

Robinson, J., "Kerygma and History in the New Testament," The Bible in Modern Scholarship, ed. by J.P. Hyatt, Nashville/New York, 1965, pp. 114-150.

____, "Die johanneische Entwicklungslinie," Entwicklungslinien durch die Welt des frühen Christentums, hrsg. v. J. Robinson and H. Köster, Tübingen, 1971.

____, "Recent Research in the Fourth Gospel," Journal of Biblical Literature, 78, 1959, pp. 242-252.

Ruckstuhl, E., Die literarische Einheit des Johannesevangeliums, Studia Friburgensia, n.s. 3, Freiburg/Schweiz, 1951.

Rudolph, K., "Gnosis und Gnostizismus, ein Forschungsbericht," Theologische Rundschau, 34, 1969, pp. 121-175; 181-231; 385-361. (36) 1971, pp. 1-61; 89-24. (37)1972, pp. 289-360.

____, Die Mandäer I: Prolegomena, Das Mandäerproblem, Göttingen, 1960. Die Mandäer II: Der Kult, Göttingen, 1961.

____, (Hrsg.), Gnosis und Gnostizismus, Wege der Forschung CCLXII, Darmstadt, 1975.

Sahlin, H., Zur Typologie des Johannes Evangeliums, Uppsala, 1950.

Schenke, H.M., Der Gott "Mensch" in der Gnosis, Göttingen, 1962.

____, "Die Gnosis," Umwelt des Urchristentums I, hrsg. v. J. Leipoldt und W. Grundmann, Berlin, 1965, pp. 370-415.

____, "Hauptprobleme der Gnosis," Kairos VII, 1965, pp. 114-123.

Schenkel, H. (ed.), Marcus Aurelius Antonius, Lipsiae, 1913.

Schlatter, A., Die Sprache und Heimat des 4. Evangelisten, Gütersloh, 1902.

____, Der Evangelist Johannes, Stuttgart, 1930.

Schleiermacher, F., Einleitung ins neue Testament, (hrsg. v. G. Wolde), Berlin, 1845.

Schlier, H., *Religionsgeschichtliche Untersuchungen zu den Ignatiusbriefen*, ZNW Beiheft 8, Gießen, 1929.

Schmidt, G., Till, W., (Hrsg.), *Koptisch-gnostische Schriften I*, GCS 45, 2. ed., Berlin, 1954.

Schmidt, K.L., art. βασιλεύς, *Theologisches Wörterbuch zum Neuen Testament*, Vol. I, 1933, pp. 573-595.

Schmithals, W., *Die Gnosis in Korinth*, FRLANT N.F. 48, Göttingen, 1956.

Schnackenburg, R., *Das Johannesevangelium, I. Teil, Einleitung und Kommentar zu Kap.1-4*, Herders Theologischer Kommentar zum Neuen Testament, Band IV, Freiburg, 1965.

_____, *Das Johannesevangelium. II. Teil. Kommentar zu Kap. 5-12*, 1971.

_____, "Johannesevangelium als hermeneutische Frage," *New Testament Studies*, 13, 1967, pp. 197-210.

_____, "Die Messiasfrage im Johannesevangelium," *Neutestamentliche Aufsätze*, (Festschrift J. Schmid), Regensburg, 1963, pp. 240-264.

Schneider, J., "Zur Komposition von Joh 10." *Coniectanea Neotestamentica XI*, Fridrichsen Festschrift, Lund, 1947, pp. 220-225.

Scholem, G., *Jewish Gnosticism, Merkabah Mysticism, and Talmudic Tradition*, New York, 1965.

Schottroff, L., *Der Glaubende und die feindliche Welt*, Wissenschaftliche Monographien zum Alten und Neuen Testament 37, Neukirchen-Vluyn, 1970.

_____, "Heil als innerweltliche Entweltlichung," *Novum Testamentum*, Vol. XI, 1969, pp. 294-317.

Schrenk, G., art. πατήρ, *Theologisches Wörterbuch zum Neuen Testament*, Vol. V, 1954, pp. 974-1017.

Schulz, S., *Das Evangelium nach Johannes*, Das Neue Testament Deutsch 4, Göttingen, 1972.

_____, "Die Bedeutung neuer Gnosisfunde für die neutestamentliche Wissenschaft," *Theologische Rundschau*, 26, 1960, pp. 209-266; 301-334.

_____, *Komposition und Herkunft der johanneischen Reden*, Beiträge zur Wissenschaft vom Alten und Neuen Testament, 5. Folge, Heft 1, Stuttgart, 1960.

_____, *Untersuchungen zur Menschensohn-Christologie im Johannes-Evangelium*, Göttingen, 1957.

Schürmann, H., "Joh 6,51c —ein Schlüssel zur grossen johanneischen Brotrede," *Biblische Zeitschrift*, N.F. 2, 1958, pp. 244-262.

Schütz, R., "Ev. Joh 10,25-29," *Zeitschrift für die neutestamentliche Wissenschaft*, 10, 1909, pp. 324f.

Schwank, B., "Damit sie alle eine seien (17,20-26)," *Sein und Sendung*, 28, 1963, pp. 436-439.

Schwartz, E., *Aporien im 4. Evangelium*, Nachrichten von der königlichen Gesellschaft der Wissenschaften zu Göttingen, Berlin, 1907/08.

Schweitzer, A., *The Quest of the Historical Jesus*, London, 1956.

Schweizer, E., art. σάρξ, *Theologisches Wörterbuch zum Neuen Testament*, Vol. VII, 1964, pp. 98-104.

_____, art. πνεῦμα, *Theologisches Wörterbuch zum Neuen Testament*, Vol.VI, 1959, pp. 436-443.

_____, art. υἱός, *Theologisches Wörterbuch zum Neuen Testament*, Vol.VIII, 1969, pp. 364-395.

_____, *Church Order in the New Testament*, Studies in Biblical Theology 32, (trans. by F. Clarke), London, 1961.

_____, "Das johanneische Zeugnis vom Herrenmahl," *Neotestamentica*, Zürich/Stuttgart, 1963, pp. 371-406.

_____, "Der Kirchenbegriff bei Johannes," *Neotestamentica*, pp. 254-271.

_____, "Die Heilung des Königlichen," *Neotestamentica*, pp. 407-415.

_____, *Ego Eimi*, FRLANT N.F. 38, 2. Aufl., Göttingen, 1965.

_____, "Jesus der Zeuge Gottes," *Studies in John*, Supplements to Novum Testamentum 24, Leiden, 1970, pp. 161-168.

_____, "The Church as the Missionary Body of Christ," *Neotestamentica*, pp. 317-329.

_____, "Zum traditionsgeschichtlichen Hintergrund der 'Sendungsformel' Gal. 4,4f. Rm.8:3f. Joh.3:16f. I Jn.4:9," *Zeitschrift für die neutestamentliche Wissenschaft*, 57, 1966, pp. 199-210.

Sevenster, G., "Remarks on the Humanity of Jesus," *Studies in John*, Supplements to Novum Testamentum 24, Leiden, 1970, pp. 185-193.

Smalley, S., "The Johannine Son of Man Sayings," *New Testament Studies*, 15, 1969, pp. 278-301.

Smith, D.M., *The Composition and Order of the Fourth Gospel*, New Haven/London, 1965.

_____, "The Sources of the Gospel of John: An Assessment of the Present State of the Problem," *New Testament Studies*, 10, 1964, pp.336-351.

Soltau, W., *Das 4. Evangelium in seiner Entstehungsgeschichte dargelegt*, Sitzungsberichte der Heidelberger Akademie 6, 1916.

Spitta, F., *Das Johannes-Evangelium als Quelle der Geschichte Jesu*, Göttingen, 1910.

Stauffer, E., art. εἷς, *Theologisches Wörterbuch zum Neuen Testament*, Vol. II, 1935, pp. 432-440.

Stendahl, K., *The School of St. Matthew*, Philadelphia, 1968.

Strathmann, H., art. λαός, *Theologisches Wörterbuch zum Neuen Testament*, Vol IV, 1942, pp. 49-57.

_____, *Das Evangelium nach Johannes*, Das Neue Testament Deutsch, Göttingen, 1951.

Talmon, S., "The Sectarian יחד --a Biblical Noun," *Vetus Testamentum*, 3, 1953, pp. 133-144.

Taylor, V., *The Formation of the Gospel Tradition*, London, 1960.

Teeple, H., *The Mosaic Eschatological Prophet*, Journal of Biblical Literature Monograph Series X, 1957.

Thüsing, W., *Die Erhöhung und Verherrlichung im Johannesevangelium*, Neutestamentliche Abhandlungen XXI, 1, 2 Aufl., Münster, 1970.

_____, *Herrlichkeit und Einheit. Eine Auslegung des hohenpriesterlichen Gebetes Jesu*, Düsseldorf, 1962.

Tiede, D.L., *The Charismatic Figure As Miracle Worker*, SBL Dissertation Series 1, Missoula, 1972.

Torrey, Ch. *Our Translated Gospels*, New York and London, 1936.

Tröger, K-W. (Hrsg.), *Gnosis und Neues Testament*, Studien aus Religionswissenschaft und Theologie, Berlin, 1973.

Van Hartingsveld, L., *Die Eschatologie des Johannesevangeliums*, Eine Auseinandersetzung mit R. Bultmann, Assen, 1962.

Van Iersel, B.M.F., *'Der Sohn' in den synoptischen Jesusworten*, Supplements to Novum Testamentum III, 1961.

Van Unnik, W.C., "The Quotation from the OT in John 12:34," *Novum Testamentum*, Vol. 3, 1959, pp. 174-179.

Vielhauer, P., "Ein Weg zur neutestamentlichen Christologie?" *Evangelische Theologie*, 1/2, 1965, pp. 24-71.

Völker, W., *Quellen zur Geschichte der christlichen Gnosis*, Tübingen, 1932.

von Campenhausen, *Kirchliches Amt und geistliche Vollmacht in den ersten drei Jahrhunderten*, 2. Aufl., Tübingen, 1963.

von Rad, G., *Old Testament Theology*, Vols. I & II, (tr. by D. Stalker), Edinburgh and London, 1963.

von Walter, J., "Ignatius von Antiochien und die Entstehung des Frühkatholizismus," *Reinhold Seeberg Festschrift II*, Leipzig, 1929.

Walker, R., "Jüngerwort und Herrenwort," *Zeitschrift für die neutestamentliche Wissenschaft*, 57, 1966, pp. 49-54.

Wead, D., *The Literary Devices in John's Gospel*, Basel, 1970.

Weiss, H.-F., *Untersuchungen zur Kosmologie des hellenistischen und palästinischen Judentums*, TU, 97, Berlin, 1966.

Wellhausen, J., *Das Evangelium Johannis*, Berlin, 1908.

_____, *Erweiterungen und Änderungen im 4. Evangelium*, Berlin, 1907.

Westcott, B., *The Gospel According to St. John*, London, 1958.

Wetter, G., *Der Sohn Gottes*, FRLANT N.F. 9, Göttingen, 1916.

Wikenhauser, A., *Das Evangelium nach Johannes*, Regensburg, 1961.

Wilckens, U., art. σοφία, *Theologisches Wörterbuch zum Neuen Testament*, Vol VII, 1964, pp. 497-529.

Wilkens, W., *Die Entstehungsgeschichte des 4. Evangeliums*, Zollikon, 1958.

_____, *Zeichen und Werke*, Abhandlungen zur Theologie des Alten und Neuen Testaments 55, Zürich, 1969.

Windisch, H., *Johannes und die Synoptiker*, Leipzig, 1926.

Winter, P., *On the Trial of Jesus*, Studia Judaica I, Berlin, 1961.

Zimmermann, H., "Das absolute ἐγώ εἰμι als die neutestamentliche Offenbarungsformel," *Biblische Zeitschrift*, N.F. 4, 1960, pp. 54-69 and 266-276.

_____, "Struktur und Aussageabsicht der johanneischen Abschiedsreden (Joh 13-17)," *Bibel und Leben*, 8, 1967, pp. 279-290.